A Celebration of Poets

of Poets

Grades 7-12
Summer 2008

creativeCOMMUNICATION
A CELEBRATION OF TODAY'S WRITERS

A Celebration of Poets
Grades 7-12
Summer 2008

An anthology compiled by Creative Communication, Inc.

Published by:

creativeCOMMUNICATION
A CELEBRATION OF TODAY'S WRITERS

1488 NORTH 200 WEST · LOGAN, UTAH 84341
TEL. 435-713-4411 · WWW.POETICPOWER.COM

Copyright © 2008 by Creative Communication, Inc.
Printed in the United States of America

ISBN: 978-1-60050-212-5

Foreword

Thank you for joining us in this "Celebration of Writers." We are proud to provide this anthology for you to read. Inside this book you will find the hopes and dreams of a generation of students.

This fall, I received a letter from a young writer. In the letter he thanked Creative Communication for being "A truly courageous group who is willing to invest in the adults of tomorrow." We thank him for these kind words. However, more importantly we are glad that we can contribute to a student's success. Each class that is taken and each project that is completed in school moves a student closer to a successful life. When we invest in our children, we are investing in our future.

I often hear from teachers who tell me about the atmosphere in their classroom when their students are accepted to be published. I am told that it creates an energy and excitement that cannot be created by regular classroom instruction. These feelings can be remembered for a lifetime and can be used as a catalyst to help these students continue to love education. I hope that publishing these writers will make the world a better place.

Thomas Worthen, Ph.D.
Editor
Creative Communication

WRITING CONTESTS!

Enter our next POETRY contest!
Enter our next ESSAY contest!

Why should I enter?
Win prizes and get published! Each year thousands of dollars in prizes are awarded in each region and tens of thousands of dollars in prizes are awarded throughout North America. The top writers in each division receive a monetary award and a free book that includes their published poem or essay. Entries of merit are also selected to be published in our anthology.

Who may enter?
There are four divisions in the poetry contest. The poetry divisions are grades K-3, 4-6, 7-9, and 10-12. There are four divisions in the essay contest. The essay division are grades K-3, 4-6, 7-9, and 10-12.

What is needed to enter the contest?
To enter the poetry contest send in one original poem, 21 lines or less. To enter the essay contest send in one original essay, 250 words or less, on any topic. Each entry must include the student's name, grade, address, city, state, and zip code, and the student's school name and school address. Students who include their teacher's name may help the teacher qualify for a free copy of the anthology.

How do I enter?
Enter a poem online at:
www.poeticpower.com
or
Mail your poem to:
    Poetry Contest
    1488 North 200 West
    Logan, UT 84341

Enter an essay online at:
www.studentessaycontest.com
or
Mail your essay to:
    Essay Contest
    1488 North 200 West
    Logan, UT 84341

When is the deadline?
Poetry contest deadlines are April 7th, August 18th, and December 3rd. Essay contest deadlines are February 17th, July 15th, and October 15th. You can enter each contest, however, send only one poem or essay for each contest deadline.

Are there benefits for my school?
Yes. We award $15,000 each year in grants to help with Language Arts programs. Schools qualify to apply for a grant by having a large number of entries of which over fifty percent are accepted for publication. This typically tends to be about 15 accepted entries.

Are there benefits for my teacher?
Yes. Teachers with five or more students accepted to be published receive a free anthology that includes their students' writing.

For more information please go to our website at **www.poeticpower.com**, email us at editor@poeticpower.com or call 435-713-4411.

Table of Contents

Essays from Canada are included in this edition
as well as essays from the following States:

Arkansas
Iowa
Illinois
Indiana
Louisiana
Michigan
Minnesota
Missouri
Ohio
Wisconsin

Summer 2008 Poetic Achievement Honor Schools

* Teachers who had fifteen or more poets accepted to be published

The following schools are recognized as receiving a "Poetic Achievement Award." This award is given to schools who have a large number of entries of which over fifty percent are accepted for publication. With hundreds of schools entering our contest, only a small percent of these schools are honored with this award. The purpose of this award is to recognize schools with excellent Language Arts programs. This award qualifies these schools to receive a complimentary copy of this anthology. In addition, these schools are eligible to apply for a Creative Communication Language Arts Grant. Grants of two hundred and fifty dollars each are awarded to further develop writing in our schools.

Algonquin Middle School
Clinton Township, MI
Jane Pickelsimer*

Arrowhead Union High School -
North Campus
Hartland, WI
Elizabeth Jorgensen*

Ascension of Our Lord Secondary School
Mississauga, ON
Maureen Ahmad*

Bristol Elementary School
Bristol, WI
Cheryl Fowler*

Cannon Falls Sr High School
Cannon Falls, MN
Stacy Mittag
Cal Vande Hoef*

Clintonville High School
Clintonville, WI
Julie Rohrer*

Destrehan High School
Destrehan, LA
Donna Lynn Thompson*

Eastmoor Academy High School
Columbus, OH
Carla Phillips*

Ecole secondaire E J Lajeunesse
Windsor, ON
Annette Richard*

England High School
England, AR
Barbara Barkley*

Fairfield Middle School
Fairfield, OH
Mary L. Villareal*

Gwendolyn Brooks College Preparatory
Academy
Chicago, IL
Donnie Boyd
Chrishan David

Hartford Union High School
Hartford, WI
    Mark Boyd
    Lin Mooney Courchane
    Heather Weise

Haynes Academy for Advanced Studies
Metairie, LA
    Teresa Bennett
    Sandra DeMers*

Hazelwood West Jr-Sr High School
Hazelwood, MO
    Marie Boesch*

LeRoy-Ostrander High School
LeRoy, MN
    Samantha Miller*

Linwood Public School
Linwood, ON
    Mrs. Enns-Frede*

Little Miami Jr High School
Morrow, OH
    Melinda Carter*

Mount Carmel Academy
New Orleans, LA
    Karla Amacker
    Melissa Gayé
    Kristen Hode
    Jennifer Kadden
    Scott Richard

Nativity of Our Lord Catholic School
Etobicoke, ON
    Jennifer Blandi
    Mr. Dsoza
    Dorothy Kleine
    Sarah Lopez*

New Albany Middle School
New Albany, OH
    Suzanne Cooper
    Kerry Fuller
    Allison Martini*
    Shannon May*
    Patty Randall*
    Melissa Withers*

Oak Creek High School
Oak Creek, WI
    Penny A. Kapitz*

Parkway Middle School
Rockford, OH
    Abbie Braun*

Paw Paw Middle School
Paw Paw, MI
    Jane E. Cowin*
    Annette Markovich*

Prairie Lakes School
Willmar, MN
    Cathy Erickson*

Rib Lake High School
Rib Lake, WI
    Gail Curran*

Robert Bateman Secondary School
Abbotsford, BC
    Alana Coombs*

Sandusky Middle School
Sandusky, MI
    Desiree Benavides*

Shakopee Area Catholic School
Shakopee, MN
    Ann Heyda*

Southwest Jr High School
Springdale, AR
    Janet Cupit*

Springfield Boys and Girls Club ABC Unit
Springfield, IL
David Boggs*

St Clare Catholic Elementary School
Woodbridge, ON
Ms. Capobianco
Ms. Deacetis
Mrs. DePaulis
Ms. DiVincenzo*
Mr. Esposito
Miss Fabris
Deborah Fazari*
Ms. Galloro
Ms. Inglese
Ms. Mamiani
Ms. Montesano
Ms. Ortega
Ms. Pacitti
Ms. Porto
Ms. Pucci*
Mr. Ruberto
Ms. Santangelo
Mrs. Vigliatore

St Monica School
Mishawaka, IN
Mattie Willerton*

St Peter Catholic High School
Orleans, ON
Melodee Mulligan*

Taylorville Sr High School
Taylorville, IL
Janet K. Kensil*

Tremont Elementary School
Upper Arlington, OH
Julie Fryman
Patrick Hurley*

Trinity Lutheran School
Utica, MI
Deborah Wesenberg*

Troy High School
Troy, MI
Meagan Foster*
Donna Guith
Linda A. Pavich

Wainwright High School
Wainwright, AB
Heather Rentz*

Waseca High School
Waseca, MN
John L. Moon*

Weledeh Catholic School
Yellowknife, NT
Lori Bailey*

Whitewater Middle School
Whitewater, WI
David Tuten*

William Fremd High School
Palatine, IL
Gary Anderson
Marilyn Berdick
Gina Enk
Sabra Gerber
Judy Klingner
Leah Ross*
Theodhora Shaka

Language Arts Grant Recipients 2008-2009

After receiving a "Poetic Achievement Award" schools are encouraged to apply for a Creative Communication Language Arts Grant. The following is a list of schools who received a two hundred and fifty dollar grant for the 2008-2009 school year.

Acushnet Elementary School, Acushnet, MA
Benton Central Jr/Sr High School, Oxford, IN
Bridgeway Christian Academy, Alpharetta, GA
Central Middle School, Grafton, ND
Challenger Middle School, Cape Coral, FL
City Hill Middle School, Naugatuck, CT
Clintonville High School, Clintonville, WI
Coral Springs Middle School, Coral Springs, FL
Covenant Classical School, Concord, NC
Coyote Valley Elementary School, Middletown, CA
Diamond Ranch Academy, Hurricane, UT
E O Young Jr Elementary School, Middleburg, NC
El Monte Elementary School, Concord, CA
Emmanuel-St Michael Lutheran School, Fort Wayne, IN
Ethel M Burke Elementary School, Bellmawr, NJ
Fort Recovery Middle School, Fort Recovery, OH
Gardnertown Fundamental Magnet School, Newburgh, NY
Hancock County High School, Sneedville, TN
Haubstadt Community School, Haubstadt, IN
Headwaters Academy, Bozeman, MT
Holden Elementary School, Chicago, IL
Holliday Middle School, Holliday, TX
Holy Cross High School, Delran, NJ
Homestead Elementary School, Centennial, CO
Joseph M Simas Elementary School, Hanford, CA
Labrae Middle School, Leavittsburg, OH
Lakewood High School, Lakewood, CO
Lee A Tolbert Community Academy, Kansas City, MO
Mary Lynch Elementary School, Kimball, NE
Merritt Secondary School, Merritt, BC
North Star Academy, Redwood City, CA

Language Arts Grant Winners cont.

Old Redford Academy, Detroit, MI
Prairie Lakes School, Willmar, MN
Public School 124Q, South Ozone Park, NY
Rutledge Hall Elementary School, Lincolnwood, IL
Shelley Sr High School, Shelley, ID
Sonoran Science Academy, Tucson, AZ
Spruce Ridge School, Estevan, SK
St Columbkille School, Dubuque, IA
St Francis Middle School, Saint Francis, MN
St Luke the Evangelist School, Glenside, PA
St Matthias/Transfiguration School, Chicago, IL
St Robert Bellarmine School, Chicago, IL
St Sebastian Elementary School, Pittsburgh, PA
The Hillel Academy, Milwaukee, WI
Thomas Edison Charter School - North, North Logan, UT
Trinity Christian Academy, Oxford, AL
United Hebrew Institute, Kingston, PA
Velasquez Elementary School, Richmond, TX
West Frederick Middle School, Frederick, MD

Grades 10-11-12

Top Poem Grades 10-11-12

Insomnia

I toss and turn in my tiny, twin bed
Trying to catch a wink
But sleep eludes me like a mouse to a cat
Thus driving me to restless frustration

I've tried counting sheep
And softly humming lullabies
Yet, still, sweet dreams evade

Now, I have resorted to glaring angrily
At the raging, red digits on a clock's bland face
I stare it down like the proverbial bull —
Daring it to move

It lazily blinks its rectangular eyes
Flashing five o'clock, Five O'Clock!
Signifying a mere two hours left
Until I have to be up

Oh how this infuriates me!
I moodily turn from its smug, luminous smirk
And into the darkened abyss beyond

Paola Atienza, Grade 12
Kwantlen Park Secondary School, BC

Top Poem Grades 10-11-12

Strokes of a Paradox

It was a dream.
That ashen velvet voice;
wrapping up fairy tales in promises and pretty words
spit out like stars on a blank canvas sky,
and it was no exception to the notion
that white stains so easily.

Though pallid now are the lavish words that graced our lips,
I'd still be caught a fool
for the smile that captured the spring sunset
with the warmth of the summer's ocean breeze.
The one that mentions times when we dreamt in lilacs and rain;
danced in the park, kissed under falling leaves,
when these eyes wore our vivid colors of love;
splashed and swirled in caramel, and blue-green irises.

But time has faded,
and now we hide; refusing to admit:
our masks can never make us blind.

And we will only be called naive
when the brilliant hues we've strived to contain,
spill through our crumbling concrete disguises,
and our canvas will flourish again.

Danna Boughner, Grade 11
Newbury High School, OH

Top Poem Grades 10-11-12

Like Fine Wine

Like fine wine,
our relationship is.

He would always tell me,
old…men with hats can't drive.
However,
whenever he and I left the house
he would always throw on his Yankees hat
and hop right into the driver's seat
and remind me that
old men with hats can't drive.

He always knew how to make me laugh.

He has lived a long life.
Not all of his life was happy.
I know the times we spent were.

I haven't visited him much in years past
except at Christmas time,
and when the Yankees came to town.

Our relationship only gets better with time,
just like fine wine.

Zac Carbone, Grade 10
Troy High School, MI

Top Poem Grades 10-11-12

Changing Seasons

A gentle breeze toys with the tendrils of a willow tree.
Its sweeping branches tickling the flowers dancing below,
the petals glisten with the life of spring as they waltz
back and forth in a continuous body, colors fusing as one,
moving in time with the rhythm of life.

Then, a heavy blanket of heat covers the land,
pressing down on the flowers, ceasing the dance,
stopping the breeze, only stagnant heat remains.
The petals droop under the heavy moisture.
The joy has been replaced with drudging fatigue,

until the return of the breeze.
No longer gentle, it alters the colors.
Stealing away the greens and pinks,
replacing them with reds and yellows that fade into death.
Freezing winds bring the final chill.

As Hades swept Persephone down, death sweeps over the land.
The barrenness of the Earth is swiftly covered in white.
Innocence drifting from the sky, hiding the world with its beauty.
Through the bitterness of nights, the day still comes,
melting snow, promising the return of life.

Morgan Ebert, Grade 12
Taylorville Sr High School, IL

Top Poem Grades 10-11-12

Ms. Fuller

First: I am like artwork, a collage if you will,
A mix of emotions that scream, they all scream with excitement.
I paint a picture, with pictures alone, and for every thought, I think.
Second: Some say I am closed in like a caged animal,
But this animal is just that.
A rhino, charging hate, discrimination, war,
An animal like a rhinoceros that sings like a bird, and this cage is its rules.
But rules are meant to be broken.
Third: I am as refreshing as the summer rain,
A cool relief from the blazing sun.
Rain, that trickles down your house's shingles, and fills every pore in the earth.
I give hope to the dehydrated, and bring life to the unborn.
I give the hungry food to end humanity's drought.
Finally: I am as alive as a parade, hundreds flock to receive happiness.
My advertisement reads, "Bring your loved ones!", "You'll love the floats!"
You read it, as I throw lollipops to your children, spreading love and joy,
Like multiplying cells, rapidly.
I leave an outstanding feeling.
And I'll be back again.

Jeanna Fuller, Grade 12
St Louis Park Sr High School, MN

Top Poem Grades 10-11-12

Arlington

Rolling hills stretching as far as one can see.
The grass is green; the air is clear.
But something hushes me.
Across the hills stretch stories of lives that were once dear.

Gravestones stretch across the lawn;
Each row is straight and the same.
Each headstone represents a life that is gone.
It shows that war is not a game.

Each stone has a different story,
But each habitant once breathed the same air as the other.
They did not die for the glory;
They fought to defend their sister and brother.

They fought for what is ultimately right:
To bring peace to earth and show what is true.
That each person deserves the same and each life is bright.
To undo the treatment some suffer through.

The stones are the same shape and size.
Some are tattered and others are new.
There is reason for this I realize.
For each life is equal; it is true.

Chelsey Johnson, Grade 10
Windom Secondary School, MN

Top Poem Grades 10-11-12

The Makings Of…

Anything is attainable; it's about how hard you work.
Don't listen; it's a facade — a minuscule quirk.
Challenges are met with strength and aplomb.
Forever second-guessing, you're never that calm.
It's not about diplomacy or grace under fire,
Worthless, insignificant and nothing to admire.
Quality of spirit that renders one speechless,
Yet, the tragic flaw is a stunning success.
With a shake of the head, and a very quick smile,
You might just realize what has taken others awhile:
Courage is not about bravery, strength, and never being afraid:
But overcoming such a fear is how a hero is made.

Megan LeBlanc, Grade 12
Grimsby Secondary School, ON

Top Poem Grades 10-11-12

Winter Night

The silent snow whispers its hushed sound.
In the stillness of the night,
Feathery flakes swirl 'round.
Sparkling in the moonlight,
Cold frosty flakes kiss my face
Turning the world
Into a magical place.

Downy banks cover the ground;
Under it all green grass is found.
Undisturbed, the blanket of ice.
The tranquil calm of a winter night.

The world is filled with glistening light,
A world where all is perfect, where all is right.
Shimmering diamonds filled with grace;
Fluffy, soft, frosty, and wet.
Powdery snow decorates each window with lace.

The whole world is set
With a feeling of wonder.
Like a million grains of sugar,
They catch the light;
The world transformed on a winter night.

Audrey Sutherland, Grade 11
Home School, MI

Top Poem Grades 10-11-12

The Symphony

It pulls at my fingertips
As the keys' hearts beat in time with mine.
They feed their emotions into my soul
And my soul pours it back.
I don't even know the notes
But my fingers welcome the right sound
Like an old friend.
They pound and press
And inflict their beauty
On the air surrounding.
They caress and stroke
Like two lovers embracing.
Even a single note is a definition
Of the word beauty.
The keys sing of their own accord
And I merely accompany them
In their sweet lament.
As we finish our dance
The music smiles at my radiant face.
For we have created our own
Symphony.

Mickeelie Webb, Grade 10
Huntsville High School, ON

Top Poem Grades 10-11-12

Starlight

The charcoal canvas stretches overhead,
A thousand gems spilled 'cross the midnight sky.
The breeze breathes gentle secrets yet unsaid,
As Luna gazes from her heavens high.

The jewels weave stories through the pearly black,
Their tales of heroes wrought of ancient lore.
A tapestry so rich, nothing to lack,
A band of the horizon's shimm'ring shore.

Each shard a unique iridescent beam,
No need to be concerned by earthly time.
A magic, potent as any could seem,
Embodied inspiration. Pure. Divine.

Some evening soon I'll find a star who sees
Beauty in night and the starlight in me.

Julie Weiner, Grade 12
Shaker Heights High School, OH

World Between Worlds
Can you see the blankness?
Feel the nothing on your skin?
Hear the thundering silence,
and taste blandness within?
Do you wonder where you are?
You've entered my domain
The place between the places
The corner where walls meet
Where there is no more good
than there is evil
Where there is no more pain
than there is pleasure
This is no more hell
than heaven
So, ladies and gentlemen
Welcome to Purgatory.
Sarah Breiter, Grade 12
De Forest High School, WI

Theoretically Speaking…
We're taught that Earth is
Round, gravity pulls, and
Oxygen weighs 8.

We learn to distinguish sounds,
Words, from noise, how to
Revel in greatness formed by
Poe, Da Vinci, and Galileo.

We learn to walk, we learn to talk.
We learn to read, to write,
To equate and combine.
We learn to love.

But what good will it
Do us when the world
Explodes?
Jamie Burkhead, Grade 11
East Union Middle/High School, IA

I Am
I am a bird with broken wings
I am a baby turtle racing for the ocean
I am a single-teen parent
I am a struggling high school student
I am the life of my daughter
I am a victim of abuse
I am the eyes for my mother
I am the cane for my father
I am the oldest of seven children
I am a teacher to my siblings
I am the bonding of my friends
I am courage
I am Cha Lee Vue
Cha Lee Vue, Grade 12
St Paul Area Learning Center, MN

Three Fat Largemouth
They are what I seek every day on the lake.
I am who they fear will get a hold of them.
Three Fat Largemouth sitting under stumps and tree limbs engulfed in the water.
Three amongst thousands in the lake.
But I only want three. Three just calling my name.
Three in the hardest spots to fish.
From my boat I can see them swimming gracefully through the water.
Their power is unannounced.
They might be only 20" long but they will strain your muscles and wear you out.
They will dart around in the water with the agility of a 10" fish.
They are deceiving, but it is possible to catch them.
Man has never wanted anything more than he wants those three fish.
For food and for the challenge.
It takes a patient being to catch them.
They sit amongst weeds and stumps.
One wrong move and he is stuck, never to see his Rapala again.
When I am tired and think there is no hope.
When I am the fisherman who has been skunked the last six fishing trips.
When I am about to give up. Three who still wait patiently.
Three who sit there despite of my mood.
Three whose only reason is to teach me to work and then enjoy my work.
Jon Leonard, Grade 12
Arrowhead Union High School - North Campus, WI

Tremble
I tremble with thoughts of when you first met.
I tremble with thoughts of her as my eyes are getting wet.
I tremble with thoughts of the laughter you first shared.
I tremble with thoughts of when you realized you never cared.
I tremble with thoughts of your first date.
I tremble with thoughts that maybe it was fate.
I tremble with thoughts of that first walk to her front door.
I tremble with thoughts of that first hug and when you lingered for more.
I tremble with thoughts of how much of her you miss.
I tremble with thoughts of your first kiss.
I tremble with thoughts of when you first cuddled in bed.
I tremble with thoughts of when those "3 words" were said.
I tremble with thoughts when you first realized that she is something I'm not.
I tremble with thoughts of the day that I was first forgot.
Tara Ruggeri, Grade 12
Windsor High School, MO

Expression of Depression
Who am I?
What is the purpose of my life,
Rather than being the topic in everyone's conversation?
A feeling of emptiness like an evicted renovation.
No body likes me, I'm considered an outcast,
never experienced love, relationships fast they don't last.
But look at me, who and how could someone love such a being as me?
Day's go by, sometimes, don't even notice
Maybe if I had money, or drove a yellow lotus
people would notice…Me…but I doubt it.
This is my very expression of depression.
Sam Taylor, Grade 11
Eastmoor Academy High School, OH

The Cacophony

The cacophony I cannot hear
The cacophony that affects my ear
Affects my ear, so I cannot think
I cannot think when I am near
The brutal sound, in my thoughts resounds
My thoughts are noise that blend in the around
So much that the noise is common to my ear
Therefore, this cacophony it will no longer hear

Jessica Habib, Grade 12
Ecole secondaire E J Lajeunesse, ON

A Mere Shadow

Past the benches, in which we whispered the truth of our love,
  my memory hits me hard.
The leaves fall and twirl,
  landing on me like your soft hands,
  searching for a way into my heart.
The cold presses against my chest,
  ripping the healing wound within me.
A crow caws far away in the distance,
  it is too late —
  too late for omens now.
I catch a glance of your shadow,
  a blur,
  black as a starless night.
I reach out to grab, to hold, to claim you my mine,
  but my hands turn to dust,
  and your shadow only fades away.
Far away, you travel,
  only a shadow causing a cold draft,
  leaving me to bleed on my own.

Gamze Yarayan, Grade 11
Hickman High School, MO

Manifestation

Ripples
like waves —
increasing power, moving fast
tremors stirring the immobilizing oceans
breeze moving the mirroring sky
heavens reflected and supremacy contained
images reversed and depictions unviewable
likeness of vague,
replicated images

— Reflect —

Images replicated
vague of likeness,
unviewable depictions and reversed images
contained supremacy and reflected heavens
sky mirroring the moving breeze
oceans immobilizing the stirring tremors
fast moving, power increasing
waves like —
Ripples

Adrian Fong, Grade 10
St. Augustine Catholic High School, ON

Seven

Seven little ducks are swimming in a pond,
  Seven little fishes are swimming along.

Here come seven trucks driving down the road,
Passing a house with seven children in sleep mode.

Seven kids playing some street basketball,
  Seven kids playing in the leaves of fall.

Seven carolers at your house on Christmas Eve,
When morning comes there's seven presents under the tree.

Seven stars are dancing in the night,
Seven campers in the woods having a fright.

And here comes seven little boys,
All of which carrying seven little toys.

Jennifer Kemp, Grade 12
Prairie Lakes School, MN

Upside Down with My Feet Up the Wall
Looking Out the Window at an Unfamiliar City

I am a tiny spider living on the roof of this hotel.
I leave no marks.
The city falls down around me
while I wait for a quiet moment
to stand up straight.
All old things become new again
in a burned-out world
where gutted brick buildings shuffle sideways
to make room for
the Faster Life.

Anna Moore, Grade 12
Esquimalt High School, BC

Daddy's Little Angel

Daddy's Little Angel
Has a wonderful life
As so she thought
She was so beautiful and loved
She had all she ever wanted
She was loved by all
So that's what people thought
She would always be
Daddy's Little Angel
Well they were wrong
Daddy's Little Angel
Will never be the same
She will never fly
With those broken wings
She will never be
The cheerful
Happy little one
She once was
She will never be
Daddy's Little Angel

Jackie Shangraw, Grade 11
Weyburn Comprehensive Bridge School, SK

Water

Water.
Flowing so calmly.
Through the small creek.
Soothing sounds as it glides over the rocks.
See the fish swimming below.
Through the transparent fluid.
Water.

Kevin David, Grade 12
St Francis De Sales High School, OH

Our Dreams

Dreams we had when we were young
The hopes we had
The people we wanted to be
The grades we hope to achieve
The constant pressure we face
The constant urge to achieve
The urge to be the best
The lives we live
are possible
but hard to achieve
close but far
far away
We live
one
day
at
a
time

Jason Qian, Grade 11
William Fremd High School, IL

Two's Solitude

The daylight is slowly disappearing,
The silky moon is coming out,
Your presence? It's enchanting,
And your love's what it's about.

Time is slowly drifting,
Like the shadows before dawn,
Your silhouette is milky smooth,
And our fear, desperately gone.

Cushioned deep beneath us,
Is the magic of the night,
Soft droplets punching all of us,
We're concealed from abstract light.

The cream light calms your cheeks,
And the dust will swim on by,
Because tonight, we're in a safe place,
Because tonight, it's you and I.

Laura Anderson, Grade 12
Dr G W Williams Secondary School, ON

My Empty Room

To not exist,
Sometimes or usually I wish for.
It has come true, after all.
I fear death, but welcome the idea.
However, there is always someone
Any person, who pulls me back
From the shadows
And lets the piercing sunlight
Penetrate my weeping soul.
My hopes are too high
Too easily broken
Are easily consumed
By most of my life
To end up in the trashing memories
That did not live to happen,
But only in my fantasy.
Always a worse outcome,
In this empty room,
Where nothing will be scared by me —
With the melting glow of day,
I made my inevitable sorrow.

Catherine Tran, Grade 11
Turner Fenton Secondary School, ON

Are You Watching Over Me?

I've never felt your presence,
Never felt like you were near.
The times I tried to talk to you,
I bet you didn't hear.

I've wondered if you cared at all,
If it bothered you to leave.
With you left a part of me,
I never will retrieve.

You've always been a mystery,
The notes to music that didn't flow.
You were not here to help me,
So, without you, I had to grow.

I've blamed you for a lot of things,
I always thought it was your fault.
Because I wasn't even born yet,
When your life came to a halt.

So, nowadays, I think a lot,
About the places you could be.
And sometimes it kills me to wonder,
Are you watching over me?

Hannah McCormick, Grade 10
Highland High School, IN

Sierra

Sierra is my dog
She eats like a hog.
When in the house
She is quiet like a mouse.
Her big ears
Make it hard to hear.
With her short legs
She can barely climb pegs.
Even though she is big and round
She is still my favorite hound.

Jennifer Churchill, Grade 10
Fairfield Community High School, IL

The Cause of Tantrums

I bet you think you're funny
Going where you please —
Jumping left, then right, then left again,
Bouncing off the trees.
If you did as I requested,
I wouldn't be displeased.
I think I should simply go home;
I wouldn't lose as many tees.

Grant Molen, Grade 11
Taylorville Sr High School, IL

Hope

Bombs away
the wars continue.
Hunger bites
the children's bellies.
Some of us don't know
the consequences
of desire,
of imperialism,
of nationalism.
Some of us don't care.

Children playing
in the garbage.
Mothers praying for strength
Fathers paying for a meal
The only one.

Desire bites the children's bellies
War kills the innocent families
Exploit for profit, hunger pays
Desire kills in many ways

But hope withstands.

Emma Loop-Drouillard, Grade 12
Ecole secondaire E J Lajeunesse, ON

Summer Time

Memories of the cool blue water of swimming pools
Salty smells of the ocean
Sounds of seagulls searching for leftovers
Smell of suntan lotion
The pink tint of children's cheeks from the sun
The long hours with the warmth of the sun on your neck
The nights looking at the stars while sitting by camp fires
These are the times to relax and enjoy
These are the days and nights of freedom
This is summer

Allison Gauthier, Grade 11
William Fremd High School, IL

What Happened

How did we come to this?
Everything happened so fast.
I thought it was okay.
Guess I must've been mistaken.

The things you said cut like a knife.
We weren't that close anyway
But that doesn't make it right.
I got tired of chasing you like cat and mouse
And I told you what I felt.
I guess you didn't feel that way.
Could've ended better but you choose to leave it this way.
You should've said what you felt
And it wouldn't have come to this
But you did what you wanted
Now we see how it all fell apart.

So now I've come to the conclusion
That karma comes back around
That's why I sit here in my room
Patiently waiting for what you did to me
To happen to you!

Laura Moore, Grade 10
Carl Schurz High School, IL

I Can't Believe

I still can't believe he's gone
How could he leave me behind
How am I supposed to move on
When he left without saying good-bye
I miss him so much, that I can't help but to cry
Just to think of his face, and his beautiful smile
Makes me be more in denial
Why did God do this to me
When I can't be
Without my brother
Oh Father
Please help me move on
Help me believe he's gone
Well Mario rest in peace
May your soul be released
Into the beautiful world of Heaven

Patsy Paredes, Grade 11
Prairie Lakes School, MN

The Courage

Heaven's embrace; hold me tight
I am not ready to stand on my own.
Give me the guidance; show me the Light
show me the warmth that I long to know.

Do not leave me now,
I am begging you to stay.
I still need you; but don't know how
to keep you from slipping away.

But now, you have gone
and I must spread my newfound wings
to fly into the unknown.

I will never forget what you have given me,
the courage to stand on my own.

Kelli Malott, Grade 10
Troy High School, MI

Right Here

I was thinking of you today
And I simply wanted to say —
I know that sometimes you lose hope
And no one's there to help you cope.
But I hear every tear you cry
If you only knew how hard I try.
When life seems too much for you to bear,
I will be here with a prayer.
And though I am not always near,
I will always be right here.

I see more than a scarlet letter
Because I know that you can be better.
You wonder if there's something more;
Something truly worth living for.
Longing, aching, bleeding heart —
I know how it feels to be torn apart.
And no matter what you do,
My heart will always go out to you.
Through every trial, every fear,
I will always be right here.

Emily P. Gandy, Grade 12
Heritage Academy, MO

Lyndsey

Lyndsey,
Small, skinny, friendly, blonde-haired,
Daughter of Lisa,
Loves friends, family, and being happy,
Who feels joyful, excited, and sometimes stressed.
Who fears ladybugs, thunderstorms, and growing older,
Who would like to see Paris, London, and the world.
Resident of Franklin,
Lisowski.

Lyndsey Lisowski, Grade 10
Oak Creek High School, WI

Fear

I sit alone in a dark forest cave
Resting my tired limp body
On the comfort
Of the soft cool sand
Just outside the dark of night
The sounds of the wild animals
Fill the night air
Slowly my body tenses
With fear
And the sound of the alarm
Brings comfort and joy
For I'm back to reality
Safe once again
My fears are washed away
Taken from within and taken away

Andrew Koelln, Grade 12
Prairie Lakes School, MN

I Perish

Closing eyes, body sleeps.
The sound fades.
Falling to the ground,
Vision gone, memories unwind.
Yelling for help,
Freedom is not mine.

My throat goes dry,
Heart skips a beat, body numbs.
Where am I?
I'm not home.

Headaches emerge,
Lay on my back, waiting.
My beating heart slows,
Take a deep breath.

It stops.
I go.

Tamara Lemoine, Grade 10
Kennebecasis Valley High School, NB

Guilt Is…

Sitting on pins and needles
Sharp, stingy, prickly
Anticipating the punishment
On edge, ashamed, anxious.
Pondering the what ifs.
Controlling your actions.
A feeling that never goes away.
Always there,
To remind you again,
And again,
And again.

Karis Waldner, Grade 11
Decker Colony School, MB

America

"I celebrate myself, and sing myself,
And what I assume you shall assume.
For every atom belonging to me as good belongs to you"*

Night descends
As the shadows of tragedy
Creeps across the open field.
The towers have fallen.
As destruction's dust settled on today's horrific tragedy,
She cries. She worries. She shakes her fists in rage.
And she questions, again and again how such
Needless death and destruction could ever be allowed.
She has been climbing the concrete stairs of heaven
Traveling the mortal pathways
Between grace and humanity, her days
Are not numbered nor counted,
Just lived.
She can look out over God's steel garden
And see her children pass to and fro between the petrified flowers,
Smiling and frowning as chance may take them.
And in the last numb moment her right hand gripped for the intervening centuries.

*Opening lines of "Song of Myself" by Walt Whitman

Mekka Garcia, Grade 11
Centralia High School, MO

Bittersweet Shattered Glass Escape

As your hand slipped away, the lights collapsed.
I'm now walking in the dark, on nearly shattered glass,
Wondering what's going on, why is my heart throbbing in my throat?
Struggling to find you, you who were the light,
Afraid to move, conscious you aren't here no more to make things right.

Blurry vision not helping me seek you in the dark,
The silence becomes painful, stabbing me in the heart,
When all I can hear is tears, as they drop and hit the floor.
I shout your name out, seeking a response,
But discouragement is the only answer, I can't believe you're gone.

How could you leave me here, all alone?
Tears start to drown me, as memories of you resound in my mind,
Can't figure out, where I took a wrong turn.
There's no arms in which I can hide,
No more warmth to protect me from the cold nights.

But in the horizon, a sudden spark appears,
I can't run, for the glass might into pieces break,
And I can't bear to fall, knowing I can't fall into your arms.
So I've got to slowly make a bittersweet escape,
For there is always hope, and in the end it's always okay.

Patricia Saad, Grade 10
École secondaire catholique Renaissance, ON

4th Down

It starts in the huddle
While we're standing in a puddle
The play's called break!
The glory is almost ours to take
Everyone gets set
I'm soaking wet
My hands in the mud
The ball's snapped Hike!
I burst off the line and hit my opponent with a thud
I only got to pass block
Look up the times ticking on the clock
The ball's thrown
I pray that our one shot isn't blown
Yes! He caught it
Touchdown we won
Now it's time to have some fun

Jacob Mason, Grade 10
Oak Creek High School, WI

Friends

Petty fights, deep conversations
different ideals, different home lives,
always there for each other,
working through losses together,
love them as much as my family.
Comfort

Best friends by coincidence
know things about me that I don't even know,
always warn me, and tell me 'I told you so'
people don't understand how close we are.
Support system

Being nerds together
wondering what is heat lightning,
going camping and watching the moon.
Refuge

Going separate ways
missing them terribly.

Amanda Bondy, Grade 12
Ecole secondaire E J Lajeunesse, ON

My Love Is Like an Open Book

Read me like a story,
Because with every letter,
And every word is like my
Heart beating with mystery.
Every page has a different emotion.
Every sentence has a meaning.
My eyes will illustrate my love while
My smile will seal my promise.
Because my love is my own copyright to you,
And to never be plagiarized.

Jamie Perry, Grade 12
Vassar Sr High School, MI

That Night

These salty tears fall.
Gripping onto an old forsaken friend,
The one tucked away for so many years.
Lungs gasping for the dark air.
Hidden under the blankets
Hoping no one finds you,
But really wishing they do.
Scared like a child,
Unsure of everything
Not knowing what's outside
The bedroom window.
Tear covered eyes search around the dark room
Imagining the worst.
Hope disappeared when the sun went down.
And tonight no stars shine.
Tissues pile up on the floor
Until the body is tired,
And slowly drifts to sleep.

Jessica Scheidler, Grade 12
McNicholas High School, OH

Questions

Will tomorrow ever come?
The day drags on and on
Will the sun ever go down?
It hangs in the horizon for hours
Will I ever become tired?
I lay in bed for hours
When will I be able to shut off my brain and sleep?
Thoughts racing through my head
Will my eyes ever shut?
Or will I lay here awake forever?

Jake B., Grade 12
Prairie Lakes School, MN

My Dreams Will Go On

I didn't want to like you,
but now I really miss you.
I just wish that camp could go on.
A play brought us together.
I'd hoped it was for forever.
But now I can see I was wrong.
A dream that is lived one time
will last for a lifetime.
It shines in our hearts like the sun.
My dream was for that one play.
I lived it for that one day.
In my heart my dream will go on.
Hearts may break, but it's the chance we take
when we live out the dreams in our hearts.
Dreams soar, I'll dream all the more
'cuz you're here in my dreams
and my dreams will go on and
We'll soar and dream all the more.
You are safe in my dreams
and my dreams will go on and on.

Rachel Horzewski, Grade 10
St Croix Lutheran High School, MN

Water/Fire

Water
cool, blue
waving, splashing, rippling
tears, lake, light, flame
sparking, igniting, burning
red, hot
Fire

Zavier Davis, Grade 10
Cabrini High School, LA

Love

Beautiful brown hair
Blowing in the wind
A blown kiss
I shall send
Not only is your hair brown
Your eyes are too
I love opening my blue eyes
Just to see you
I'm pouring my heart out
Can't you see
My only hope is that someday
You will love me
I want this
To be known
You're mine
And mine alone
Our love is so warm
And true
Maybe just maybe
Someday I will marry you

Gage Reynolds, Grade 10
Leeton Middle and High School, MO

Love

Eyes meet. Heartbeats skip
Cheeks flush. Smiles flicker.
Nervous laughs. Sweaty palms.
That gut-wrenching feeling of love.

Thoughts stray. Hearts pound.
Gazes linger. Hands clasp.
Engulfing hugs. Passionate kisses.
That exhilarating feeling of love.

Eyes meet. Heartbeats skip.
Cheeks flush. Scowls flicker.
Dismissive laughs. Clenched fists.
That heartbreaking feeling of love.

Thoughts stray. Hearts pound.
Gazes linger. Minds recall.
Reminiscent smiles. Lasting memories.
That enduring feeling of love.

Emma Florio, Grade 11
William Fremd High School, IL

A Good Friend

Do you have a good friend?
A good friend is someone that cares
A good friend helps you when needed
A good friend don't talk about you
A good friend is a good person to you
A good friend doesn't flirt with your man
A good friend is someone that will come to your call
A good friend is someone that loves, cares, and respects you.
A good friend is someone that you know that will be there with you
Through thick and thin no matter what happens

Kaylee Pickett, Grade 10
Leeton Middle and High School, MO

My Last Days

Life is beautiful once you think about it,
I try to live each day calm and easy,
Intelligence and happiness are my themes,
Life is too short to have a heart full of stupidity and hate,
I know one day I must leave,
The same way I came,
With nothing;
I hope my last days I can sit back and rest,
Knowing that all the work I have accomplished has paid off,
I don't want to spend my last days hearing screams and tears of pain,
But screams and tears of joy,
I want to leave seeing a place full of health and growth,
Each generation bringing something new to the world and for the future,
My last days will determine,
How I rest in peace.

Erica Coleman, Grade 10
Auburn High School, IL

My Little Buddy

He loves McDonald's, pizza and candy.
We go there every week just for him.
He always gets kids meal and fish sandwiches.
Cute, chubby, playful, mama's boy, cheerful
are all the things that describe him.
I love spending time with him,
and I'm grateful to have a brother like him.
He can never sleep without his blanket around him at night.
The first word he says when he wakes up is "mom."
He loves to watch cartoons and plays with toys.
Imitating Spiderman is one of his favorite things to do.
He is extremely outgoing and loves to make friends.
He can be a suck up sometimes,
which makes me laugh when I'm upset.
He always makes the house a mess
and I have to clean after him.
He may be annoying sometimes,
but I always miss him when I don't see him.
I love spending time with him,
and I'm grateful to have a brother like him.
Our memories we've had together will surely stay within my heart.

Mei Sun, Grade 10
Troy High School, MI

Hole

I have a hole inside of me,
A hole so wide, where my heart should be.
A hole that hurts, digging deep;
Aching every time I breathe,
Holding back my every plea,
Making my whole being bleed.
A hole that spreads fast within me,
That through a darkness enters easily,
Giving thoughts that just won't leave,
Knocking down my self-esteem,
They just don't die, won't let me scream,
And shred my thoughts without a heed.
I have a hole inside of me,
A hole so wide, so dark, so deep,
A hole that none of you can see,
A hole that love just couldn't reach,
A hole that ate up all my dreams,
And in their stead left anxiety.
Now I can't escape the hole inside of me,
Which has consumed the person I used to be.

Elisabeth Kreykenbohm, Grade 12
Holy Cross Regional High School, BC

Sticks and Stones

You look at me and scorn for what you see
Hate filled eyes bore down on me
Those eyes…
Those two piercing blue eyes which narrow so low
Is like a physical blow
So severely…
So clearly…
Do I see the message in those eyes
Loathing words brush your lips
But not a word is said
Then with a shift of a head
You turn from me
Leaving me hurt and alone
Whether it were sticks and stones
Or spoken words
The pain was all the same

Rebecca Frymire, Grade 11
West Central High School, IL

My Father

Six feet tall, big blue eyes,
when he leaves, I know I'll cry.
15 years has come too fast,
15 years have come to pass.
I know my father, and he knows me,
but what will come, we shall see.
One big hug and one big kiss,
this I know I will surely miss.
Time flies by, it's 5:18,
this I know, for I have seen.
I love my dad with all my heart,
now I know it's not the end, but just the start.

Becki Trcka, Grade 10
Montgomery-Lonsdale High School, MN

Deadlock

Beings trapped in a silent battle
One remains on the sidelines,
The other yearns to live in the moment
Neither can succeed, yet only one can prevail
On the outside: the skin of a dragon:
Weathered yet unfazed
Parroting the norms of a tainted society
While this being conforms, the other remains invulnerable
Unaffected by the corrupt opinions of others.
Within a tensity lingers.
Surfacing only in the confines of his domain.
Like a peacock: never revealing that which makes him unique
Until comfortable with his surroundings.
The struggle to the surface continues
Gasping for air; unable to compromise
Eternal deadlock.

Tyler Bogdan, Grade 12
Melville Comprehensive High School, SK

Happy Mother's Day

I know I've been spoiled,
Just like a little brat,
But you keep on spoiling me,
And I am fine with that.

I may have an attitude at times,
We fight in arguments I'll never win,
But know I always will respect you,
Though it doesn't seem like it every now and then.

Compared to other moms around the world,
I would have to say you are the best.
You are really cool and helpful,
That's what makes you better than all the rest.

And now I end this Mother's Day poem,
I'll just leave enough room to say,
I love you always.
Happy Mother's Day!

Kira Craft, Grade 11
Eastern High School, OH

I'm Still Standing

You tried your hardest to keep me down,
but when I stood up you had a frown,
why you hate me, I will never know,
I guess you're putting on a heck of a show,
trying to kill my spirit
but you didn't hear it,
the voice of my God, the Lord dearest,
He keeps me on my own two feet,
so I won't be below in the heat,
you tried your hardest, you were very demanding,
but at the end of the day, I'm Still Standing.

Joseph Smith Jr., Grade 10
Holy Trinity High School, IL

To Swim Competitively or Not to Swim Competitively

To swim competitively or not to swim competitively
To go to a two hour practice every day
To wake up at 6:00 a.m. and drive hours each weekend to meets
To be able to eat as much as you want and not have to worry about getting fat
When winning a race or dropping time you feel as if you are on top of the world
Would it be easier to just float around in the pool?
To lay out all day and get a tan
Having more time for sleeping and homework
Is it worth it to be tired and sore?
To have skin like sandpaper, constantly cracking and aching
Hair that is like straw, stiff and full of chlorine
To never get a break at practice, constantly out of breath
To feel as if your whole body is going to fall apart if you swim another twenty-five yards
To feel trapped and each minute you get closer to the end of practice you are closer to escaping
Would it be more fulfilling just to relax?
To have time for friends outside swimming, schoolwork, and to do whatever you want
To have soft moisturized skin and silky smooth hair
The ability to go to bed early and feel rested in the morning
To sleep in on Saturday and Sunday mornings
The real question here is to work for something in life or to just live a lazy, carefree life

Jamie Puls, Grade 11
Normandy High School, OH

Things I Cherish the Most from My Childhood

Childhood is
Never getting out of my comfy sapphire blue hoodie and brown Hersey basketball shorts and
My cousin's blue Mustang convertible that sped like a comet racing through the starry night sky.

Childhood is
Playing beach volleyball with friends under the red, orange, and yellow setting sun and
Playing it on the Caribbean beach before having a big bonfire with s'mores, hot dogs and pop.

Childhood is
Rushing home after school to eat and watch *Arthur*, ritually, before doing anything else and
Having a stupid rule like "no nail polish" on my fingernails because my dad didn't like it.

Childhood is
Watching *Beauty and the Beast* over and over again 'til the DVD didn't run clearly anymore and
Taking the first plane flight ever to India and seeing my family overseas after many years.

Gloriya Solanki, Grade 12
John Hersey High School, IL

Friendship

Skin, the color of cinnamon pouring over a boiling body of beauty
Eyes, the orb to her soul, calling you, demanding you to look deeper than what's on the surface
Nose, breathing in a lifetime of emotions: sorrow, happiness, mournful, enjoyment
Ears, examining everyone, everything
Lips, sealed tightly behind the ruby red of her lipstick whispering to your heart, capturing it

Seizing you, taking you
Now you want her, need her
Feeling her touch is more than comfort now
It's a small piece to the puzzle of your chaotic life
A piece that soars through a sea of cinnamon skin

Jasmine Joseph, Grade 12
Destrehan High School, LA

Here with Me

Here with me,
Is this really where you wanna be?
Here with me,
Is this the place in your dreams you see?
Here with me,
In your future do you see you and me as a we?
Here with me,
Is where all your problems and stress will be freed.
Here with me,
Is where fulfilled will be more than your wants and needs.

Salome Tseggai, Grade 11
Eastmoor Academy High School, OH

Monochrome Will

To turn a phrase, or to render anew
a few scant lines of my feelings for you
is so hard to do, why should I even try.
What is the point in me hiding behind,
timely words, and metaphorical hues?
Just colors of lies, to hide me from view.
If I could lay it straight, I'd lay it out:
a black and white portrait, no stupid spouts
of those red roses and these blue violets,
and allegories of dogs playing fetch.
No narrative flows with hopeful endings.
Just plain black ink with my heart on a string,
and feet to the ground and head in the sky,
eyes straight to the floor, ears high open wide,
to ride the rampant, wild whispering winds,
'til the sound of your voice brings me back in.
A saying. An answer. Simply yes or no.
If only that easy. Oh how I wish it so.

TajRoy Calhoun, Grade 12
EA Johnson High School, MI

Special Gift of God

How I miss my friend Darian
Whom I enjoyed so much
Whose smile which could brighten the heavens
He taught me the meaning of true friendship
The way to live life without regret
People who understood him felt his gift and his presence
His loyalty, and trustworthiness
His capability and determination
Sometimes my decision to disagree with him made me
Lost and confused that's why I sometimes feel like
I've abandoned and disgraced him I look back at the times
We've cherished and I've never forgotten what we've
Been through and accomplished
We were like a mother's 1st sight at her newborn
He would have grown to admire what I have done
Learning, paying attention, and respecting
They might have took his life
But his memory they will never take.

Justin Lacy, Grade 10
Oak Creek High School, WI

Restless

Heart racing, mind rushing, blood pulsing…
Oppressive, anguished thoughts
Beckon ravens to the sight
Pain deepens its caress
Pupils dilate in fright.
Heart racing, mind rushing, blood pulsing…
The horizon seems endless
Taunting the tortured mind
Skin is the only restraint
To manic energy, the worst kind.
Heart racing, mind rushing, blood pulsing…
The mists of terror,
Delight in the confusion
Exhaustion is welcomed,
It would end the delusion.
Heart racing, mind rushing, blood pulsing…
Staggering, stumbling,
Willing it to appear —
An escape, a serenity,
For insanity draws near.

Restless.

Casey Knoll, Grade 12
Bowness High School, AB

Happy as a Pebble

I love sitting
In street middles, and
I keep sunning
My quirky sides, but
I'm quiet mostly,
Until fate from a truck's tire
Flings me into your windshield — Whack —
Hi! Where are you driving to today?

Garrett Wilkes, Grade 11
Forest Hills Central High School, MI

Do You Love Me?

Do you still remember me?
Or have I become a dream?
Do you still fill that empty space?
Or did I drain it with all the pain?
Do you still remember my sweet brown eyes?
Or have they become dark, dull, dumb colors?
Are you still there waiting for me?
Or are you gone and moving on?
Remember what you promised me?
Remember what I meant to you?
Or did you forget?
Or listen to somebody else?
So will you be there?
Are you gonna fall into my arms again?
Will you be by my side no matter what I did?
Even knowing that I'm doing whatever it takes?
So do you?
Love me?

Gustavo A. Guerra, Grade 12
Prairie Lakes School, MN

You

All I ever did was
kiss you.
And I'm really going to
miss you.
I will never ever
forget you.
I really hope she doesn't
use you.
My first kiss was
only you.
And everyone else knew,
even you.
I think my heart has been crushed
by you.
But why does it matter? It was
just you.

Ashley Foster, Grade 12
Unioto High School, OH

Companion

The one who has been there for me,
from night to dusk,
as I crouched down
and did profuse amounts of homework.
I was stared at,
watched by what seemed like a hawk,
till I got the job done.

For new things,
I was pushed —
not encouraged
by one who is optimistic,
till I accepted them.

Though through tough times
I stumbled and tripped,
I was helped up
by what seemed like a guardian angel
who guided me through,
till I was up on my feet.
All thanks to
the one who has been there for me.

Joe Chue, Grade 10
Troy High School, MI

A Cry in the Night

I cry in the night
and the night cries in me
and together we sit,
we sit in our tree,
I in the night
and the night in me.
For only together can either be free.

Gregory L. Bryant, Grade 10
William Fremd High School, IL

Top Secret Cargo

She may not be OK
Yet she is alive
Frantically tearing around
Screaming for him to see into her barren soul
To reach in and gather up the pieces of her heart
And delicately place them on his love-written arms

Her eyes dart around
Hoping that someone will appear to sew her shattered life back together
Always believing in the mirage of hope
Diving like a hungry animal into what is on the plate before her
Every time she is left yearning for more
The thirst in her mind which is now in her heart is never quenched

Who he was made a dramatic exit
Carrying who she was as a heavy burden, as top secret cargo
Sometimes she'll see herself
Rippling through life like a wave that gracefully laps the shore
Always coming back one more time, never without strength
Desperately she extends her arms to embrace the person she's becoming
But she can never quite reach herself on the endless journey
    of discovering the thoughts
Which stand like guards at the door of her mind.

Julene Kaethler, Grade 10
Robert Bateman Secondary School, BC

I Play the Guitar

Deep down, there is a person inside,
Waiting to jump out — it screams.
I tell it to be patient.
"Tonight, you may tiptoe out." I softly whisper.

Tonight, I am going to release my inner self —
I am going to let my emotions rush through the tips of my fingers
To shatter all the secrets — imprisoned under the smiles, laughter, and joy,
Especially the unrevealed, my dismay.

I play the guitar.

I will play hard and loud —
I will play 'til the sun goes down.

I play the guitar.

Tonight, will be no ordinary night,
I will escape from reality. I will let the world feel my day;
My tensions; my dreams;
What's underneath it all; I will not be stereotyped.

I play the guitar.

Catherine D. Carnahan, Grade 10
Bethel Tate High School, OH

About Me

Austin —
Loving, caring, thoughtful, sharing
Brother of Jenna
Lover of fresh smell of grass, the sound of thunder,
and the whistle in the wind
Who feels lonely, happy, and sad
Who needs friends, family, and love
Who gives support, respect, and love
Who would like to see himself being successful in life,
the love of a mother, and a lovely future wife
Who live in a house that is supported by his own mother,
in a city called Hutchinson
— Colon

Austin Colon, Grade 11
Prairie Lakes School, MN

Sadness Is a Rainy Day

Sadness is a rainy day
One of which won't go away.
Don't bring me downward, spiral fall.
They leave at last this waterfall.
Sinister shadows, grey and blue.
You'll never guess what they can do.
Boom, bang, bash through the night.
Covering up what's now not in sight.
Hoping it will once turn right.
The end of this will soon be here.
The rain will run without a fear.
Nor a tear will fall down.
Slowly crashing to the ground.
With this now said, it will be fine.
To open up these sores of mine.
To take a chance on sadness and a rainy day.

Chelsea Scott, Grade 11
Lake Cowichan Secondary School, BC

A Daughter's Love

This is a poem to my mother.
Who has been there for me,
Whenever I was down.
Who was there for me at my best,
And fixed me at my worst,
As her joyful self was always there.
Those brown, hazel eyes twinkle
With joy as she smiles with happiness.
There were times of pain,
And times of heartache
Yet those times that we have connected
Were what meant the most to me
The thought that my mother was a role model,
The thought that she was amazing,
To know that she is my best friend.
For the love I have, and for the life I live,
My thoughts on this person, who means the most,
Will never change.
So I write this poem to my mother.

Machaela Schultz, Grade 10
Oak Creek High School, WI

Summer Is

Bathing suits and tan lines from the golden sun
Taking a quick dip in the pool just for some fun
Chocolate ice cream dripping down the cone
Staying up till midnight talking on the phone
Barefoot walks on the sandy beaches
Drinking smoothies made from peaches
Watching fireworks illuminate the sky
Being with family on the 4th of July
Late night parties, sleep until noon
Leaving relaxing vacation way too soon
Best friends and bonfires every single night
Being so free feels so right

Jacqui Brummer, Grade 11
Solon High School, OH

Physics Class

Physics is not for those with a weak heart.
You can get stressed if things do not go well.
Firstly, you must try to find where to start,
Then find out how fast and far someone fell.
There are too many numbers you must use,
Sometimes they cause all sorts of weird pain.
Physics is like a way to abuse
The delicate parts of your brain!
Although getting marks is not that easy
Hard work and studying do pay off.
Bonus "rock" marks are kind of sleazy
All you have to do is correct the prof!

Physics is useful, so please do not shun
Mr. Miller's Physics class, it is fun!

Bartek Jakobik, Grade 12
Mother Teresa Catholic High School, ON

Best Friend

Our meeting was unique,
I got up,
so did you.
We walked across the room,
together.
A journey.
We started growing.
Talks got longer,
deeper.
I could tell you secrets,
things I didn't tell anyone.
Trust.
Always there.
Now I need you,
depend on you,
count on you.
Don't know what I would do without you.
No longer a friend,
you're family.

Michelle Bézaire, Grade 12
Ecole secondaire E J Lajeunesse, ON

All That You Are

Does my happiness upset you?
Did you want to break my spirit?
Sex appeal is all you offer;
Your eyes now fall.

I'm still a free bird,
Riding on a cool breeze.
I have named the sky my own.

You look at the stars
And see your lost dream.
Your dream that has confessed,
To being your disease.

Your eyes and heart are locked in hate.
Stuck in the past,
Wishing it was present.

I spread my wings and fly away,
Wishing you weren't living a lie.

Katie Pennington, Grade 10
Fairfield High School, OH

I Want to Be Like Her

She's the best mom
To my brother and I
I love to see her laugh,
I hate to see her cry

She's taught me so much;
I don't think she knows
The little things I appreciate
There's only so much one can show

If I could be just like her,
That's a chance I would take
If ever I lost her,
How my heart would break

So whom do I speak of?
Like whom do I wish to be?
My role model, my hero
And best of all, my mommy.

Alexandra Franke, Grade 10
Reynoldsburg High School, OH

Her Reflection

Could I see right through her, if I tried?
To the real person underneath:
Sometimes I wonder who she is?
With her eyes painted on upside down
By an unforgiving culture;
The result of a distorted reflection
Shown by a broken and tainted mirror.

Kat Weltha, Grade 12
Joplin Sr High School, MO

Me

Esteban
Funny, active, nice, and well dressed
Brother of Alex, Angie, Sandy, and Rene
Lover of money, family, and food
Who feels happy, sad, and mad
Who needs money, love, and family
Who gives laughs, love and listens
Who fears losing a loved one, no happiness, and not having a home
Who would like to see my mom happy, new people, and sunrise
Who lives in a nice size town in a yellow house with a loving family
Vargas

Esteban Vargas, Grade 10
Prairie Lakes School, MN

Mirror, Mirror

Mirror, mirror,
Still and clear, a surface untouched and untainted.
Your reflection contains contentment and bliss,
Your rejection contains malice and self hate.
Mirror, mirror,
Your sight shows shattered dreams,
Your voice tells a vindictive tale each day.
Mirror, mirror,
I look at you with open eyes yearning for harmony.
I avoid your gaze as your cruel stare pierces through me.
Mirror, mirror,
My flaws are visibly displayed in your expression,
Cemented in my face is the characterless appearance for humanity to see.
Mirror, mirror,
You judge, you hate, you ridicule,
You are nothing more than a piece of glass.
Yet, I need your approval before I can be true to myself and to others.
You are only a mirror,
Mirror, mirror.

Alexandra Jecklin, Grade 12
Queen Margaret's School, BC

Spider Girl

You spin your web —
Waiting to be fed.
Feeding from their affection,
Just to get an extra helping of attention —
Everyone sees you as pretty…
But, oh, dear spider girl you aren't so witty.

Your web of silky satin —
Their hearts you soon will flatten,
They'll see you then as cold,
Your silk heart isn't meant for gold.
Spider girl, please don't be surprised to see them mourning!
After all you should come with a warning!

Spider girl, someday your outer shell will shed —
Then everyone will see your true colors…Orange, Black and Dead!

Jennifer Magda, Grade 12
Jonesville High School, MI

Friends

Friends are the ones who will be there for you
Friends are the ones that will tell you they love you
If they are true friends they will listen to you,
Hug you,
Love you,
Care for you!
They will bring smiles to you
Brighten your day
I value my friends
Don't want to lose them
I will do anything to keep them as a friend
I will do anything
Go out of my way to be there for them no matter what
You need others to get through life
You really need love to live a happy life
That's why I think friends are important

Trent Westerlund, Grade 10
Prairie Lakes School, MN

I'm Counting

I counted the squares on the ceiling
There were forty-two in all
Those squares represent the times you left
Or never even called at all

I counted the tiles on the floor
They totaled one hundred and ten
More than the times you kissed me
More than what could have been

I counted the number of pictures of us
More than I would ever want
The pictures of places we'd had stupid fun
Were just stupid little jaunts

I'm counting the stars in the darkening sky
The amount is growing and will never end
It averages those times I wished for you
To just maybe be my friend

Bailey Poolman, Grade 12
Centerville High School, IA

Time

It never stops, nor does it go backwards.
It has and will always be important.
Though it's important, people forget.

Without time, nothing would be the same.
All that will be left is void.
There wouldn't be a past, a present, nor a future.

Thus time should not be forgotten.
We should always cherish the time we have.
After all, no one can go back in time.

Shin Ae Lee, Grade 11
William Fremd High School, IL

Meant to Be

Me and you were meant to be like a perfect picture drawn
I hope I never see the day when you and I are gone
I wanna come back home and feel your soft skin
I feel like everyone's against me it's too hard but I can't win
I'm doing all I can to make this thing work out
I still have to stop and think my head is full of doubt
I love you so much and that is not a lie
And if I can't live the way I want then I am prepared to die
Feelings jumbled up pain inside my head
There's not one exaggeration in every word that you just read
If I had it my way I'd see you every day
It's too bad I don't so here is what I have to say
I'm always nervous first I stand then I sit
You are always on my mind an addiction I can't quit
You've blinded me from the world all I see is you
Anything you say tell me what to do
Your intoxicating smell it lifts me off my feet
I love it when you look at me you love it when I wink
I'll never say goodbye I'll never hold you back
I just want to thank you for keeping me on track

Aaron Howell, Grade 10
Lincoln High School, MI

Tick Tock…Tick Tock

Second by second passes as I stare,
at the clock on the wall, tick tock.
How much more can I bear
of this wearisome class talk? Tick tock.

It has hands and a face, but ceases to speak.
There is one too many past every door.
Imagine if there was a leak,
all the parts that would fall.
No more ticking, no more tocking,
just the endless Raven's rapping.

But yet, I cannot live without it,
or I would no longer know when the bell will ring.

Kayla Pickel, Grade 12
Taylorville Sr High School, IL

I-5

Inertia swings us down I-5,
Ponds lay dead yet sparkle alive,
Gazing upon loons in fields of glass,
Wrapped in a maze blanket stitched in grass.

God puffs beneath His purest smoke,
Divine streams multiply, dividing schools of oak,
But just I was granted the grandest view,
A ten ton steel semi blocked a beauty too few.

Countless trees now stumps, paralyzed cripples,
Lifeless as confetti inserted bulletin board staples,
What excuse exists?
A day where shining rivers run dry of sands,
When our children point to the empty barren lands.

David Zhang, Grade 12
RC Palmer Secondary School, BC

Over and Over Forever

Over and over I try
Over and over I'll die
It feels like you're gone forever
Over and over I'll deny
What I feel inside
I'll tell myself you're gone
When you're right here
Over and over I'll try
Over and over I'll die
I can't lie
I won't deny
I hope you feel like I'm gone forever
When I'm staring you in the eyes
Over and over you'll try
To deny what was
Over and over I'll die trying
You're gone forever
And so am I

Heather Milburn, Grade 11
Washington Park High School, WI

The Perfect One

He made me smile,
he made me frown.
He made me laugh,
he made me cry.

I tried so hard to be the one,
the perfect one, the only one.
No matter how hard I had to try,
I'd lay in bed and cry and cry.

I made him smile,
I made him frown.
I made him laugh,
I made him cry.

Now I know he's not the one,
the perfect one, the only one.
I no longer have to try,
for the one, who made me cry.

Megan Call, Grade 11
MACCRAY High School, MN

Part Blue, Part Black

Part of me is black —
Guards up ready for war
Mean and unlikable
Never caring, reckless
Another part of me is blue —
Loving whoever shows love
Living life day by day
Having loyalty to all friends and family

Kamau Evans, Grade 11
Prairie Lakes School, MN

Why You

Every time I look your way there's a part of my heart that breaks.
Then there's another part that just can't stop fluttering.
I can't stop myself from thinking about you,
And when I finally get over you, then all of a sudden there you are
With your eyes that capture me and your smile that melts me.
I can't stop myself from falling for you.
You're the one, who makes my day,
Yet you're the one who can also break it.
Every day I tell myself that I can't have you, that your heart belongs to another.
Still though, there's this part of me that wants you to want me.
And as badly as I want to be able to walk up to you and say I no longer need you,
My heart tells me stop being a fool, you know that you need him.
I can't walk away, nor can I look away,
Why is it that you have such a strong hold?
My head says leave, but my heart is screaming no.
How do you tell the one that makes your heart ache how you really feel,
How do you stop the tears from coming and how do you get the one you love?

Hilary Thums, Grade 10
Rib Lake High School, WI

You Are My Music

The music blows gently through my hair; I can feel it running over my skin.
It is the surface that I walk on, and it is the force that pushes me to live.
I can hear you smiling through it:
You are so happy, and you are looking at me.
The music reminds me of laughter; it reminds me of better times.
I can feel your happiness when I listen to it; I can even feel your lips against mine.
The music is a blanket I wrap myself in when I am alone and scared.
The music is also arms around me when I am crying.
My music is the only thing I have when you are not there.
But I can feel you through my music:
I can feel your embrace; I can feel your warm skin against mine.
I can feel you wiping away my tears, and I can feel your love.
I can feel it all over me…my skin is tingling.
My music brings this sensation, this feeling of passion and security.
My music does not bring you to me; you bring music into my heart.
You are my music.

Megan Leanne Halston, Grade 12
George Elliot Secondary School, BC

Anatomy of My Colors

Red is the color of my scarf,
It resembles the blood that beats from my heart.
Who carries oxygen from the end through the middle to the start
That fills my lungs with hope and sets my mind apart

Purple is the color of my heart
Which resembles that of a lion's which sets me apart
It pumps ambition through my veins resembling that of my scarf
And though I'm down I will never be torn apart

Miles Edinburgh, Grade 12
Prairie Lakes School, MN

Deliquesce

What beauty there is in the cold —
In that one day soon it will thaw
And bleed out into the surrounding earth.
That — with winter's embrace —
There is rebirth:
A great hollow carcass breathes life to maggots.

Jeremy Segal, Grade 11
Ecole Saint Georges de Montreal, QC

His Name Was Indifference

You can't touch me
I'm untouchable
That is what I make myself to be
Emotionless
Plead for comfort when it's needed most
I will give you nothing
Ask for reassurance, I give you silence
Cry for acceptance, I give you none at all
You can't touch me
Wishing for friendship you look at me with hope
Prepare for disappointment
For all you will obtain is my scorn
Acknowledgment is what you seek
But I pass you by without sparing a glance
Filled with grief you ask for a shoulder to cry on
Rejection is all you receive from me
You can't touch me
Try as you might you will not succeed
Your efforts are futile
I'm untouchable
That is what I make myself to be

Tiffany Marie Frymire, Grade 11
West Central High School, IL

Ode to the Fallen Leaf

You lay there,
left alone, abandoned, disregarded.
The winds whorl as you float along
finding new places to settle each and every time.
Your color changes as time passes,
and the air stretched the life right out of you.
If only, if only that orange and black Frisbee
had not landed on your tree branch
and knocked you off.
Now you float above the ground
until the roaring winds die,
and you drift to your new home.
Never to see your old life again.
Never to fully understand
the meaning of home.
Never to find that true meaning of love.
ou could understand
freedom that you possess
o find, to be yourself,
t again you are
bandoned, disregarded.

Mandy Walsh, Grade 12
John Hersey High School, IL

In the Vase

All the flowers are standing tall,
All but one, that one falls.
The standing are the proud,
The numerous, the loud.
The crooked one is me:
Unique and carefree.
All are still in the same vase,
I'm just bent different, I have the same face.
So, we are the same, me and you,
But also different at the same time too.
Judging should not be done by your shape and size,
You should be judged by what's inside.

Mallory Makl, Grade 12
Vassar Sr High School, MI

Father Like Son

"Stop!" stated fear
"No!" echoed joy
Laugher spread, "You go play."
The sound of tiredness, "Go run around."

A silence.
Slithering — an excited jump!
In happiness, both slide down the slide.
"Like a falling star, his falling star."

Shoes come flying. All exhausted of course.
Slight movement, kiss one sleeping child.
Father like son.

Dakota Olson, Grade 12
Prairie Lakes School, MN

A Different Kind of Shadow (Time's Shadow)

A shadow that clutches the hands of all life.
Not a day goes by that eyes don't see you.
But if everyone and no one can see you,
then who will notice you when we're gone?
Your demise is increasing at not being noticed.
Not a day goes by when you aren't there.
Every day is the same.
The sun sets,
and the moon rises.
The years go by,
and generations fade.
The balance of life and death,
is strung like a bead on a shredded string.
A bond between us has grown into my daily life.
You are my friend and my enemy.
We will come to know each other though.
You are not a shadow,
yet you cling to all life like one.
You are…
…a different kind of shadow…
…that never disappears.

Paige Mundy, Grade 12
Belleville High School West, IL

Homeless*

I guess I don't really know
What it must be like
Day after day
Under that old rusty bridge

That box that once held
A home appliance
Holding you at night
Your only shelter

A small contaminated creek
A product of peoples littering
Washes your face in the morning
You drink from it at night

But you came to me
Today and now I know
The hardships of being
Homeless

Chelsea Grider, Grade 10
Carmi-White County High School, IL
*Patterned after "Luxury"
by Nikki Giovanni

The Question

Why is it hard to be a teen,
Trying so much to fit the scene,
Why must we all go away,
And soon be gone the very next day.

Joseph Perez, Grade 10
Thomas A Edison Jr/Sr High School, IN

Blindness

I used to look at women,
Picking apart their physical qualities.
I used to stare at their bodies,
Objectifying them,
Comparing them,
Belittling them,
Criticizing the ones I didn't approve of.
I used to only look at women.

Then the accident happened.
I woke up in the hospital,
Both eyes bandaged shut.
I could see only darkness.

The nurse talked to me when I awoke.
Her soothing words flowed into my body.
I could sense the concern in her voice.
Her personality surrounded me.

I am blind,
But now I see perfectly.

Nate Thome, Grade 12
Troy High School, MI

To Be

What is life?
Is it found in the grass we walk on?
Or the cry of a newborn child?
It doesn't come with a manual;
Has its own set of ups and downs.
And in the winding road to the top,
We get lost.
End up in dark, desolate places,
Or end up in the arms of the right one.
The one who gives meaning to every new day,
The one who stands by us as we find our way,
And the one who holds our hand when we're scared or go astray.

Life,
It's a learning process,
And we learn by doing.
So I cannot learn to love you,
I just do.

Denise Santos, Grade 10
Mary Ward Catholic Secondary School, ON

Demolition Day

There is a wrecking ball hurtling towards my life
It doesn't bother to slow so I won't bother to act surprised
I wait for the demolition like I wait for the midnight train
The calm before the storm, I have one request and whisper your name
Everything is shaking, things tumbling to the ground
Out of mind, out of sight, I'm with you so my heart is sound
Glass shatters in picture frames over all the photos of you and me
But that's okay because I have you and I have my memory
They can take everything from me, in ruins my life will lay
They can take the rain, the joy of the night, and the beauty of the day
But no one can take the love that you have so willingly given to me
We will lay in the damage and wreckage holding hands together in peace.

Ashley Tadlock, Grade 11
Rantoul Township High School, IL

The Birth of Civilization

A civilization was born in ancient times,
So let me tell you the story in my best rhymes.
Between the Tigris and Euphrates Rivers were no barbarians,
But a people who were called the Sumerians.
Mesopotamia birthed many Sumerian city-states.
They were similar in culture with many gods controlling their fates.
Worshiped in Ziggurats by the city's middle,
The rulers were people, but agents of the gods' tricky riddle.
Social classes consisted of nobles, commoners, and slaves.
Though in the end, their destiny was the graves.
Families began with a marriage arranged.
Men headed the household, while women were shortchanged.
Sumerian clay bricks built arches, columns, and ramps.
While using cuneiform writing made them the champs.
Fall of the Sumerian Empire came after years and years
For Sargon and the Akkadian's military, brought forth their tears.

Madeline Osbrink, Grade 10
Mount Carmel Academy, LA

Close to You

As I am walking through the silent cemetery,
I get a chill throughout my body.
I look around at all the headstones
and notice how lonely they are.

As I make my way up the hill,
I feel lonely myself.
The place where she lies,
is the place where I stand.

I am trying hard
to hold all these emotions in.
I think to myself:
this is the closest I'll ever be to you.

I light the candle and stare at the grave.
The tears by now are rolling down my face.
This is the closest
I'll ever be to you.

Manuela Miclea, Grade 10
Troy High School, MI

Hard to Rise

Why do we do what we do?
People killing each other over money, drugs, and power…
To think that we have come so far,
Yet we're barely scratching the surface,
Of this so called "world of ours"…
How do we start?
Where do we start?
Because it's our choice to rise,
And our choice to fall…
But sometimes it's hard to rise…
When everyone around you is falling…

Michael Sanchez, Grade 11
The Ranch Program at Salem, IL

Getting Over You

A word, a sigh,
A slight smile as you're walking by?
You act like you don't see me anymore.
How could you just up and walk out the door?
Do you not remember what we had,
Just thinking about it makes me sad.
I see you and all the feelings come back with a rush,
And the world around me goes into a deep hush.
I look away,
Hoping you'll have something to say.
But you just walk by
And I feel like I want to die.
It's hard to get over you,
But I'm finding the way through.
I'm finally walking away,
And I don't care what you have to say.

Megan Pettet, Grade 11
Morgan High School, OH

The Sun Had Shone So Brightly in the Morn

The sun had shone so brightly in the morn.
The farmer rose out of his creaky bed.
The winds whipped fast; the little farm they scorned.
The wilting flowers and the fading corn
bent in the winter wind while darkness spread.
The sun had shone so brightly in the morn.
The wired fence the awful wind had torn.
The farmer ran out to the crooked shed.
The winds whipped fast; the little farm they scorned.
The farmer snatched the shovel that was worn.
"I must get out there fast," the farmer said.
The sun had shone so brightly in the morn
The trees could not hold on to the acorns.
All over the dirt earth the acorns spread.
The winds whipped fast; the little farm they scorned.
After the destruction the farmer mourned
the loss of the life that he always led.
The sun had shone so brightly in the morn.
Of the farmer's sleep the winter winds warned.
No longer did he rise out of his bed.
The sun had shone so brightly in the morn.

Kayla Watson, Grade 12
Destrehan High School, LA

Baseball

The sun is shining out on the battlefield.
Two men are locked in an epic battle.
They stare at each other showing no fear.
Then one makes a sudden move and fires a rocket.
The other quickly reacts, he swings and misses.
It hits the glove with a thud, Strike Three you're out.

Tim Kaye, Grade 12
Arrowhead Union High School - North Campus, WI

Eternal Love

My mellow mother is the one I turn to
whenever I need a shoulder to lean on,
or ask for advice, or simply share a laugh with.
She multitasks very well;
that is what I admire most about her.
She cooks, cleans after us,
and provides us with all of the essentials.
Yup, that's my mother.
I cherish all of the precious moments we have together.
Every time I'm with her,
I feel that our bond is unbreakable.
She influences me, and I influence her.
I give her all of the latest fashion trends
and what's hot and what's not,
while she tells me to work hard in school
and what's right and what's wrong.
As I get older, all these loving memories and the ones to come,
will certainly stay with me throughout life.
My flesh and blood, my best friend,
who I will love eternally.
Yup, that's my mother.

Mayer Trenh, Grade 10
Troy High School, MI

Who Loves Me

Dad is someone who teaches you right from wrong, who loves you no matter what, who cooks for you when your stomach "talks" to you. The smell of his french toast from across the room brings warmth to my heart and makes my tummy say "hi." The sight of his finger pointing when he is giving his lectures. The hugs he gives when I do something wrong or need security. He squeezes so tight enveloping me with a blanket of love.

I remember my dad coming in my bedroom and telling me children's stories and doing different character voices as well. I remember the football, basketball, and baseball games he took me to though he could not remember where he parked the car after the game was over. From the games we play on PlayStation and Wii to the television we watch, especially *Different Strokes*. I remember the time we played *Who Wants to Be a Millionaire* on the computer. I imagined the sound of money appearing in my hand once we WON the game.

Dad loves me with all his heart, from his head to his toes. He teaches me valuable information that I will carry with me from head on. His pancakes are delicious and his blintzes are scrumptious.

The sun will set and it is time to go to bed. I will say my good nights and pray for my family.

Katie Muyleart, Grade 10
Oak Creek High School, WI

Confessions of a Broken Heart

Heartbroken and despaired, I became aware of just how wrong you were, you played me and played her.
Just when you thought you had me at my weakest stage, I showed you common sense has nothing to do with age.
Thought I wouldn't notice? Thought I couldn't see? My eyes are wide open, you didn't fool me.
I feel bad for her…not you, 'cause I already know what she's going through.
She thinks it's love when it's no more than lust, she believes in you and gives you all her trust.
Faithful loving, sinful lies, lonely nights and teary eyes.
She thinks you're true, no matter what you do.
Young and foolish, innocent of…losing herself and falling in love.
Awakening to the truth and all you had done, suddenly being in love isn't so much fun.
He begins to lie and come up with new excuses, when will he realize his talk is useless?
She gives up on him and decides they're better off apart. It's not just a poem, it's memoirs of my heart.
I know how she felt and what she went through. I was in her shoes once, I cried those tears too.

Shacree Hamilton, Grade 10
M L Winans Academy of Performing Arts – Detroit, MI

I Am New and Old

I am new and old. I have only unconditional love.
My knowledge, many seek to understand.
I do not discriminate, I see only you
Stacked in rows I wait, for hands to set me free.
I am a friend, a travel companion to all who seek me.
The darkness traps me, engulfs me; keeps me from freedom.
I yearn to take you away, to hold you in my arms,
Taking you to places you dream about on a flying carpet.
I can turn your dreams into realities, and take you from this world and its realities.

Now, I am aged with years, my world no longer new.
My visitors come slowly and irregularly now.
My back is broken with age, my heart crinkled and yellowed.
The dust I have gathered shows my story is old and well traveled.
I sleep now dreaming of our adventures.
Oh, how I miss seeing your smiling face.
But look there you are, your face still smiling.
I weep inky tears as you pass me for someone new.
I wait silently hoping your hands will choose me someday and scatter the shadows around me.

Elizabeth Oberlies, Grade 12
Union High School, MO

Genuine Fervor

Sitting upon hours, gazing into space,
'Tis marveling of love and affection;
Lovers convene, await others' embrace,
Gentle to my heart, thou art perfection.

Thoughts of existence, transpiring joy,
Thou brings such gratifying adornment;
A love nourished, a yearning to enjoy,
'Tis light as soft a touch of contentment.

Others he has courted, flouting my heart,
Shoved away with un-passionate desire;
Letting out a cry, for the time apart,
Engaged in foolish conduct, thou art a liar.

Three spoken words, a blissful 'I love you,'
Thou cannot question fervor purely true.

Brandi Trzop-Goodick, Grade 11
Prince Andrew High School, NS

Much Like You

I scrutinize the infinite flame suffocate, mesmerized
by its mass murder
Much like the ring fixated on your left hand
I hear the ingeminated melody of the grandfather clock
Much like your feet prowl towards the door
I speak wrathful and rueful tongues
Much like you attempt still merely mumbling
I question the success of holy matrimony
Much like you have your married life
I criticize unsettled and uncertain values
Much like you do this union
I vindicate those who have mistaken
Much like you demur father-some figures
I become curtained during ruptured crusades
Much like you derive from rigid hands
I witness the infinite flame suffocate
Much like you have this life of yours
I am much like you

LaTeesha Beck, Grade 12
Melville Comprehensive High School, SK

Don's Sonnet

"How do I love thee? Let me count the ways."
To begin would take more than one night,
For the count is not near small if done right.
It is a worthy wonder
To see where my sonnet will end,
For I shall make a list of immeasurable number
And word each way which will my love defend.
My essence is disturbed like heaven by thunder,
But this thunder is wanted for all of God's days.
It is not possible to describe my love's might.
Neither word nor number can express how bright
Compared to what my soul and essence send
To my holy love who is above and without slumber.

Michelle Aertker, Grade 12
Zachary High School, LA

A Smile to Hide the Frown

Look at the girl sitting all alone
She always puts on a smile to hide the frown.
She looks at the people who have it all
But what they don't know is at night she bawls.

Walking down the halls at school
All the people act so cruel
If they were in her shoes,
They wouldn't know what to do.

She'll always wait for that day
When you'll be by her side
So she won't be all alone
Putting on a smile to the frown.

Kaitlyn Van-Y, Grade 11
Swan Valley High School, MI

The Once a Year

Carly. Her name makes me smile.
Things I love about her I could write for a mile:
her pretty eyes and accent are things that I love.
If she were the baseball, then I'd be the glove.
I love the choice of words that to me she would teach.
I cherish our dancing and long walks on the beach.
Her company is precious. When we get together for dinner,
when she's by my side, I know I'm a winner.
My favorite times are with her when we watch the sun set.
A smile stayed on my face from the day that we met.
Carly. Her name makes me smile.
Things I love about her I could write for a mile.

Martin Hella, Grade 10
Troy High School, MI

I Have Love

I have loved.
So too then, have I coveted,
So too then, have I thieved,
So too then, have I killed;
Such acts may be categorized together,
According to what so many who oppose me have said.

If I am denied one right,
I may as well be denied all right;
To admit I deserve less
Is to admit I am less;
To admit I am less
Is ultimately to wish me gone.

But on I love,
In spite of the hate,
Knowing I have done nothing but love,
I accept my fate,
For in my mind,
There is nothing that great.

Daniel Reed, Grade 11
Waseca High School, MN

The Breeze

The sun is setting
I'm slowly dazing
This passion overtakes
All reality and entity
That could ever take place
Appearing in front of me
Your arms surround me
A heart beating to the rhythm of mine
Here in this moment in time
For this one minute
Distance isn't an issue
I felt you
I saw you
I held you
Until the night's breeze
Came to steal that ease
Fantasy could no longer last
This distance between us remains vast

Zeinab Zeidan, Grade 12
Ecole secondaire E J Lajeunesse, ON

Dreams in the Morning

For once in my life
My dream came true.
That dream
Was you.

But it did not last,
My fairy tale romance.
We had no
Second chance.

You left me to cry
With every other girl,
Who let you
Crush her world.

I should have known.
I should have seen.
But seeing only
Ruins the dream.

Lea Hair, Grade 11
Episcopal School of Acadiana, LA

Life

Life is a long, dark corridor.
You don't know where you are going,
Will the path ever become clear?
Are you doomed to walk alone,
In this black and cold corridor?
It's up to you to find the light.
The question is…
Can you?

Aaron Schueller, Grade 12
Prairie Lakes School, MN

Pain and Sorrow

Pain and sorrow, lust and love,
Buried deep within a lonely soul,
You gave me a chance to show you
Who I truly am and a chance to be me
My pain you saw through when no one else did
My sorrow you felt when no one else acknowledged it
My nights became yours as we sat up together
Holding each other laughing and crying
My days became yours
As every thought that crossed my mind was of you and no other
It was by you that I felt that I could be free
It was sitting with you that I felt that healing glee
Joy and happiness had for a time lost their meaning
You not only restored them in my life but imprinted them on my soul
My love, how can I convey to you
That what I feel for you is not lust but actual love
These words are not words
They are the melody that my soul sings
At every dusk, dawn, noon and twilight
Now there remains little to say except that
I love you, I have loved you, and I always will

Zainab Chaudhry, Grade 12
Crescent Academy International, MI

Today

The ground is still wet
The dirt is stained a dark chocolate shade
Stray leaves soaked to the floor
Plastered against the concrete like thieves hiding a raid

The trees stand strong
Their leaves glowing a vivid green
Never wilting but instead sticking straight out and long
Sucking up water to live longer and recreate this scene

Shadows play on the ground
Waiting to be moved by the sun
Their dark figures flicker
The day has just begun
The sun beats down on the surroundings
The ground slowly drying and changing from black to a dark grey
The birds start chirping
It is a new day

Now everything is dry
The trees, the dirt, the ground
But I just smile as
I cannot hear a sound
This is today — a different day than yesterday.

Nathan Kuyek, Grade 10
Robert Bateman Secondary School, BC

Death by Eraser

Dizzy, faint, slowly to disappear
voice becoming a whisper.
You feel weak; your energy is gone.
You see no light in the darkness
which has blinded you from what had
once made you happy.

You feel you are closed in, trapped
by a bounding, suffocating force.
Of course you cannot see it, so how are you to defeat it?
You stagger around life, unsure of what to do.
You have no reason to feel like this,
but in the end you know it's true…

It has consumed you.

Marie Morris, Grade 11
Hillmond Central School, SK

Declaration of Love

Come live with me and be my love
You'll fly greater than the clouds above
You'll be my rose, my tulip
And your heart will never rip.

I will hold you close
As of your beauty I take a dose
I will care for you when you are sick
And be by your side when you are down and weak.

Oh! My heart blooms with passion for you
My only hope is that you love me too.

Luisa Vidales, Grade 12
Farragut Career Academy High School, IL

The Sweet Loss Of…

One winter night my bones stiff as ice
but I sweat with love
the wind tears my face apart
with the freezing slap of Mother Nature
I grab her hands
she leaps on two toes
I arch my neck down
to feel the soft warm touch of her lips on my frozen lips
I am as hot as an oven set to broil!
I wander home in a cloud
but it was the first day of a terrible after-feeling
my bones are no longer stiff it is my heart
I no longer sweat with love, I pour tears
the frozen slap on my face comes from her hand
she gives her love to this "football playing has-been"
on my face lies the handprint of Jasmine
inside I am rotting to the core
and I will never kiss those sweet lips
never more

Michael Gonzalez, Grade 10
Carl Schurz High School, IL

My Love*

I love you more than you could ever imagine,
You're all I think about day and night
Your laugh I could listen to for hours
I am so so glad I met you.
But as of right now I cannot live without you.
You have my heart please be careful.
It has been broken before
I don't think I could take the pain once more
So remember, no matter where you may go
A piece of my heart will be with you.
You have the most precious part of it also
And no matter where you go
That piece will be with you forever.

Brandy Nicole Mooney, Grade 10
Delta C 7 High School, MO
*Dedicated to Denny

Another Day in the Marsh

Whistling wings sail overhead
Twisting and turning like a fighter pilot
They bank dropping speed and altitude
Wings set and feet down they pass by

The hens talk to each other overhead
They circle again this time fully committed
Their iridescent green heads shine in the sun
They start dropping in one by one

Pop, Pop, Pop…echoes through the marsh
No feathers float through the air
No ducks hit the water
Oh well, it's just another day on the marsh

Chris Meschke, Grade 12
Waseca High School, MN

Treasure

Countless treasures, some lost, some found
Decorates our days.
The luster in the midnight sky
And golden gleam of the sun's sparkling rays.
The laughter of a mama's babies
Or a breathless view
A memory worth a thousand smiles
Learning things you never knew.
An ancient quilt stitched with old, loving hands
A string of grandmother's pearls.
A song played softly just for you,
Like you're the only soul in the world.
The warmth of hands intertwined,
Underneath the stars.
The comfort of an embracing hug,
The beat of another's heart.
Of all the treasure, all the love,
And all the things that shine
There is nothing that is more valuable
Than that of precious time.

Ellie Rodenberg, Grade 12
Eureka Sr High School, MO

Me Myself and I

My insides feel black —
Alone and afraid
Desperate and depressed
Destroying me by the minute
But at times I feel green —
Happy but mellow
Excited and cheerful
Smiling at each person I see
But when you mix those colors together
You always get me

Kyle Renowski, Grade 11
Prairie Lakes School, MN

Food Obsession

Bursting into my mouth.
Jell-O slips
And runs
Playing tag in my mouth.
Slapping one another,
And racing away.
Squirting me.
Killing me with flavor.
Squishing to dust,
Sloshing around,
Gathering together,
Ready to take a plunge.
Sliding down my throat
Tickling me on the way,
Smacking me in my stomach.
Waiting until others follow.

Kaitlyn Multhauf, Grade 11
Hartford Union High School, WI

Blush

A word was spoken
prematurely.
Wet and sticky —
tricky, trickling out
into the sterile silence.

I tried to hide it.
Covers draped my coffin legs —
a flag salute to all the dead
who failed to scale
the silence.

But you struck it.
Apologies cleansed and purged and
Hallelujah, sin is dead:
scalded down the sink.

Still the words march free
in your memory
and we'll never kill them now.

Nicholas Surges, Grade 12
Lisgar Collegiate Institute, ON

The Human Stages of Desire

Baby is born, to discover desire.
Wants, needs, sensations grow higher.

Adolescence comes along, so does desire
dreams of first love, burn inside like wildfire.

Adulthood comes with change, as well as desire
longing for love, wealth, and children to inspire.

Old age creeps along; creeping beside it is desire
as well as peace, harmony, which all come together once you retire.

Justin Lepine, Grade 12
Ecole secondaire E J Lajeunesse, ON

How It Is

School, I simply just don't even know the words to describe,
Sheer boredom? No, simply something to do,
To get me out of your life, but only for a moment.
Parents, well I think more than half my life I was being ignored,
Unless I did something wrong that is.

You think what I write is nonsense?
Well I'll show you; one day I am going to be a poet and when that day comes,
Who am I going to thank?
I am going to thank you, Dad, for feeding the anger that lives inside me.
For supplying me with the tools I need to express myself,
Even if you disagree, I thank you from the bottom of that anger that lives in me.

I applaud you for doing what you had to do,
I am not your little angel anymore, nor had I ever been,
You will always be my father, and that I am going to have to live with,
A world without me.

Allie Bergman, Grade 10
McKinley Sr High School, LA

Every Breath I Take

Every breath I take, and every smile I wear
Brings up only the prevailing past and current feelings I compare
Surrounded by the truth of what is no more
The ended existence of someone, I cannot ignore
The truth preserved in every waking moment I live
A continuous reminder that you no longer live
That unforgettable moment that still lingers in the air I breathe
With the everlasting pain carried beneath
The internal scars that still lay inside
The acceptance of it not truly complied
Because of how long it took for these tears to cease
It was letting you go that compelled these tears to release
That extended all the fears I carry with me
The feeling I may be carrying with me for eternity
Every breath I take, is felt so deep within
Every smile, is an effort in forgetting something I never wanted to happen
Something I never dreamed could ever be true
Something I found was wrong once I had lost you

Sophia Affleck, Grade 10
Killarney Secondary School, BC

Champions!

The diamond was perfect, green, brown, and white,
Two teams stood waiting, about to begin the fight,
It's game time, the ump shouted "Play Ball,"
The pitcher slung strike one, a breaking curveball.

It's now the top of the tenth, ten to ten,
I start to the plate, wondering how we can win,
The fans cheered me on, like I was their show,
I stepped into the box, wanting a massive blow.

The pitch was a fastball, nice and high,
I swung, delivering a devastating fly,
It sailed over the fence, and even over Venus,
I rounded the bases, everyone cheering for us!

Cody Riché, Grade 10
Holy Savior Menard Central High School, LA

Volleyball, Volleyball, and More Volleyball

Hearing the whistle and serving the ball
The feeling of getting ready to play is amazing
Getting a floor burn from a hard hit ball
Watching the ball fall into your setter's hand
Enjoying every hit that your hitters make

I could play volleyball in the hall
I could play all day long
Volleyball is my life
To win a gold ball I will strive

Even though it's time to go
The team just wants to play ball
I can't wait for the next day to come
We are a team that doesn't give up

Jordyn Anderson, Grade 10
Rib Lake High School, WI

Only So Much Fire

I've been making mistakes my whole life
I'm still going down those bad roads
I keep trying to find the positive side
But it gets hard
I bend my head down and realize
There can only be so much fire
Before I get burned
I'm crying and lying
And trying my hardest to learn
From my mistakes
And I have what it takes to make it
Sometimes I feel lost and alone
Even when I'm with my family
Sometimes when I'm with my friends I get angry
But I know they'll always save me
I realize someone cares
And they'll always be there
That makes me so much higher
There can only be so much fire.

Holly Smith, Grade 10
Cartwright High School, ON

The Board

To skate, is to live.
It's hard to understand.
Picking up a board is changing
The way you live.
You get judged,
And not always in a good way.
It enables you to see places
In a whole new perspective.
Building spots, holding it down.
With infinite possibilities.
Something you have to live to understand.

Daniel Herrera, Grade 10
Haynes Academy for Advanced Studies, LA

My Heart

He was a wolf in sheep skin to the eyes,
A weed pretending to be a red rose.
His smooth-talking tongue, the perfect disguise,
A prince charming in modern day clothes.
What he made up for in alluring words,
He lacked in empathy and wisdom.
Unsure and unstable like a flock of birds,
His eyes were cold and his love even more seldom.
But when the fog and my eyes had cleared,
All renewed hope had been brought to the light.
Nothing was left though my heart had been seared,
My sorrow had flown out into the night.
At one point I thought we could never be apart,
But there is still some fight left in this heart.

Cailey Bekker, Grade 12
Grand Forks Secondary School, BC

Seduction

Seduction
Love and betrayal
Joy and pain
Sunshine and rain
Dark nights and cloudy days
Seduction
Blood and shame
Love and fate
Why does love seem so fake
Treachery mesmerized
Enjoy don't hate
Maybe this chance you'll take
To do something great
Don't miss your shot
Before you reach the gate
Seduction
Don't hate
Love everything from up above
Help me feel the love
Seduction
Love and hate.

Alexis A. Hudson, Grade 11
School of Leadership at South Shore Campus, IL

My Darling Rae Anne

I remember
Those days
The day when you were born
The days I held you in my arms
I was so happy
To have you
But in the same time
I was scared to lose you
I remember
When you held my fingers
With your little hands
I wish I could see you
But I can't
I remember when I made you smile
That brought joy to my life
I'm sorry I messed it all up
Baby, I didn't mean to lose you
I don't want you to grow up
Be like your daddy, take care
You know I will always love you
No matter what
Ronald Anariba, Grade 11
Prairie Lakes School, MN

Waiting For…

I'm waiting for that moment,
The one that stops time,
The one that makes it hard to breathe
And the one that blows my mind.
I'm trying to figure out when,
And where this could all take place.
But all this searching makes this moment
Less and less important.
I should just wait.
Blind and held by faith.
I should just let it be,
Relax and melt into this bliss
For life, is that moment.
Ashley Roy, Grade 12
Destrehan High School, LA

E.A. Poe

This is a ballad you don't know
Of a talented poet, E.A. Poe
He died of unknown in Baltimore
With his raven perched, nevermore
A terrible life of loss and pain
Wanting, wishing to be fain
Wrote dark stories of fear and death
His lonely gravestone is all that's left
He lived his life all dull and bland
Til his very last steps in Maryland
Lukas Lindamood, Grade 11
Jackson High School, OH

Where I'm From

I am from hide-n-go-seek in the hay loft,
Tubing at the lake house,
And reunions with the family.

I am from "The River" and "Wide Open Spaces,"
Country music and classic rock.
Screaming songs with the car windows open,
And dancing like no one's watching.

I am from Grandma's macaroni and fried chicken.
Good ole comfort food,
The kind that makes you feel warm from the inside out.

I am from water fights, and King of the Raft wars
And racing through the snow on horseback.
I am from getting up early and not eating 'till the animals are fed.

I am from "Positive Attitude means Positive Performance"
And "Can't is not in our vocabulary."

Where I'm from is who I am,
And where I come from will never change.
Gretchen Syburg, Grade 12
Arrowhead Union High School - North Campus, WI

My Giants

When I am with my giants,
I feel the wild savage blood that runs through their veins.
When we run I will go wherever my giant will take me.
When we almost fly,
I feel the fiery freedom and fury that burns inside of them.

When we ride, we ride as one.
Cantering in an open field, our spirits are as the clear night sky.
Our hearts beat in unison.
And we break into a gallop, there is nothing that compares the feeling,
It's a feeling of pure bliss.

Their spirits are so noble and gallant,
You can hear it in their eyes.
You can see it in their thunderous hoof beats.
Their whole past is in their untamed souls.
Souls that could run wild forever.

Their thunderous essence has taken over me,
I am held captive in awe, of their unbroken spirit.
My giants' eyes can tell everything about them in a single glance.
Freedom, passion, fury, fight, wild, freedom.
All we have to do is listen…
Ashley Brianna Swan, Grade 10
Rib Lake High School, WI

To You!

To you, you know who you are.
I don't know how you lived the life you did!
You let the best thing in this world go.
You left her alone to take care of two amazing people
You brought into this world.
How did you live every day knowing what you were doing?
You hurt us all so much.
You thought it was ok to come and go as you please.
You taught us that it is ok to walk out on the ones you love.
I decided I loved you so much
But I don't want to be like you at all.
I want to be everything you're not.
I'm going to do something with my life.
All you ever gave me was hurt and your bipolarness.
And yet I still love you and I don't know why.
I guess it's because you're my dad.
After all you have and haven't done,
I would do anything to have you back.
Anything for one more hug,
One more time together!

Niki Tarter-Fox, Grade 12
Oak Hills High School, OH

Is This My True Fate?

As I sit here and wait
I wonder if this is my true fate
I wonder why he got taken away
I think, what did I do that day?
did I go and hurt someone
or did I just have too much fun
it's really hard for me not to cry
when I know that I never got to say goodbye
I always hate shedding tears
when I think about all the lost years
I wish you could just be back
then my life could get on track
but it cannot be true
I will never get to see you
as I sit here and wait
I wonder if this is my true fate

Brittney Gibson, Grade 12
Sebring Mckinley High School, OH

Life

Life begins with success, life begins with freedom
So we must not waste life
But waste the things that are distractions
And that ruin our life
Stay focused and life won't be a waste
But when things get tough make haste
Life begins with the pure parts of life
That make it easier for giving back to the world
Life makes it worth living
Sometimes even more appealing.

Taylor Sawyer, Grade 11
Eastmoor Academy High School, OH

The Least You Could've Done

Breaking down the stars I take a fall
I climb back up and I face it all
the people staring back at me
the moment so intense that I can't breathe
and all of this to make you happy
you didn't show
I did it all
pursued my dream to let you know that I could do it all
and the least you could've done was come
reaching for the moon it leaves the sky
nothing really matters so don't apologize
we've said it all before there's nothing more to say
nothing you do will take it all away
all I've ever wanted was all of this
and the least you could've done was join me in my bliss
all I ever wanted was my moment in the light
the universe around me beholding all my light
performing for the angels and the stars in the sky
you should've seen me baby
I was the star on the stage
and the least you could've done was come

Julie Liddell, Grade 11
Richmond High School, IN

Phantom of a Want

Emptiness abounded.
Alice,
eyes watching,
hoping for movement in the hallway.
Curses and laughter,
echoed back and forth.
Footsteps and chatter,
all went by,
unseen to Alice.
A flash of color?
Movement among the unnoticed ones?
Approaching,
singled out,
bringing hope.
Now fading away,
Alice didn't follow,
or call his name.
He had appeared,
and disappeared,
a phantom of a want,
to have a friend in this God-forsaken hallway.

Steven Chevalia, Grade 12
Adlai E Stevenson High School, IL

I Wish

I wish I was a tree so I could give off oxygen.
And so I could see all over the forest. I like trees!
I wish I was a waterfall, then I could fall over rocks
I can have beautiful fish flowing through me.
I can be clean and beautiful
I would have lots of people coming to view me.

Adan Ahmed, Grade 10
Abraham Lincoln High School, MN

Out in the Lawn

distant figures in the night
lay out lonely
trying to catch some light
broken angels
born without wings
wallow in self misery
and it shall be an age of dark
till the sun rises full again
releasing these prisoners of fate
to mix their blood and tears
in an attempt to create
wings enough
for just one soul
to perhaps save us all

Samantha L. Meyer, Grade 12
Johnston High School, IA

Us Twins

Girl and boy
Sister and brother
Called "A," and "Z"
Like mother, like father
Dolls and dresses, cars and trucks
Let's play "dress up," let's not
Happy face, joyful soul

Material girl, bricks of gold
Simple boy, blocks of cheese

Christ believer, Christ follower
Our differences, our distinctions

Zain Ismail, Grade 12
Ecole secondaire E J Lajeunesse, ON

I Will

I will try again
I will not force myself
This time it will be real
A quick moment
when my heart quenches
I will know
This time for real
No clouded judgment
I'm done fooling myself
This wall will be put to rest
because I am not afraid
I will be bold and strong
I will be confident in myself
But for now I wait
I'll wait for as long as I need
As long as it will take
for you to be there for me
And this time, it won't be anyone
It will be you and me.

Erika Lauraitis, Grade 10
William Fremd High School, IL

The Cycle

Pain. It hurts. But it's not the hurt one can see.
It's the pain of seeing someone else in the place you once wanted to be.
Once a dream, never a reality will it be.
The worst are the reminders you so often see.
The desk that will never hold your name
And the ribbon in your hair that will never be the same
As the one in the hair of the girl who has stolen your place.
Can't you see the pain on my face?
I want it. I need it. Why is life so unfair?
Why was I the one dealt with an empty hand?
But come to find out my hand is not so bare.
A new position I soon happen to land.
Maybe, I lost because that was not the girl I was supposed to be.
Maybe, I am supposed to be here to help with this side.
Wait. Do you see what I think I see?
It looks as if there is something wrong with her on the inside,
The familiar look of pain and jealousy that her eyes behold.
Maybe, just maybe, this is the cycle returned fourfold.

Catherine Cranfield, Grade 11
Mount Carmel Academy, LA

Rise and Fall, Rise Again

The silence is piercing, as the sun.
No words are needed, it says it all.
The pain is deep, the heart is sore.
The damage is done, the love has torn.
We need some time to make things right.
My heart will be sore on this lonely night.
"Where art though Romeo?" Why aren't you here?
This really pains me, then escapes a tear.
My pillowcase is soaked now, lights out for my happy ending forever.
Today I wake with eyes swollen shut.
Scared and lonesome, wounds on my heart still cut.
A three year relationship thrown away,
I guess there was nothing left to say.
Whatever the reason, the sun rose again today.
But this doesn't mean I'll be okay.
Again I rise but this time with an open mind.
There will be no memories to cloud my sky.
I feel lighter, it worked. I'm free.
I will always remember you, but my heart is healing
Day by day, this much is true.
Goodbye to you, my one and only somebody…

Estefania Gasca, Grade 12
Beardstown Jr/Sr High School, IL

I Didn't Tell You

I didn't tell you when we were hanging out, I saw a shooting star.
I didn't tell you that I still love you, you were right there, and not too far.
I didn't tell you what I was thinking, or about how I still feel.
I didn't tell you I wasn't kidding, and I know for sure my love is real.
I didn't tell you that I don't want it to be him, only you that I want to kiss.
I didn't tell you that I think of you, then I make a wish.
I shouldn't have to tell you that I love you, you should already know this.

Brianna Rodriguez, Grade 10
Ottoville High School, OH

Fame

A lonely boy wanders through town
His dream was to have fame
Everybody told him he looked like a clown
And he hid his face in shame
He looked at his reflection and saw a frown
Then looked himself in the eye and set an aim
He told himself that he will be the best wearing a crown
His conscious told him no one will ever call him lame
He thought to himself saying no one will bring him down
Soon it all became a fair game
Since people came from all around town
To see the boy who finally made a name
And see the sinister thoughts drown
All around the world they came
Those who called him a clown, started to frown
The boy was finally able to stand on his own two feet
And never accepted defeat
So he wouldn't end up back on the street
The boy's eye drew with angelic flame
When everybody saw what he became
The boy knew his aim, and finally had fame

Deepak Sharma, Grade 10
Strongsville High School, OH

Morning Flyaway

Motoring across the glass like water,
The feel of the temperature getting hotter.
Sitting there in the morning dew
Watching the decoys get set up by the crew.

Hiding in the weeds listening to whistling wings
While all the songbirds sit in trees and sing.
A flock buzzes over the top
Shots are fired and waiting for ducks to drop.

The birds crumple as the dog goes to retrieve
All the hunters start to believe.
Seeing all the birds head to migrate south
Yet soon one will be fried and in my mouth.

Cody Jackson, Grade 12
Waseca High School, MN

The Traveler

On the long road home,
The traveler stopped in,
Many places, and saw many sights,
But on the long road to home,
The traveler never forgot the
Woman that awaited him.

And after many long years,
On the long road home,
The traveler saw the end of the path,
And as quickly as he could,
He rushed to the end of that long road,
And into the arms of his long awaited love.

Jonathon Roseberry, Grade 10
Leeton Middle and High School, MO

Love Is a Hockey Stick

Love is a hockey stick,
There are many different brands,
Every person has their own,
And a reason it's in their hands.
Without it you can't hope to win,
That game which is filled with pain,
Unable to stickhandle through obstacles,
Isolated and filled with shame.
The stick is very unique,
Its different designs show the trends,
Possibly the most vital feature,
Is under pressure it just bends.
Although at times it may break,
The shooter must be aware,
That not all sticks last forever,
And receiving another is only fair.
A stick performs many tasks,
From scoring goals to making a pass,
The player must use it well,
Or the game shall be lost and life will be hell.

Jared Heger, Grade 10
Windom Secondary School, MN

A Veil of Blue

Scarred first with white
which turns to gray and then
through phoenix blood of fire and sun
to shapeless black, and black
itself the sky, now, the bed
of a thousand shining song –
full stars alight with sleepless night
the also-songful souls enamoured of
the view above, below with necks that
cry of craning up; and love,
they cannot see enough except to be,
to be the sky which stabbed of late
by moon and star that share the
fitful feeling of a sky which plunges
deep into the blanket under which
they lie

Luke Sawczak, Grade 12
Toronto District Christian High School, ON

New Beginning

My eyes: purged by luminance,
My sight: pure as the stars,
The door to society was reopened,
Radiance smothered the darkness.
The invigorating sky left a fresh dusting on my sleeve,
Only the heavens shared this tranquil moment.
I put up my flag, making peace with the others,
There was no going back, a new beginning had arrived,
The slate was clean,
My life, now white.

Brandon Materna, Grade 11
Solon High School, OH

Amazing to Me

I'm at my doorstep,
I've just left your presence again.
I was with you all last night,
I have never felt so right,
With anyone other than you.
You make my world turn,
My heart stops when you say my name.
The only time I cry,
Is when it involves you.
And no matter what time of day,
No matter what mood I am in,
You will always be amazing to me.
When I stand beside you,
I get butterflies.
Your kisses are so sweet,
They leave me breathless.
My insides hurt,
When you're not around,
You keep me stable and secure.
And no matter what,
You will always be amazing to me.

Kassandra Tennant, Grade 12
Eckville Jr/Sr High School, AB

Memory

When I was a child
I like to play video games
In my room.

I hated it when
My brothers would
Come in to wrestle me,
They were so much bigger.

So if I heard them
Coming to the room
I would quickly hide
Under the bed.

When they would leave
I would come out
And continue what I was doing.

Cody Claus, Grade 10
Leeton Middle and High School, MO

Flight

Let go of the string
It's lighter than air
Watch it flip, fly and float
As it soars farther away
A pinpoint of color in the sky
The balloon is soon out of sight!

Amanda Oliver, Grade 11
Hillmond Central School, SK

Pain Is My Companion

My heart can't sleep in peace
For you, I keep walking toward the horizon
Ocean waves mimic the melody of my heart
And these scars you've placed on my body won't vanish overnight
You are the reason I could feel so strongly
But you departed as if you were a stranger, I felt alone
Just a trace of hope in your last words holds me together
In this everlasting dream, days are imaginary
I lie in the meadow of endless twilight
The howling wind reflects the rhythm of my pulse
Overflowing emotions swell across the sky
Someday, I will stand by your side
Until then, this pain is my companion
The winding road is blurred with plight
But severed ties will heal with the welcomed cries
Someday, I will show you the horizon
My heart finds serenity in your hands
For you, just a glint of joy behind my eyes
Suppose the hurt withered away
Perhaps then I will awaken to a new dawn
Until then, this pain is my companion

Ana-Maria Castillo, Grade 12
Gleneagle Secondary School, BC

What Is Poetry?

What is poetry?
That is what I would like to know.
Is it truly the window that leads to our artistic soul?
Or is it the strikingly impressive use of words to achieve one's goal?

Some say it's a gift,
A very rare one given at birth.
Made only for the creative minds,
Is the ability to manipulate and play with words.

Others think it's just a skill,
Something one does only by his or her free will,
A form of art with insignificant rhymes,
The foundation of a song expressing hard times.

Again I ask, "What is poetry?"
That is what I'd truly like to know.
Is it every period, comma, and apostrophe?
Or a little more than a collection of words we know?

The more I ask, the more I realize
That there are more than a million ways to epitomize.
For a poem is of no such worth
Than that of which is held by the beholders' eyes.

Michael Perry, Grade 10
Greaves Adventist Academy, QC

Losing You

I always thought I knew what I wanted, I didn't think this day would ever come.
A month seems so long, the days race by, and I think what have we done?
As the hours keep passing, and I keep thinking I never knew how far you'd be.
A million miles, another town, another life, where can you fit me in?
I lost you twice, and got you back, I didn't think it would happen again.
Summers ending, days are fading, I just want to see your smile.
I'm afraid of losing you, afraid of letting go, I don't want you to leave, not tonight.
In my heart I knew you would always go, but not with me here all alone, it's not the way it should be.
Soon our lives will be busy, and we'll think of each other, maybe, once in a while.
But I realize although we may be a thousand miles apart, we could never be.
And your leaving is sad, but we will not say goodbye for so long.
We could say it as much as we want, but it would only mean until next time, not forever.
Forever is too long for me to wait, but waiting's not the hard part.
All I mind is losing you.

Carly Eichner, Grade 12
Kettle Moraine High School, WI

Face the Facts

Sin-free. Flawlessness.
It's all a continuous challenge; a never-ending idea shoved and forced into our heads.

Perfection. Superiority.
We are pressured and poisoned with unachievable conquests. Until we finally
POP! Letting our emotions be released freely, in a fierce, flow, of feelings.
SMACK! goes reality as it knocks us off our feet and onto the cold, heartless ground as it hits us relentlessly in the face.

Weakness. Tears.
Coming down our face like water falling off the Niagara.
Accepting our problems and soaking in the truth like dry, brittle sponges absorbing water.
Silence, sitting. Stillness, aimless. We work our minds, asking them for all the answers.

Stand. Face the facts.
Be different than this colorless, changeless creation called the world.
Rebel as you prove to our constant, cowardly civilization that I am different and decisively myself.

Maggie Daly, Grade 10
McNicholas High School, OH

Invisible

I could go to you and scream for not asking what I dream.
But you wouldn't notice me because I'm impossible to see.

I live in hope and fear that my silent tears you would hear.
I want to say that you don't care. But I know that isn't fair.

I've never told you what I'm really feeling even though my scars need healing.
Sometimes I just want to shout all the things you should know about.

I desperately want to tell you all the things I want to do.
But what if you just laugh in my face and put me back into my place?

Or worse, what if you believed in me? And set all my hopes and dreams free.
Then any failure would send me into despair. Because I would be letting down those who care.

Maybe it's just better to keep it all inside. Just go back into my room and hide.

Dakota Vock, Grade 10
St. Mary's Home School Academy, IL

Two Delightful Flavors

They are the only two that satisfy me. I am the one who cannot choose between them. Two sweet ice cream cones with flavors of chocolate and vanilla. Two sweet flavors that I am forced to choose from. Two who rest in my freezer, waiting for the bulb to turn bright.

Their flavor is universal. They appear on every entree. One is rich while the other is creamy; each one pleases the pallet till it churns in our belly. This is how they taste.

Let one not be able to choose between the two, both of them lay in their frozen sanctuary, mocking me. "Choose, choose, choose," they shout, "you cannot have both so who will it be?"

When I am too flustered to just grasp a flavor in my hands, when I am too torn between chocolate or vanilla, it is then when I stop and think. When the door is opened, the light shines bright. The two just stare with their smiles wound tight. Two hands snatch both and the door slams shut. Two lids pop open and two spoons sprout out.

Morgan Janssen, Grade 11
Arrowhead Union High School - North Campus, WI

The Dancing Angels

Today I saw an angel standing on stage and even though it was standing, this was not the case.
It moved its fingers and toes to play a melody and drew me in to linger and cause myself to be…
speechless and wonderful, to be myself for once, and to show my heart before everyone else.
The heavens released my fleshy skin and let me free; free to dance among angels is where I wished to be.
Nobody around, just the presence of their souls and even on the ground we were too precious to hold.
To release our spirits and let our emotions speak, is something so incredible it flows from my hands, to my feet.
Today I saw an angel in the reflection of a tear; she was full of equal sadness and of equal cheer.
She wasn't perfect, full of flaws and hardly any strength but she continued on as proud as a queen.
The angel in the tear and the angel on stage is the same and only angel that wrote this page.

Joanna Sawyers, Grade 11
Neosho High School, MO

Change

I am the girl who wants a change.
I wonder why God has put you through this.
I hear you say "I love you" or "Goodbye" and I hold back tears and pray to God it won't be the last time.
I see you suffer through this and start praying that this will change soon.
I want you to go back to your old self, where you were always smiling.
I am the girl who wants a change.

I pretend that this is all in my head.
I feel the pain you're going through but it will never compare to what is really happening.
I touch our old pictures, when I was little and you were happy.
I worry that one day you won't be here when I need you, or when I want to talk.
I cry every time more test results come in, I'm scared it's gotten worse.
I am the girl who wants a change.

I understand that this is part of life.
I say I'm okay and that you'll be fine.
I dream that there will be a cure.
I try to stay positive so you won't see my tears.
I hope it's not hurting you.
I am the girl who wants a change.

I beg you, God, help her.
I promise I'll change this time, for good. Just make her okay.
I am the girl who needs a change.

MaryAnn Crowley, Grade 10
Bellefontaine High School, OH

My Full Court Resort

My escape from stress is not an island in the sun,
But rather a basketball court on which I can stun.
I'd pass up tanning on a deserted beach,
Just to put on a fresh pair of sneaks'.
There won't be any need for sun tan lotion,
As long as I'm rehearsing my free throw motion.
Away from the three point line I will fade,
While beach goers hide from the heat under shade.
Set sail for a cruise on an expensive yacht,
I'll be right here practicing my jump shot.
Vacationers put on their sunglasses and leis,
As I work in the gym making up plays.
Instead of laying seaside on a towel,
I'd sooner choose to commit a foul.
Rescue me from that island breeze,
Stick me in a full court press if you please.
Destroy my castle made out of sand,
But never take the basketball from my hand.
Don't make me leave for an exotic resort,
I'd rather stay home and tear up the court.

Maureen Carey, Grade 10
Magnificat High School, OH

Sleeping Beneath Creation

My midsummer day
Waiting for the sunset
The sunset that brings me pain
Holding my pain in different cargo lanes
Gripping my lungs to set fire to my eyes
Watching my hours turn to minutes,
And my minutes turn to seconds
I can only count down and watch the birds fly by
I look at measurements of how long I wait
Do you remember times?
Because I do
See the months go by,
But it's the days I can't take
Sleeping in the tall grass
The wind pushes me awake
I am God's creation of man
But for right now
I can only breathe.

Tyler Koutny, Grade 10
Antioch Community High School, IL

Jordan

Tall, shy, skinny, long-haired
Bassist of Lament the Tragedies
Love of music, food, and candy
Who often feels tired, nervous, and confused
Who fears life, spiders, school, and losing everything
Who would like to see the world, war stop, pollution stop
Resident of Oak Creek, WI
Schneller

Jordan Schneller, Grade 10
Oak Creek High School, WI

Love Is Like Wine

Love is like wine
Spectacular flavours
A wonderful taste
When you drink,
You do not guzzle it down,
You sip it, to savour it a while longer.
Love is like wine.

Time goes by and the wine stays fresh,
As if it can never lose its savoury goodness
Many of us will save it to open it again someday
And it will taste as if it were brand new.
Wine is one of few drinks that can be preserved
Which can last long periods of time.
Love is like wine.

Love is the most powerful emotion
That may last an eternity
Much like preserved wine,
It can be that glass that brightens up your day,
A pick-me-up after a long day at work.
Love, like the wine, will be savoured to the last drop.
Love is like wine.

Marcel Beneteau, Grade 12
Ecole secondaire E J Lajeunesse, ON

She Awaits the World

Blackness covers the world in grey.
The trees shadow the wood.
The Moon engulfs darkness with her light.
Forever looking at her world below.

Her shining rays caress the ground.
Luminating the place she's cursed to dwell.
The sky hugs the Moon in its ebony waves.
Showing her off to the world around.

The Moon begins to grow exhausted.
Her lunar power begins to fade away.
At a waning pace she grows dull.
Slowly, she sinks into eternal light.

The Sun arose with his bold light.
He opens his eyes to see the universe.
Ebony turns to light, as water to ice.
Warmth strengthens the world around.

The sky feeds the horizon.
The Sun is swallowed whole.
As the Moon welcomes the night's hug.
She opens her eyes and waits to fade away.

John Francis, Grade 10
Eastern High School, OH

Seasons

In the winter the snow will blow,
In the spring the grasses grow,
In the summer the sun beats down,
In the fall the leaves hit the ground,
It's the circle that lasts forever,
It's the circle that never ends,
If you stand before it, it will never begin,
If you stand behind it, it will never end,
It's the circle that lasts forever,
It's the circle that never ends.

Candice Wilkinson, Grade 11
Huron Heights Secondary School, ON

I Miss You...

It's been 3 years,
And still, you're gone.
And I'm left wondering
What went wrong?
I said I'd never leave you,
That I'd always be there.
But still you turned and walked away,
Like you never even cared.
You tell me that you're sorry,
That you don't push me away.
But every day that you don't answer,
Makes it harder for me to stay.
I still think about the days
Where everything was wrong.
But still we smiled, and even laughed;
Now just like that, you're gone.
I miss you more than ever,
And I think of you each day.
And even though you've faded out,
I'll never walk away.

Jennifer Nicholson, Grade 12
Home School, IL

Fly

Will I be able to fly
Into that blue sky
With these tattered
And broken wings?
I want to fly but,
Will I be able to fly
With guilt and hatred
Weighing me down?
My fears of flying away
Keeps me grounded.
Will I be able to fly
And face my fears?
If I clean my soul from darkness,
Fear, and hate,
If I become someone else
Will I be able to fly?

Jessica Brown, Grade 10
Norwell High School, IN

Adoration

Feet on the ground, cold and unforgiving.
It stands unaffected by my shaking body.
My bruised, trembling heart is suspended over an emptiness
That I never thought I'd see from where I once stood.
And now,
I stand here peering over the edge, paralyzed by fear.
No words can satisfy, no letters be sufficient,
To portray Your mercy piercing my heart.
How it waits to be woven into great ballads,
Seemingly, to be forever resonating in the hearts of all who love Him.
Peace inebriates my soul, calming,
I cannot escape it, yet it is welcome and I embrace it.
An awareness awakens somewhere deep inside me allowing me to realize
That I am being cradled by something so precious, so infinite.
And now, at last, I can see what I have longed for
And what was known to become of me.
All this time, walking with my hand in His,
Being guided, never alone,
Held by something which is holding me now:
It is love,
It is my God.

Mary Ganser, Grade 11
Marian High School, IN

Fake

Alone is what you would like me to feel
Silence makes an awful wreckage of a girl
The whispers resounding in my ears
They are all that you would like me to hear

Happiness, you would never wish upon me.
But that is exactly what I feel. Your looks have no affect.
Fake is what matches your faces.
Smiles and kind words are what you try to make fall from your lips.
All I hear is Fake.

Trust built up for so long
And broken so easily.
Laugh is what I will do
You cannot break the girl who thinks nothing of you.

Rana Tayar, Grade 12
Ecole secondaire E J Lajeunesse, ON

James

This is a poem to my brother James
Whom I care about so much
Who's athletic and smart
Has won awards and medals for his hard work
Short hair and happiness that blows in the wind
Helps me when I'm down and sick because he knows what to do
to make me feel better about myself
So I thank my brother James who turned 14 for all the thoughtful and grateful things
to help my life get better and I will always be there for you when you need caring.
So I write this poem to James.

Jessica Tobias, Grade 10
Oak Creek High School, WI

Listen to the Sky

The stars in the dark, evening sky,
remind me of memories too tired to fly.
Without them our hearts have nothing to hold,
nothing to please them as they grow old.

The cool, shining moon during the night
acts as a guide to give our dreams flight.
Had we not dreams, empty is life,
filling it with our unhappiness and our strife.

The rising sun when you look to the east,
looks like a wild and untamed beast.
The bright rays that shower us all,
give us hope if we happen to fall.

The beautiful sky, pure and blue,
shows us how to act and gives us a clue.
It proves that when your heart's in line,
it allows the sun to shine.

The majestic clouds of the sky,
remind me of the souls that fly.
Tells us when you let the wind blow,
it pushes you farther than you thought you could go.

Katrina Campbell, Grade 11
J L Ilsley High School, NS

Graduation Navigation

Now that school has come to its end,
Recall the bizarre and heal the scars
And try to keep every last friend.
We'll shoot afar and aim for the stars
As we discover who we are.

We're set to sail goodbye on boats.
But scared to know if they will float,
Departing on seas of hearts and hopes.
Through crazy folks and inside jokes
What memories later will our minds evoke?

Past the math and teachers' wrath,
Friendships grew and maybe minds, too.
As we continue through the path,
Remember those few, the ones you most knew,
And what they did for you.

Past senior skip and freshman lip,
Hearts will rip and friendships will tip.
Prepare the ship for its maiden trip.
Just raise the sails and blaze the trails
And never shall your fails prevail.

Robert Utterback, Grade 12
St Clair High School, MO

Friends

Life is a struggle
Life is a puzzle
Ever since we all met
It's like our paths of destiny were set
We are always here for one another
Like sisters and brothers
Family forever
Always together
Our hearts are connected
Emotions are reflected
It's more complex than math
We each walk our own path
But we all walk under the same sky
One sky
I love y'all so much, no lie!

Brad Bensel, Grade 10
Haynes Academy for Advanced Studies, LA

Me

Cory
Athletic, carefree, relentless
Brother of Haylee, Gabby, Makayla
Lover of basketball, football, and outdoors
Who feels joy when I'm around my family and friends
Who needs sports, family, and friends
Who gives support encouragement and hard work
Who would like to see the Super Bowl and NBA finals
Who fears highest and bees
Who lives in a small town with few people in it
Frericks

Cory Frericks, Grade 11
Prairie Lakes School, MN

Gone But Not Forgotten

Unwanted protection, smothered me, until I was distance
Feelings, put the wedge between us
Anger, made sure it stayed there
Friends, is what what we were
Once, you were my closest friend
Time, was our enemy
Dominance, was what you wanted
Complete, dominance is what I would not give
Control, to who became and were my friends
Judgment, lead us back to anger

Regret, that everything came between us
Worry, that only one of us moved on
Pain, the last thing I wanted to cause you
Knowledge, that I did
Happy, as just friends
More, is what you need from me
Less, is what I gave

Sorry, will never be enough

Lyndsay Fletcher, Grade 12
Iroquois Ridge High School, ON

The Love He Gives

Red is the blood He sheds
Blue is the tears we weep

Black is the feeling we dread
Gray is the sorrow we keep

Yellow is His reassuring smile
Pink is His eternal love for us

Sky blue is Him rising from His grave
White is the holy light that will save us
Samantha Frymire, Grade 12
West Central High School, IL

Innocence

Is an innocent really an innocent?
Who knows? Who cares?
You stare with stricken eyes.
Without respect,
Without care,
It pains me.
I am motionless as you profess
That you are innocent.
I think it's not that you are innocent,
I think the case is you're safe.
Not innocent safe.
Safe from myself and other perspectives.
But are you guilty?
No one knows but you,
You corrupt my subtle mind.
I stride toward you,
Stare into your eyes,
The people hear three words from me,
Quiet yet profound,
Subtle yet unnerving,
I am guilty!
Rebecca Parsonage, Grade 12
Red Earth Creek School, AB

Boogie Men

As final rays of sun sink down,
Under covers, look around
To question everything in sight,
Wary of what comes at night.
Tall dark figures, sharpened claws,
Ripping, snarling, snapping jaws.
Live men, dead men, in-between,
Only in the dark are seen.
For, while you gape in silent screams,
Nothing there is what it seems.
Wait a while, and come the day,
Boogie men will run away.
Cassandra Whalen, Grade 10
O'Fallon High School, IL

Z.S.L.

When people ask me why we are no more,
I give them a quick stare and say, "We were just too different."
Then I shrug melodramatically. I know it is not true.

He was afraid, but braver than anyone I know.
Would he have gone that far had he known the outcome
What kept him in place?

How did he cope to confine his feelings in no one
For a best friend knows less than close to nothing about him?
He would try to befriend others just to get them to maybe
Try to see that inside he was alone.

He would continue to give a grin for my own happiness,
Even when he had none of his own, to hold me when I would cry
Over the little things that did not even matter,
To ask me how my day was, showing me that someone cares.

Love, I am sorry. I guess we were the same.
I should have tried harder. Maybe you would be here
If I had just given the same as you had done for me.

How often do you lie awake under the stars
Wishing I was there counting the years in which forever stands?
Felisha Cashio, Grade 10
Destrehan High School, LA

The Orthodontist

Consultations, questions and visits, I am too young to understand,
I listen with full attention,
I think this might hurt,
I get an x-ray done, it wasn't so bad,
I wait, while the paperwork is completed,
Befuddling lights and sounds all around,
They call it the Operatory,
Snapping, grinding, bending and twisting,
Pain shoots from my mouth, ouch!
Light shines bright into my eyes, I shut them, now I listen,
There is a bad song on the radio,
They talk in code. Saying "put a 2-3 on this" and "bond that."
I still don't understand,
Next they take "impressions,"
They force my mouth wide open, ahhh…
I gag and spit onto a tissue, a tear rolls down my cheeks,
"I can't breathe," I say,
"You're all set" says the assistant,
I hop out of the chair, smile to myself in the mirror,
My mouth is full of metal and plastic,
There is a long way to go…
Brendan Clouthier, Grade 12
Ecole secondaire E J Lajeunesse, ON

The Writer

Head in her hands, pencil lying still,
She can't think of anything to write.
The gears in her mind are working overtime,
Trying to come up with something, anything.
Like an owl she sits there, unblinking,
Staring blankly off into the distance.
Like a shoe without a foot,
Her body is motionless as her mind races.
Like a cold, icy winter's night,
She seems frozen in time, unable to move.
Then, suddenly, like the first day of spring,
A smile like bright yellow sunshine erupts on her face.
She grabs her pencil and begins to write,
Her hand moving swiftly and smoothly
As her heart hits the paper.

Katie Thacker, Grade 10
Covenant Christian School, IN

Learn

Why is it, that when we walk,
there is a path we leave behind?
Those footprints through the snow,
so embarrassing to look upon,
where we have fallen, stumbled,
and sometimes, even crawled.

Could they be there to remind us
not to walk that path again?
Or show others what happened
when from the straight and narrow we bend?
That others might be spared the misery
of mistakes that can't be unmade,
and know by the path behind us
which pathway not to take.

Colleen Waldner, Grade 12
Decker Colony School, MB

Personal Envy

Her blue eyes, her light brown hair,
She's all I need, she's all I beware.
She's confident and strong, she's assertive and smart,
She's all I need, we're so apart.
She's talented and outgoing, she's friendly and gifted,
She's all I need, apart we have drifted.
She's popular and cool, she's the one everyone wants,
And everyone wants to be, my brain, she haunts.

I'm uncertain and weak, I'm timid and stupid,
I'm all she isn't, I'm no one's cupid.
I'm inept and shy, I'm alienating and unable,
I'm all she isn't, I'm so unstable.
I'm alone and uncool, I'm the one everyone hates,
And loves to hate, my brain she debates.

She is all I want to be, and cannot.
She is my true self, with others around, she is forgot.

Laura Hendriks, Grade 12
Archbishop Carney Secondary School, BC

Big Red Balloon

I hold in my hand
An object of pure wonderment
It flies above my head
I cannot relinquish my gaze
This big red balloon fascinates me
How does it remain heavenward?
The string slips from my grasp

Up, up it goes
There is no more to be seen
Save a little red dot in the sky
My cheeks grow wet with sorrow
My heart is heavy with grief
I should have been more careful
Why oh why did I let it slip away?

A man appears, smiling
He says, "I've been saving this balloon just for you,"
My tears dry as he hands me a new one
I tie it to my wrist
We have been given a second chance
My big red balloon and me

Shayna Renaud, Grade 12
Ecole secondaire E J Lajeunesse, ON

Life

Life is a big lump of clay.
It's dark and cold, feels very alone.
Sits there with no color, no shape, very hard.
It's like something's trapped inside yet trying to get free.

Suddenly I see light and change.
It's beautiful and soft, easy to form.
Bright and blazing colors, so much shape, very smooth.
It forms into a wonderful changed girl.

Miranda Swearingen, Grade 11
Prairie Lakes School, MN

War Zone

I grab his hand and try to run away.
All around us, there is the smell of fear.
They panic when someone resists their ways.
Soldiers: they attack us, mock us, and jeer.

Now we are trapped on the battlefield,
Shells explode: ground beneath us shakes.
He then protects me like a human shield.
Why are we the ones that the world forsakes?

I hold onto him tightly. Remember:
We always smiled during kisses,
Only felt right when we were together.
Why is that what everybody misses?

While society sends the troops to war,
We realize what we are fighting for.

Jen Taggart, Grade 10
Troy High School, MI

Getting Over You

I pass you in the hallway
It's just not the same
I'm broken hearted
With only me to blame
I try to ignore you
Even though we both know I never could
I try to forget you
Because my friends say I should
My heart is so hollow
I never knew you would be like a pill
Hard to swallow
My throat gets dry
I start to shake
This is something I just can't take
This needs to end
To stop right now
I just need to know somehow
Some way
Sometime
Someplace
If I could just ever forget your face

Michelle Lucas, Grade 10
Rib Lake High School, WI

Me

Part of me is a magnificent green,
smiley and pleasant,
crisp and joyful,
relaxing and cool,
But dig a little deeper and be careful,
dark black like the Great Depression,
anger and destruction,
agony and hopelessness,
loneliness and sadness,
Yes it is true, they are both me,
Be careful no one knows my reactions,
but don't worry I try to stay green!

Eugene B.-W., Grade 10
Prairie Lakes School, MN

I Cry*

I cry when you're away from me
because I want something to hold
I cry when you're with me because
I don't want you to go
But I still love you when you are
here or away, day or night
I want you to know no matter what
and no matter where you are
I will love you always and forever
Love,
Ashley Collier

Ashley Collier, Grade 10
Iowa Juvenile Home, IA
*Dedicated to Michelle Collier and
family and friends

Unforgiveness

Nothing is as painful, as unforgiveness to the soul.
A heart that's torn asunder, with forgiveness becomes whole.

A single kind word spoken, means more than countless words.
The three words, "I forgive you," are all that need be heard.

To a soul that has been wounded, like a healing, cooling balm.
Forgiveness soothes and comforts, till at last the soul is calm.

For the soul that seeks forgiveness, when forgiveness can't be found.
It struggles vainly every day, to hear that simple sound.

The power in those three kind words, can heal a heart that's broken.
But that heart cannot begin to heal, as long as words remain unspoken.

Compassion in its purest sense, reside in those three words.
The three words, "I forgive you," are all that need be heard.

Shailpreet Bajwa, Grade 10
Ascension of Our Lord Secondary School, ON

Waiting

The power of the light was more tempting than any food,
all the materialistic things were gone and they were finally through.
They ripped up their hopes and dreams and washed them down the drain,
hoping not to feel the awful piercing pain.
Day after day while sitting on the air,
they finally lost the perception that this wasn't fair.
They tried to obey the awfulest of commands
until God finally lended out His big, giant hand.

Ashley Brown, Grade 11
Marshall High School, AR

Secret Me

"I love you," he said. But in my heart I know this couldn't be true.
If you loved me you never would have left.
You were never there when I fell off my bike and scraped my knee.
You were never there to pick me up from daycare.
You were never there when I lost my first tooth.
You were never there when I had my first crush.
You were never there when I needed "boy advice."
You were never there when I failed my math test.
You were never there to see me go to homecoming.
You were never there to see me go to prom. I looked so beautiful.
You won't be there to see me graduate high school.
You don't even know I'm graduating early, because you left and never called.
I hide the pain I feel inside. I tell everybody I don't care.
But I cry myself to sleep at night
because it hurts to know that you never loved me.
I hope one day you realize what you're missing.
But by then, it might be too late.
You see, Daddy, you can't be proud of yourself
for who I am today, because you were never there.
Mommy was always there.
She was the one who cared, and you never loved me.

Brooke Mueller, Grade 11
Hartford Union High School, WI

Only Family

You are the only one who has been here for me
You are the one who gives me only your love
I have loved you from the first time we met
We have never been lonely again

When we are together we don't feel sad
We don't feel lonely when we are together
We love one another
And we will always be together

I will never leave you
You will always be by my side
You will always be in the middle of my fun
You will never be left behind

We sleep together so we don't have bad dreams
We play together so we will have endless fun
We talk about our problems any time we want
I will never leave you

We will always love one another
We will always have our bond as kids
Even when I'm grown you will always be my best friend
I love you my one and only friend

Eric Case Jr., Grade 10
Norwell High School, IN

As Long as I'm with You

The sparkle in your eyes,
could light up the sky.
The feeling that you make me get,
are feelings I never want to forget.
It doesn't matter where we are,
even if it's far,
as long as I'm with you.

You stay in my head throughout the day,
I never thought I could feel this way.
How happy I get when you hold my hand,
is something I will never understand.
I know that I can be myself,
and I don't have to prove anything to anyone else,
as long as I'm with you.

The way you make me laugh, when I don't even want to smile,
definitely makes this all worthwhile.
I never get scared, and I never have fear,
because I know you'll always be here.
Through the roughest of times,
I know that I'll be fine,
as long as I'm with you.

Brittany King, Grade 10
Westlake High School, OH

The Special One*

The one I know as special, I used to hate.
The one I know as special, others see as dumb.
The one I know as special, I did not appreciate.
The one I know as special, thinks everything is fun.

The one I know as special, I used to make fun of.
The one I know as special, has gone through pain and sorrow.
The one I know as special, overflows with love.
The one I know as special, never thinks about tomorrow.

The one I know as special, that's whom I'd fight for.
The one I know as special, she need worry no more.
The one I know as special, is special can't you see?
The one I know as special, has always taken care of me.

David J. Reimer, Grade 11
The Ranch Program at Salem, IL
*Dedicated to Tricia Reimer my handicap sister

Spring Colors

Spring colors rise anew
Gone is that winter hue
Trees blossom as flowers bloom
Nature's rebirth is coming soon

As the snow fades away, so does the cold
In with the new, out with the old
I go outside to enjoy the vibrant sun
Children play across the street filled with fun

Green grass flourishes along with my mom's flowers
After all, they have been dormant for so many hours
As the final pink buds on the apple tree emerge
A massive amount of pollen seems to diverge

As allergies spread throughout the air
Nobody seems to give a care
Everyone's in the spirit of the season
The wonderful spring colors must be the reason

Garrett Ripa, Grade 11
Solon High School, OH

Sun Cycles

I run, barefoot over parched golden
Grass under me, the sun beating
Down, down diving through the water to pick up a handful of
Sand in buckets, building
Castles, kittens, sunflowers made form the clouds
Shapes draw on the sidewalk in pink and blue and
Red sunsets, streaked with purple over the
Ocean stretches out before me, vast, deep,
Big ice cream cones, melting and dripping down my
Arms, legs faces tinted by the
Sunshine pours in through the
Windows, wide open, as we speed down the
Roads, hot black asphalt, burn my
Bare feet, running over parched golden grass.

Katie Gusba, Grade 12
Ecole secondaire E J Lajeunesse, ON

Trying to Find All the Love
Michael —
Funny, loving, trusting, and generous
Brother of Josh, Jasmin, Vince, Hunter, and Kody
Lover of Haley, racing, and hunting
Who feels loneliness without his lover, anxious in the night, and joy when with his family
Who needs the love of his life, his dog, and mostly his friends
Who gives all his love, happiness, and laughter
Who fears losing his fiancé, his parents' trust, and his friends' love
Who would like to see better paying jobs, happiness in EVERYBODY'S life, and to make his parents proud
Who lives in a treatment center with little freedom, and A LOT OF HOPE!!!
— Bahr

Michael Bahr, Grade 10
Prairie Lakes School, MN

Perfection Is Color
What makes a color?
What makes a rainbow so beautiful?
What makes the sun rise and set with such majestic tones and character?
It is the expression of God
The sky is His canvas
And the color of the world His paint
It is like the world would be nothing without the colors God has given to us.
Such a wonderful and perfect gift has never been given quite like the first snow in December
The way the snow just makes everything look so clean and simple
Color is perfect.
The way it dances along a lake with the ripples
And the way the leaves turn from green to golden in the fall as if it were just a simple pass in time.
What makes a color?
What makes the world so beautiful?

Carmela Schwalbach, Grade 10
Oak Creek High School, WI

Two Lovers
A story as old as time, a love as timeless as night.
A heart's beat through destiny, but enemies through blood.
One as fair as the sun's light, and one as charming as the stars in the sky.
A once in a lifetime love, and a once in a million circumstance.
His eyes laid on her. His heart beat faster and widely, but his soul moved slowly and calmly.
All he saw was her glow of purity and beauty.
She saw only him and thought of only him.
His eyes were glistening as stars, but his lips were the sonnets of time.
Words were useless to their yearning, but a kiss quenched their thirst.
Together they were strong, apart they thirst for each other.
Their love was not at a price, for their love was forbidden.
Each family burned for the other's death, and only the lust for battle could calm their souls.
But love has a ways of moving, and love for each other they couldn't lose.
A forbidden marriage, for a forbidden love.
A hard reality they came to terms with, for love wasn't on the houses' minds.
Grief from banishment fell upon them both.
Death was all that was left, and death was all there was.
A poison fell upon the charming man, and a dagger fell upon the fair woman.
The story of their love was told, and the true love of the lovers calmed the feud of houses.
Love withstands hatred, and love withstands death.
Love gave them time, and love will set them free.

Morgan Roberts, Grade 10
Quincy Sr High School, IL

Slopes

The anticipation kills as I journey higher and higher
As the aroma of pine fills the air
What lies before me, I do not know
But that's the thrill
I arrive at the summit, my senses alive
The sound of wax and steel carving through snow,
Brilliant and white and specked with diamonds
I relish the rush of wind against my visage
Aww! The adrenaline of acceleration
And with each turn a new treasure is revealed
However I do not have time to notice
I feel as if I'm in a tunnel
All I see is straight ahead
Once again my senses alive

Alex Beck, Grade 12
St Francis De Sales High School, OH

Car Rides

Escape
Searching, the road stretches out before you
Anywhere you want to go
Directions
Losing yourself, being free the thrill of abandon
Finding your way, experiencing new things
Purpose
Gaining wisdom about life
Absorbing the sights all around
Time
Going slowly out the window
Measured in trees and houses passing by
Return
Disappointment, the journey is over
Happiness at the thought of reaching home

Katie Roberts, Grade 12
Ecole secondaire E J Lajeunesse, ON

Solitary Soul

The night is quiet
Distant guns silent
He sits and rests to keep from falling
Whining bullets,
Screaming men,
Clobbering bombs shaking the ground,
Still rattle his consciousness
Waiting for first light
Longing for family,
The horrors of the war sickening him
Pressing the blood-soaked bandage to his forearm
His mind, like the menacing moon, alone.
Abandoned in the night
He scans the heavens, thinking
Amidst his trapped condition
He can't get home until it's over,
His duty,
  His life,
    …His death.

Gideon Wollman, Grade 10
Decker Colony School, MB

Silence

Silence was once an escape
But now it's a never ending nightmare.
I can feel myself change
Nothing is the same.
Things I used to love
Now bring only pain.
My mood changes like a flicker from a flame.
The earth slowly disappears from below my feet.
I feel myself drifting away from things
That used to make me smile.
Feeling so sad, so alone, is not new to me anymore.
This constant feeling nipping at me like a bug.
I just want things to snap back into reality
But I just lay there, daydreaming.
I beg not to be left alone
But no one is there to hear me.

Andie Casterlin, Grade 10
Hastings High School, MN

Stab

What is that? Another tickle in your ear,
As your "friends" take another shot at you behind your back.
Never actually hearing it, but you know it's said.
Thoughts bouncing back and forth inside your brain.
How could they be doing this to you?
Lying to your face again and again, or just saying nothing at all.
Stand back, take a second,
Think.
What should you really be doing here?
Sitting around like it doesn't matter?
Of course not!
Do something about it you knit wit!!!
Letting them continue will get you no where fast.
It will just spiral until it becomes out of control;
A hurricane plowing through a town made of your self-esteem.
Stop it before it starts,
Before you end up a worthless waste of time.

Becky Poynter, Grade 10
William Fremd High School, IL

We're Not in Destrehan Anymore

Standing on the edge, amazed at what I see.
The wind whipping as I looked out,
so cold I could barely breathe.
There are horns blowing,
people pushing,
you can't barely even think.
Cars at every turn,
people moving so fast you can't even walk,
buildings with no end,
people hounding you just to get a buck,
hotels, restaurants, plays,
the bright lights never dim.
Where does it all stop?
The city that never sleeps is what it's called,
but to me it was the city that never even blinked.

Sabrina Clement, Grade 12
Destrehan High School, LA

Kelsey Lee's Poem

Our love is the one thing
That makes my heart sing
And helped to give you that ring.

If I was given that chance
To take one final glance
I wouldn't glance because of the trance
Of our romance.

Our love put me under,
Which left me asunder.

And when I had come too
I could only see you,
Which proved that this is true.
And I will always love you.

Kreger Tooker, Grade 12
Badger Public School, MN

Cows

Cows
many kinds
and many colors
Red, white, black, brown
Cows like to eat grass
and lay in sand all day long
Cows are my favorite animal
I love their spots
and big eyes
How pretty
Cows

Amanda Schwartz, Grade 12
Fillmore Central High School, MN

Actors*

They are nomads
Changing to become new characters
Bringing a piece of themselves
Into every one
Some are dashing heroes
For every hero
There is another playing an evil villain
While others portray both
These people give us stories
Ones that lift us up
Ones that are shared
Ones that must be talked about
These people live to entertain
To lift our spirits
To tell stories

Kyra Morgan, Grade 10
Home School, IL
*Dedicated to the Actors of
"Stargate Atlantis"

Big Buck Down

My breath was staggered as I put my range finder up to my eye
"30 yards," I said.
I picked up my bow and knocked an arrow,
still keeping an eye on the 12 point buck.
Drawing back my bow my eyes zoomed in on the vitals
Thud! Arrow making its mark on the Styrofoam target

Niko Markos, Grade 12
Arrowhead Union High School - North Campus, WI

A Bad Decision

It all happened late at night,
Cars drive by as they see the cop's flashing light.
They were not prepared for this,
One family is going to have a child they will miss.
The cops walk step by step to the front door,
Take off their hats to explain who they are here for.
The mother drops down to her knees,
Begging that it must be a mistake, please!
The parents holding each other tight,
As they know their son won't be coming home tonight.
Sitting with no smile and a tear,
A car accident is a parent's worst fear.
No words can explain how they feel,
Can't take anything back because everything that happened is real.
The guy that killed their son shouldn't have been drinking,
But once he got alcohol in his system, he stopped thinking.
He did not think before a decision,
Now there is a smashed car along the road due to a collision.
With a son just lying there, no more life is left in him to spare.
The drunken driver walks away with only bruising,
But the innocent one ends up losing.

Shelbie Vander Feen, Grade 11
West Sioux High School, IA

Shoreline Scenery

Trains on a track, like most of my feelings,
Wait, better yet,
I'll describe them scenically.
A subtle whistle wind, a rusty old Ford,
By the trees on the streets,
With the waves slowly rising.
There's a sting in the wharf's air,
Like breathing in too much aerosol,
Spending forever in reverie.
So if this is about life,
Then life comes in and bows down,
While we ebb and flow,
But let me sow my keep in blue.
The cliffs littered with tourists, stomping for a recount
With a quick camera angle, acute like the bend of an arm.
And every teenager's wounds abstruse.
The currents of their watered wrists run deep.
But the Fundy before them,
Won't be the reason they drowned.
And Murphy's Law of, "what can go wrong, will,"
In my ears, as I sleep, till waves break and salt this bare sunrise.

Sarah Quayyum, Grade 10
Grand Manan Community School, NB

Speeding By

Top dogs at the school, smiling with excitement
count downs plastered on the walls
college talk bounces off one another in the halls
invitations gradually passing from one hand to the next;
pictures exchanged,
life's future plans start to unfurl.
Do any of us stop to think?

All our firsts turn into lasts
Sports we've played, we may never play again.
Extracurricular activities fade away.
Field trips gone forever.
"I am a Hornet" now becomes "I was a Hornet"
Familiar faces of students and teachers we might not see again.

Homework piles on the closer we get,
unsure of what is to come next.
Everything seems to weigh me down.
Time flies on by.
Tears well in my eyes.
The door closes.
Memories are left behind these walls, forever lingering;
As a new chapter begins.

Megan Waite, Grade 12
Central Montcalm High School, MI

Tainted Love

All night I lie awake
'cause it's too much to take
knowing what we could've had
and how things have gotten so bad.
I'd give anything to return to the days
When we weren't going through this terrible phase.

Every day gets harder to get through
knowing I can no longer trust you.
I miss the way you made me feel.
Now I question if our love is real.
You don't realize how much pain you give my heart,
but it's slowly ripping us apart.

I miss the days when we didn't fight.
Now we go at it morning, noon, and night.
I wish you knew how hard things are for me.
I wish you would open your eyes and see
deep inside I am screaming.
I only wish I was dreaming.

All I want is to be happy and have your love
and be with you forever, as I always dreamed of.

Caitlin Willis, Grade 10
Sheridan High School, AR

Big Screen TV

Each day I come home to watch you on my break
From a tortuous day of suffering I can hardly take.
There in my living room you stand,
Waiting for me to give you the wake-up command.
With a flicker or two you spark to life,
Making weird noises like a pterodactyl in flight.
The images you process and the sounds you emit
Make me pretty happy, I have to admit.
Life without you, big screen TV, is something I cannot endure,
If it weren't for you, I'd be reading books. What a bore!

Christian Bell, Grade 12
Northshore High School, LA

The Heart's Song

The heart sings — praises,
The heart dances — jigs,
The heart waves — and smiles,
And the heart also forgives.
The heart thinks — the unthinkable,
The heart weeps — for others,
But heart breaks down — because of me.
It accepts
What the brain refuses to acknowledge.
It soothes
The spirit into cooperative behavior.
It feels
The first twinges of happiness.
But it also
Feels the last mournings of sorrow.
It tries to be happy for others' sake,
But cries out for another understanding — heart.
It isn't just a part of our bodies,
It's more than a part of our souls,
The mind does realities,
But the heart controls.

Jae Shin, Grade 10
Haynes Academy for Advanced Studies, LA

Silence

Silence, but the humming sound
Of the machine
Such loving care, such paying of attention
Hours
Black plastic box love, liquid crystal love
New window
Vassal being, robotic being, enslavement
No more humans
Inverted role, serving the crafted servant
Pathetic
Willfully alienated, wittingly atrophied
Rotten
Something must be, (unexpected error encountered)
. . .
Something is rotten in the state of post-modernity

François Fournier-Gendron, Grade 12
Ecole Antoine Brossard, QC

The Day That Poetry Died

The day that poetry died,
I was standing on the moon
producing silly, useless rhymes,
all precisely out of tune.
The day that poetry died
the mountains shrank with fear,
and the song the blue jays cried
forced from the sun, a tear.
The day that poetry died
some will be keen to say,
that all of life would henceforth bleed
out of beauty, night, and day.

The day that poetry died, however,
was not any of these lies.
The day that poetry died, 'twas when
our love did break its ties.

Amanda Klump, Grade 12
McNicholas High School, OH

Trapped Inside

No ink in the pen, pencil's out of lead,
Can't write your mind is dead.
Feelings inside you can't put to words,
Whatever you try just makes it worse.
Trying to come out you're going crazy,
You're trapped inside.

Rafael Pena, Grade 10
Carmi-White County High School, IL

Magical Pen

Oh magical pen
thou breaketh this wall
which bemuses mine own thoughts.
Malevolently, you masticate
what sanity was mine —
spewing bloodless fluid from
the cavity.

You help to preen my
'pious pejoration.'
Pick at each solecism
like an awl on metal —
less insidious
than the true intention.

Oh magical pen,
thou breaketh this wall,
to beguile me to speak but truth.
I scour my mind to rid
memories of you,
but you always come back
for like…not that of youth.

Nicole Guley, Grade 12
Portage Collegiate Institute, MB

A Tribute to My Mother

This is a poem to my mother
Someone that I respect and see her as more than just a mother
Someone I see as a friend
Someone I can talk to whenever I need to
Strengths that I see in my mother is to take good care of her kids
— two kids that she calls spoiled
Weaknesses of my mother is when she has to see her kids hurt
My mother's personality is the fun type
She's funny and all of my friends see her as a real cool person
My friends also see her as their "second mom"
My mother is not the overprotective type, but she does still show concern
We share common interests in music and type of music we listen to
This is why I see her as more than just a mother…she is just like a friend
So I write this poem to my mother.

Kamisha Harris, Grade 10
Oak Creek High School, WI

Caught in the Rain

The remaining leaves shudder in the harsh wind,
The already fallen treasures dancing along the damp sidewalk.
The wind rushes by, taking with it every of the sky's tears.
Cars struggle through the downpour, screeching to a halt,
Honking callously at the stranded pedestrians with
Umbrellas turned inside out —
Hassled workers hurrying along, trying to escape His wrath.
Though all are trying to evade the cascading waves of water,
None remember that this outburst has been caused by Him —
Except a homeless old lady, amidst all the confusion,
Oblivious to the chaos around her.
She thinks only of Him, hears only silence,
Feels only the power of her clasped hands,
As she remembers what the rest of the world has forgotten:
Taking one step towards Him would bring Him a mere 100 steps closer to us.
As she chants divinely in her devoted trance, she transfers her message to Him.
Her frail body quivers in the wind, her stringy, unkempt hair blowing wildly.
Moments later, a lone Samaritan passes by, offering blankets, money and a hug —
As if the hand of God is reaching out to her,
Offering protection from His storm
And truly proving that He is with her always.

Jaya Raghubir, Grade 11
Middlefield Collegiate Institute, ON

Unanswered Question

Does he still love me?
Well the real question is did he ever start?
Does he still cheat on me?
Will this relationship last or am I just wasting my time?
I tell myself yes he does love me and he tells me that he really does.
But is he telling the truth or another lie?
I kept asking myself these questions but I never seem to get an answer
Can anyone answer them or do I have to wait and see like everyone else?
And if he needs more time to answer this one question
Do you love me?
Then I will wait for him no matter how long it takes!

Dana Hollenback, Grade 10
Springfield Boys and Girls Club ABC Unit, IL

The Book

I walk across the field of wildflowers
Holding in my hand The Book.
I see a figure moving towards me
I run over, attempting to get closer.
He beckons to me, to draw nearer, to embrace.
I am getting tired, and I stumble and fall
The Book flies out of my hands
Its pages exposed for all to see
My future, my past, everything.
I look at the pages, look around me,
People are staring, with eyes wide,
What to do now?
Just forget, let the rising dust settle.
Ahead of me, the figure still beckons
I get close enough to hear him say,
"Look back and learn through the mistakes of your past,
It's not yours anymore: you gave it to me"
I no longer feel lonely or sad
I go looking for The Book; I find It, open It
And written there were the words of life,
I sit and I read and discover my teacher.

Shawni Wipf, Grade 10
Decker Colony School, MB

Love

Love can be good and bad at the same time
Love can be respected by that loved one
or destroyed by that guy
Love can be true love, love can be false
but when you fall deeply in love
the truth reveals itself

Tiffany Mckenzie, Grade 11
Ascension of Our Lord Secondary School, ON

Gabby

She can open a door with the flick of her nose
A big ball of fluff, and a smile that glows.
The greatest friend a girl can wish for,
Always ready to greet you at the door.

A big ball of fluff and a smile that glows,
She barks at all the neighborhood joes.
Always ready to meet you at the door,
Loves to lay on the cold, cold floor.

She barks at all the neighborhood joes,
Rolls in the leaves and the grass and the snow.
Loves to lay on the cold, cold floor,
Wants to be loved more and more.

She can open a door with a flick of her nose,
Rolls in the leaves and the grass and the snow.
Wants to be loved more and more,
The greatest friend a girl can wish for.

Nora O'Connell, Grade 11
Solon High School, OH

You'll Be Disappointed

Sitting there all by yourself,
on the bar stool,
thinking about who knows what.
Listening to your iPod, singing to yourself.
Coloring on a piece of napkin.
Your little green shirt and ripped jeans,
Gold necklace dangling,
Shining in the sunlight,
Along with your big bright eyes,
and bright red nail polish.
You wait for me to show up.
In the meantime you order something to drink.
It's a diet Pepsi with lime.
You drink your drink,
still waiting and wishing.
Wishing I would show up.
In an hour you'll leave,
go home and sleep in your nice comfy bed,
but it didn't feel as good tonight.
You'll think of me before you fall asleep,
still waiting — wishing.

Trenton Biersack, Grade 11
Hartford Union High School, WI

Day by Day

Life is like a giant book,
With pages written day by day.
But no matter how hard you try,
You can never rewrite a chapter.

As the years go by,
Chapters just fly.
But the lost words are only written,
When you close your eyes for the final time.

Taylor Sears, Grade 10
Mount Elizabeth Secondary School, BC

Guardian Angel

Wings of light, now take flight
Become my guardian angel.
All through the night, with all your might
Guide me, my guardian angel
Stay out of sight, lips shut tight
My secret guardian angel.
To enormous heights, high above the lights
The neon's and greens the very obscene
Take me, my guardian angel.
With your heart so pure you are my cure
Your beautiful looks found only in books
My loving guardian angel.
You protect me, you select me
From all the souls in the sky
You are all of these things I can't lie
This love you cannot buy.
You are my guardian angel
And I'll love you till I die.

Ryan Carpenter, Grade 10
Napoleon High School, MI

Lost

Some people mark me for crazy
Others believe I am disturbed
Some people think I am empty
Others think I am absurd

I lost my friends
I lost my family
I can't keep this up
I have to stop trying

I feel so broken
Worn to the core
I feel so empty
I keep wanting more

I can't believe I feel this way
I can't believe you think that
I feel so incomplete
I can't believe you'd do that

Stephanie Schimpf, Grade 10
Northview High School, MI

Stuck in Time

As I'm stuck in time
Listening to these mad rhymes,
My head starts spinning
Like a washing machine
Stuck on its spin cycle.
I feel like a pendulum
With so much momentum
That no human can stop me.
I feel so lost in thought
And time that I have neither a thought
Nor the time to pay attention
To Father Time's withered hands
Slapping me in the face
Like I was being struck
With a sledgehammer from
All directions all at once.

Dana Thomas, Grade 12
John Marshall High School, OH

Jealousy

In walks the man
That I have only heard of
Running at full speed
I get slammed by jealousy
It holds me tight
It won't let go
Not while he's got
The one thing I want.

David Miller, Grade 12
Prairie Lakes School, MN

It Is My Place

Being outside allows me to see beyond the horizon,
To think and analyze my thoughts.
Trees sway in the wind as possibilities are tossed in my mind.
It is my place.

Stephanie Runyan, Grade 12
Bethel Tate High School, OH

Eraser Rubble

I didn't have an eraser, so I pretended spelling didn't matter
and crossed bits out when I changed my mind,
I suppose you could still read it if you tried.
Whiteout on graphite
 unnecessary, unnatural, always whiter than the page
 ink seeps through your back
 it's so extreme, to type up a rough draft
To hand it in perfect:
double spaced/double killed pages/over kill clean/spell checked and smudge-free
 the most perfect of people
 with no traces of history
 So there's no way to know…
I suspect you're all plagiarized
just copied and pasted
machine-made humanity is much more reliable
 Take me for example, I might be spelt wrong
 But at least I exist, And will always remain
 even after I accidentally delete you — oops — fatal error!
I hope someone saves you…
The human touch,
Marks off for neatness

Jenny Smart, Grade 11
London Central Secondary School, ON

One True Love

It is the only thing that keeps me going.
I am the only one that it affects.
One true love with roots so deep it is impossible to uproot.
One who is with me and belongs with me.
One deep in my heart and permanently there.
One who shares a room with me and makes us sleep like babies.
The Love is forever.
Sending waves of affection all throughout my body.
It grows deeper and deeper with the promise of forever never, never going to die.
This is how it works.
Let this one go, never to be found again, there is only one,
And without it I wouldn't be, no reason of living.
Love, Love, Love I keep telling myself, however it's not hard with the way that we are.
When I am old and graying, my wish is that you will still be by my side.
When I am too weak to keep pressing on, I hope our love is still going strong.
When there is nothing left to live.
One who loves and doesn't forget to be loved.
One true love keeps forcing me on.
One who is completely devoted to me.
One whose reality lies in my hands alone and mine in theirs.
For the real reason is to love and to be loved.

Rachel Rasmussen, Grade 12
Arrowhead Union High School - North Campus, WI

Disaster of Love

The disaster of love left me flat on my face.
My heart aches with disgust
Don't feel sorry for me, it's just a phase.

Lose your innocence, lose yourself, I'm in a daze
To you, foolishness is written on my forehead,
The disaster of love left me flat on my face.

I try to sleep; my room feels empty, get off my case
The beats of my heart can't escape my chest.
Don't feel sorry for me, it's just a phase.

Walk away; I won't be noticed, I won't be chased,
Close myself to the outside, I hide;
The disaster of love left me flat on my face.

My mind and heart, broken in two separate ways,
I hurt to feel, and I'm hurting for you,
Don't feel sorry for me, it's just a phase.

I enter through the exit, and try to hide away;
Your words and your memories eat at me,
The disaster of love left me flat on my face.
Don't feel sorry for me, it's just a phase.

Veronica Buccola, Grade 12
Destrehan High School, LA

Ms. (apt) Diagnosis

Let's lie in the field of feline flowers
where the blades pierce and the whiskers tickle —
    There, can you be free?
where the air is too thick to breathe?
Your lungs will suck dry
and your tortured tongue will swell,
but with no gasp to scrape your vocal chords
you can't scream *I'm fine!*

The Doctors and Gawkers use your choking face
as a gingham bull's-eye and claim *death*,
though you haven't even died.
Can't they see your fingers
fishing for mine in the sea of stress?
It's just natural…
But I can't convince you to take that breath
for the Doctors' gloves are the same ones
that suffocate your speech.

How I'd love your lips to split apart —
for me to kiss and you to speak:
It's just natural.

Suzanne Myszkowski, Grade 12
Fox Sr. High School, MO

Love

Love, more than oneself.
No more ME always WE,
To what extreme would you go for Love?
A lifetime?
Sacrifices made.
Trust needed
Love between TWO makes two forever ONE.

Perla Ghanem, Grade 12
Ecole secondaire E J Lajeunesse, ON

The Performance of My Life

Leaves rustle through a field,
while crickets warm up their strings
for an orchestra by twilight.

The tenors begin to soothe their throats
by going through their croaking scales.
The sun sets and spirits rise,
as my life begins.

Under the stars and out of mind,
I fall into myself.
The harmony of the night sets the stage
for the performance of my life.

My fingers tremble as my fears shut down.
I tie back my hair and lay down my cluttered mind.
I lie back and drink it in…
this is the living part of my life.

Alyssa Loman, Grade 11
Taylorville Sr High School, IL

Wildflower

You can cause me much happiness
When you smile —
Yes indeed you may have no teeth,
But one day they will come
You may not be able to stand on your own —
But that day will also come
And I will be there to see you grow
Like a wildflower in the sun
You will become big and strong
You will become a teenager and then a man —
And I will always be there —
To see you grow, to see you cry,
To see you succeed, and to see you fail,
But most of all, I will be there
I will help you when times are the hardest,
And the times when they are the easiest —
I shall be your rock,
So I can make you as happy as you make me
But until those times are to come:
I will watch you grow
Like a wildflower in the sun —

Kyesha Blakey, Grade 12
Eastmoor Academy High School, OH

Fake

I put on my pretty clothes
I put on my pretty makeup
I tell everyone I have a pretty family
I put on my pretty smile…
    but it is all FAKE
    a cover up
    a scam
    so my pain
    my worries
    won't be seen
Amber Brownell, Grade 11
North Polk Jr/Sr High School, IA

Self Sacrifice

I'd rather everyone be poor
Than a few select be rich
Gaining as the bullets pour
And bodies fill the ditch

I'd rather that I be dead
Than China still survive
Waving its flag red
While its civilians die

I'd rather live in a tent
Than this pollution continue
But the First World's intent
On constantly blinding you

I'd rather feel maddening agony
Than people know addictions
No more black market economy
No more self-hurt afflictions
James Douglas, Grade 11
The Woodlands Secondary School, ON

The Immortal

A
shadow
at dusk
swaying back and forth
taunting your courage,
engrossing
the mind
confusing and silent
yet following faithfully
like a begging black ghost
searching for its soul

undetected at night
unscathed by the light
Omnipresent
for all eternity
Lyndon Wollman, Grade 11
Decker Colony School, MB

All You Are

School is the source of all frustration
a jumble of people you can't stand
courses you can't get
but then there are the Few

The Few that you can stand
and then all you are is with them
and you're left all the day in the great throng of those you despise
and all the Few do is make the rest of the day more frustrating

Day to day the world bears down
hunching your back against the weight
homework, scholarships, clubs and yet
your frustrating Few remain on the edge of the daily horizon

Waiting for you
and all you are is with them
but you're far away, trapped
behind a stack of books that keep you away from your Few and yourself
Simon Bild-Enkin, Grade 11
Esquimalt High School, BC

Stereotypical Syndrome

I'm not after your money, I'm not a bully at school,
I don't hang out every day, I know drugs aren't cool.
I'm your average teenager…

I'm not a gangster off the streets, I'm not a criminal in disguise,
I don't sleep in the ghetto every night, there isn't mischief in my eyes.
I'm your average Black man…

I don't wear a turban on my head, I don't smell of curry and rice,
I'm not that taxi-driver you called for, I don't check fifty stores for the best price.
I'm your average Brown man…

I am not "fresh off the boat," I am not an animé freak,
I don't have that Asian accent, I can distinguish between English and Greek.
I'm your average Asian man…

I strive for change around me, for equality and justice everywhere,
But I fall short with all those stereotypes, that haunt my world like a nightmare.
I'm your average person, stereotypical syndrome-struck…
Arnav Agarwal, Grade 10
Father Michael Goetz Secondary School, ON

I Wish

I wish, I wish to see my country become a peaceful place.
I wish, I wish I could go back to my country.
I wish, I wish I could see soccer players
of my country playing on our beautiful beaches.
I wish, I wish I would become a doctor and help the sick people.
I wish, I wish to see my parents.
I wish, I wish to live with my family.
I wish, I wish, I wish to see everything going ok.
Fartun Ali, Grade 11
Abraham Lincoln High School, MN

Battle of the Hearts

There's a question in the air
Three commands and the search for it begins
Only when the clock stops can the question be answered
You and your marked path is all that matters now
You're with yourself, but not alone
Fighting for the prize everyone longs for
Months of diligent training put to the test
A mighty battle is at hand
The question: which heart wants it more?
The answer?

Mariah Georgetown, Grade 11
Bethany Christian School, LA

Breaking Writer's Block

Creating a puzzle of words;
Putting the pieces together
Was thought to be impossible
Yet the words flow and run
Like the cool waters of a river.
A poet, a magician of words,
Asked to "time in" at their personal occupation,
Gives in to the brick wall that keeps out
Imagination and creativity.
A fragment of dialogue is overheard
And the impenetrable wall collapses
As if the wrath of the Heavens have been unleashed.
And the chaos of the crowds of imprisoned words
Is controlled as the paroled words
Are released in an orderly fashion.

Kara Hart, Grade 10
Leeton Middle and High School, MO

April

When she comes around
She makes everything shine like a new beginning
Her beautiful sound
Sounds like new birds singing
The smell of her hair
Smells like flowers blooming
And her eyes that glare
Are like warm stars that are soothing
Her heart warm as fire
Unthaws the love I have for her
With such soothing desire
Something has occurred
Just as our love that is new
The birth of little creatures is too
The river flows
And the wind blows
So soothing like her touch
She makes me laugh
Just like a fool
I love April
And all of what the future holds too

Donald Wayne Richards Jr., Grade 12
Unioto High School, OH

True Gold

If all that glistens is not gold,
Then why have I so been told?
Of all the men that I do know,
They have all informed me so.
But if this is true of men I've met,
Why haven't they found their treasure yet?
Could they be so badly blind?
For gold is not so hard to find.
Perhaps it is not gold they seek?
But something found by the meek?
Something easy, yet hard to find,
But to do without, we'd lose our mind.
So we hunger and so we thirst,
Looking for something we all want first.
Yet half the time we do not know,
For what we seek, or where we go,
But seek we must, for so we feel,
That without it, nothing's real.
And find it we will, one grand day,
For love we cannot keep at bay.

Clare Cianflone, Grade 10
St. Jude's Academy, MN

When Little Girls Play Pretend…

She's 5 years young.
He's 5 years old.
His eyes make her sick.
A little girl with a common cold.

Strike up a conversation, he'll digress
After just one look at her pretty little dress.

Someday she'll notice,
Someday he'll pretend,
That falling in love
Is more than just a trend.

But his sight makes her rewind
Erase the tape,
Fall behind.

Throw out the rule book,
Tear up the dictionary.
Hook, line and sinker…
No need to worry

Her life is perfectly imperfect,
His life is full of possibilities.
What's one more little flaw
To the list of liabilities?

Alexandra Raines, Grade 10
North High School, IL

I Love You I Hate You I Can't Live Without You

I always let the good things walk out of my life
I never realize the good things that are standing in front of me,
I just walk right on by like it's nothing.
You tried so hard for me for so long but I told you I wasn't interested
And that relationships aren't for me so move on.
You kept trying until the day I snapped, and then you were really gone.
I realized what I needed
You came back and made me happier than ever.
But I noticed I was the only one who was happy.
When you left you met someone else but came back
Because you felt like it was meant to be but you weren't 100% happy.
Day in and day out our fights got worse
We were constantly at each others' throats yelling and screaming about nothing.
You meant the world to me but I can't go on with the fighting and unhappiness.
We need to move on. The days go by and all I think about is you
As much as I know you're who I wanted it wouldn't work the way we planned.
I wish I could go back to when you were crazy in love.
I tell you all the time I hate you for the pain you put me through but the truth is I don't.
I love you and I will forever. But I can't tell you that.
When I think of you I think of a bunch of different conclusions that don't make sense.
I love you, I hate you, I can't live without you.

Heather Chapman, Grade 11
Hartford Union High School, WI

Alone Without Love

They place their flowers along beside her; these past few days have been such a blur
They stare and wonder what went wrong; their little girl is forever gone
They've shed their tears and now wonder why; what didn't we do…what passed us by?
The answer love, does not come to mind; but that is the answer deep down inside
Their daughter watches from up in heaven…"Why don't they get it…I don't understand them
All it would have taken were three simple words…I love you; but they never were heard
They did not care, their lives were too busy; I was always alone, for no one to miss me
Not one person noticed the trouble that grew; I covered it well and nobody knew
I couldn't linger, as days passed to years; my heart couldn't hold all my troubles and fears
With no one to talk to or listen to me…I couldn't go on, it was obvious to see
I took the easy way out, though it was hard, I'll say; but it was the right choice for me on that day
Am I sorry for what I've done?…no, for now I see the light of the sun!"

Mary Dye, Grade 11
Kingsford High School, MI

I Am From

A closet of memories and a Facebook of pictures I will never delete.
My friends saying, "Getting dat fo' sho'!" to my mom saying, "Did you forget to call?"
A yard with dog toys lying around, a garden that used to be my playground, and a trampoline I have fallen off of way too many times.
My mom's apple pies, breakfast casseroles, tacos and my aunt's sugar cookies.
Getting in trouble for clogging the vacuum from my bobby pins being left around the house.
The vacation to Barceló, Mexico where every night when 9 PM rolled around we met up with strangers who are now our friends.
Kim and Greg, whom I seem not to like, but have my mom's paranoia and my dad's craziness.
A neighborhood where I've seen the same people for the last 12 years walk their dog, drive home, swim in their pools, and do a summer cook-out.
A garage with a black, rusted, old Eagle Vision which I drive around.
My parents saying, "I love you!" and "Drive safe!" will never get old.
All these people, places, and things make up where I am from, and after this poem I realize it's safe to say it's all just my home.

Mandi Hake, Grade 12
Arrowhead Union High School - North Campus, WI

I Wish I Knew What the Future Will Hold

I wish I knew what the future will hold.
Should I turn to the left or to the right?
Am I to make the choice that is most bold?

Which choice will I eventually scold,
To find my head on a damp pillow at night?
I wish I knew what the future will hold.

Will my God's hand eventu'lly turn cold?
Oh, I hate pondering over this plight.
Am I to make the choice that is most bold?

I am the only one who has not told
I am holding my true emotions tight.
I wish I knew what the future will hold.

Into what kind of person will I mold?
Is my love above the eternal light?
Am I to make the choice that is most bold?

I fear the most that my soul will be sold,
And I will lose my grip by love's strong fold.
I wish I knew what the future will hold.
Am I to make the choice that is most bold?

Chelsey Thomas, Grade 12
Destrehan High School, LA

World Today

The world today is an inferior place,
In which we live with violence and hate.
But what does it take for all this to break?
Chip away the mask off our own true face.
Set an example for all to see,
'Cause what you do is a reflection on me.
I know it's easy to turn the other cheek,
But world peace, friendship, isn't that our first priority?
Lend a hand to those in need,
Make a difference in their being.
Nourish the children in need of feed,
So they don't have to beg and plead.
Be a good person for society,
Face the facts of reality.
It bothers many people like me,
Only fifteen, but we still have to see.
The world today is an inferior place,
But tomorrow might be a better day.
It takes us all to chip away,
The mask that covers our own true face,
To stand up straight for goodness sake.

Jing Emilie Han, Grade 11
Westdale Secondary School, ON

Friendship, Heartbreaks, the Teenage Life

Days and days go by, each and every day filled with pain.
I know life goes on, but still there is pain.
Breakups with the ones you care about.
Backstabbers, the unexpected and trusted.
Hours of crying and red eyes.
Just a normal teenage thing.
Years of searching for the perfect friend or lover.
Those are one in a million.
Everyone backstabs, and breaks hearts.
Gorgeous guys and petite girls.
Envious kids wanting to be the perfect vision of a teenager.
The minute things go bad everything gets worse.
Hormones, shocking truths, deaths.
Suicides, tears flowing.
Through it all shines the greatest power of all love.
A little goes a long way.
Find the right one and hold onto it,
Be it romance or friendship.
It heals the broken heart.

Kaytlyn Eidal, Grade 10
Fort Zumwalt East High School, MO

Love

The love I hold for you
is very dear.
When it's cold
don't worry I'm here.
I feel sad
when we're apart
even though
you're always in my heart.

Marsha Wyllie, Grade 11
Ascension of Our Lord Secondary School, ON

Love

Love
Is like lying in the lost night,
With your partner beside,
Secrets are shared,
With nothing to hide,
It's like words being put into a jar,
Shut with a lid,
And none to leak.
As I repeat the meaning of love to myself,
I feel as if though I'm a lonely book on the shelf.
I'm like an icicle in the sun,
Just waiting to melt,
As I feel my heart being whipped
With the metal part of the belt,
And as pain fills within me,
Deep and all in the dark,
My emotions cannot be kept inside of my heart.
So this is the reason why I express myself,
To show the people the way that I once felt.

Wa-el Nasser, Grade 12
Whitmer High School, OH

You

Every time I think of you
I am in awe
You are everything to me
Though our relationship is yet raw
You look at me from above
I feel your presence in my heart
You hold me in your hands
Therefore I am your dart
You aim my life at your will
What you have prepared for me is best
My future is in your hands
To pass my life I take your test
I want to get closer to you day by day
Please don't let me go
Hold me close and hold me tight
For I know you are not my foe
With you all things are right

Yanna Pitsul, Grade 11
Normandy High School, OH

The Stutterer

Sad,
trapped,
beautiful mind.
Eager to prove yourself, you try so hard
and yet you can't seem to get there;
you don't stop trying.
Unattainable, unstoppable.
Reach;
a far, high, strong reach.
For what you want…
You keep reaching.
Love,
hidden knowledge,
you are my sister.
The S-s-s-stutter prevails.
But does that matter?

Krista DiCecco, Grade 12
Ecole secondaire E J Lajeunesse, ON

Let Me Be

My progress stifled by my doubts;
The more I try, the more it hurts.
Let me live a poem
More beautiful than any before.
May my words be my wings
That I may digest all the nutrients of life
And suck out all the venom.
My intentions trapped in a cold world,
Let it no longer be two-dimensional
But driven by the soul.

Emily Phillis, Grade 10
Troy High School, OH

Time Is Running Out

Time…waits for nobody
Tick-tock-tick-tock when does it stop?
Never! Because time waits for no one
No matter who you are,
No matter what you do
Time is running out, running away from me and you

Grace Oti-Osei, Grade 10
Ascension of Our Lord Secondary School, ON

The Winds of Change

Tall weeds swaying in the cool tantalizing breeze,
Gently swaying, swaying, swaying,
To the sweet soft whispers of the wind.
Bits of foil and negligent leaves dot the flourishing hillside,
Wrappers, bottles, and incessant trash tarnish its pristine beauty.
The stalks of tortured grass fidget in pain from their presence,
And subtly scream their pleas of sorrow.

Ants scurry hastily through the forest of green,
Trying to escape their gargantuan two-legged oppressors.
The crows resort to murders
And gorge themselves on heaps of plastic carrion.
Their ravenous caws are the only ones
Speaking of adaptation and coexistence.

Lean stalks of future flowers shrieking in the smothering smog,
Quietly pleading, pleading, pleading,
For silent solitude.

Their cries go unheard,
And are swiftly swallowed up by the winds of change.

Forrest Paul, Grade 10
Robert Bateman Secondary School, BC

For My Hmong People

We gotta stop the hate and appreciate
What our parents went through.
They didn't do it for themselves.
They did it for you, cuz they wanted you to live a happy life
And live freely. So tell me why y'all still kill
And talk smack about each other
When we really should be helping out and making things better
By working together.
We are a strong nation side by side, so let's stop all the crimes
And stop serving time.
Why can't we just get along with our own kind?
Everybody is special and is somebody's sunshine.
Our parents emigrated from Laos.
We gotta step it up and help them out
Cuz they are getting too old to handle the work
Like how they used to when we were a young buck.
And now we're walking around like we don't really care.
We gotta respect each other cuz we're like a brother from another mother.
Skip what others say.
They got nothing — that's why they brag.

Xao Yang, Grade 10
Starr Academy, WI

If Only

If today was your last day,
What would people say?
If today was your last chance,
Would you take a second glance?
If today be your last goodbye,
Could you savor the moment and be ready to try?
It today was your last prayer,
Would your love fill through the air?
If today be your last gift,
Whose soul would you selflessly lift?
If today you could transform,
Would your life stay the same or would your heart be torn?
If you realized someone dear was lost,
Would you pay the ultimate cost?
Now, here comes a tremendous loss,
See Him, hanging there on that cross,
Looking down unto the crowd filled with anger and despair,
Does anyone out there even pause to show they care?

Katelyn Gardner, Grade 11
Mount Carmel Academy, LA

They

They live
They wait
They bear life
They are mentors
They are lodestars
They are custodians
They do so much
They do so little
They try so hard
They sometimes do right by doing wrong
They sometimes feel they are ridden with a sense of failure
They always feel it is all their own fault
They never know what to do next
They do not forgive themselves for their own mistakes
They do not always see their success
They are blinded by devotion
They are blinded by pride
They are blinded by love
They are human
They are out-and-out
They are mothers.

Jacob Berg, Grade 12
Kwantlen Park Secondary School, BC

Sunrise/Sunset

A new day arrives, as the golden sun touches the sky.
Each struggle is taken one step at a time.
New friendships are made.
Endless memories are written in our minds with invisible ink.
People are happy.
The day ends as the sun sets.
What will tomorrow bring?

Kendall Koepke, Grade 12
Arrowhead Union High School - North Campus, WI

Dizz

You're always by my side
when I'm down or sad.
You get me through my life,
you're more than just my dad.

You make my world safe
by providing me with protection,
one day I'll be like you:
Intelligent. Perfection.

No matter how mad you get
I know you'll always care.
I love how you're easy going,
and I dig your crazy hair.

You always have good ideas,
you'll always have that spark,
but you save time for yourself
when you watch *South Park* after dark.

You're always by my side
when I'm down or sad.
You get me through my life,
you're more than just my dad!

Camille Elsea, Grade 10
Troy High School, MI

War

The hesitation of leaving them behind
Wondering if this decision was right
One last glance and I disappear *forever*?
The future is unknown
Anticipating the moment I see them again
Emotions are set aside reality is here
Prepared to survive the challenge
Staying alive
Enduring the obstacles all for them
Defending the country
Wishing it would come to an end
The bombs appear, the fire breaks out
The tears are held back
I struggle to make it through
Running the others drop one by one
I imagine it all ending here and now
I see them, and I run faster
Soon, it is all over and I am back on the plane
On my way home
Rewarded by their faces everything was worth it
I am home I am with them.

Alessandro Petrucci, Grade 12
Ecole secondaire E J Lajeunesse, ON

Green

I am green,
I take over the land as grass,
Yellow is my best friend,
Without her, I would be nothing,
Red is my one and only love,
I am very shy around grey,
For he casts a shadow over the land,
I do not like blue,
Blue is both the sky and water,
Why should I only be grass?

Erin Rome, Grade 10
Oak Creek High School, WI

Father

She feels empty
As if a part of her isn't here.
So she'll look elsewhere
For a love that wasn't there.
In the process, she'll feel pain
Sometimes good, but always bad.
She'll feel many emotions
The sad, always overriding the glad.
All because of a love
That she thought was never there.
Until she realizes the love she needs
Was and will always be there.
In God she has a father
Who she thought was never there.

Alexia P. Burton, Grade 11
Belleville High School, MI

Cobalt Blue

What a colour cobalt blue
Azure, intense and primarily true
Mixed with yellow procures green
No nicer a pair can be seen
Combined with red produces purple
And now the end of the circle
Only two colours can be made
But cobalt blue will never fade
Far too vibrant, and far too pure
The nicest colour forever sure
If not the best then why a dye
Why its presence in our sky
Surely now you understand
No nicer colour can be had
Everywhere you look or turn
Its reflection will then burn
There is no escaping cobalt blue
There is nothing you can say or do
So for those who despise the colour
I regret so say there is no other
Whose essence is equal to this blue

Ryan MacInnes, Grade 10
Robert Bateman Secondary School, BC

Moon Bow

The moon's whole face unnormally shrouded,
And Artemis' bow paints the heavens with light.
Stars twirl from her dark-fletched arrow to settle on the silken sky,
Lighting the night in one smooth release of the string.

To own a bow that great.
A bow, upon being touched by godly hands, lights,
And shining brighter than Apollo's face,
Gives forth miracles sent by the shadow edged string.

A bow of yew is not so strong as her moon bow.
There she rests it strung and waiting for her hand each clear night.
Easily within the grasp of my sight.
How I wish my hands reached quite as far.

Allison Meadow Weick, Grade 11
Esquimalt High School, BC

I Wrote This

We were…peanut butter & jelly, Batman & Robin
We talked for hours…until her mom told her it was getting too late
We hung out…unless her mom said she couldn't
We were best friends…until I wrote those things
I was just trying to be nice…apparently I crossed the line
A line I didn't even know existed
How could my comments get so misinterpreted?
People I talk to say its her fault…I blame it on me
It's my fault…I wrote those things
Why is that she never said anything before he came along?
But it's still my fault…I wrote those things
She says it's because of what other people might think
Who would've thought they'd think that?
I always said I didn't care…but apparently I should
How am I supposed to feel?
Trust me…If I only knew
But it's still my fault…I wrote those things
We're still friends but you can tell it's not the same
I'm probably ruining it as I write
But that's my fault too
After all…I'm writing it

Carolyn Nevarez, Grade 10
Fremont Ross High School, OH

Me

Mike —
Content, confident, anxious, and intelligent
Brother of Cheyenne, Candace, Vince, and Todd
Lover of myself, basketball, business, and opportunities
Who feels joy when successful, traveling, and learning
Who needs food, water, and shelter
Who gives respect, effort, and honor
Who fears failure, death, and bad heath
Who would like to see less hatred, less disrespect, and the terrible music to just stop
Who lives where I hang my hat, currently with my mom in Redwood Falls
— Norcross

Mike Norcross, Grade 11
Prairie Lakes School, MN

Nick Was More Than Someone

Nick was someone who,
Could make you happy instantly,
Would do anything for a smile,
Would giggle when someone makes fun of him,
Was your shoulder to cry on,
I thought was the happiest person I knew.
I remember,
The message that brought me to tears,
The phone call that had an endless ring,
The crying I was holding back,
The smell of the flowers I was holding,
The blank face he had while lying in the coffin,
The pills that took my best friend away,
The suicide that changed my life forever,
Nick was,
The greatest friend I ever had,
Having problems but wanted everyone else happy,
Trying to make the world a better place,
The reason my life changed forever,
My best friend
And may he rest in peace.

Alexia Schey, Grade 10
Oak Creek High School, WI

My Search for the Treasure

The water crisp and clean in a stream of life
Filled with hope for tomorrow,
I stand alone.
I search for the treasure that can't be found, I look but can't see
I stand alone.

The water whispers my name;
Could it be the treasure?
I stand alone
Not knowing what happens next. I wait, I watch, I commiserate.
I stand alone.

Silently I search for the treasure long gone
Emptiness, loneliness and grief flood my soul
I watch the moments fade farther and farther away
My search fails
The treasure vanishes like sand slipping through my palms
I stand and wait for tomorrow

My mind made up
I discover the meaning
That forms my life.

Independently, I rest alone

Delila Wipf, Grade 11
Decker Colony School, MB

Mom

This is a poem to my mom Marlo
Whom I have disrespected a thousand times
Whose glossy and colorful eyes
Have glazed in pain of my attitude
Still up and ready for whatever to do
Because when I needed help
You were there to be helpful
I thought you knew
You are beautiful and fair
With your bright eyes and hair
But now I see that no one knows
About yourself, but must be told
And retold until it's taken hold
Because I think anything can be killed
After a while, especially beauty
So I write this for life, for love, for you
My sweetest, young, beautiful mom, age none
Going on none

Gadge Merrill, Grade 10
Oak Creek High School, WI

Phantoms

You left me alone in the world,
My heart beats for you,
Yet you left me to my own darkness,
I wandered through the night,
To the end of the Earth,
Yet you left me,
Now I walk alone, cold, forgotten;
I walk through the walls of my memory.
You haunt me, I cannot sleep;
The walls scream to me of you,
They are the phantoms I cannot forget,
They remind me every day, every night;
In my sleep I hear them screaming to me.
I cannot take it,
My heart cannot take it,
My heart aches for release,
"Things fall apart; the center cannot hold,"
My heart aches, Release me,
Release me from my pain;
The phantoms of you haunt me,
Release me.

Jasper Richardson, Grade 12
Roosevelt High School, MI

Love

My love is infallible with a never ending surplus
Love makes me think before acting
I would give anything to be with the one I love
Without love the world would suffer
In this world with so much anger and hatred
We need love, less anger, so much more acceptance
In this world we need *LOVE*

Jordan Pierce, Grade 11
Prairie Lakes School, MN

Brandon Lee Miller

B aseball fanatic
R eally good friend
A wesomely artistic
N icknamed Kenny
D oesn't like school
O rdinarily likes to help
N ever been mean

L ikes to be helpful
E nergetically helps people
E nthusiastic

M aintains a good attitude
I dolizes his grandpa
L ikes the outdoors
L oves his family
E njoys fishing
R eally doesn't like to read books.

Brandon Lee Miller, Grade 10
Rib Lake High School, WI

Love

Love is like a fairytale.
Love is blind,
Needs no words, sees no evil.
Talking, listening,
Trusting, cherishing, memories.
Heart and soul.
Unexplainable, confusing,
Simply amazing.
Taking chances, being strong,
Doing anything for each other,
Can happen to anybody.
Hard to find,
Harder to forget,
Impossible to define.

Jordan Menard, Grade 12
Ecole secondaire E J Lajeunesse, ON

Life

Life is a construction site all torn up
Rainy days and sunny days
Hot and cold
It goes up and down
You never know when it can go downhill
It's a long working process
You make mistakes
But you patch them back up
You try to put it together
But sometimes fails
Never give up!

Adam Flategraff, Grade 11
Prairie Lakes School, MN

Love

Love is a cool blue like a moonlit sky
Love is the sound of songbirds in the morning
Love is the taste of sweet sugar to the tongue
Love is the smell of freshly cut grass
Love is the beauty of a sunset on a summer's day
Love is a warm bed on a cold winter's night

Zach Gregor, Grade 12
Prairie Lakes School, MN

My Last Grandfather

The last time I saw you alive, you were in a wheelchair
With your harmonica in your hand always willing to play for anyone
Who would listen. Lord knows I would love to hear you again.
I would love to hear the music from your harmonica one last time
Just so I don't forget.
As a young child I looked up to you.
You were one of my heroes
Every time I came you would always throw down some change for me to pick up
Just to make me feel good because I had something I could call my own.
You were an amazing grandfather.
There for amusement at Christmas
Always making the day brighter with your sense of humor that never got old.
Now you have passed away
It is probably for the better
You don't deserve to be in pain,
You've been through a lot through the years,
Concentration camps, immigrating to the US,
Falling off of a ladder, stroke, and finally
You pass on to a better life
I'll see you there when it's my time.

Thaddeus HarriSon, Grade 12
Hartford Union High School, WI

Home Wrecker

Now some people might hold hostility towards me
Because I broke up their marriages despite their sad plea
Friends let other friends borrow me and that's how I start
Then they fight over me leaving their friendship torn apart
Be careful don't introduce me to your spouse
I can guarantee you you'll fight over the house
Because of me divorced fathers resort to being a dead beat
And forget their kid's support now mom wishes dad was dead meat
I pit brother against father and mother against daughter
I love when I make nations go to war and cause mass slaughter
But I only get a small fraction of satisfaction
When various poor factions decide to take action
I am what and who every one of you work for
I am the cause of the slave trade and for Darfur
I am why ancient civilizations sent out their war ships
I am the one modern civilizations decide to worship
I am what your grandparents and parents always chase
What you chase but sadly every time seem to misplace
If I am the root of all evil then what in the world does that make you?
You created this evil it's true I'll say it until my face turns blue

Khaleefa Hamdan, Grade 12
Brookfield High School, ON

Hello Child

Deep in the slumber of a dream I haunt you
Misery and darkness seeps through
Your sugarcoated mind
You don't know me —
But I know you
In your dreams
I am what you're trying to hide

I am the fire burning under your skin —
But you choose to ignore me
Sorrow was never part of your plan
Sometimes I feel that I inspire you
For in the silence of writing —
My darkness spills out.

You can run, but you can't hide
Well maybe you can hide —
But you can't run away from me.
I am the brilliance in the corners of your mind
If you would only live out your brilliant side.

Liz Dobski, Grade 12
John Hersey High School, IL

The Importance of a Title

My name's just a facade,
therefore I will not decorate my face with such a mask.
My achievements,
attitude,
and admiration declare this soul of mine.
And in the end,
you shall realize who it IS that I am.

Tim Brown, Grade 11
Carmi-White County High School, IL

Freedom

Freedom is something we want
It's what we strive for
The independence
It's how we want to present ourselves
In the way we talk
How we dress
The words we choose to express ourselves
Freedom,
It soars above the rest
It unites us
It makes us who we are and who we want to be
Creating a family
With a common ground
With a similar perspective on life
Having one goal
A "fight" for freedom
This artificial yet true family
Is committed to each other
Fighting for the word that to some means nothing
But others it,
Makes who they really are.

Maciej Konczewski, Grade 10
William Fremd High School, IL

freedom's temptation is but a futile hope

i am tempted
to break the fragile glass surrounding me
the glass prison they have put me in
just to see their fear
to stop their whispers and wandering hands
their attempts to keep me silent

but no.

instead i sit at attention
waiting for an errant rock to hit
the glass — watch it shatter
raining silver shards
sharp yet delicate
piercing my skin while setting me free

but no.

i am still waiting
afraid as the glass walls watch on
seeing all
saying nothing
never parting their lips
to let slip their secrets

Rebecca Hare, Grade 10
St John's Preparatory School, MN

Can So Much Be Felt?

How they point and they stare I didn't care
And I didn't mind when they laughed at my kind
Walked the empty road and left the sorrow behind
But I knew my limit
Never walked too far
Because the world and what's in it
Ain't nothing near pretty
I never been outside my city
Then I asked myself what's the matter with me
I stepped out the house, and stood at my place
Closed my eyes, and pictured my face
A different color maybe another race
My foot made a step then I quickened the pace
Smelled the flowers felt the breeze
It's so quiet I hear birds and trees
I felt far from the sadness far from the grief
And this isn't madness for I felt as light as a leaf
Heard no cries
Flew over the skies
I felt so safe
So I opened my eyes

Ahlam Almulaiki, Grade 11
Frontier International Academy, MI

Memories

Everything was like a dream.
The soft billowy clouds floated above me,
Pillows for me to snatch from the blue sea,
To curl up under the welcoming cool shade offered by a sturdy wooded man rooted nearby.

Small hands, gently grasping the black bike handles, pleasantly moist,
Tissues to wipe away the sun's hot tears.
Waving.
Gentle signs of happiness to the open arms around me.

My naked feet tickled and massaged,
By the hot, charcoal pavement ready to burn away my worries.
And by the rough pedals of my bike.
A sensation that made my smile grow like the blossoming flowers around me.

Lungs inside of me filled,
With bonfires past,
Accompanying yesterday's hot dogs.
Smoky air that burned away sour school days of months gone by.

My thirsty mouth, dry and empty, was quenched with thoughts more rich and flavorful than any soda or slurpee,
Of old school jokes, smiles as plentiful as blades of grass,
Of fruity Popsicles that filled my summer and childhood memories,
Of satisfaction only brought on by days such as those.

Kristine Werling, Grade 10
William Fremd High School, IL

It's Just Us Two Now — A Dog's Tale

He used to play fetch with me, so many days ago, out in the backyard, at a park, at the beach, or in a field somewhere.
It's just us two now.
He used to be so happy, such a very long time ago. I was his best friend and he was mine, before his mother left us two alone.
So long ago it was.
I remember it like it was just yesterday, when he took me for those joyful jogs.
Once upon a time he was happy with his life, so long ago it was.
Why'd she have to leave?
When it all came: the sadness, the sorrow, the crying, and the hate, when it all fell apart.
It all came crashing down.
His mother thought she could do it; handle both of their lives. Supply them with the simple necessities, but fell upon her knees at the price of life.
She couldn't handle it.
She once took me to the store with her to sell me to a begging soul upon the street,
but found she could get nothing, and returned me to the open arms of the boy.
She needed to survive. Now he just sits there staring at those magazine covers,
With the actresses and their fake beauty, and imagining them as the mother that left.
It's just us two now.

AJ Morales, Grade 10
Starr Academy, WI

My Christmas…

Christmas is a time for rejoicing. The smell of pine trees when walking in the house. The sound of jingling bells telling you when Christmas is finally here, the touch of different shaped ornaments, seeing the different bright color lights on a big tree, sleeping by the window, waiting for Santa to come with the presents, the opening of beautiful decorated presents with a big bow on the top, but the happiest thing is, when it brings you and all your relatives together. Spending those wonderful moments at the dinner table, Christmas is a time for joy.

Janet Muro, Grade 10
Oak Creek High School, WI

This Key

Must my life be a dream
Or must this be God's vision
This thought consumes the minds of many
Many people dream of love
Shall these dreams come true
I believe we should stop wishing for it and just embrace it
This must be,
This must be,
A vast case of emptiness that my heart suffers from
Must I die with this key
This key that only my mind can control
This key that hides many of God's secrets
Shall anyone understand this
Oh how naïve I was
I used to wish upon a star for love
But now I shall dream of love in an endless dream
Before I die I shall feel this grip
This…grip
…this touch that fills my heart with such satisfaction
This…touch that only a woman can fulfill
This divine feeling we shall call true love.

Tommie Burns, Grade 11
Mel Carnahan High School, MO

Apathetic Survival

We wear blue jeans and cargo pants,
We pull waistbands down to our knees.
We dye our hair to make a statement,
And we have little regard for aged approval.

We play our music loud to drown out our problems,
We like our music edgy to kill our fears.
We sing along though we have no voice,
And we do not care for outside opinions.

We go to war and fight the misunderstood,
We fight for peace with an ignorant premise.
We strive to do good, but do not know what good is,
And we detest guidance from experience.

We see disease in its many forms,
We believe it is wrong but cannot be stopped.
We fear carcinogenic repercussions for our actions,
But we reject warnings to think before we act.

We put on a face, an attitude, and a personality,
We live with it throughout the day.
We practice an apathetic survival,
To shield ourselves from who we really are.

Matt Hersha, Grade 11
Hilliard Davidson High School, OH

Sight

Look through my eyes.
Can you see what I see?
Do you see?
Black
White
Or shades of grey.
Tell me.
I can't remember.
How can you be sure,
Of what you see
When you can't believe it
Yourself?

Gretchen Ertz, Grade 11
Arrowhead Union High School - North Campus, WI

Dear Grandpa

You were a great man
Who grew up in a town that was striving to grow,
That was later taken over by Nazis.
And they forced you to fight for something wrong
For which you didn't stand for.
After the war, you became an engineer
Made a lot of money and took crap from nobody.
You always had the final say in everything.
You were the first person in this town
To ever own a car,
You later bought a motorcycle, too.
You became one of the most powerful men in the country,
Now you're in a better place.
Grandma's sick, too.
I hate to say it
She'll later be right by you in that better place.
Say hi to Tupac for me.
R.I.P. Grandpa.
You were a great man.

Stefan Risca, Grade 10
Troy High School, MI

Chances

Aghast at the notion
That it's time for change
Time simply flies by
One thing begins, and other things end
The clock ebbs away
Like the oceans with a tide
Swiftly moving in and out
A simple, quick, sincere goodbye
Shed a tear or give a smile
Run away or stay awhile
Beautiful once you get to know her
Not as obnoxious once you see past his layers
So many things are changing
Yet, nothing meets the eye
Take a little time while there's
A little time left
Don't wave these chances aside

Cassandra Bergh, Grade 11
Heritage Christian School, BC

Believe

Glistening among the black night sky,
To choose just one is a challenge
Twinkle, twinkle little star
Each one stellar in its own way
How I wonder what you are
Which one will grant the wish
Up above the world so high
The most luminous of them all, found
Like a diamond in the sky
Brightly shooting along the skyline
Twinkle, twinkle little star
Quick, hold our breath, make a wish
How I wonder what you are
And believe that anything
Is possible.

Dylan Gore, Grade 11
Hartford Union High School, WI

Graduation

An end
We'll never return
Though we yearn
A celebration?
Separation?
Standing in black robes
Among faces we know,
A pass or a fail
Can determine our tale.
A handshake away
With no way to stay,
Tearful goodbyes
No more surprises.
Our journey advances
We must take some chances
Ready to proceed
Discover, succeed.
End results
Children to adults
A beginning

Kelsey Jariett, Grade 12
Ecole secondaire E J Lajeunesse, ON

The Angel Before You

The intensity of that piercing glare
The inspiring image of innocence
The glowing presence of motivation
Is bright like the descending of the
Fervent glow of the second coming
The passionate tenderness of the voice
The motivational tale of the tune
The genuine humility shines bright
Like the infinite fire-filled flame
Of the spirit within the angel before you

Diana Chahine, Grade 11
Kelowna Secondary School, BC

So Far Away

In a place where you feel so alone, but yet surrounded by people.
When we're at two completely different ends of the worlds,
But looking at the same moon, the same sunrise.
I'll never forget the look on your face when you took my hand for the last time,
Knowing there was a possibility you could never see me again.
You were so far away from me, but so close to my heart.
I wanted you to come home, but you couldn't.
I knew that everything would be okay,
And someday I would find myself trying to stay by the phone
Because your voice would always help me when I felt so alone.
I remembered replaying the memories we shared over and over in my head
Until I would go to bed.
You don't know what you have until it's gone.

Chelsea Ballas, Grade 10
Oak Creek High School, WI

Friends Forever

Four more months.
Everybody leaves.
"Keep in touch, we'll be friends forever!"
Empty words.
Clumps of friends will be spread out like a fan soon.
"I'm gonna miss you so much!"
They're lying.
"I'll call you every day and come visit you!"
No they won't.
Everybody will drift.
Splitting apart is a way of life.
People say real friends stay.
How do you know which ones are real?
It seems like everybody is fake.
Since when did the word forever get thrown around to mean nothing?
In four months, everybody will be somewhere different.
Borderlines are dividing friendships.
In four months, is the term friends forever still going to mean anything?

Stefanie Miller, Grade 12
Rolling Meadows High School, IL

Now I Do

My love for you is dying.
I can't take this pain anymore.
I am trapped in a dark room
with all my problems surrounding me,
I don't know what to do,
I have no one to turn to
it's killing me inside.
You don't know how much you mean to me
I feel like I am never
going to be with you again
but deep down in my heart I know that some day we will be together.
You stole my heart the first time I saw you
and my heart will always be with you.
My problems are all surrounding me
but when I was with you I never had no problems but now I do.

Kimberly Harrison, Grade 11
Ascension of Our Lord Secondary School, ON

I'm Sick

I'm sick of losing the ones I love to the streets, it only seems that once I lose someone, here goes another gone like the wind. I try and tell them life is too short to be doing what you are doing, but it only seems like they want to speed up the day that their family and friends last hear their heart beat. I try and help the lost and confused by my words, but what do my words mean to someone that's already dead inside? I think they just have to find out for themselves, but by the time they do that it's already too late. When will people just face the fact, that once you they are gone there's no coming back. They fail to realize a bullet has no age, sex, or name to it. It just flies in the sky like a shooting star. So, many people I have lost to violence. When will it be over, when will it be safe enough for us to walk down the street and not get hit by that one bullet that will take our life? What will the world come to, what will the world be like when our kids take their first walk on this Earth, will they have to fear too? Will it ever be safe? Every time I hear another young one has lost their life to this violence it makes me sick.

Aleysha Williams, Grade 12
Thornton Fractional North High School, IL

Death

Denial — not accepting — do not want to admit — too young
Loneliness — distanced — scared — sad
Fear — alone — scared of where you will end up
Dark — everything does not seem so happy anymore
Sadness — depressed
Quiet — nothing you hear seems to matter anymore
Revenge — anger — hate — confusion
Heavy air — something bad is happening — you feel the loss already
Weighed on heart — do not want people to be sad because of the loss
Sick — weak — lack of strength emotionally, mentally and physically
Distraught — do not know what or how to think and cannot focus on important issues
Soul — thinking of where your soul will end up (Heaven, Hell, or somewhere else)
Cold — a feeling of loneliness
Grim Reaper — the feeling of death standing next to you and knowing what is going to happen
Unknown — where will your soul go — what is next — is there a next step — ???
Death…

Ian Fraser, Grade 12
Ecole secondaire E J Lajeunesse, ON

Girl on the Beach

The full moon glares down on the wet and sandy beach.
A beautiful girl walks down the shoreline, her bare feet sink into the sand.
Leaving an imprint that will soon be erased by the next wave that encounters it.

She stares at the beautiful face of the moon, wondering how such a thing was created.
Was there anything else as unique and beautiful as the moon? Where could it be found?

All this passes through her mind as she walks down the beach with perfect silence
Other than the waves lapping the shore.

She thinks so much and gets dizzy. After being hit with a cold wave,
She laughs and sits a bit farther back, letting the waves hit mid-calf.

After enjoying the walk on the beach, she heads home and thinks of it all again.
The thought of it brings romance to mind.

How nice it would be to spend some time on the beach with the guy of her dreams.
In the brightness of the full moon, a gentle breeze,
And the quiet waves lapping the shore covering her tracks.

Kurt Dyck, Grade 11
Institut Collégial St. Pierre, MB

Dark Side

There is a dark side to me
One you never wish to see
But push me the wrong way
And you'll see it anyway
There is no limit to my pain
So never look for its source
Just hope you never see it again
And let my anger run its course
This is your fair warning
So go and swallow your pride
I wake up every morning
Knowing there is a beast inside
You never wish to see it
Or what this side can do
But if you push me to my limit
I swear I will destroy you
So never try to see me
And my darker side
I think I feel it coming now
Maybe you should hide

Bryan Olson, Grade 10
Portage Collegiate Institute, MB

Puddles

God inflicted
   damnation of the
     gifted
differentiation of the different.

Passing from plausible to dubious
in   merely   seconds

   Forbidden fruit
knowledge results in
   social isolation
     desolate interior

Exist thoughts with no escape
   for fear
    rejection

produces self-awareness

   Reflection
introspective
  analytic
    deviant
      fragile
Identity shattered

rain.

Canaan West, Grade 11
Chalmette High School, LA

True Vision

We rely on our eyes solely
They have become our definition of trust.
A potter cannot shape clay with her eyes.
Blind, she trusts her hands.
True vision does not come from the eye
But by reinventing our individual reality.
Believe what you see, or see what you believe.

Alyssa Leinweber, Grade 10
Destrehan High School, LA

Hidden Soul

The way you look,
so happy, so soft,
quiet blue eyes,
as if saying everything about you.
So you dig deeper, looking into your soul
with bleeding eyes.
Searching so desperately,
for something you can't control.
Questions of fury and sympathetic emotion overlook everything else.
Your rage takes over you,
as you get more and more lost with each fall you take.
Failure always was your success.
Stepping back,
further back into reality,
nothing's clear,
take one step further.
Tripping over the obvious,
yet you're still so oblivious.
So turn around,
face the truth.
Nothing comes easy when you're left in denial.

Brittany Kreklewich, Grade 12
Melville Comprehensive High School, SK

Broken

I'm not afraid of the fall.
I'm not afraid of the landing.
But it's the fear of being broken that scares me the most.
It's the fear of believing that once you fall, you will be broken forever.
It's the fear of getting up and having those who you thought cared,
Actually turn their backs on you or gawk in your face.
It's the fear of YOUR fear shining right through you
So that the whole world may see you,
All of you, in your state of brokenness.
The only thing you want at the moment is, get out, get away, get lost.
You can't! because when you are in this state
You have to realize that this was just a test.
A test to jump off the spring board and into the water.
The water that engulfs you, suffocating you, blinding you.
All you have to do is swim. Swim to the light and don't look back.
Don't turn around till you know you are safe.
Remember, this was just a little test.
In the end you will make it. In the end you will be in your prime.

Krystal Burggraff, Grade 12
Owatonna Christian School, MN

Life Is Water

Life is water oh so calm
But when it's windy waves surface
Waves are what's holding me back
Pushing me towards shore not where I wanna go
I wanna go to the other side when the water is calm
Where nothing is pushing me back
With no waves but I must push ahead
To overcome the waves
That are holding me back
Otherwise I will never reach the other side
Where all is calm and peaceful

Joshua Cole, Grade 10
Prairie Lakes School, MN

River Swimmer

Wading gracefully,
I dive in with both hands,
to the cool, predictable river,
and its pulling demands.
I stroke methodically,
against the refreshing surface,
with its strong current,
and directional purpose.
The green transparent water is filled with abundant fish
They glide along the sticks and stones, to eat, their only wish.
I walk along the bottom,
periodically immersing my head,
recalling all the day's occurrences,
and everything I've said.
Splash after splash,
the fun is never done,
I will continue swimming,
until the setting of the sun.
The water is my place of thought and release,
where I enjoy my surroundings, and all troubles seem to cease.

Emily Cybulla, Grade 10
Bellaire Public High School, MI

There Is No End to Your Greatness

You have always had the best grades
You never look bad,
I have always wished to be just like you
You have the right friends and know when
You should not hang out with certain ones.
You never do anything wrong.
Your mom thinks that you are perfect
And never asked for a better daughter!
You know when one of your friends are upset or hurting
You know just the words to say to make them better.
One thing that I wonder
Is why do you let people push you around.
You let them tell you what to do and when to do it
Why do you not stand up for yourself
Just once?

Amanda Oldenhoff, Grade 12
Hartford Union High School, WI

Leaving

Leaving inside just peels my skin until I'm bare
It hurts like my flesh burning in a fire
When I leave to turn my back
I look back and see you crying
I want to turn back around
But I can't handle the pain that you put me through
At times I have this piercing heart with pain so undying
It fluctuates my emotions so badly
I cannot explain in words how much
Because you taught me something
Something very special
Something no one else can teach me but you
How to love and how not to love
So by this I want you to forget about me
Have me in your dreams and memories
But I'm leaving
I will always love you
But I'm not in love with you
I'm sorry, but I will move on
And so should you
So goodbye my first love and live well

Johanna Workman, Grade 11
Conway High School - West, AR

Final Time

I stood at the entry gate waiting to take the field
For what would be my final time
My final time as a Marching Jay

My emotions ran wild through me
I could not believe this would be
My final time as a Marching Jay

I took the field one more time
All I could hear was cheering
I could feel this performance would be prime

Bang! The show had started
Before I knew it the show was over
Tears started falling heavily
As I marched off the field
For my final time as a Marching Jay

We made our way back to arcs
Where we heard our final remarks
We received our last command
Thoughts raced through my brain like a movie
As I went at ease for the final time
My final time as a Marching Jay

Molly Borcherding, Grade 12
Waseca High School, MN

My Father Is King

I am a cherished princess;
My Father is the King of kings.
He loved me even when I rejected Him,
And to Him alone my heart sings.

Through life I try to honor Him,
In all I say and do.
For He alone gives life to me;
His words are forever true.

Although this world is filled with evil,
I do not have to worry.
In the shelter of my Father's wings I rest;
I'm a daughter of the King of glory!

Allison Horst, Grade 11
Horst Home School, LA

Number 2

2 choices to make
2 sides of the brain
2 people affected and
2 years gone to waste
2 months to go
2 types of outcomes
2 kinds of emotions
2 cars crashed and
2 ambulances came
2 people in critical condition
2 days past and
2 people gone

Brent Hall, Grade 12
Prairie Lakes School, MN

Forever

How could you do that
when you know how I feel
I love you Chyler
and we have a deal

I said I wouldn't cheat
I said that I did care
and my heart started to beat fast
it got me wishing you were there

In that house beside me
as I hold you close to say
it's your choice to see
that I'll be here every day

I need you just like you need me
I don't want to be apart
baby can't you see
you're forever in my heart.

Jessica Parise, Grade 12
Northland High School, MN

Finding You

You were always there hidden in the dark.
Singing out like the morning's lark.
I never noticed the work you did, never realized how important you were.
Now you're gone I see it all.
Who will I go to in times of need, who will I call to have a laugh.
All I can do is reminisce on times we had and things we shared.
Until we meet again.

Ifunanya Mba, Grade 11
Holy Trinity Secondary School, ON

Never

"It's better to have loved and lost than never to have loved at all."
It's hard to believe.
Having loved and only lost,
It seems to not get much better.
Falling in "love"
(can it even be called that by a teen lacking maturity?)
Is a slash at the heart a tear at the soul?
Taking your time which can only be spent and never gained
Love ticks away to the beat of a heart somewhere.
Being a sucker, I tend to fall into its warming arms
I often forget to watch to see if it can catch me
"Amanda" — Boston —
True love is only wasted words and wishes to which sad looms
only building upon itself and it never grows in the way you'd expect
from marriage to divorce it never lasts with dreams smashed and hearts broken
you'll wonder on wondering why what's next
time seems to drag on without a finish but you wish it had no beginning
Tearing, tearing
What's the difference?

Rob Michalak, Grade 12
Hartford Union High School, WI

Written Majesty

She struggled to look past the ashen surface to the murky truth beneath
Fingers swirled through currents of pewter shavings
Removing the single sword from its coveted sheath
She focused on the sacred engravings
Hand poised the arsenic lines flowed like water
Creation and destruction in a matter of a single moment
Elegant movements bathed in slaughter
Not one leaden smudge an accident
Slate panes of a soul appeared as if by magic
The smoke filled depths taking any onlooker as a prisoner
No one could ever call the somber judgment as tragic
Each victim becoming an innocent believer
Pewter sparks flying in every direction
Final strokes captured in an intimate embrace
A perfect inner reflection
Mislaid feelings at a final resting place
She caressed her silver sword with a tender gesture
Her fingers released her intimate lover
Emotions she tried to capture
Amidst a charcoal field there were no longer feelings to uncover

Rachel Edelman, Grade 11
Solon High School, OH

Me? I Left My Hate in My Other Pants

If beauty is there, why do we not see it?
Why are we looking when lost without sight?
We take what is there and coat in molasses
Until we have blackened what used to be white.

Come, let us walk.
I know of a stream.
There we will talk
Of all that things seem.

Look at those flowers.
Do they look lonely?
About what they're grinning
Is known to them only.

What of the leaf that falls
Down in the forest?
It doesn't cry.
It sings with the chorus!

Why so much bitterness? I see not why.
The water is clear, and so is the sky.
No hating. We'll hold hands for a while,
Until the hour comes when you learn how to smile.

Daniel Ralston, Grade 10
Robert Bateman Secondary School, BC

Parents…

How can I manage something
just me by myself?
No older sibling to dwell with anymore.
Who can I talk to?
Not my dad, but sometimes my mom.

My dad calls me names and puts me down.
I can't go to him for help when in need.
They ground me.
Can't do anything.

My parents both drink.
They're not alcoholics, but they both drink.
My mom just blows up and yells at me
for no apparent reason.

So, how can I manage something
just me by myself?
No older sibling to dwell with anymore.
Who can I talk to?
Not my dad, but sometimes my mom.

Charlotte Misuraco, Grade 10
Fort Zumwalt East High School, MO

Rethink, Reorganize, Rebuild, Recover

Dey sayin' we ain't worth it,
Bein' rebuilt, that is.
The water was a' risin'
Like mama's voice durin' a Sunday sermon.
Ya mom 'n dem,
Well, they was lost in the flood.
It took only seconds to destroy us,
And years to recover.
Dey sayin' we ain't worth it,
Bein' rebuilt, that is.
Well look who was right.
First the Saint, now the Hornets,
Baby, we got our soul back.

Leah Smith, Grade 11
Mount Carmel Academy, LA

Nature's Beauty

Ducks fly free over the mighty Mississippi River.
Ducklings swim in the current of their mothers.
Pheasants roam free in the S.D. plains.
The Whitetail deer grazes under an apple tree.
The buck chases the doe around during the rut.

The ice cracks beneath my feet on the shallow pond.
The cattails have a layer of frost that never seems to go away.
The sunsets are everlasting in my memory.
The cold wind blows the leaves by my face.
The smell of the fall will never be forgotten.

Trees stand outside for their entire lives.
Braving all that we can't.
They adapt to the temperature.
Give us oxygen to breathe.
They support our life.

Nature provides us food.
It provides us life.
The memories I've shared with my dad.
They will never be forgotten.
Nature has shaped me into the person I am today.

Jacob Menden, Grade 12
Hartford Union High School, WI

Senseless

A life before me has gone by fast
I try every day to recreate the past
The ideas and sounds have taken a pause
Leaving us with no direction, no sense for a cause.
We're one in the same, every faceless being
We turn two blind eyes to what we've been seeing.
Our mouths reflect our minds, two windows closed
We keep them from running, the free dancer is posed.
Our crippled limbs are rooted and planted,
These gifts for expression have been taken for granted.
We can't even see the dawning of a new day,
No freedom for what we've been trying to say.

Kyle Ballou, Grade 12
Avon Lake High School, OH

It's Here

It's here.
The moment we've both dread
sense the beginning.

The moment where
our souls become distant.

Our hearts,
hanging on by a thread.

Our minds,
slipping further away.
Further than we ever
thought possible.

I need you.
She said.
You keep me sane.

I can't lose you.
He said.
You ARE my heart.
And without it I'd die.

Macy Loupe, Grade 11
Thibodaux High School, LA

Bingo

Triple random, double perfect
Triple perfect, double random
So many cards
So many choices

I argue with the seller
But choose the right card
I grab my dabber
And I have my lucky charms

I sit down at a table
But require a refreshment
"One Pepsi please"
Now I may start

With my cards all set up
I tightly grasp my dabber
Listening to the numbers being called
I dab away

Dabbing left and right
The pressure is on
O 69
B-I-N-G-O

Nicolas Brousseau, Grade 12
Ecole secondaire E J Lajeunesse, ON

Arboreal

Twisted in beauty,
But pointed out for its flaws and imperfections.
Saturated with ancient wisdom over time.
Mistaken for arrogant,
While radiating pure humility, bowing in the frosty air.
Always and forever sincerely yours,
Humanity's life supply of oxygen.

Neda Anvari, Grade 11
Fraser Heights Secondary School, BC

Wait

Sure, we're friends and that can be great
But my heart won't lie so I continue to wait
Wait for the day that you may change your mind
Because I know there's something there and it's up to you to find.
My heart will be strong but will soon start to die
So I'll wait for your rescue as the days fly by.
Night after night I sit here and pray
Pray for the day that you'll take me away.
Away to the stars and into the sun
I'll wait here forever until my whole life is done
You represent my smile and why I'm still here
So I'll wait for the day that you take all my fear.
The fear is so fierce and it holds me so tight
I want to break free, fight with all of my might.
I'll fight 'til the end, 'til you feel the same way
So I'll continue to wait here day after day.
Wait for the love that has been here so long
Until you finally realize that you were all wrong
You'll know I'm the one and you'll know I was right
Our love can be strong so hold me real tight
Hold me forever and never let go, I'll wait for that way, it'll come…I know.

Carly Crouse, Grade 10
Leo Hayes High School, NB

More Than a Word

A man can hold his shoulder and wait for the next boulder.
He keeps his head up as the world gets colder.
Climbing that hill until he reaches the top.
Fighting for the freedom, never to stop.
Pouring out his heart to life,
when all they do is bring agony and strife.
If you have the desire put one foot after another
you'll find him slippin' and hang onto your brother
you say yes but the world says no

you fight for peace but they put on a show
the world says stop but you say go
determination, life's intimidation, you prove the accusation that starts from the lung.
You prove the validation that ends at the tongue.

From the words of Malcolm X "Nobody can give you freedom.
Nobody can give you equality or justice or anything. If you're a man, you take it,"
I say you're more than what they pick you're more than a statistic.

Latasha Owensby, Grade 12
Speedway Sr High School, IN

Where I'm From

What kind of place molded me into such a form,
where I've felt at home since the day I was born?
Is it the house or the hundreds of trees,
or the wheel barrow of frogs or the lake I can see?
From stacks of newspapers and magazines,
lemon-scented Lysol and clean laundry,
where it's calm and quiet and comfortably lit,
the dishwasher hums and there the candles sit.
Extreme sledding and rock 'n roll,
where volleyball comes from the soul.
As long as you're "just saying," it will be cool,
like "what it is, is," never made anyone a fool.
The meows and the snores heard all through the night
The boys are in the military, but they'll be all right.
Casted from the Theory Man and Ma's point of view,
I've become an Abby and I like it, too.

Abby Tindal, Grade 11
Arrowhead Union High School - North Campus, WI

You Are the Moon Which Casts Its Silver Light

You are the moon which casts its silver light
down upon my face, lighting a bright smile
filling my being with tremendous might
to bear the long day through and walk the mile.
The look I give will surely not defile
such tenderness I see within your eyes
that will cast away any thoughts so vile
within my pervert mind like grey cloud skies.
With you I could mend any broken ties
that were destroyed when the past sun did set
to ne'er arise again, I do surmise,
but yet I do not lament the sunset
for my feelings have now been set anew
and my sights are only set upon you.

Cat Folvik, Grade 12
George Elliot Secondary School, BC

Days Gone By

When I was younger, I used to cry.
Now that I'm older, I often wonder why.
As I sit and think of my younger days,
I remember all the games that I used to play.

Games like tag and hide and go seek,
Although it is hard you cannot peek.
Dodge ball, tether ball, and football too
Then home for dinner, oh boo-hoo.

My days to roam free like the buffalo had come to an end,
For off to school I went with my friend.
Now that I'm older and high school is nearly complete
The things that I've learned will help me compete.

From fun and games to poetry
My life now has responsibility
Those delightful dreamy days of running wild
Are gone forever now that I'm not a child.

Austin Clayton, Grade 12
Valmeyer High School, IL

Angel Cries

Never thought that you would take it this far,
Shows me just how unfeeling you are.
I'm scared to see what you've done to her
How you've ruined all the fun for her.

I don't want to see her face,
When she has to come back to this place,
And finally has to face,
I'm trying not to cry,
But it's not working.
I'm trying to make things better,
Praying that we'll all come together,

Praying in vain,
Waiting in vain,
Dreading the pain,
When I see her face,
I just don't know how much I can take.
It's so easy to picture myself in her place.

They say it rains when angels cry,
Well I wish these angels would wipe the tears from her eyes,
Instead these angels continue their cries,
Cause they also know what lies.

Lebene Numekevor, Grade 12
St Benedict Catholic Secondary School, ON

Your Meeting

When I looked at you I thought of the moon
When I looked at you I thought of your dream
When I look at my heartbeat it was out of control
I couldn't stop looking at you
My eyes were glued to you
I know you were looking at me but why did you have to go
Days went, and you never came
Years came but you never came
Do you know that I was there
There forever waiting for you
When we met you talked to me
When we met you praised me
When we met you liked me
You took my heart, I couldn't think anything else other than you
I couldn't talk anything else besides you
But why did you have to
I loved you
But did you love me
I consider you my own but did you consider me
Don't play with my emotions they are like a rose petal
Touch and it dies

Ruqaya Syeda, Grade 10
Haynes Academy for Advanced Studies, LA

The Silent Diamond

Standing there upon the earth
sent from heaven, straight to birth
from the clouds came whitened spears
from the sky came heavens' tears
silent diamond, in a loving flight
fall swiftly down and glitter bright
hit the ground and splash the light
the light shines on in a flawless sight

Lance Hambler, Grade 10
Kelly Road Secondary School, BC

Step Up

Step up to wild ambition,
calling out your name.

With every inspiration,
and explosion of confidence,
answer back to its chant.
Answer with your own clarifying call.

Walk with caution,
but don't inhibit passion's stride.

Ambition does not want,
hidden secrets,
with hidden meanings.

It needs your spirit,
through self-sacrifice and truth.

Ambition is taking a chance on you,
so take a chance on it,
and step up.

Jacqueline Kleinholz, Grade 12
Oak Hills High School, OH

Passion

Bodies entangled
Bounded by rope

Passions erupting
Covered from head to toe in sweat

Hearts pounding
Limbs entwined and straining

Mind is fogging
The grunts and moans grow louder

Bodies collapse
The pleasure induces relaxation

Three legged race!

Kaitlynn Swinn, Grade 12
St Basil Secondary School, ON

Childhood Treasure

The figure walks out of the thick fog
With every step taking human form
Down the abandoned railroad tracks
Stepping over railroad spikes and throwing rocks into a nearby creek
He places pennies on the rail in a long line
Just as he has done before
Stepping on the rail, the boy walks until he loses his balance
He takes a seat beside the tracks
Eyes closed, he listens to the ever-present nature
The pale boy lifts his head
And bounds further along the tracks
Sprinting now, he leaps over a fallen tree
Bare feet on the gravel
He cuts off and runs down a worn trail
Weaving in and out of mature trees
He stops dead next to a tall oak
He begins to dig near the base of the tree
A few minutes pass and he uncovers a box
The boy picks it up and walks triumphantly back to the tracks
He skips down the rail
And disappears around the bend

Elliot Frank, Grade 11
Hartford Union High School, WI

Tyler

Caring, loving, sharing, and generous.
Brother of Chris, Mike, and sisters Megan, Randy, and Joyce.
Lover of the hot summer days, and the fresh blue water,
and the first day of opener fishing,
and hanging out with my wonderful girlfriend at the lake.
Who feels joy when with my girlfriend,
and sad and lonely when thinking about my friend that have passed away,
and moved on to a better place.
Who gives smiles to friends and family,
encouragement for people not to go in my footsteps.
Who fears losing another friend, loneliness,
and most of all losing the most perfect girl I'll ever meet.
Who would like to see myself at a freestyle event.
Who lives on Green Lake.

Tyler Panitzke, Grade 12
Prairie Lakes School, MN

No Matter What

It's times like these where it all sets in.
My mind runs free and I can only hope for the best.
That you mean it as much as I do.
It's a promise that I'll always keep.
But to you, is it a predetermined broken promise, or the real thing?
Just let it out, so that I have forever to pick up the pieces.
But when I hear those promises back and see that look.
I know it's true and sink deeper.
The look that makes it real, and I know you'll stay by my side.
A look that means; no matter what I say, or what we argue about.
This is for keeps and you are my bluest light.

Beth McCall, Grade 12
St Michael Catholic Secondary School, ON

Society's Identity

The sweet sounds of slumber swirl in my head,
But my body refuses to sleep.
The mask I wear, hidden in the abyss,
Wanting to dive into the depths of a reborn person.

I have been living a masquerade,
Hiding what I truly am.
Observing what the world wants,
Not what I want.

I'm not a natural leader,
Not even a trained follower.
What am I?

I am a drone,
Robot to the world's norm.

Do I want to be known for being normal?
I want to make a difference in the world!

I want to be…
AN INDIVIDUAL.

Josh Appell, Grade 12
Melville Comprehensive High School, SK

Forgotten

The flowers on your grave are fresh today.
They brighten it with beauty
    Along with the morning light.
I stayed for hours talking to you
    And read you chapters from your favorite book.

The flowers on your grave are a day old today.
They still lighten it with beauty
    Along with the morning light.
I stayed for an hour talking to you,
    But I left your book at home.

The flowers on your grave are a week old today.
They are withered and dead;
    They do nothing for your grave but show the truth.
I only stayed for a few minutes today,
    And I sold your book at the garage sale last weekend.

There are no flowers on your grave today.
    When the sun shines
It shines on your grave like it does all others:
    With no beauty
        Or meaning.

Amy Schaefer, Grade 11
Taylorville Sr High School, IL

My Best Friend

I'm falling for my best friend
But I cannot let him know
For fear of his reaction
I mustn't let my feelings show

Because once it's out there's no going back
Into the way it was before
It will stir a change and break a bond
Only leave me wanting more

I must fight my fate, no matter what the cost
So many teardrops will fall
But just keep it inside and bite my lip
Rather than lose it all

My secret is safe inside my heart
Where it shall always stay
Bear the hurt and conceal the truth
Deep and locked away

Erin Lang, Grade 12
Montmartre School, SK

You Bring Out the Stereotype in Me

You bring out the government in me.
The lies. The promises.
The smile of contradiction in me.
You bring out the Indian act in me.
The money in me. The labels. The rez.
You bring out the pity in me.
The bribe in me. The forgotten in me.
You bring out the destruction in me.
The stolen in me. The accident. The promise.
You bring out the belief in me.
The strength. The law. The weakness in me.
You bring out the ancestors in me.
The wisdom. The stories. The power I hold.
The feather. The peace pipe and the chief.
You bring out the Native in me.

Brianna Dick, Grade 12
St Andrew's Regional High School, BC

Beauty of Nature

The beauty of nature is all around you.
You can see it wherever you go.
Flowers swaying in the breeze.
A bright sunny day.
Crickets singing in the night.
Puppies and kittens running around playing in the grass.
Birds singing in the trees.
A glistening lake at sunrise and sunset.
A full moon lights up the night.
Stars shining on a clear night.
Leaves of different colors.
Animals eat peacefully in fields.
Horses running in meadows.
These are some of the beauties of nature.

Ayla Brossow, Grade 10
Rib Lake High School, WI

I Needed You

To be there for me but you're never there from the beginning. And I don't know what else to do you left me there by myself. And I sat there oh so lonely with no one by my side to hold me when I was blue. And now I just don't know what to do anymore. So now you want another chance because you need me now don't you. Well you're just too late now because you're no help from the beginning and I did so many things for you but you didn't need it. I needed you because I love you but you didn't need me at all.

Markeda Perry, Grade 11
Lincoln West High School, OH

My Anonymous Sweet Heart

She is as sweet as M&Ms,
though, candy can't make me smile the way she does,
interestingly enough, both can make me crave them.
Whether it be for attention, or to taste the chocolaty goodness.
Candy cannot create the pain and agony that a crush can.
Pain that makes me want to SCREAM at the mistakes that I have created in attempting friendship.
Though, the pain is eased with the thought of a new day, a new chance, new opportunities.
Especially since I'm timid and prone to saying stupid things!
She is as sweet as M&Ms, simple words cannot describe how I feel about her.
Love is certainly not it. "WHAT!?!" you say.
Then I ask you, "Define love. Describe the emotion to me."
To me, I use the word very carefully as if a bomb that may explode if tempered with.
Erupting in an explosion of disappointment and depression, as my history has shown.
Using the word doesn't set it off, it's when you try to define the word.
Incorrectly matched to someone or some emotion, that doesn't fit, will result in a catastrophe.
Which would describe my previous years of life.
But not anymore, now, I stand tall and await each new day's gift of opportunity.
She is as sweet as M&Ms.
Ironically, I am allergic to M&Ms because they contain nuts,
which is the only way you can describe how I feel about her.

Dean Michael Krokos, Grade 10
Troy High School, MI

Questions

Why do we reminisce about the days gone by?
Why do we cling to nothing with a tortured sigh?
At what point do our hopes and dreams fall away?
When we are weak, delayed, angered or decayed?
Where is the place where everyone belongs?
Where was the time when everything went wrong?
Why do we hunt for solace in all the unknowns?
Why do we search when we know we are alone?
Is there nothing we can do, nothing we can stop?
Is there nothing we control, are we the worst of the crop?
Is this all a dream or a nightmare?
Whatever the case, no one seems to care,
We preach to ourselves that life is not fair,
We scream for help, but no one is ever there!
But there is not a soul to fix us we're already torn,
We are so quickly depleted, abandoned, and forlorn,
Everyone is destitute with no chance of being reborn,
All my good intentions are locked and caged,
All my insecure questions have crept onto this page,
It seems pointless to create such a mindless banter,
But what makes me feel the most vulnerable is knowing I don't have any of the answers.

Eric Bolduc, Grade 10
Lake Region Christian School, MN

Me

Josh
Athletic, smart, honest, caring
Brother of Nichole and Leroy
Lover of pumpkin pie, excitement of a newborn baby,
and the happiness of a child
Who feels loneliness when traveling alone,
scared when in the dark, and nervous when testing
Who needs family, friends, and courage
Who gives love, support, and effort
Who fears bears, darkness, and loneliness
Who would like to see Hawaii, Disneyland, and the rainforests
Who lives in a large white house on Independence Ave.
Vandiver

Josh Vandiver, Grade 11
Prairie Lakes School, MN

The Snowing Drift

We ride and glide
Across the snow covered ground
My sled is turning me around and around
Hitting bumps, sending me flying in the air
I hit the ground
Cracking my back
Rolling down the hill
Stopped, and then lay on my back
Almost broke my back
Like an old wooden bat
That the Twins broke
With only one crack of a home run

That snow drift's my challenge

Cory Lamb, Grade 11
Prairie Lakes School, MN

Precious Cargo

We shall never view our mission lightly
Like those who have nothing to lose
Rather, we carry our brothers tightly
Precious Cargo in those times we choose

Heaven will help not those who come between
Our home, our path, our goal
For fury shall be brought to bear;
Against oppression, death or toll

What becomes of you, my friend
Whence we release you from our eagle's grasp
Only a few shall ever know

But believe during those long hours
That Night Stalkers are near
And fear your enemy will know
That Night Stalkers will always,
Always carry our precious cargo, back home.

Tim Yoo, Grade 12
John Hersey High School, IL

The Departure

Please do not hide your lovely face from me.
I'm here, My Love, and I'll take care of you,
though final breaths are all what's left may be.

While smiles and laughs are now but memory,
which fades away as darkness takes your hue,
please do not hide your lovely face from me.

Through pain and sickness, strain your eyes to see
the man who'll wait 'til skies again are blue,
though final breaths are all what's left may be.

I'll hold you close, now clinging desperately.
You look your worst, or so you think you do;
but do not hide your lovely face from me.

Don't close your eyes, Life, please come back to me!
For frozen lips, a kiss and, "I love you,
though final breaths are all what's left may be."

God rest you now at peace eternally.
As you depart, beginning life anew,
please do not hide your lovely face from me,
though final breaths are all that's left to see.

Ian Hollenbaugh, Grade 12
Saline High School, MI

Well Known Fact

Water falls downward,
It's a well known fact,
And that is that.

I am a droplet in a mighty waterfall,
Rushing down to the stones below.
I splashes everywhere in the gleaming summer sun,
It's a well known fact.

I am a stream with pebbles in the middle.
I go up their gentle slopes before quietly falling down again,
And that is that.

Now I am a small drip from a tap,
Trapped in a plumbing trap.
I go up along the pipe to my freedom,
It's a well known fact.

It is not impossible to defy gravity.
It's a well known fact,
And that is that.

Mary Jie Yang, Grade 11
Woburn Collegiate Institute, ON

The Vietnam War*

People fighting,
People dying,
Women and children crying.
Husband and father gone to war
This world is no good any more.
But what choice do they have
Because of the United States' draft?
Eighteen years old
And no choice but to go.
Now what does this show?
Where is our freedom?
Where's our rights?
What must we do
To show this isn't right?

Vanessa Howell, Grade 11
Marlington High School, OH
*Dedicated to my teacher, Mr. Albrect.

Misinterpreted Fate

Now I wonder as the shadows fall
Why I bother with you at all
Yes I made you wait a while
Maybe because you never smiled
The hate I thought I felt from you
Is now a sure thing through and through
Now you dismiss me with naught a wave
All I try for is our friendship saved
But exile seems what you want
Your gaze to pass me as a taunt
Though I shall not simply slink away
This battle will be fought day to day
As you leave me now, sitting on the brink
It gives me time, time to think
That one day I shall understand my fate
But by then I'm sure, it will be too late.

Tim Rogers, Grade 12
Esquimalt High School, BC

Heartless

"You have no heart."
I have a heart. Can't you hear it beat?
Can't you hear it break?
"Your emotions take the back burner."
No, I just don't flaunt them like you.
It feels just as good to me.
It hurts just as much to me.
I just keep quiet.
I want to scream, shout, stomp and cry.
But I don't.
Because with all the noise you make,
Nobody would hear me.

Natasha Mitrev, Grade 10
William Fremd High School, IL

What I See

I see many who take their life as a game
They don't care if they win or lose
I see people dying for AIDS and drug abuse
I see many who live a life filled with deceit
I see people getting killed and becoming stains in the street
What I see is chaos and it's very strange
I see that this world needs a change

Kara Davis, Grade 11
Eastmoor Academy High School, OH

Ghost Family

Always used to be whole,
Always used to be together
An argument being unusual,
Love filled the air making no room for hate.
They'd laugh and play together
For hours and hours
Not allowing any silly interruptions
Like the ringing of the phone, the catchy jingle on the TV, nothing.
Playing games is what they did best
A round of Uno or Aggravation was their favorite.

Now separated with their father out of state working.
That part's always missing.
Never returning to the old family of happy go lucky times.
Tension rises in the house with their mother.
And even when they're whole again,
When he's back home,
It's not the same,
There's still something missing.

Brittany Zenisek, Grade 11
Hartford Union High School, WI

Flying

If I could fly
O the things I would do!
I'd do a few aerial tricks to impress my friends
Then I'd fly to Chicago
I'd fly over Wrigley and watch a Cubs game
If I could fly I'd never use a car again
So Al Gore and I would be best friends
I would also travel the world
I would see the most wonderful places
I'd go to the Eiffel tower in Paris
The pyramids in Egypt
The Great Wall in China
And I'd still have time to come home and finish my homework
If I could fly I'd help out the fire department
I could save kittens in trees
I'd be the hero of the town
If I could fly I would also fly up next to an airplane
Then I'd tap on the glass just to see how startled a passenger would get
I could fly around dropping water balloons on people's heads
Life would sure be interesting if I could fly

Alex Klein, Grade 11
William Fremd High School, IL

Just This One Time

From the smooth porous carpet of grief,
A single blast of flood,
Hidden in a traveling bag
Strode with serious speed towards the
Crystal floor.
The ground was shaking with the flood
Yet to hit, a flood which was to change
A lot in the life of a young girl.
Through the hairy, microscopic pores of friction,
The flood droplet streamed with a steady speed,
Pacing itself on each ground.
Suddenly, the droplet increased in speed,
Flying and suddenly hitting the crystal floor with
Violence.
The droplet exploded in a catastrophic manner
While engulfing microcosms.
A fallen flood, an engulfed generation,
A tear droplet of a wild young girl
Only if, only if she had listened.
Just this one time, look, a droplet, a flood,
Changes all things.

Robert Okyere, Grade 12
Westerville North High School, OH

Holocaust of Spirits

Six million spirits caught and maimed
With the black blood of Hitler's spell,
That poured down bodies, ripped and flamed
Or gassed to death in man-made Hell.

Six million hands forced to cremate
Those they loved most, fed down to die
While blood clung to the tainted gate
That pierced young cheeks too torn to cry.

Six million lips, nigh drowned in death
And ashes burning out their eyes,
Through which they strain for one…last…breath
As their last thread on life unties.

Six million hearts made to betake
Their tortured beats to Rest with knives.
A prayer said, one last keepsake,
As anguish draws out souls from lives.

And now, years since, their memory
In rivers of spilt souls enframes
Hearts that singe through destiny,
For that same blood hangs from their names.

Abrielle Fuerst, Grade 12
OHDELA Academy, OH

What's Better Than Cross Country?

It all started August 13, 2007
Cross country is a gift from heaven
It was our first year combining with a team from the north
We were enemies at first but I was the first to come forth
When we almost won our meet at Timms Hill
All of us knew this year was going to be a thrill
With Peterson and Schirmer leading the pack
We all started talking smack
When Jason and Charlton hit the eighteens
Everybody knew what that could mean
With me, Jeffrey, and Cal bringing up the 5th and 6th spot
We definitely had a reassuring shot
Our Hawks Cross Country team started to dominate
That's right we made our goal and we went to state

Jeffrey Quednow, Grade 10
Rib Lake High School, WI

This Feeling

Once I thought love was just a story,
A story meant to give false hope.
Hope for true happiness.
A happiness I would never find.
But now,
Holding you so close so eager but yet so afraid.
Afraid because I never felt this way.
The way I feel isn't bad it's new.
And the funny thing is I only feel it when I'm with you.
No it's not lust.
Lust is a feeling of greed.
No this is so much better.
I don't feel it in my head or in my heart,
I feel it throughout me.
This mix of joy excitement and the strongest of all peace.
Now I'm not one to believe in fairy tales,
But somehow I think maybe just maybe,
This might be the thing I've longed for all my life.
Something I never thought could be real,
True Love.

Theresa Green, Grade 10
Windom Secondary School, MN

Life's Changing

Life is all about anticipating change
Some you can help some come without warning
That is what defines our character

How you wake up every morning
And face the judging world
With a somber smile or a bright frown

It can be the smashing sound of a game winning grand slam
It could also be the news you never wanted to hear
Take each change as a life long lesson

Never forget what you learned each day
Take advice and never look back
Every obstacle will get you on your way

Jenna Hines, Grade 12
Waseca High School, MN

Love Is Like a Tear…

Love is like a tear,
Falling from your eye,
You never know where it will land.
Your tears last forever,
But not when you try.
Drying your eyes,
Seeing the light,
Walking on clouds,
This is love.
Tears come and go,
So does love.
Rainy days pass you by,
Sunny days are by your side.
Strive for your future,
Leave your past behind,
Love is where you are.
Life passes you by,
Love stays its path.
Dry your tears,
Love is near.

Ashley Lenoir, Grade 10
Windom Secondary School, MN

Snowmobile

S now
N ight
O utdoors
W inter
M orning
O pen trails
B lustery
I ce
L ight
E xhaust

Joel Ekern, Grade 10
Blair-Taylor High School, WI

The Future

Afraid, but confident,
That is what I am.
Fearing the future,
But yearning for tomorrow,
Though I believe in myself
I am still afraid I will fail.
When I was young,
I desperately wanted to become an adult,
But now it scares me half to death.
Prepared but clueless,
That is what I am.
Planning in advance,
Though I don't know what lies ahead.
Though I want to go to school,
I don't know what for.

Joshua Herrington, Grade 12
The Ranch Program at Salem, IL

Life in Love

Once in a while, you'll hit some rough spots.
You'll look back and have some weary thoughts.
You might wonder who you could've been or what you could've done.
It might not mean much, but it could mean a ton.
Your life will move on, changing pace and direction,
But when you look to your left or your right, you'll see the connection.
He'll be there to make you smile;
He'll lift your chin when you're sad or in denial.
He'll be there to pick you up or push you that extra mile.
He'll accept you; love you for your own personal style.
She'll kiss you and hug you; she'll tell you she loves you.
She'll miss you; she'll wait for you, she'll go on late night trips with you.
She'll gripe and she'll moan, but you're still her own.
She'll laugh, she'll cry; but she'll always have a loving gleam in her eye.
As you leave here today, as you go hand in hand, remember that together…
Forever and stronger you stand.

Jacob Shawver, Grade 10
Leeton Middle and High School, MO

Dreams

A dream triggers inspiration,
Inspiration triggers drive, determination and desire,
Which triggers heart,
Heart triggers hope,
Hope triggers fear,
Fear triggers sadness which ends in tears.
Sadness equals a dream lost,
Which restarts this cycle.
Finally, when the dream is obtained,
We realize the pain suffered has made us a *better, stronger* person.

Brett Hickey, Grade 12
Ecole secondaire E J Lajeunesse, ON

Something Missing

This man who loves his wife and children very much
Doesn't understand the feeling in the pit of his stomach
That spreads to his toes and up to his head
To the ends of his hair, or what's left of it

This woman who gets up early every day, except Saturday
To go to work at a job that she likes, not loves
Wonders why it feels like she's always on the outside of the loop
And wonders who's on the inside

This child, who talks about things that children talk about with their friends
Such as action figures and who can jump higher
Asks his mother about this feeling in the pit of his stomach
He says it feels like perhaps there's a hole there
His mother checks under his shirt and says there's no hole

So the child goes away, his question unanswered
He wonders to himself why he didn't get an answer
Maybe it's because his mother
Wonders the same thing.

Hannah Smith, Grade 10
Robert Bateman Secondary School, BC

My Angel

I like to fly between the skies
and I feel your protection wrapped in your wings
I like to fly between the skies
and I lose myself with the light of your eyes
Because you are an angel in my life
that with your look you provoke my happiness.

Mario De La Rosa Moreno, Grade 12
Abraham Lincoln High School, MN

In One Moment

It all happened in one moment.
As I came out of the kitchen
I saw something jump
out of the corner of my eye
as if someone flinched.
I turned around, and saw
three-inch palms on the floor,
with back crouched,
and knees bent, in a crawling position.
He smiled his adorable, toothless smile,
even the sun would envy upon.
Feeling a bit guilty that I made him jump,
I walked towards him.
He stretched his arms
out for me to pick him up.
Oh! I still can't get over his small, chubby arms.
As I picked him up,
his soft lips brushed my cheeks.
It was the first time he learned to kiss.
And…
it all happened in one moment.

Nora Sakpal, Grade 10
Troy High School, MI

The Falling of Serenity

The artist called it war,
And the poet, a silence
It could have been so much more.
Colourless, talentless too —
All that we abhor.
Strangle held, earth bound,
As that which tragedy wore,
The ruin and the writing,
On the dark unsightly sighting,
By the painting of a heaven,
Which we did long adore,
As every little creature,
Of contemptible size,
Sought every single feature,
Another might prize,
To tiny demon dynasties,
We now solemnly depart,
With vengeance on our breath,
On our brushes, pens and heart.

Josh Winter, Grade 12
John Paul II Catholic Secondary School, ON

Outside the Window

Here I sit upon my chair,
Looking out the window, feeling a slight breeze;
The smell of the fresh clean air,
As I gaze out at the evergreen trees.

The crisp spring leaves like crunchy chips,
All painted a delicate green;
They would taste like heaven if put up to my lips,
And smell as sweet as the best scent you've ever seen.

But the beauty will come and will go,
What's left is left, and what's to come will come;
The city is prospering and will always grow,
No one knows when it will stop, not even my mom.

Thankful for the times when I've gone out to play,
As more buildings are taking up space;
Who knows when it will come to that day,
When this city is not the same place.

The soil may not be as healthy or brown,
The trees around the corner will then be around the bend;
I could still be living in this town,
When it all comes to an end.

Paige Dudzik, Grade 10
Robert Bateman Secondary School, BC

The Last Memory

I decided to walk home alone
In the darkness of the night
Attempting to fight my emotions of
Emptiness, sadness, and anger
I couldn't believe this happened to me
So I walked the roads of my reservation
With no fear, no heart, no respect
As I look to the left
I decide to
Walk the dark and unpredictable trail
No moonlight
Just the shadows of the night
I continue to walk…
Just then I hear footsteps, a voice,
A sudden warmth came over my heart
He gave me a big hug and grabbed my hand
He looked younger, stronger, and sad
"I love you boy" he cried!
"I love you too Dad" I stated with confidence
As we walked I knew
I was safe during this, Last Walk.

Justin Johnson, Grade 11
Prairie Lakes School, MN

Life

Don't take life for granted,
For it could leave you empty handed.
Don't ever leave your friends behind,
Because you will never get out alive.
Remember to take chances,
You never know what might happen.
Always be yourself,
Don't pretend to be someone else.
Live and learn, forgive and forget,
Live your life with no regrets.

Brittany Peche, Grade 10
Rib Lake High School, WI

Hidden by the World

Emotionless face
Hidden with fear
Stone cold eyes
That won't shed a tear

A hardened heart
Frozen with sorrow
Floating in nothingness
No faith in tomorrow

A life spent alone
Teaches the heart not to feel
To hide it from the sadness
The pain so unreal

But a smile, a laugh
From a friend that's grown near
Can unfreeze the heart
And save what's left here

Sarah Bommarito, Grade 11
Christian Academy of Indiana, IN

Black and Blue

Any little twist of truth
Every single "secret" lie
Make my heart more black and blue
Make me wonder why

Every moment I'm with you
standing in your warm embrace,
Makes me more and more a fool
conceiving memories I can't erase

My heart gets beaten with your words
and I know you don't really care
But as it bruises more black and blue
at your face I still sit and stare.

Ashley Ferguson, Grade 11
Vegreville Composite High School, AB

The Storm

The air gently moves across my face.
The sun begins to fade.
The clouds become a fearsome gray, and then it starts to rain.
It sprinkles, drips, flows, and pours all around me now.
I sit and ponder of this wonder as it's falling all around.
I get up onto my feet; and throw my hands out wide.
I twirl and dance, laugh and sing.
This was nature's awesome surprise.

Alexia Mannel, Grade 10
Rib Lake High School, WI

Remote Friendship

This is a tribute to my friend Tyler
In first sight his eyes full of shyness
Comforting him in a new location is what I did
Life is what he found
Getting to know him, getting to see through him
The world roamed around us as we sat gently under the sun
Best friends we became
Then struck problems at home
Fear and hate flowed through him
Fights were broken out
His mother was in pain
Too much time I spent to help
Now wishing I spent more time
Problems struck again
Adoption was a choice, Tennessee was his new world
Yet sadness still struck
His hopes fell for a good life
Even though I felt alone, tenacious I felt
Until shyness refilled his eyes, more problems seemed to strike
He was cold and numb, until the day he felt no more
Life was found but betrayed him at dawn, life is no more for my friend Tyler.

Tim Harmeyer, Grade 10
Oak Creek High School, WI

Waiting*

Waiting can do things to people.
It can make them go insane,
If it's something really important to them.
Like, love, for instance.
If someone is being patient with you
And waiting 'til you're of age,
It can strain you.
You don't want to wait,
But to avoid conflicts,
You wait anyway.
Waiting can sometimes kill,
Figuratively speaking anyway.
I don't like waiting,
But, I guess I'll have to endure the insaneness of waiting.
I'll endure it because I truly love the person and am willing to wait.
How long would you wait?

Ashley Poppe, Grade 11
Neillsville High School, WI
*Dedicated to Mike Fisher - my soul mate

Summer Is Here

The city feels just wonderful,
With everything so colourful.
Be brave do not fear,
Winter is gone, now summer is here.

Beautiful flowers start to grow,
Standing straight in a row.
Look at them it makes you calm,
There is no need for therapy or balm.

The truck arrives that sells ice cream,
Moments later you hear the kids scream.
To buy ice cream they're out on the street,
They don't care about the roaring heat.

On the beach, there is nice ocean breeze,
Which pleasantly moves through the palm trees.
This makes you feel that the world is fair,
Not in winter, but in the summer air.

Sparrows chirp, sing and play,
Starting from May, every day.
They ask me "How are you doing, dear?"
I say, "I'm good 'cause summer is here."

Zenia Unwala, Grade 12
Birchmount Park Collegiate Institute, ON

Darkness Inside

So this is what it's like, to be lost,
lost in the darkness of yourself?
To be trapped,
trapped in time?
Where is the light, you ask.
It left, gone forever, stolen from me,
with he who has my heart.
Do not bother in vain, to help me.
I am eternally wandering,
wandering until my heart stops beating.
I am but a shell,
a shell of the past.
Wanting what is forbidden,
needing a touch forever denied me.
I'm sure it will pass.
After an eternity, the hole will scab over,
when I am too old, and alone to remember.
I wait for the day, that I reunite,
with he who was stolen from me,
when I will be whole and young again.
I wait for my death.

Halsey Shaheen, Grade 10
Vanier Collegiate, SK

Dear Walleyes

Dear Walleyes,

I hope you had a quiet winter,
Because the smoker-craft and I are coming this spring.
You have until May 10th to run and hide,
But don't worry I know your secret spots.
You will be deep in your freezing cold water,
But the fenwick and our patented snap jig are ready for battle.
But don't worry,
If I win one of you might be over a nice
Warm fireplace for the rest of your days,
Hopefully not alone.

Tyler Ous, Grade 12
Grand Rapids Sr High School, MN

My Jealousy of Mike

When Mike skated around the rink
I trailed behind him.
How did he do it?
He is so fast.
During the game he shot
Goal after goal.
All I heard was spectators cheering him on.
Then, a shoot out, naturally he wins.
Trophy time for most improved player.
Another decoration for his mantle.
During math class I see him again.
Tests are being handed back.
I catch a glimpse of the big fat red "F"
On his paper.
I always thought he had it made.
Maybe I don't really know him well enough.

Neal Potvin, Grade 12
Hartford Union High School, WI

Good Luck, Not Goodbye

Twelve times sounds the bell,
Upon which last words of farewell,
Accompanied with passionate hug and kiss,
Mark the closing of a reunion of bliss.
They have both arrived at that fork in the road,
Neither knowing what the future shall bode.
For her, a return to her elite station,
For him, abroad to fight for his nation.
For both, the heartache of separation.
For both, a despairing sense of trepidation.
As he held her in one last embrace,
Neither wanted to utter what both must face.
For in that one word lays an ocean
Filled with finality, closing, termination,
Acknowledging barely suppressed fears,
Bringing pain both deep and fierce.
Finally, he, standing strong to the last,
Looked into her eyes and held her fast.
Wisely, he spoke, with a single bottomless sigh,
"I'll say good luck…not goodbye."

Mendy Yang, Grade 10
Okemos High School, MI

Volleyball

Spiking the ball is lots of fun
But you have to run
Passing is a key thing too
But make sure that you tie your shoe
When you set the ball
Make sure that you don't fall
When you go to block and touch the sky
You feel like you're going to fly
Serving up that final point
Don't throw your shoulder out of joint
When you score
It is not a bore
And then when you win
You want to play again

Mallory Gebers, Grade 11
Patrick Henry High School, OH

Summer Fires

Summer night bonfires
Dark bedrooms
Burn of fire
Caught in my net of hair
Smoke ring eyes
Rub ash out
In morning's routine
Of washing my face
And mouth's sticky corners
Victim to charred marshmallows
I purposely burned
I twist my hair
Around my finger
Pull it across my lips
To smell last night's smoke
Which my shampoo
Didn't want to wash out either

Kristen Kupstys, Grade 10
William Fremd High School, IL

Small Town Girl

Big city lights
Fill the streets at night
I am just a small town girl
Without much knowledge of the world

So many sights to see
What a variety of things to be
Yellow shapes blur through the street
People walk by and don't even greet

For some this lifestyle is okay
But I could just not live this way
I am just a small town girl
This is where I belong in the world

Brynn Anderson, Grade 10
Carmi-White County High School, IL

Face Value

You look at me like an article of clothing in a store.
Either you like me or you don't.
You take it as face value: That girl is fat. That boy is stupid.
You judge me on how I look and not on what I am.
I am the only one who understands.
You take it as face value: That girl is hot. That boy is fly.
You think you are better than me. The truth is we are all the same.
You take it as face value: That girl is dumb. That boy is dangerous.
You talk about me behind my back or even in front of me.
We all do the same.
You take it as face value: That girl is weird. That boy is a loser.
You feel better by putting me down.
If someone does it to you it's a big deal.
You take it as face value: That girl is smart. That boy is fun.
You place a tag on my friends and me. The same goes for you.
You take it as face value: That girl is rich. That boy is poor.
We do the same thing to each other. Face the truth, we are all the same.
We take it as face value: That girl is mean. That boy is aggressive.
You are the only one that knows the truth.
Our happiness is someone's pain.
We only hurt each other in the end. Face value only goes so far.

Victoria Jambretz, Grade 12
Arrowhead Union High School - North Campus, WI

The Beauty of Memories

Memories are treasures that are kept in our heart and soul forever.
They are puzzle pieces of the past that our mind puts together.
And that always reminds us of people and moments we held dear
That brought smiles, joy, laugher and even tears.

They bring back the souvenirs of our words to our last day on Earth.

Life has such treasures that time's always stealing;
So while you are still young, capture each feeling and moment,
And make all the memories you can every day
Because there's nothing dear to your heart that can ever entirely stay.

Soha Fakih, Grade 12
Ecole secondaire E J Lajeunesse, ON

Anxious

School's almost over —
No more waking up early to catch the bus
And no more stressing over tests
Or trying to finish homework last minute because you forgot to get it done at home
Now is the time to relax —
For THREE months
Meanwhile a lot of kids are getting ready for their summer/fall sports
And that three months gives you time to dedicate your time to perfect your craft
Because you don't have to worry about
Having to get back home early to finish some homework
Or some project that you got yesterday and it's due tomorrow
So kick back, relax, and get ready for that 2:30 bell to ring
To send your summer into full swing

Darryl Wood, Grade 11
Eastmoor Academy High School, OH

Hope Is…

Hope is not a rich man wishing for more money;
Hope is a poor man wishing to make it through the day.

Hope is not a young girl longing to go shopping;
Hope is a young girl longing for a pair of shoes.

Hope is not praying you can go to the best restaurant;
Hope is praying you will get to eat today.

Hope is not wanting your parents to leave you alone;
Hope is wanting your parents to be there.

Hope is not being able to have everything;
Hope is being able to have anything.

Hannah Freeman, Grade 12
Taylorville Sr High School, IL

Tiger

Drive, chip, and putt
These are words of golf.
Golf is Tiger's game.

When Tiger puts on his spiked shoes,
He owns the green course.
His swing is like a knife going through butter.

Tiger is loved by fans,
And feared by competitors.
Tiger can make the snow white ball come alive.
He can make any shot.

Tiger can boom a 300 yard drive,
Or putt for eagle from any distance.
No shooting shot is impossible.
He is invincible.
He is Tiger Woods.

Nicole Draheim, Grade 12
Waseca High School, MN

Who Are You

I don't know who you are anymore
It's hard to believe our bond is being torn
I know you've been busy and I have too
But the way you've been treating me lately:
What am I supposed to do?
I never know what to do next
Haven't you noticed that lately I've been vexed?
Maybe you don't realize
How you've been pushing me away
But how could you possibly expect me to stay?
What if I were to disappear quick and fast
Then would you ask:
"Why did you leave?"
You replaced me with a mutual friend
And you expect me to bend?
I'll go along with this little charade.
No matter how hard you two parade!

Emily Johnson, Grade 10
Haynes Academy for Advanced Studies, LA

The "Normality" of Nature

Normal means natural, calm and casual,
We use this word to explain the Earth.
But to the greater Gods, against us are the odds,
For they see us as what we're truly worth.

They try to remind this world so unkind,
That to them we are put in perspective.
To the nature we disrupt, animals we corrupt,
And souls we leave unmended.

The way thunder screams at absurd self-esteems,
And the Earth quakes as we start to command.
Do we not see? A coincidence this can't be,
Just the gods holding out their hands.

Without these seemingly rude signs of gratitude,
Believe it or not we would be insane.
For a superior human who's looking to ruin,
Could drown out any amount of rain.

And of course with not a wink of remorse,
We continue to receive these signs.
But let's all just agree, as far as we can see,
Normal is wrongly defined.

Julianna Hamad, Grade 11
Ellet High School, OH

Mother Nature's Song (Abridged)

Mother Nature sings her song, She calls far and wide
But no one is there to listen
She shouts out for peace, but Her patience is running thin
She will make them listen

She sends out diseases, the floods are unleashed
Some start to listen
The winds are Her fingers, The water, Her weapon
The fire is Her fury, The people, Her victims

She lashes out with fire and She throws at them storms
People are listening
Her fury has peaked, She sends herself forth
She is not listening

Now her anger has past, She shows what She demands
The people are listening

The world has changed,
Now they are in tune,
When Mother Nature starts to sing

Alex Chila, Grade 10
Robert Bateman Secondary School, BC

Gymnastics State 2008

Gymnastics State 2008 was the time of my life;
it was so much fun just to be with the whole team and to even be competing up at State!
I remember driving up with the whole team, painting the big truck we took and writing on it,
competing and trying as hard as we could to win, getting 4th place,
going out to dinner with the team to Pizza Hut, staying up all night and having a lot of fun.
I heard the crowd cheering for their school
I saw the gymnasts trying to be their best
I tasted Propel right before I was ready to go up and compete
I smelt feet and sweat on each gymnast as they were trying to win
I touched the vault, floor, beam, and bars
State 2008 was definitely the best time of my life!

Alexis Czuta, Grade 10
Oak Creek High School, WI

Me

Maritza
Generous, funny, caring, and grateful
Sister of Mario
Lover of Ashly, Delsie, and Claudia
Who feels happy, sad, and moody
Who needs family, friends, and support
Who gives advice, love and affection
Who fears death, heights, and love
Who would like to see more happy people, peace from everyone, and respect from everyone
Who lives in a blue/gray house in a very small town called Montevideo, Minnesota on 4th Street
Lombrana

Maritza Lombrana, Grade 10
Prairie Lakes School, MN

Thunderstorm Impressions

Men bowling from Rip Van Winkle, lightning dances across the sky, lights up clouds in a brilliant streak
Thunder rumbles, roars, all the while rain pours, belts, like something from Tim Burton
Never gets less spectacular, that eerie beauty
Scary and deadly yet can't look away, like a moth attracted to a flame, aware it's inching closer and closer to its impending doom yet powerless to look away
Stirs something primal, senses alive; on fire
Electricity literally and figuratively in the air, sparking the atmosphere with dangerous excitement
Intensity comes and goes as it gathers and releases strength to strike the Earth
Jumps clouds, thunder lets out ear-splitting, hair-raising, glorious claps and peals
Blinding flashes of light, some miles away, others terrifyingly close
Illuminating the ground at brief intervals
No warning for when the next one approaches
I lean forward out my window
Stretch my hand towards the sky and feel rain slide down my arm
The crazy desire to become closer to nature's lethal forces
And I am not alone in my stupidity
Countless others have ignored their safety in pursue of an impossible intimacy
Yet logic holds no reason with them for they try anyway
The existence of such tremendous destructiveness is only comprehensible by witness
Nothing compares; everything pales in comparison, it leaves all who behold it awestruck
Amazing

Michelle Deas, Grade 10
Francis Libermann Catholic High School, ON

Waiting

Silently she waits for him,
She's waiting for his footsteps
To hit the hardwood floor.
How long has it been?
She asked herself…
Much, much too long.

How long since she received a letter?
How long since she heard his name?
She's received no word,
So she keeps waiting.

How long should she wait?
When should she worry?
When is he coming back?
And then the phone rings…

Her waiting is done,
She no longer has to worry
She thinks to herself,
As she silently places the flowers on the grave.
Now he is the one waiting.

Beth Weise, Grade 10
Rib Lake High School, WI

Our World

Look at the world we are living in
Safe streets becoming havens for terrorists
Gangsters, the people that kids are idolizing
Equality is still not happening
Can anyone live without committing a sin
Whatever happened to the dream of Martin Luther King
People still judging others on the color of the skin
Or segregating them on the basis of religion

Just look at the situation in the Middle East
Priests killing each other, turning into living beasts
Bombs blowing up, disturbing the peace
Gun shots heard over the kids' sweet melodies
There is only one solution to all this
To look over our faults and ignore the differences
Create a world we'd all love to live in

These questions aren't so ambiguous
But actually all very contiguous
Let's make the right choice
Come together, speak with one voice
End the hatred and stop the bad noise
So one day we can all rejoice.

Dhruv Sekhri, Grade 11
Troy High School, MI

Secrets

I kept it from you for your own well-being,
I thought if I stayed hush it would vanish,
Once out, I feel like I'm not worth living,
And now our trust seems to rust, tarnish.
Wait! Please listen and try to understand,
Acknowledge that this is my decision,
But is there really true evil at hand?
What I did without your permission,
There is no balm for the fire you spit,
There's no refuge from the hate in your eyes,
It is okay just to strike me, take a hit.
Because you will only believe I lie,
The words that you speak brings me deep sorrow.
Beware! There might not be a tomorrow.

Michel Collins, Grade 11
Cabrini High School, LA

i fall

i watch the world through a sheet
of glass seeing but unseen
numbers and squares
burning an image of a life outside
my own
doors lead to it but i
am left in the wake
as the moon calls to the sea to dance
a voice cries and i turn
eyes raised curtains drawn
smile nod murmur 'til
echoes pass to stillness
and finally i find
measure melody reason rhyme
building crescending
words and notes dancing
around me on ebony wings until
i fall
to myself
missing the place
where one is missed

Cathy Nygren, Grade 12
Melville Comprehensive High School, SK

Too Late

This is a poem for my grandpa William.
Who has come and gone so fast.
My memories I have are good and bad.
But all of them will last.
Your time was up, you had to go.
My everlasting love for you that you will never know.
One fateful night in dark November.
The Lord beseeched your soul to come.
And now you rest up in Heaven.
Never to feel pain again.
My only regret I have today
Is that I never had another chance to say I love you.
So I write this poem to William Perry.

Thomas Perry, Grade 10
Oak Creek High School, WI

Dream

Our minds get twirled
as we enter bliss
we enter a world
where the world doesn't exist
Reality is no more
even a rabbit can roar
why can't we wonder for days?
why come back
to a world of disgrace?
what this world lacks
can be found in that place
that perfect illusion
why can't it be real?
it leads to confusion
a world so ideal
we live our dull lives
and then escape to paradise
to a world beyond our eyes
a world with no lies
a world with no cries
a world with no goodbyes
but why stay in this world and weep?
when all we have to do is count sheep

Victor Nzeata, Grade 11
Merrillville High School, IN

Land

Land everywhere should be saved
No one cares
They keep building
And don't stop
They don't understand
Land is more important
Than just building on

Animals homes are there
Without buildings
There would be a beautiful view
For all to see

Beautiful healthy trees
And grass
Animals out in the open
Not fearing anything

Air nice and clean
No worries of pollution
Unknown flowers blooming
Enjoying the sun's
Beautiful rays

Stephanie Vincent, Grade 11
Hartford Union High School, WI

Love

Love is an unexplainable feeling; it's like a never-ending dream,
You never want to wake up.
Love makes you do things you would normally not do.
It's not just one person anymore it's two.
Love is like a drug, an addictive drug,
A high that you never want to come down from,
A place that you want to stay forever,
Love is an escape.

Lauren Brooke Turner, Grade 11
Eastmoor Academy High School, OH

Under the Bridge

I look under the bridge and see your face,
Wondering how much more you can really take.
How did you even get to this hell of a place?
All you have left is a sheet and your faith
But being that low doesn't your faith fade away;
Asking for money because you have no other way.
You're low and feeling like there's no way,
But being that low, all you do is pray.
I respected you for your strength, for waking up each day;
Have you ever wanted to give up so the pain could evaporate?
Trust, I know having to eat only crackers every day,
But we will never have to go back to those days;
Even though Katrina hit and we felt like our faith was stripped.
But don't give up
Jesus didn't; He gave His life so we could live.
No matter how low you fall,
He will be there to catch and hold you, like He does to all of His children.
Poverty can make you want to give up,
But trust in God so that one day you will stand up and become strong.
And feel alive; so you can look back at all of this and know
You have survived.

Jasmine Adams, Grade 11
Cabrini High School, LA

Stranger Soldier

Left right left right
Walk little soldier follow the ranks
Like you always have
Sorry I won't be following this time
I learned long ago that following you means to lose myself
Forgetting who I am and betraying myself
Sorry if I don't want to be like you are sorry if I can't be what you are
Sorry if I want things to change sorry if I'm not that little angel
Who's all you want her to be
I'm sorry that I have my own thoughts I'm sorry you can't understand them
I'm sorry you can't like me and take me for all the oddity that I am
If you love me would you please let me know?
If you hate me just move on in the ranks
I'll be there and look onto your disappearing face
I don't know you anymore
Happy life, stranger.
Farewell, dear stranger.

Ariel Drolet, Grade 11
Ecole Secondary Louis Philippe Pare, QC

Hidden Talent

Reach out and touch —
The peace which evades you
Break out and show —
The world what you can do
Do not hide it away —
Talent smuggled beneath your coat —
The soft, warm assuredness
That no one will know what you wrote
The words which flow —
But must not be seen
Nestled next to the fuzz in your pocket —
The sheltered pocket which keeps you serene
You will make it in this world —
If you are another so-and-so, you think —
But hope will tug at you in the night —
That you are on the brink
Of shedding this coat of doubt —
Hot and stifling, smothering your pride —
And you know, just know,
That this talent will not die.

Katelyn Boulton, Grade 11
Ida High School, MI

Roses

Our love is like a red rose sprinkled in dew
Each little drop, it reminds me of you
The petals are like my heart
Soft and easy to fall apart
The thorns are like our fights, they can be tough
And sometimes we want to give up when we've had enough
But the stem is what we're like when we're together
We hold each other up and we'll make it forever

Katrina Budgell, Grade 10
King's Christian Collegiate, ON

On the Road Beyond the Midnight Passion

On the road beyond the midnight passion,
We anticipate this world of hypnotic mystery.
Have you seen the markings beneath the sun,
Where we embrace together to celebrate our birth?
The rhythm of creation continues to beat,
As we remember the warmth of the promised land.
Now we're consumed by fear and mistrust,
And kill those who have once done the same.
The hunt for survival is now a religion,
And war is our temple of worship.
Still we try and change the repetitive mantra,
But dwell a cast under Lucifer's wing.
Our essence seems to no longer exist,
The future is an atrocity.
Destiny can be ours to control,
If we reconstruct this eternal damnation.
Look inside your own reflection,
And transform these dreams into an establishment.
Immerse within the pure and divine,
As we enter the glorious city.

Matt Panetta, Grade 12
Br Andre Catholic High School, ON

Silent Downfall

You pull a piece of me,
as I sit by and envy how you numb away the sorrow
with smells that remind me, my friend,
of just how far you've fallen.

And you pull a piece of me,
when I follow you blindly into the darkness,
spewing hatred about things we don't know
and heaving anger at anyone in view.

You all pull a piece of me,
sitting in your abyss of the world
blind to the cries of humans who aren't good enough for you,
shooing away the good things
to make room for your fast paced lives.

I pull a piece of me,
while I sit quietly complacent
to change myself, if fake and perfect
is all that you need.

You're all me.
You take away the bits of me,
and behind it all, you're causing me to crumble.

Shelby Hewerdine, Grade 10
Fort Zumwalt East High School, MO

Save Me

Please someone help me.
Someone set me free.
Set me free from this loneliness.
I want it all to go away.
The depression,
The loneliness,
The hurt,
The pain,
I want it to go away.
Please someone set me free.
From all of this insanity.
I cannot take it anymore.
I want someone,
Someone who would be with me,
Someone who will make this all go away,
Someone who will stay with me,
Someone who will fight off all these feelings.
Please someone save me.
Save me,
Before it is too late,
I fear it might be.

Holly Daigle, Grade 12
Higgins High School, LA

A Man

No man is a portrait of himself,
Nor a mirrored reflection of his identity,
A man bares the colors of his soul
And those who have made him so,
Eyes of those of many sides
A heart welded into gold,
A man can care, a man can hold,
A man continues to grow.

Meagen Grossmann, Grade 10
Mount Elizabeth Secondary School, BC

You May Not

You may not see it,
But it's there.
You may not feel it,
But I care.
You may not want me,
But it's you I crave.
You may not think so,
But you're so brave.
You may not know,
But it's you.
You may not believe it,
But it's true.
You may not hear it,
But that's my heart.
You may not think so,
But you are still so smart.
You may be amazing,
But she won't see,
How bad I need you,
But why would you want me?

Caitlin Schnipke, Grade 10
Ottoville High School, OH

The Feeling of the Woods

A drop of water on the leaf
Sends shivers
On the green, that in return
Whispers in the wind.
The sunshine dances
With the woods like blades
Cutting air through
Illuminating the retreating fog.
The sight explodes in action.
It electrifies my senses.
The color floods the mind,
And the unity of
Sound produces the utmost
Song of wild, that in return
Vibrates my imagination
Sending shivers
Down the spine of my being.

Elena Apsatarova, Grade 12
Northwest High School, OH

Prisoners in Black and White

There is a piano carved into every heart, made with black and white keys,
a place where the freedom of color is lost, and the music is unbearably beautiful,
for every heart fades in the melody of memory.
Every time a strong and fragile note is struck, we become stuck
in the knowledge we were never supposed to have;
accidentally informed, and let down, to discover that
love is a prisoner of circumstance.
So cast your stones at me for having the naiveté — or the courage — to dream,
to reach for, to scream for the moment
just beyond the fingertips of my soul
that will make the music run cold and freeze in my ears,
for I don't want to hear every story retold.
Cast your stones at me
and I'll say that I don't want to hear,
but I do,
for I need that faint glimpse of your face,
and the piano that is played in the black and white place
is played by you.

Kiersten Wones, Grade 11
William Mason High School, OH

Beauty from a Park Bench

There he is
Just sitting there
I wonder what he thinks of
Is it love, is it hate
I could never tell
But still he sits
Concentrated, and still
So I watch, closely
Admiring the beauty of him
Everything about him
From the way his breath would smell in the morning
To the way he would placidly sleep at night
I always watch when he sits
But somehow I get this feeling that he knows I'm watching
I don't know, I guess if he wasn't a picture, he could've been my love
But I guess I'll never know.

Cookie Richardson, Grade 12
Waynesville Sr High School, MO

I Wish You Were Here*

I wish you were here to say, Throw a little harder!
I wish you were here to say, Swing a little faster!
I wish you were here to say, Don't eat too much candy!…then give me the 'wink wink'.
I wish you were here to fight with my dad,
I wish you were here to make me laugh.
I wish you were here to take me to baseball games.
I wish you were here to teach me how to eat sunflower seeds,
I wish you were here to yell with me, Yay! Home run!!
I wish you were here to call me hun,
But most of all, I just wish you were here to be with me.

Brittany Krause, Grade 10
Centennial High School – Red Building, MN
*In loving memory of my Uncle Mike

Love Forever

Love is the warm hug the sunshine brings on cold days
It is music of the soul
That plays games with the heart
Without love the mind, body, and soul are free as birds
Birds soaring through the skies
Falling in love gives you someone to fly with
Someone to be your companion
For the closeness and compassion
Love turns up the volume on the stereo of the heart
The heart beats faster and faster
Like the rhythm of a drum
As a single drum turns into an orchestra
You fall deeper into love
That special someone to make your day
With just a simple smile or kiss
When two people fall in love bells are chiming in their ears
They are meant to be
Like PB and J
And as a butterfly is meant to fly
Soul mates

Carly Kroll, Grade 10
Oak Creek High School, WI

Love Is Forever

Love is forever…or at least that's what they say,
though my love for you will never go astray.
So when you tell me that times will be tough,
or our love rough
all I think is, "will we be ok?"
Then a sharp thought is thrust into my mind
it tells me to try and stay with this love through time.
It shows me the way to make it all seem right,
and tells me to tell you each and every night.
Even without my so called "if" my love would still be true.
Though deep down you don't believe it, I forever do love you.
I know it might be impossible to prove.
God knows I will try all I can.
When it comes right down to it,
I would do almost ANYTHING for your hand.
You are my beautiful angel,
I like it that way.
Damned be I if some guy steal you away.

Daniel Wilczynski, Grade 12
St Francis De Sales High School, OH

The Dim Hallways

No money in the schools
Kids turn to the streets
No food in their stomachs
No shoes on their feet
Viewing the world through their ear buds
And tapping to the beat, ignoring the teacher
And sweating from the heat
No pats on the back and no drug free
No love in their hearts and no facing defeat
No money in their pockets, so back to the streets.

Kurt Eizinger, Grade 12
Central High School, IL

The Storyteller

I'll tell you a tale of times long gone past,
Of princesses, mermaids and kings,
Of the mighty triumphs of sons that were last,
Of dragons and goblinish things.

So sit by my fire, you travelers, you two,
And list' to me whilst I reveal,
The tale of two travelers, much like yourselves,
Whose deeds were both mighty and true.

And while my yarn is spinning,
And the embers fading 'way,
Don't be ashamed to marvel,
At the happ'nings on that day.

Larissa Clotildes, Grade 10
Duchess Park Secondary School, BC

The Invisible Curriculum

We're an educational institution
We teach children and it's your turn
I hope that you are here to learn

Of course they will like you!
You'll get along, you'll do just fine
(As long as you can keep in line)

Don't talk to him!
Where'd you get your clothes?!
We don't like her kind you know

You can make friends — don't be so shy
You're bothering your teacher — don't be so bold
Why can't you do as you are told?

Equations and books are easy!
But you forgot these other bits
Wouldn't school be great if learning was only it?

Jessica Pigeau, Grade 12
Home School, AB

My Cat

What do you do on summer days?
Well, I talk to my cat; I'll tell you about that.
My cat is big, and dark, and grey.
He sits on my lap and we chat,
This may sound absurd but I'd do it all day.
We talk of outside and inside and what to play.
We talk of food and that pesky gnat.
He tells me of the cats next door,
And informs me when there are any more.
I tell him of my trips to town,
And of all the nice things I have found.
We share secrets and take long naps.
Then he gets up and he arches his back,
We say our good-byes then go our ways.
That's what I do on summer days.

Rebekah Richardson, Grade 11
Richardson Home School, AR

Love Is a Beard

Love is a beard if not kept well can get pretty ugly,
Love is a beard when you have something good, and you try to improve it, you can get hurt.
Love is a beard depending on which way you go it can be smooth or rough,
Love is a beard the longer you have it the more it will grow
Love is a beard some people can handle it and some cannot, young teens want to have it but cannot.
Love is a beard the longer you have it the more it blossoms.
Love is a beard some females want it, but some are disgusted by it, every once in a while you will need a trim.
Love is a beard along with time comes perks like a mustache and a sole patch, you never know how it will turn out.
Love is a beard it does not always turn out well, the young beard is one of them.
Love is a beard it never is the same.
Love is a beard it can be a beautiful thing if you respect it, which makes the beard easy to be admired by others.
Love is a beard very fragile, and if you are lucky to be blessed with a great one you should not take it for granted.

Jonathan Westman, Grade 10
Windom Secondary School, MN

The Game of High School

You'll find the sluts, geeks and jocks at any high school, everyone is just trying to fit in and be cool.
There's no one that really wants to be here, but we must get through it, to pass senior year.

Rumors, stories and lies are always told, somehow the drama never gets old.
It only takes one person to say one word, then around the school the story is heard.

Each day at lunch you sit in the same place, you never socialize with an unfamiliar face.
It's the same people that you'll always befriend, the cliques in high school could never blend.

The football players, big and buff, they wear their jerseys and think they look tough.
They walk through the halls, they're so cool, they think that they rule the school.

The sluts think that they have all the power, they fix their makeup after every hour.
They wear mini-skirts in 50 degrees below, they are dressed in designer clothes from head to toe.

The geeks walk around with a huge stack of books, everyone around them shoots them looks.
They really don't care about how they dress, they roll out of bed and come to school looking like a mess.

It's all about who you know, and what you do, to yourself, it's hard to be true.
Some would do anything, just to fit in, it's the game of high school, can anybody win?

Luckily there's only four years try to get through it without tears
In the end, it taught you a skill the game of high school, what a thrill.

Emily Lauer and Nicole Larkin, Grade 12
Arrowhead Union High School - North Campus, WI

Writing by the Limelight

Turning on the rays of my reading light, I begin the dance of poetry.
Like an ice skater on the clean slate of a rink, my pen glides along the paper revealing the expression flowing through my hand.
Thoughts of love, ecstasy, or melancholy bask in the limelight for a fraction of a moment as the blue lines are filled.
This millisecond of the spotlight fulfills the word's destiny as fate guides the ink.
Every sentence, every phrase, every letter yearns to be used for the sake of literature and of life.
Detailing the curve or the dot of a letter enhances the writing as a human does to the world.
The beauty of language mirrors the rhythm and pace of a person's spoken word.
Human nature is represented by the words on paper but human divinity cannot be described in a simple sentence lain within the limelight.
Because discovering true human divinity resembles fitting the right words in a sentence; piece by piece one must use one's imagination to reveal the final draft.

Katie Beck, Grade 11
St Vincent-St Mary High School, OH

History

Cold and restless
It reaches into your bones
Pray every night
To go home
You have kids, and a wife
"Be safe," she always says
Need to make it back somehow.
These dirty Germans don't deserve my life
Months have passed
This war isn't even close to ending
I have seen things,
I pray no one will ever have to see
Another battle
Bullets firing
Vision begins to shrink
A bite in my neck
Getting so cold
I begin to cry
And prepare myself
To leave this world
A hero to my country.

Ryan Glynn, Grade 11
Hartford Union High School, WI

Open and Shut

I open the door to her room,
maybe to say something sweet
or perhaps just to pester.
We've grown apart since we were young
when we'd always play together,
but now those intense gray-blue eyes,
not unlike my own,
annoyedly peel away from her laptop's screen.
No matter what I've said,
below those eyes,
the mouth orders that I leave.
And if I don't, I can expect a warning,
a small slap, or pinch on the arm,
but I know she doesn't mean serious harm.
I laugh it off.
Her kind heart couldn't want to hurt me.
But then I'm shoved out.
The door that lead me in is slammed in my face.
We've grown apart since we were young,
and even though she's mean sometimes,
she's still my sister, and I love her anyway.

Rachel Petrach, Grade 10
Troy High School, MI

That Girl

When I first met her I knew it was meant to be,
I knew she was the one that will be there for me.
I thought she loved me but it wasn't true,
I thought she'd make me happy but she made me blue.
Who knew love would be so cruel,
I'm sitting here knowing I got played for a fool.

Nash Boateng, Grade 11
Ascension of Our Lord Secondary School, ON

For a Moment

There I lie, alone and broken,
    Until a passerby heard me woe'en.
I said, "Here let me tell,
    How I lay broken in this hell."

This girl all majestic and pretty,
    Led me into this morbid city.
Where skyscrapers tower over you,
    And whisper their secrets all askew

She lured me in like a fish on a reel,
    And showed me love's sweet appetizing appeal.
We laughed and shared secrets about our past,
    Not knowing that this relationship wouldn't last.

We loved each other, fore I thought,
    Until she left me on the spot.
There was no explanation, no note, or letter,
    Then I found out that she had found someone better.

Michael Douglas, Grade 11
St Francis De Sales High School, OH

After the Storm

I stand alone under a tree as the rain is falling
Allowing my mind to wander…
The air is cold and the wind is brisk
As it plagues my thoughts of the sun.
Even as I'm protected by strong branches and delicate leaves,
The rain soaks through my skin and into my bones…
She begins her story of woe
With a hint of sadness
Just as her gems begin their descent.
Her tale is weaved with her most melancholy memories
As each jewel grows as it falls.
The jealousy builds in her tragedy
Making thunder rage and lightning crash
But the anger subsides as the day turns into evening
When her tale is through, the clouds whisk her away
Leaving a dead sky in her place.
But as the stars flicker through the darkness
I'm laying under the tree in the mysterious calm
Of the soft moonlight watching the roses bloom.

Kayla Aldan, Grade 12
Boardman High School, OH

Nutty, Isn't It?

Life is like a snack-size Snickers bar.
Layers of decadent chocolate cover
complications underneath.
Ambition fuels — take it all in a single bite.
But, no, it is better to savor every moments.
Hard spots — much the same as peanuts — may arise.
We wish to hang on like caramel.
Crumbling down we try to save every piece,
collect every morsel.
On the outside, it is simple, but the "case" is not the case.

Allison Copenbarger, Grade 12
Taylorville Sr High School, IL

Now That I'm Not a Child

Now that I'm not a child,
I can talk on the phone,
And go out on my own.

I can now drive a car,
And perfect a putt for par.
I can go out with my friends,
And listen to different bands.

I can now help out my dad,
And sometimes do very bad.
I can read a fascinating book,
And learn how to cook.

I can eat all kinds of foods,
And hunt in the woods.
I can watch "R" rated movies,
And slurp on a cherry smoothie.

Now that I'm not a child,
I have responsibilities,
And many new abilities.

Aaron Scheibe, Grade 12
Valmeyer High School, IL

Here We Are, We're Crying

Here we are, we're crying
Our tears each for the past.
Here we are, we're crying
For this love that couldn't last.

Just at first we felt it.
It slowly fades away.
Just at first we connected.
Then it falls apart.

And here I am, I'm crying
Because of what you've done.
And here I am, I'm crying
Because of what we have become.

I saw the signs this entire time.
Right in front of my eyes.
I saw what this was coming to.
The deception and the lies.

And there you are, you're crying.
For the pain you've caused in me.
And there you are you're crying.
For you, I have no pity.

Ashley Shoultz, Grade 11
Princeton Community High School, IN

Inside

Look inside,
See what's there,
A special person,
That is different from the rest.
If you like me, GREAT, then we're friends,
If you hate me, that doesn't change
The person I am.
I am what I am,
So please understand that I'm just being me.

Jessica Persaud, Grade 11
Ascension of Our Lord Secondary School, ON

Summer Love

sitting back soaking up the sun
being there with you was so much fun
i never thought that we would be
together like that, you and me
with our feet on the ground and our heads in the sky
we danced until the moon was high
i told you my deepest secrets
i will never regret
you kissed me in the pouring rain
all summer long i felt no pain
until that last summer day
i wanted so much for you to stay
we held each other tight and cried
"we'll see each other soon," you lied
time passed by year after year
i waited for you in our spot and i am still waiting for you right here.

Natasha Finley, Grade 11
Posen Consolidated High School, MI

Disheveled

Today I wake to the incessant blaring of my alarm clock,
Cursing as I trudge across my room to shut the
Darn thing off and giving it a hefty smack on the top of its sleek
Electronic head as I meander through the
Voluptuous mess in my room, and, unavoidably, I walk
Headfirst into the wall, causing me to yelp in pain,
Rubbing my very sore head vigorously, I manage
To massage my head into a headache;
While, grumbling all through breakfast, I choke on my toast,
I furiously gulp down liberal amounts of water, and the
Lump that clogs my throat engorges into the size of an egg;
I cough and splutter, drenching my pajamas with groggy, saliva
Infused water and I stub my toe on my door before racing to the bathroom:
My hair is a tornado recently struck,
My shirt is a whirlpool of what can't be easily described,
My toe is bloating into a light-bulb, and the
Bump on my head is steadily turning into vivacious shades of magenta;
And I hear a sickening crunch; the teeth of my comb has been
Swallowed whole by my tornado-hair,
Roaring, I sprint to my room and I stare at the clock:
Oh no, I've just missed my bus.

Elaine Duan, Grade 11
Sir Winston Churchill High School, AB

To You

Is this love true?
Can I match it up to you?
Will we make it through the thunder?
The love is like rain.
Always falling; never calming.
Can we be birds?
Let's hold hands.
Love will fly away.
Yours is empty like a hole.
Fill me up with gold.
Just buy me everything.
This love is not real.
It just pretends like actors.
Line after line.
You've won the Grammy.
Can't we just fly? Love in the sky.
A secret at night. Lie in the day.
But birds sleep all night. And chirp all day.
Just what happens, when birds cannot fly,
And the rain just stays.
My love fades away.

Alyssa Honkonen, Grade 10
Oak Creek High School, WI

On Remembrance Day

Remembrance day is upon us again,
On this day we remember everyone who were slain.
On the eleventh hour on this day,
We stand and we pray.

The ones who survived have endured much sorrow and pain,
And the world knows that their friends didn't die in vain.
As they lie in Flanders fields,
They shall rest in peace.

The poppies that we wear,
Shows that all of us still care.
And peacefully the poppies gently blow,
Between the crosses, row by row.

And today we stand here remembering them,
In their memory I recite this poem.

Fathima Hafsa Prem Nawazdeen, Grade 11
Crescent Heights High School, AB

Chapter 8

I'm standing at a door
    Trying hard to bust the lock
There's a storm out, all boats tied
    But I just set out from the dock
I'm running, chasing something that seems so far away
    I pray, hoping to God that the things I love will stay
I'm finally realizing what is really, truly real
    I'm finally learning how to express myself and feel
Filled with hope, frustration, love, newness, and rage
    I feel a new chapter beginning as I write on a new page

Marlin Jenkins, Grade 12
Michigan Health Academy, MI

Anger Management

So much anger,
So much hate,
So much lost
In a twist of fate.
All that cruelty
That never ends
As one cracks
And one bends.
Crying out bruised
For some help —
The reply is worse
Than what was already felt.
A soul confused
With words unspoken
For there is no time left,
It's been broken.

Ruth Olson, Grade 12
Centennial High School – White Building, MN

Ceases to Exist

I never knew that a love like ours could ever exist.
Some may think it was all just a dream.
But the moment my eyes caught a glimpse of your beauty,
I felt as though my world was flipped upside down.

Others may say that our love is just nonsense.
But I know best,
That when we meet
My emotions get stirred
And I feel overwhelmed with joy.

As we talk,
It feels as though someone is pressing fast forward,
And time is stolen from us.
So I always try to spend our moments wisely,
Making sure a minute is never wasted.

I never knew that a love like ours could ever exist.
I never knew.
I never knew.

Wesley Hong, Grade 10
Troy High School, MI

Dearest Denmark

Here and there, fight wars on my mark,
Here, discover greed, gluttony, lust, pride and destruction,
There, find envy, sloth, wrath, blood and pollution,
Something is rotten in the state of Denmark.
Look up and see the brave flying lark,
I think you see what I can too,
I see bits of me, bits of you,
Something's still rotten in the state of Denmark.
We are corrupting the Earth, our dear Denmark,
Here, share with me this morsel of light,
Hope to find somewhere, with all our might,
Something that's rotten in the state of Denmark.

Giang Vu, Grade 11
Ecole Antoine Brossard, QC

Tree

He sits in a field
alone waiting
for the graceful bird
or hefty squirrel
to rest upon
his branches
to keep him company
in his exposed
barren tundra
forsaken by all
except the wind
and thinks of
what he did
to deserve such a
punishment
or maybe he
shouldn't be tainted
by others like him
so his one friend
loneliness goes
for the time

Lucas Schneider, Grade 10
Cannon Falls Sr High School, MN

A Deceitful Trust

Ill thought to all minds be told:
Let us not in another place trust.
For trust lusts trust
And, in enmity, must
Call fate upon the death of itself.

Foul tales be told,
Though time make them old,
Foul still be which eminence see.
Rank hold not what is bold
Nor have be life foretold,
But what in it does hold sovereignty?

Paul Wardlaw, Grade 11
King's Christian Collegiate, ON

Existence

Sketches and wild eyes,
A blood-red rose,
A teardrop, a secret —
That nobody knows.
In one moment,
A lifetime
Will be over and done:
In that same instant,
A new one
Has only begun.
I.
Why?

Sarah Richmond, Grade 11
Grimsby Secondary School, ON

Running for Your Life

Trying to run but can't hide,
But you still walk the dangerous roads looking for a ride,
You're running for your life scared someone will find you,
Not thinking of the past because of what is inside of you,
Thoughts of what may happen if you tell the truth
Turn into fear because of people who are looking for you.
Running for your life is not as easy as you thought,
But be careful and a step ahead of your enemy or you might just get caught!

Jeremy Ridgle, Grade 12
England High School, AR

Social Boundaries

People see, people hear, people think. Every day a new face.
Who are they? Who am I?
What group are they in? They must be popular.
They wear expensive clothes. They're beautiful.
I'm not rich. Would they talk to me?
Maybe I should talk to them. Would they ignore me?
I'm not dumb. I'm not lame.
We could be friends. Maybe she would even like me.
Maybe we could hang out. Maybe we could have something.
I think she would like me.
She looked at me. I stare at her.
Maybe she likes me. Would she like someone like me?
I'm different. I don't have everything.
She's beautiful. Am I?
Would her friends like me? I think we would get along really well.
I would make her laugh. She would make me smile.
Could we be together? No we wouldn't.
She wouldn't want to be with me. I'm not good enough.
I would make a fool of myself. But, what if,
No, we will never know. Because I'm afraid to talk to her.
And she will never talk to me. Both afraid, we will never meet.

Mark Burdette, Grade 12
Arrowhead Union High School - North Campus, WI

Windy City

I grew up in the Windy City,
Where all you heard was horns honking and
Smelled the Tribune pollution in the atmosphere.
I grew up on the city streets,
That poor old man always on the sidewalk
And the red beater Pinto parked on the curb.
Then one day I became a cheese head.
It was Edith, my grandmother, who brought us here,
To this neighborhood full of cheer.
The little rascals screaming and running up and down the black top,
Then they run right through my great-grandma's garden
That was full of lilies and green pepper plants.
And as they make it out of the garden
The birdhouse gets knocked over and thistle seed
Goes everywhere and the squirrels scatter.
I am from a unique, almost square state.

Molly McIntyre, Grade 11
Arrowhead Union High School - North Campus, WI

The Coming of They That Are Men

No one marks the passing of a doe? None to find where bird roads go?
Anticipation runs like blood through vein.
The leaf shivers, the bow shakes, the hills themselves are about to break.
Fire and water, earth and sky (for the end of all is coming nigh)!
Fire, the dancer, in the storm, flame come down from heaven's torn.
Descend to renew the lands, dedicating the barren, lifeless sands.
Water, the singer on the world, waves called down from clouds unfurled.
Flowing down to birth green, flowering in mystery unseen.
Earth, the elder, under the hill, essence older than the plow that tills.
Sky, the watcher over all, sky come down before the fall.
Sending down the renewing fire. Scalding the world in heaven's pyre.
Directing the waters to quench the blaze, drowning lands in a wet haze.
Stars above become stars below, stainless moons come and go.
(rhyme and rhythm ebb and flow)
Words written in stone, scratched there by a bone, standing stones don't stand alone!
They are coming, they are near.
They quench the fire, they fill the pond, they dig the hills, they blind the sky.
The leaf shivered, the bough shook, the hills themselves have broke.
Ash and mud, earth and sky, (for the end of all has come) bye!
Ash is sodden, mud is dry, earth is over, sky is done.
Stars above become stars below, stained moons come and go.

Gregory Bryant, Grade 10
William Fremd High School, IL

Hockey Night

I could hear the National Anthem being played and the sound of skates as I shuffle my feet on the ice.
I could see the other team sizing me up and my cool breath as it hits the air.
I could taste the cold air as it passes through my lungs.
I could smell nothing that was distinct enough to care about.
I touched the ice and my stick as I prepare to enter a competition of the good ole hockey game.

Brett Pokrzewinski, Grade 10
Oak Creek High School, WI

The Pain of Labeling

In a world full of labels, stereotypes and scars, everyone's fighting to prove who they are.
They get thrown in a box, and given a name: geek, freak, prep, and jock; they're pretty much the same.
And nobody knows where these came from or who had the power to place labels on me and on you.
Still we try to fight them and we try not to perceive maybe just what our label makes everyone believe.
We have no reason to cast the blame on someone when we don't even know their name.
What happened to times where nobody cared about how to dress or what clothes to wear?
I sit here in class as the blame starts to fly. Girls start to complain about their label and why
they got stuck with a name that's so vulgar and wrong, when they put me in a place that I do not belong!
So everyone's wronged and no one is right but the labels can't change, at least not overnight.
So what's the big deal, and why such a fuss? Everyone does it; there is no need to cuss!
We use words in ways that seem awful and rude, the tension still simmers and feelings still brood.
All this hatred and loathing, based on nothing but lies, is really quite childish, and yet no one tries
to change their opinions and quit being the judge who has such a temper and holds a mean grudge.
Aren't we tired of these boxes? Don't we all want to get out? Still we keep on labeling, keep on boxing without a doubt.
What we're doing isn't right but that's the way it's supposed to be, and it's keeping them from knowing her and her from
knowing me.
There's no way to stop it and no way to heal the pain. There you have the reason that it starts over again.

Samantha Cox, Grade 12
Arrowhead Union High School - North Campus, WI

The Not-So-Lost Soul

Her frigid tears have dried,
And the tender remnants of a smile that once lay on her face,
Slowly and surely crept back into its place.
After being crushed to the ground,
Her hearts fragments scattered on the floor,
She finally realizes that she alone is the only one to restore her soul to its rightful home.
She's missed it intensely while it has been gone.
Returning, her soul kisses her thoughts,
Reminding her of who she truly is,
Strong, beautiful, extraordinary.
Reminding her of the most crucial piece of information,
That not a single soul in the universe could ever be the woman she is about to become,
The woman destiny will ensure she blossoms into.
Yes, she missed it intensely while it was gone,
But maybe, just maybe, it never left,
And the answers were inside of her all along.

Sara Sangiuliano, Grade 11
Br Andre Catholic High School, ON

Five Little Fingers

They reach for me,
I reach for them.
Five baby fingers with tiny wrinkles and still-growing nails like the ones we all used to have,
Five that were brought to this world as equal as anyone else's,
Five more reasons to love the child even more.
From our room we can hear them as a nuisance,
Yet we just sleep and never appreciate how lucky we truly are.

Their movement is unknown.
They grasp to understand this new world around them.
They grab for the dog's tail and the shiny new toy and the man's face hidden behind his heftier hands.
This is their role day to day.

Lest the thumb be forgotten, they'd all be useless, each bending with none holding.
Ha ha ha, children laugh as I watch.
They teach.

When I am too sad and too mad to keep laughing,
When I am a scrawny thing against so many others,
Then it is I look at the fingers.
When there is nothing left worth looking at in this world,
Five who reach despite the unknown thing lying there.
Five who grasp and never let go.
One infant whose only reason is to be and be.

Peter Henckel, Grade 11
Arrowhead Union High School - North Campus, WI

Peer Examination

Envy is something we do every day. Watching, staring, and thinking why not us? All we want to be is something we are not. But what is so great about them? Feeling like we are all puppeted by the green eyed monster. Afraid of how others will judge you. A unique individual hiding underneath the skin. Holding back to be itself. Too afraid to reveal. Feeling like a wasted piece of trash thrown away never to be used. When we could be not caring and just living life we're under the pressure of someone's opinion that should mean nothing, but the constant pressure of our own. So why should it matter? Block it out and have it never come back.

Andrew Sharot, Grade 10
Cannon Falls Sr High School, MN

Why Does It Have to Be So Hard?

Why does it have to be so hard?
Living without you is a nightmare!
You haunt my dreams every night,
You don't seem to go away.
Your face lingers like a fog,
Your presence is always felt.
You're just a person,
So why don't you ever go away?
I can't seem to get you out of my head,
I can't get you out of my life.
Maybe it wouldn't be like this if I hadn't loved you,
If I hadn't cared about you so much.
It just doesn't make any sense,
Why won't you go away?
Why do you linger here?
Why is it so hard to let go?

Nicole Johnson, Grade 10
Ascension Christian High School, LA

How Would the Color Blue Feel

If I was the color blue I would feel happy,
I would feel like I am the sky,
I would feel like I am the ocean,
I would enjoy the sound of the waves,
I would feel mad when it starts to rain,
Those clouds will come and take over my blue sky,
I would feel special that I make up the rainbows,
I would not like when people choose a different color over me,
I would sometimes wish I was the color red,
I would feel happy that I am not the color green,
If I was the color blue, I would change everything to color blue.

Tehami Raza, Grade 11
Oak Creek High School, WI

Time

Time
Is a human necessity.
Time
Are the hands ticking on the clock.
Time
Is of the essence.
Time
Is something we all have.
Time
Is something we all want.
Time
Is something we often take for granted.
Time
Is something we all have equal amounts of.
Time
Is viewed as obsolete in heaven.
Time
Is just a man-made creation.
Maybe it is time
We stop putting so much stock
Into time.

Kelsey Bowen, Grade 11
McNicholas High School, OH

Stare

I'm seated.
He's there.
I look.
I stare.
He looks.
I turn away.
He does the same.
At a corner, he's there.
His eyes, like a falcon
Round and brown
Beautiful.
Is he staring?
I look.
No longer.
I look again.
There they are,
His eyes
Fixed on me.
I turn.
I smile.

Minzala Mvula, Grade 10
Haynes Academy for Advanced Studies, LA

Faking First

You say I smile all the time
I wish that was my only crime.
You tell me my life is so carefree
But nobody here even knows me.
Of course I'm nice to everyone I meet
If I'm not it's only my defeat.
In this world I'll never be good enough
You look at me and think I'm not so tough.
But there are things you don't even realize
Like how all my fake smiles are just more lies.
I hide the tears that stream down my face
While everyone around me puts me in my place.
My self-esteem? There's nothing left.
Your only crime? Well that's just theft.
My love? My pride? It's all gone.
And I can't be restored by dawn.
Holding my head high is such hard work.
Killing me inside with just a little smirk.
I'm so glad I'm leaving here.
From me, you won't get a single tear.

Rochelle Wake, Grade 12
Lucas High School, OH

Holes

I walk on the earth and yet I fall.
I'm in a hole I still call.
But you won't come, and the hole gets deep.
As I fall my heart will weep,
You tell me to watch my step,
And yet I fall in a hole I met.
Each hole deeper than the last,
But each hole does hide my past.

Tamara Green, Grade 12
England High School, AR

A Young Woman's Song

Look at me
To the eye I am an old child
Mind still free
Heart still wild

Look at me
You see a little girl
Dreams too big for my city
Ideas too small for the world

Look at me
A woman in the making
My future's a pearl in an oyster
And it's mine for the taking

Look at me
A product of Mom's dreams
Holding Dad's hopes
Building my self-esteem

Look at me
I'm finally at the end
I've given you a piece of my soul
And introduced you to LaCreisha McDole
LaCreisha McDole, Grade 12
Heritage High School, MI

Now That I'm Not a Child

Every day is a transformation,
Go from living a life of no responsibilities,
To making all of one's own choices independently.

Every day is a new sensation,
Go from understanding new words,
To learning foreign languages.

Alteration, modification,
Go from living in the safe, warm walls of one's parents' home,
To living with as stranger in a tiny room.

An incarnation, celebration,
Go from being told right opposed to wrong,
To deciding oneself to correct decision.

Every day is a new equation,
Go from $2 + 2 = 4$,
To solving sin, cos, and tan.

Every day is a revelation,
Filled with information, anticipation,
On to another destination.

Now that I'm not a child.
Noelle Perkowski, Grade 12
Valmeyer High School, IL

Knock on My Door

Welcome…I've been expecting you.
Sit…so we can talk.
Smile…the worst has yet to come.

I'm looking at you, my dear
For you look quite well.
The knock on the door,
The sudden swing,
The ice in your stare,
the words when you speak
have a sharp sting,

Have replaced

The soft knock
The subtle push
the heart warming glance
The sweet words you'd speak.

Smile…the worst has yet to come
Sit…so we can talk
Welcome…I've been expecting you.
Petrê Singh, Grade 10
Woburn Collegiate Institute, ON

Don't Cry

My hair is falling out my skin growing pale
Arms feeling weak but life I cannot fail
I don't want to die but I know it may be soon
It's time for treatment may you leave my room
I'm only 7 years old I have really no fear
I don't understand the darkness so I aim for the clear
I live in this place with many people inside
A vehicle with many lights brought me here it was my ride
Treatments hurt me badly they really burn my chest
The doctor makes it better by telling me to just rest
I ask my mommy when I go home
But she tears up and cries
So I ask my daddy when we're going to play sports
I let him know I'll give all my tries
But the doctor keeps saying that I may die
It's only a matter of time
But I keep my hopes up and pray I stay fine
Well something is calling my name it's coming from a bright light
I have to go but I might see you later I just might
And if you see my parents tell them I will love them even though I'm away
I hope to see all again for now my lifeless body right here shall lay…goodbye
Kody McDonald, Grade 11
Greeneview High School, OH

The Ritual of a Geisha

At the break of dawn,
as musk creeps among cherry blossoms
a young lady awakes.
She combs her hair,
rich and kempt,
the tangles loosen,
the strands flow, without restraint,
and she slides in an ornament.
Wrapped amongst threads and silks,
the ends of the yukata flows,
her aura glows in the fragile rays of sunlight
she picks out a fan, richly adorned
with pale spring blossoms.
She glances at her reflection,
flexes her arms,
her posture poised,
her slender fingers woven around silk and fan
she dances, quite gracefully,
in tune to the morning bells.

Lindsay Kim, Grade 12
Adlai E Stevenson High School, IL

A Look into Nature's World

Red and orange rain from the sky
Rolling hills of green
Forest canopy's darkening all below
The desert's endless sea of sand
Ocean's waves wisp against the shore
Animals roam the plains
Gardens of different hues, roses and petunias
The wind carries all and forgives nobody
The weight of all, rests on dirt
Clouds of different shapes infuse the imagination
Squirrels collecting nuts to survive the winter
Snow drifts slowly, changes the shape ground
Spring rains and flowers blossom
Summer's warm sky brings soft thoughts
Falls leaves drift from the sky once more
Winter freezes everything until a new year
Volcanic power redesigns what was once
Water giving life to all
Sun's rewarding promise of light
Man of the moon couldn't find the cheese
Thanks for the view

Jacob Bergum, Grade 12
Hartford Union High School, WI

Returning to Reality

I'm waking from this dream I created
No longer hiding in myself
No longer in need of a tourniquet
My heart beats strong again
I'm no longer frightened
There's no reason for me to return to my refuge
All of my tears became suppressed
I'm returning to reality.

Bethany Pierson, Grade 10
Elgin High School, OH

Life Without Color

I feel the warmth upon my face.
I can taste the sweetness of the air
As bees buzz without a care.
Wondering about the outside world,
I feel lucky.
Life is fair.
The day is warm,
A tender breeze stirs the scent
Of flowers throughout the air.
In my world it is beautiful.
It is what I feel.
Color never matters for my eyes only see black.
It is what I hear,
Feel and taste.
Not what I see
That paints a beautiful picture of life
Without color for me.

Jessika Decker, Grade 11
East Union Middle/High School, IA

that is the question

what will it be, to wake us from our sleep —
something before we would at only weep?
what wrongs were we willing to bear
how many horrors happened before we did care?
can we do it? will we do it?
will the feeble of heart and mind pursue it?
what thoughts would creep from the deep of the mind
when all ideas before were to be left behind?
will revenge take root in our naive heart
that is haunted by inaction from the start?
what words would take a life of their own
when released from legend, story, or poem?
what feelings fresh and ideas bold
lie hidden within that frame of old?
can we do it? will we do it?
will the feeble of heart and mind pursue it?
that is the question
would the majority matter if we were but matter
would the majority matter if we did but scatter?
can compliant creatures rise and be as one
and what will we do once we think we've won?

Christine Franzel, Grade 11
Luck Jr-Sr High School, WI

Monstrosity

So put your hands together and follow me
The words of the great Mahatma Gandhi
Don't hit back but turn the other cheek
Positive words, all that we should speak
Goodness, all that we should preach
Whatever happened to the word humanity?
Has it lost the war against ferocity?
Or is it alive in the hearts of human beings?
Can anyone answer this question for me?
Do we revere generosity, or idolize monstrosity?

Anthony Jurayj, Grade 11
Troy High School, MI

One Sad Thing

I got these horrible sad blues.
I don't know what to do.
I don't know who to tell.
Nobody cares to hear
When you've been here before.

What shall I say?
Who shall I tell?
Shall I take some Kleenex
Cry my blues away?

I wonder if
Crying would do?
With so much pain,
It would probably take all night.

But I don't have
Kleenex or time
And I am too blue
To make time
   Or
      Get a Kleenex.
Rebecca Reinke, Grade 11
Hartford Union High School, WI

Pink

People say the color pink
is pretty, soft, and girlie.
But pink does not agree.
Pink wishes it was more like black,
solid, rough, and surly.
In its spare time pink hits the gym
to try to get more buff,
so the other colors would start to think,
"Boy, that pink is tough!"
Pink's only dream is to fit in
with blue and green and gray,
but when he tries, they kick him out
and say that he is gay.
Pink hates it when we think of him
as being such a girl,
and when we use him for girl's clothes,
it makes him want to hurl.
Unfortunately Pink will always have
this curse over his head.
So pink should just give it up
and be best friends with red.
Jack Rehn, Grade 10
Oak Creek High School, WI

The Ballerina

Comforted by her gentle grace
The beauty in
A crazy race
Swayed by the gentle crusade
Yet tensed in
The suspense portrayed
Dubiousness
Fills the air
With certain anticipation
That is imperceptible there
Head held high
Confident poise
Resonating in
Her delicate voice
Unblemished elegance
Porcelain face
Complementing
Her silky pace
Body meets music
Together as one
Unified in a rendered run
Megan Holub, Grade 11
Wauconda High School, IL

The Fool

I am a fool.
I gave you a chance,
And you blew it.

I am a fool.
I thought you loved me.
I thought I could believe your words.

I am a fool.
After all we went through,
I thought we had something,
And we did, lies.

I am a fool.
You never truly liked me.
If only I could have seen it sooner.

You broke my heart,
You made me cry,
But what you really did
Was make me stronger.

I guess I'm not the fool after all.
Angel Daub, Grade 11
East Union Middle/High School, IA

Just Look at Me

You see me.
But do you really?
Do you just see past me?
Or maybe you stare at me,
And think, "What a loser?"

Maybe you look at me,
And just feel pity.
You feel obliged,
And say, "Hello."
You maybe promise an invite,
But it's just another empty promise.

But why don't you look at me?
Really, just look at me,
And just see me.
And feel no pity,
Or animosity.

So look at me,
But just look at me.
Don't judge me
And assume your judgments are right.
Just look at me.
Bryan Schmidt, Grade 10
Mitchell District High School, ON

Defining Dreams

Carving words on blue lined paper
Smearing lead with tears,
Eyes of glitter and sparkled dreams
Release all feelings here.

Dreams they flutter with the wind
Clouds above us all,
Waiting for the morning fog
Dreams above us fall.

Eyesight's blocked of what's ahead
The future seems unreal,
Weighted down by dampened air
Unsure of what you feel.

Blocking vision with an opened heart,
See what your eyes cannot,
Blowing wind, let it lead you
Forget what you've been taught.

Treacherous heart, lead the way
Which foggy dream is mine?
Reversing wants for gifts of love,
Dreams I now define.
Bridget Sidles, Grade 11
Centerville High School, IA

Untitled

It falls softly as a silver dove,
Liquid glass from high above.
It shatters the stillness like a lone wolf's cry,
As it falls with its sisters down from the sky.
A lonely life is all it's known,
Surrounded by others, but still so alone.
Yearning for something written on its small glassy face,
A delicate raindrop, finding its place.
Around it come shades of blue mixed with white,
Dancing together like sparrows in flight.
Their small fragile figures grow more as they fall,
The wind's sweet whistle, to them seems to call.
But the one lonely raindrop shivers with fright,
As it plummets to its end in the darkness of night.
The joys of all sharply come to an end,
As they enter a new world full of hate and judgment.
The one lonely raindrop drifts close to a friend,
As the darkness sets in, and the sky seems to end.
It says, 'stay close together as we fall to the sea,
In this strange harsh new darkness, forever we'll be.'

Nicole Janisch, Grade 10
Robert Bateman Secondary School, BC

Hidden

Hidden, we wear a mask.
A mask of popularity, makeup, clothes.
A mask of lies.
And it's the only thing you seem to notice.
But masks can be deceiving.
For, what lies beneath, isn't always beautiful.
We lay hidden within ourselves.
We've built a wall to keep others out.
Not showing who we really are,
We've become so good at lying to ourselves.
About what should be, what could be.
And what might have been.
But please don't give up.
Keep trying to break my wall.
Chip away at every flaw.
Remove it chip by chip, stone by stone, block by block.
I promise, something beautiful lies inside.

Sarah Peterson, Grade 11
Troy High School, MI

The Unknown

Dark and murky yet calm
The water stands still and silent.
Its unknown depth allures me
Nature surrounds it,
Nature is a part of it.
A piece of trash floats by,
Ruining a perfect image
Careless people harming our environment
Not realizing the damage they are creating
Learn to enjoy nature
Allow it to overtake your emotions and become one.

Kelly McCloskey, Grade 12
Destrehan High School, LA

Tranquil

The condo on the barren beach
A solace for tired minds
Each grain of sand a memory
Each palm a lasting reverie

A solace for tired minds
A retreat for tired hearts
Each palm a lasting reverie
We never want to say goodbye

A retreat for tired hearts
The epitome of serenity
We never want to say goodbye
Our image remains engraved in the waves

The condo on the barren beach
The epitome of serenity
Our image remains engraved in the waves
Each grain of sand a memory

Jessica Forkosh, Grade 11
Solon High School, OH

The Road of Life

Life is a road that we all travel on
Going place to place from dusk to dawn.
We start on our road trip when we leave the womb
With our final destination being the tomb.
There are road signs and people to show you the way,
And billboards and salesmen to lead you astray.
We travel this road, no clue where to go,
Whether serve at a diner or star in a show.
We travel this road, seeing thousands of places,
Millions of things, and billions of faces.
On this road there are rules that you need to know
In order to get where you need to go.
Don't look behind you, 'cause you'll never move forward,
You'll be stuck in one place like a caged bird.
Don't look ahead to the next mile mark
Because it may not come, and you'll be stuck in the dark.
Keep your eye on where you are at all times
Take the miles as they come time after time.
And lastly the greatest of all of the codes
Share your travels with your friends on the road.

Joe Repka, Grade 12
St Francis De Sales High School, OH

California

Wake up half past noon
And get to the beach very soon
To soak up the sun and get a tan
And possibly find a handsome man
Skip lunch and just buy a drink
Because why would you need to think?
It's summertime and the weather is fine
So sit on back and waste some time
Take a swim, relax, and enjoy life
Because tomorrow it's back to the everyday strife

Lauren Darwit, Grade 11
William Fremd High School, IL

Freedom Waves

We salute "Old Glory," our U.S. flag;
Our forefathers have paid a huge price tag.
'Twas year seventeen seventy-seven,
The stars and blue union came from heaven.
Congress chose this "American banner";
Many think Betsy Ross was its planner.
It stands for our freedom that has been bought
In the battles that the Patriots fought.
With thirteen colonies, thirteen stripes, too,
We're so thankful for our "red, white, and blue".
Their courage is shown by the stripes of red;
Red also stands for the blood that was shed.
Liberty is shown by the stripes of white;
They fought for our freedom with all their might.
Our blue union stands for justice and care;
May we remember the love that was there.
All of the white stars represent a state,
But together they make our nation great.
Francis Scott Key wrote, "Oh, say can you see…"
May it still wave "o'er the land of the free".

Michael Livingston, Grade 12
Oblong High School, IL

Fireworks

Boom! Crash! Bang!
The sounds of the flashing
Lights, the smashing
Sounds of a world
Of reds, greens, golds,
And multitudes of others bring
Me to my knees.
I ponder the wonder
Of these sounds and colors,
How something that was small and compact
Can become so big and bright.
And I think maybe, just maybe,
If something so small like that
Can become so big and bright
Maybe I too can become
Big. Someone who starts small and
Changes the world —
All because he believed he could become big and bright.
Boom! Crash! Bang!
The sound of a person becoming great.

Vincent Calautti, Grade 12
Boardman High School, OH

Forgive and Forget

Years drifted by with no words being spoken
Til finally one day all your ties were broken
As we talked for the first time in what felt like forever
I wondered how we had never managed to be together
Because I feel so secure with you about
You'd always be there — I have no doubt
But your multitude of signs don't correlate
Ruining the perfect future I mentally create
Call me up late just to see if I'm awake
I really don't know how much more I can take
You say you're not ready for anything serious
Then why so much effort, I'm just curious
Just know I'll be all right with whatever you choose
I want you to be happy, even if that means I lose
So now I'm begging you, just make up your mind
Then maybe I can move on and leave this all behind
Now it's up to you to decide and commit
I pray you don't force me to forgive and forget

Katie Smith, Grade 12
Troy Christian High School, OH

False Denial

The eyes of deception blink one more time
From the walls inside an house full of lies
Up to the ceiling they quietly climb
To see everyone in their own disguise

Afraid of the cover's tide to arise
Wandered paths no longer have any guide
Directed to a passage of demise
Stranded and locating somewhere to hide

Identity's truth has been put aside
Faded away into a private mind
To settle in and be forced to reside
Or be locked up and to ever confined

Fabrication travels freely around
Truth's pitcher won't even step on the mound

Chad Wolfe, Grade 12
Frances Kelsey Secondary School, BC

Life Is a School

Life is a school with it's never-ending lessons
You show up and sometimes pay attention
Stick with a close group
Only like certain things about it
Don't always hate it, but don't always enjoy it either
Always asking for help and having to be patient
At the start it goes by slow and drags on,
But in by the end you're wondering where the time went
It may not always be understandable
But it's always a new learning experience

Josh Pourrier, Grade 12
Prairie Lakes School, MN

Last Dance

With her in my arms,
Thinking nothing could be better,
Dancing the last dance,
Dancing on clouds,
In the sky high above,
The stars twinkle in her eyes.
One kiss is all I ask,
Before she leaves forever,
Hands slide down her smooth beautiful face.
Holding her tightly so she doesn't leave,
But she's already gone.

Kaleb Grossman, Grade 11
Covenant Christian School, IN

Grades 7-8-9

Note: The Top Ten poems were finalized through an online voting system. Creative Communication's judges first picked out the top poems. These poems were then posted online. The final step involved thousands of students and teachers who registered as online judges and voted for the Top Ten poems. We hope you enjoy these selections.

Top Poem Grades 7-8-9

Dreams Distilled

Dreams escape into the mist
Becoming what they were
Secrets of a sleeping mind
Hidden from the world
If only for a fleeting moment
Wishes were fulfilled
Now the flame of wonder has been doused
And night's ecstasy distilled

Jennifer Beall, Grade 8
West Middle School, IA

Top Poem Grades 7-8-9

Summer

Summer is like a photo album
Holding memories that make us smile
Hot days intertwined
With late night bonfires
Watching the starry sky
Fill up with the burst of fireworks
On the 4th of July
Going to South Haven
And joining friends on the pier
Swimming in pools
Soaking up the sun
Summer is like a photo album
Just waiting to be filled

Courtney Congdon, Grade 7
Paw Paw Middle School, MI

Top Poem Grades 7-8-9

Wind

In my writing I am wind,
completely alone to create my piece.

I am warm and cold,
ever changing my direction:
mood, topic, and genre.
I speak to everyone like wind whispering in the trees.
I move the pieces to create my art
like the flower petals and leaves on the ground.
Moving words to arouse an emotion.
Bringing along the smell of the season,
my voice.
Sometimes I help others,
giving them energy and refreshing their minds.
Sometimes I will leave them cold,
begging for another warm gust,
another page, another paragraph, another word.
They can see the aftermath of my actions,
though I am never finished creating.
Always editing my movements.
Always present, even when I am not recognized.

The wind is me.

Molly Conroy, Grade 8
Tower Heights Middle School, OH

Top Poem Grades 7-8-9

The Secret of Life

If you can help someone you don't know,
And expect nothing in return.
If you're crying inside,
But never let it show.

If you meet someone you love
And would risk anything for them.
Even if it means going to heaven above,
Then you have found something most people can't.

If you can have fun,
But never take it too far.
If you never forget where you came from,
Or who you are.

If you believe you have succeeded
Even though you've been through hardship and strife,
Then you have found something most people can't.
You have found the secret of life.

Jen Grubb, Grade 7
New Albany Middle School, OH

Top Poem Grades 7-8-9

Freedom

Freedom gazes through the eyes of a soldier.
She has soft wavy brown hair with sensitive brown eyes.
Freedom appears in dirty camouflage clothes.
Her identity is undetected from the smudged agony —
seeping through her face.
What does it take to have freedom.
Blood spilled. Tears cried.
Loud bangs crowd the sky.
Now lives are taken —
without a good-bye.
Bodies layer the ground.
Freedom's hands reach out to save us —
we take advantage of her and dispose her kindness.
Violence is seen in the eyes of innocence, giving influence.
Her ambition is shatterproof.
Freedom fiercely fights for our individual rights —
we all should be worthy of.
Like a bullet proof vest protecting us from harm.
Her presence unseal obstruction.
Freedom screams for peace, she is thirsty for unity.

Stephanie Klegin, Grade 9
Clintonville High School, WI

Top Poem Grades 7-8-9

The Jack Pine

Upon a tongue of ancient stone
Worn smooth by years of gust and rain,
A rooted figure stands, alone
Yet parried in its last domain.

A brushing, soft caress of wind
Unites the granite with the sky;
Fingers hissing on graceful limb
Content their reach with evening light.

When owls their abodes move on,
Bent trunk remains unstirred
In snowy mantle, awaiting dawn
With patient knowledge, silent heard.

Heaven's mirror of deepest blue
Reflects the haunting high-held song:
Anthem as the warm glows through,
Lifting out the resting prong.

Shining on the rocky mist
Atop the figure's pontic face,
The crowned rose regards its list
In simple theme of jack pine's grace.

Kyle MacDonald, Grade 8
Codrington Public School, ON

Top Poem Grades 7-8-9

Autumn's Splendor

Through the year there are changing seasons,
God made them all for different reasons.
Winter, spring, and summer, too —
But to autumn's splendor what did He do?

He dipped His brush in red and gold —
To paint the trees of summer.
Then did their real radiance unfold,
Then were their leaves a'numbered.

Then the corn all green from rain,
He tinted a golden hue.
So that a good harvest came —
Filling the cupboards with food.

He made then the leaves to fall,
He made the wind to blow.
So now the birds on warm lands call —
To beat the ice and snow.

But soon autumn's haze will lift
Into another season.
From Our Father, another gift —
For thanking Him another reason.

Rose McClanahan, Grade 8
Our Lady of Victory School, MN

Top Poem Grades 7-8-9

Santa House

Through my grandma's old door
Almost run into the old,
Brown bench that people relax on
The cats sitting on the hay bale
Fall through the cracks
Next to the cash register
Going cha ching
I sit in the chair with wheels
Ready to have people come in
Sipping their hot cocoa
And pay for their fresh Christmas tree
Watching kids run up to Santa
So the parents have some memories
And people look at pictures
While taking a chance to win a free tree
The day is done
Turn off the lights and unplug the sign
Thank you for sharing your day with me
Turning back to ponder on my day of work
Exhausted

Jake Schertz, Grade 9
Clintonville High School, WI

Top Poem Grades 7-8-9

What's Going on Here?

Our ancestors lived as if the world
Would never let them down.
That the Earth would meet their every need
And would always be around.

We build factories and big cities,
Industry is on the rise.
Automobiles pump out exhaust;
Smokestacks pollute the skies.

Our generation populates the world
As none before.
We cut down forests, drain the land of her blood
All to make room for more.

Our children's future seems far away,
But is closer than we think.
It's up to us to save the world
Before we're all extinct.

Lucas Skjordal, Grade 8
Gilbert Middle School, IA

Top Poem Grades 7-8-9

Blueberry Stains

Blueberries.
A little girl and an old man eating together in the summer sun.
Splotchy indigo stains imprinted on my dress and fingers and mouth.
Smiling face, a canvas of well earned wrinkles.
A few teeth missing, but not missed.
Lined crooked above a white beard,
Long and haywire; Santa Claus.
Single outfit: tweed cap, black boots, suspenders.
Long underwear in ninety-degree weather,
A confused inner thermometer.
Years ago he would trek
Through fields and gardens, planting, fixing.
Now he putters; small cautious steps,
Trying just to make it from here to there.
Sleeping more and more on his big brown chair.
Hearing less, talking less.
Still he laughs; small chuckles which brighten my day.
To some it may seem he forgets
The life he lived and the things he loves.
But there is proof he has not
As he wanders through the kitchen, in search of blueberries.

Tahra Wilkins, Grade 9
Maharishi School of the Age of Enlightenment, IA

A Dragon's Flight

A dragon's flight,
nippy on your nose,
may give you frost bite.
A dragon's flight,
face in the wind,
in the middle of the night.
A dragon's flight,
when she comes near,
she will give you a fright.
A dragon's flight,
so far in the sky,
hope you aren't afraid of heights.
A dragon's flight.

Dakota Longley, Grade 7
Triopia Jr/Sr High School, IL

Poetry

P oetry is fun
O pen-minded people expressing selves
E veryone has feelings to express
T ry it once
R eally fun to do
Y es, you can write poetry

Trent Ellis, Grade 8
Kewaskum Middle School, WI

I Am From

I am from an island
where the sparkling waters surround.

I am from the snowy land,
where I love to speed through trails.

I am from a fun community,
where we play with friends outside.

I am from a cold deep lake,
where we go tubing.

I am from the bush,
where we play paintball.

I am from a place,
where I call home!

Cole Turner, Grade 8
Weledeh Catholic School, NT

Sovereignty

First, I spread out my roots
as I bloom to a new life's creation.
Then, I stretch out my stems,
that grow unique in their own way.
Finally, I set off to flee up and away
I am a gorgeous flower.

Ladie Elizabeth Gyamfi, Grade 8
St Peter Catholic High School, ON

Sadness

Sadness is the color of a rainy day sky;
It sounds like a grown woman weeping her heart out
And tastes like flavorless chocolate.
Sadness smells like a scentless candle;
It looks like a gravestone that's almost completely chipped away
And it feels like your life is over.

Sadness is the color of a burnt rose;
It sounds like a violin being strung for its last time
And tastes like a miserably salty tear.
Sadness smells like cremation in the process;
It looks as if the end of the world is here
And it feels like depression deep down in your soul.

Sadness is the same color as a thundercloud;
It can sound like a baby bawling its eyes out
And tastes like perfume being shoved down your throat.
Sadness smells like the flames of a fire;
It looks like a coffin being lowered into the ground with a single rose on it
And it feels as if you're getting shot in your heart.

Sadness is the main thing that dominates us, and it always will in so many ways.

Kristin Montgomery, Grade 8
Little Miami Jr High School, OH

Crotch Rockets

The thought of *speed*,
    Chills your body down to the bone.
The sights you may never see in the largest jungle.
The thrill of a life time,
    Most don't acquire.
The wind in your face feels refreshing on scorching hot days.
The roads aren't always the best, with the never ending holes.
Going through the gears is like a million dollars in your newly stitched pocket,
    Giving you confidence of the performance.
The smoothness of the ride is like sleeping in a hammock.
The excitement is irreplaceable like a life you love.
The racing wind around your helmet,
    Howls like the owls,
        Perched in the dusk of the night.
The air is fresh,
    Like being in a hard wooded forest,
        Producing air for you and I to breathe.
Now, don't think twice about getting a crotch rocket.

Joe Hauser, Grade 9
Clintonville High School, WI

The Sky

The sky is not just blue
    It shines with a radiance called hope
        It's what brings everyone outside to play or keep them in on a rainy day
            It is the greatest portrait of beauty that has ever been painted by an artist
            It is almost as though it was spread onto the Earth with an enormous
                Butter knife so we could call it beautiful.

Taressa Boyd, Grade 8
Oakland Christian School, MI

Bound

He doesn't love you.
He'll find somebody new,
As soon as he's done using you.

What will it take
To make you realize, you're making a mistake,
That boy of yours is a fake.
All you ever do is give, and all he does is take

Hold yourself together.
Stand up and shout "I am leaving you forever!"
When he says he wants you to stay say "NEVER!"
Because you won't need him ever.

Don't you let him bring you down!
He is never even around and,
He's probably with every girl in town;
Never giving thought to how it will make you frown.

Plant your feet on solid ground!
Tell him you don't need him around;
You don't want him around,
Unless you want to be emotionally bound.

Cori Linn Page, Grade 7
West Branch Middle School, OH

I Am From…

I am from a country,
Where the blazing sun gives you an easy tan.

I am from a busy city,
When 5:00 p.m. is not the best time to go downtown.

I am from a place,
Where pop seems safer than water.

I am from a fast moving hands city,
Where texting is the only way to go, rather than calling.

I am from knockoff designer clothes,
Where being careful of what you buy is a good idea.

Rogine Olayvar, Grade 8
Weledeh Catholic School, NT

Pink Is…

Pink is roses and Bubble Yum and my nails.
Pink is the taste of pink lemonade.
Perfume and powder smells pink,
Love makes me feel pink.
Pink is the sound of laughs and smiles,
Pink is my favorite color,
My love and my favorite sucker.
Hearts are also pink.
Pink is known as me.

DeLana Hagerty, Grade 7
Algonquin Middle School, MI

Wakeboarding

Wakeboarding is a blast,
It's amazing how long the pros can last,
I like the feeling of hitting the wake,
I get so high it feels like it's fake,
Doing a back flip is an amazing feeling,
I like landing and hearing everybody cheering…
I hope to wakeboard for a long time
And this year I'm going to learn how to grind…
This summer I won't be hard to find,
Because I'll be on the lake all the time…

Taylor Fahlen, Grade 8
Grant Christian School, MI

Embarrassed

My face gets hot like I am gazing at a flaming red fire.
It's a radiant bright tomato,
My heart starts pounding
What is the teacher going to ask me?
I hate this…
I start talking fast I feel like it is as fast as a cheetah
I'm scared, shaking, and shivering, not knowing what to do.
Make it stop…
The pressure's on
Make it go away!
STOP!
STOP!
STOP!
It's too late…

Jessica Dunbar, Grade 7
Linwood Public School, ON

Final Breath

I hear the train pass by,
People in there, not knowing that they might die.
All I can taste is the disgusting bread,
Still aching from barely getting fed.
All I can smell is burning flesh,
The Crematoria coughs, the smoke is fresh.
I look around, seeing children getting beat everywhere,
I can feel the fearfulness in the air.
The Nazis like devils, taking one life at a time,
Not knowing if one will be mine.
I've lost all my loved ones, so why should I care?
I hear so much screaming all over the place,
I fall and taste blood, there's dirt on my face.
Ha! At first we all thought it was just a joke,
Until we arrived and smelled all the smoke.
The noise was almost unbearable,
From all of the crying and screaming people.
Salty, wet tears touch my tongue.
I watch people get killed; I hope I'm not one.
My nose like a vacuum for the scent of death.
In my mind I'm taking my final breath.

Miranda Temple, Grade 8
Parkway Middle School, OH

The Titanic

The Titanic was the biggest.
The best of all the ships.
With all its glitz and glamour,
With that we cannot quip.

There were people rich and poor,
They flocked to see the sight
It was hard to get on,
Without putting up a fight.

"The unsinkable Molly Brown"
Also known as "Molly"
Mrs. James Joseph Brown
Took an oar and rowed by golly.

People ran, cried, and hoped
Titanic was the ship to never ever sink,
It was built in 1910, sunk in 1912
It hit an iceberg, went into the brink.

The band played
"Nearer My God To Thee"
As the ship sank
This was their plea.

Joshua Ridley, Grade 7
Isaac Newton Christian Academy, IA

Powerful Words

I hate you, you hate me,
You hate my whole family.
I keep wondering when,
It will stop.
If it ever will,
No one knows.
I don't think it's worth it.
Are we just going to keep,
Hating forever.

Dustin Weiss, Grade 8
Kewaskum Middle School, WI

Music

M elody
U nique
S inging
I nstruments
C horus

Bill Quinn, Grade 7
St Gerald Elementary School, IL

Love Me

Love me or hate me,
I swear it won't make me or break me
We don't know what will happen next.
We have to pray for the best.

Misty Dyer, Grade 7
Fairfield Middle School, OH

Lake Songs

As the Earth gasps and sighs, much like my tired soul
Its breath swirls about in my ears
The wind a booming train that flows into a whisper
The flora and fauna an orchestra of enchanting tunes
Reed grasses kiss one another and the air
Vibrant, lively stalks unperturbed by the weight of the world
Lilies bob and crunch under my kayak
As is cuts through the ripples in the wind
Birds, mystified by foreign intruders, voice their disapproval in a clamor
As their delicate wings brush the breezes
And their feathers glow like shining sun catchers, radiators of heat and light
Bass choirs of bullfrogs serve as an encouraging metronome
To the racket of the feathered band, and their director, the wind
Therapeutic, the music seeps into my aching soul
And washes away pain with its vibrational current
With healing hands, the music cradles my heavy heart and rocks it to and fro
It lovingly unlatches the little door within me
That allows my troubled mind to escape and fly free in jubilation with the birds
In unison with the lake songs, my soul, my heart, and all of my being
Sing
Thanking the Creator for this wilderness salvation

Angela Como, Grade 8
Central Middle School, WI

Deer Hunting

In bed is really where I really want to stay,
The beeping of the alarm clock tells me to start the day.
My heart beating fast as I see a big buck in my mind as I put layer on after layer.
My gun painstakingly cleaned last night,
The smell of solvent still lingers in the air.
I step out the back door and see my breath,
My cheeks feel instantly cold.
As I walk down to the barn,
A beagle barks
A cool East wind bites at my cheeks.
In my stand you hear the leaves rustle,
Is it a deer? No, it's a squirrel.
Then I hear twigs cracking,
A big buck is headed my way!
My heart pounds and my hands get sweaty,
I wonder if I'll get a shot at him,
I click off the safety.
There he stands 25 yards quartering towards me,
BANG! The shot echoes through the woods,
He runs through the thickets and crashes in a field,
What a day, and what a rush!

Jared Gitter, Grade 9
Clintonville High School, WI

Solitude

The ink from my pen flows to the paper, trying to express the words I can't speak.
The feeling in my heart can't relate, to the feelings in my head.
That I write on this slate.

Erin Paragin, Grade 7
Fairfield Middle School, OH

Healing Waters

It is supposed to be beautiful
Supposed to make dark days brighter
　　　And lonely nights bearable
But in our sick and twisted way of life
We have destroyed it
Made it what was once a breathtaking mansion into rubble
　　　COMPLETELY DIMINISHED
From the meaning it once claimed

And as we continue on this path
My only hope is that there is a stream to
CLEANSE us of our ways
To bring love back to what it was

Amy LaFay, Grade 8
Oakland Christian School, MI

Shadowy Reflection

I am independent and protective
I wonder which seed I will sow
I hear the subtle hum of silence
I see the chaotic strife of my peers
I am independent and protective

I pretend I am a far, far, star
I feel the stubbornness of a dormant volcano
I touch the scales of a silver dragon
I worry that boredom will strike true
I cry for my shrinking freedom

I understand the dirges of vengeance
I say time leads to understanding
I dream of timelessness
I try to be the diamond in coal
I hope for the protection of a hundred thousand
I am independent and protective

Ryan Volkman, Grade 9
Archbishop Carney Secondary School, BC

Christ's Crucifixion

It all started with the kiss,
That kiss upon His cheek.
Then came the soldiers and they began to hiss,
They beat Him mercilessly until He was weak.
Oh, such hatred! That rose up from the crowd,
As the son of man took up His dreadful cross.
"Crucify Him!" Those Jews were oh so shroud!
They kept their eyes hidden from the what really mattered!
That life that is not an acceptable loss!
In went the nails,
Thunder shook the skies.
Knees shook of those who believed the ruthless lies.
The world has been destined to be diminished,
From the night the son of man cried, "It is finished."

Shane Spear, Grade 9
Southwest Jr High School, AR

What a Wonderful World

In the morning before the world awakes,
I listen to the sounds.
I hear the things before I see them;
The birds chirping and the swoosh of the wind in the trees.
I come out from my tent to look upon the world
And its astounding brilliance,
The huge golden oak tree with its wonderful collection
Of birds and butterflies.
Now, I have the pleasure of laying my eyes
Upon a vivid gleaming rainbow.
I lift my head up high and smell the sweetness
Of everything around me;
That crisp smell of dew on anything it touches,
That fragrance and life of wildflowers in the meadow,
And I know when I sleep it will be there tomorrow.

Matthew Quance, Grade 7
Sir Ernest MacMillan Public School, ON

My Friend

My good friend,
Where are you?
With your short tan hair,
Your big hazel eyes,
And your overall friendliness.
I miss you the most.
Who am I supposed to play with now?
Who can I race around the yard?
The sadness seemed to fill my body,
Until I realized that you probably feel better now.
Did you know that you were my best friend?
Or since I wasn't always around,
Did you think that I didn't love you?
No,
I know that you loved me too,
My favorite dog…
Windfall.

Erik Salyer, Grade 7
New Albany Middle School, OH

Beach

Calm surf creeps toward me
Returns to reveal a million shells
All the same
Like beads of a necklace
Freckles of sand
Cling to my feet
Small as sugar
Salty as the waves before me
Sunlight blinds me
Paints my skin
Wraps me in warmth
A comforter around me
The crash of waves
A never-ending song to my heart

Pandora Wadsworth, Grade 9
Maharishi School of the Age of Enlightenment, IA

Love Notes Never Wrote

Love notes never wrote
You always filled me up with hope
Smiles built me up
Words tore me down
Cried every night
Because of little fights
I'd lock all the doors
Fall to the floor
Scream at the mirror
Till the pain was no more

Maddie Woodrow, Grade 8
Covington Middle School, IN

Singing

I love to sing
because the feeling
is like a bird.
When I sing
my heart opens
like a butterfly beginning to fly.
My singing is like the wind.
My voice flows.
The eyes looking at me
wondering what to do.
When I go on stage
I am laughing at you.

Ryan Bourke, Grade 8
Weledeh Catholic School, NT

Strength

When all I want to do
Is curl up and cry
I'll stand a little straighter
And look you in the eye

When I start to feel
Inferior to you
I'll think real fast
And maybe outsmart you

When I start to wonder
If it's all worth the pain
I'll know that you
Don't know what I'll gain

When all this is over
And I'm looking back
I'll know that I'm not
The thing that you lack

I'll give you a call
And you'll pick up the phone
I'll tell you once again
"You're still never alone."

Melody Stalnaker, Grade 9
Shenandoah High School, OH

A Day in a Concentration Camp

Waking up from a short night's sleep.
Getting up is hard because you were laying all different ways.
Then you get an awful stench that burns your nostrils,
after that you get up
you are sent to out in front of your cabin to be counted
for hours standing in the cold.
You hear screams of pain from people that sound like a wolf howling.
the bread you eat is like eating dirt,
but to some it tastes like a fresh piece of bread.
The Nazis are as mean as snakes,
they beat you for no reason.

Cody Severns, Grade 8
Parkway Middle School, OH

I Am

I am a crazy but cool girl who knows when to be understanding
I wonder about what the world will be like when I get older
I hear the sound of love whisper in my ears from the angels above
I see the way that love is supposed to be like around them
I am a crazy but cool girl who knows when to be understanding

I pretend to be in control of my inner self when I am not
I feel the touch of happiness from the hand that I love
I TOUCH the hand of the one I love with all of my emotions
I worry that people won't like me for me
I cry when I think nobody is looking
I am a crazy but cool girl who knows when to be understanding

I understand that I am not unusual but YOU just have to get used to it
I say "why not try" when something new comes upon me
I dream about the day when I will be able to spread my wings wide open and fly alone
I try to hide from what I should be facing
I hope for a marriage that will last
I am a crazy but cool girl who knows when to be understanding

Justine Dewyer, Grade 8
Otsego Middle School, OH

Nervous

Reading in front of the class,
you're digging in the floor
trying to hide your face,
your mind is blank like a surprised turkey.

Clickity-clack down to the office,
your belly becomes a playground for butterflies.

Running slowly in a race,
your legs are as weakly and wobbly like a calf's first time on feet.

Seeing new friends,
your brain gives the message to keep your moving mouth shut
time to hide…

Nervous

Levi Martin, Grade 7
Linwood Public School, ON

The Watery Swamp

The water zigzags back and forth
Through the swamp.
It is an unending snake
As it cuts a jagged line through the landscape.
The reeds on the river's bank sway in the wind
That whistles through the watery bog.
The rushing water flows
Through the swamp
Like an army of ants
Racing furiously across the soil.

A turtle climbs out of the water
Causing leaves to be crunched under its weight.
The leaves sound like firecrackers
As they break the silence around them.
Then the turtle slides back into the river
While the water zigzags back and forth
Through the swamp.

Tanner Dye, Grade 7
New Castle Middle School, IN

Looks Deceive

The ocean, it flows
It glitters and glows
In the sunshine it dances,
In the moonlight entrances
Its peaceful waves caress the shore
Recedes in itself, and goes back out for more.
Yet it's not always peaceful
And not what it seems.
At times it rages and its waves are rough
It stops for nothing, although it's enough.
Not all is well, or what it seems,
Sometimes good things,
Are just in our dreams.

Jessica White, Grade 9
Hazelwood West Jr-Sr High School, MO

No Way Out

Pain, sorrow, regret
What do you think about that
Try to get away from it all
But you always end up to fall
You shed a little tears
For the pain and problems in your years
Why, why me
Why not just let me be
In a hole with no way out
HELP ME PLEASE you shout
Then an angel appears and says
everything will be all right
Only if you hold on to me tight
You will be out of your hole
But in the world with hope and a new soul.

Brittany Frazier, Grade 7
Alexandria Middle Magnet School, LA

Rock Climbing

R ising up to the heavens,
O ne foot at a time,
C rack of stone, like a bullet in a barrel,
K eeping the balance.

C alming wind caressing me, like a loving mother,
L ooking down, seeing the miniature model that is the world,
I nfringing against the laws of gravity,
M omentarily stress-free,
B arely hanging on, "like a lizard on a window pane,"
I nching my way to the top of the world,
N ow I am nearing the frigid, frozen, foggy peak,
G oing up through the clouds, passing into the sky.

Kevin Wilson, Grade 9
Hazelwood West Jr-Sr High School, MO

The Voice Inside Your Heart

Faith is bigger than the world.
Faith is invisible to the naked eye.
At every second,
Of every day.
Faith lives in your heart,
But never picks a moving day.
She's there when we choose her to be.
She's invisible when we don't.
She preaches advice and inspiration, and always paints a smile.
She whispers, "You can do it, don't give up."
She helps inspire others, while she glides over the ground.
She knows the right and wrong thing to do.
She's the voice inside your heart.

Liz Aceto, Grade 9
Clintonville High School, WI

Facade

Could it be?
The girl you look at every day,
but never really see?
Hiding behind her nice clothes and pretty face,
creating the perfect disguise,
to hide how she really feels inside

She could be amazing,
the best at everything,
or she could be sad and lonely
behind that smile she keeps painted on her face.

But who are you to say?
You never gave her the time of day.
Or could it be that maybe, just maybe,
she hides behind the smiles and laughter,
to find the one person
who could see right through her flawless facade,
and help her find her way.

Amanda Robinson, Grade 8
Holy Savior Menard Central High School, LA

I Am From

I am from dragging yo-yo's behind me and dropping slinkies down the stairs.
I am from my sister pushing me down the sidewalk
on my first two wheeler and just counting the seconds until I fall.
I am from late summer nights under the stars and slurping ice pops.
I am from the *Rugrats* and *Hey Arnold*.
I am from the Spice Girls and the Backstreet Boys.
I am from Runts, Gobstoppers, Sweet Tarts, and gummy bears.
I am from Junie B. Jones and the Hungry Caterpillar.
I am from running down the lacrosse field and slapping sticks with Elaina.

I am from a place where squirt guns replace real guns.
I am from a place where segregation only means when you don't eat the green gummy bears.
I am from a place where when someone said you were "popular" that meant you were nice.
I am from a place that doesn't exist anymore.

Chelsea Wilson, Grade 7
New Albany Middle School, OH

Hospitals

Dragging your feet through the creaking automatic doors
For people who can't walk to their own miracle
Front desk asking what room are they in
Looking down the dreary hallway
You feel like you have just gotten off a roller coaster after riding it fifteen times
Trudging down to the room you hear a moan coming from someone dying directly beside you
As you freeze in your tracks staring in shock
Numerous doctors and nurses dressed in all white
With their stethoscopes around their sweat-dripping necks
Rushing past and through you to get to the patient
You can almost taste the scent of the Lysol they use to clean the instruments
Rethinking the visit you continue on staring blankly ahead
Disease there must be millions here everyone waiting for the bad news to come
Staring at you with the evil eye look the janitors and workers stare you down
As if trying to yell at you to get out since you have no business being there
Your frown droops even lower on your terrified face
Your throat becomes tighter and tighter
Holding back the tears of fear as you make it to the door of whom you are visiting
You try to fake a smile so they can't see your pain underneath
Knocking on the cold door a nurse drags herself out asking to see who you are visiting
She says the person has left us all

Laura Engel, Grade 7
St Katharine Drexel School, MO

Dear Daddy

Dear Daddy, I'll miss you so, dear Daddy, you're in a better place, I just know.
Dear Daddy, why'd you have to go? Oh Daddy, my heart's gonna blow.
Dear Daddy, this isn't fair! But Daddy, this is my prayer.
Dear Daddy, you were such a good man, but don't worry Daddy, this is my plan.
Dear Daddy, I'll never give you up, but Daddy, I don't want to grow up,
Dear Daddy, you're choking on your breath now, dear Daddy, I have faith this isn't your final bow,
Dear Daddy, you squeeze my hand tight, no Daddy! Don't see a bright white light!
Oh Daddy, speak to me once more, please Daddy, don't open the door!
Dear Daddy, I know this is the end, dear Daddy, you were my best friend.
Dear Daddy, we shall never part, yay Daddy! Maybe this is a new start!
Oh Daddy, I'm too late, oh Daddy, that was your last heartbeat.

Alessia Mastrorillo, Grade 7
St Clare Catholic Elementary School, ON

The Tormenting Tsunami

The water erects into a colossal skyscraper,
And then it strikes like a venomous rattlesnake without warning.
The tsunami dashes forcefully through the city
Leaving nothing behind in its wake.
The ocean recedes beyond the horizon
To confront the city another day.
The tsunami slaughtered the desolate city
Without even giving the city a chance.
People try to cope with the devastation
Of the swift, strong, sinister tsunami.
Another day the tsunami coils up
And rattles his tail like maracas, shhh,
And then strikes upon a city.
A person sees the wave in the distance
Getting larger and larger, but then it breaks
And washes upon the shore no more
Than a minuscule wave.

Nathan Cain, Grade 7
New Castle Middle School, IN

Night Time Creep

Shhh you won't be able to hear him,
He creeps up on us,
Like a thief in the night,
He keeps little kids up because of his gloom,
I'm talking about the night that brings,
Beauty in the sky,
And frights at the same time.

David Grant, Grade 9
Hazelwood West Jr-Sr High School, MO

Romance

Romance,
Such a passionate creature
Peaked high above the streets
On a soaring branch
With her long silky brown hair
Soft hazel eyes
Her beautiful white feathers flutter in the breeze
As she watched from up above
Waiting silently
To drop a feather
For that very first kiss
Or the exchange of vows
When she leaves
Will no more feathers fall
Is everything a lie
So what is she
Good or bad
Next time, watch her
Waiting in the trees
To drop that next feather
For the next love to be

Nichole Paisar, Grade 9
Clintonville High School, WI

Kindness

If you find something valuable
And return it to its owner;
If you see someone having trouble
Or needing some direction
Yet you offer to give them help;

If you find it hard to understand
But listen through it all;
If you hear gossip being said
Or feel it tough to not spread the untold
Yet you keep your mouth closed and not waste your breath;

If you are not trusted through peers
Yet you trust them back;
If someone you know doesn't try to figure you out
And you are interested in their thoughts and feelings;
You are a kindhearted, generous person.

Natalie Kassoff, Grade 7
New Albany Middle School, OH

Under the Mind

This is a story about me and you,
This is a trip to what we see and do
If you reach deep down beneath your heart and soul,
You'll find something hard, black, and cold, like coal.
If you use common sense,
The feeling won't be so dense.
For this is beneath your mind —
Telling you to be unkind.
I would not dare say its name,
For if I do it will not be the same.
If you let this deep dark secret go,
It will not let you say no.
For this is beneath your mind —
Telling you to be unkind.

Miranda Marie Keller, Grade 7
Greenfield Middle School, OH

Sojourn

I stand inert, a piece of stone I am
Life's journey has carried me along my path
A dirt road, with an end covered in fog
Life has many tempests, filled with echoed turbulence.
I stand my ground and wait for a saviour
A hand, a face
Although the winds do trouble, they polish every time
And I emerge a diamond
The polished eyes do cry, the polished lips do whine,
The polished soul does wander
Into the fog those diamonds do shine
With lessons learnt in time
I am not a diamond, I am but a stone
Being carried by the wind of life
I stand inert, while moving forward.

Isabelle Thibault, Grade 8
Lower Canada College, QC

Nightmare

You fall into a sleep,
That is very, very deep.
And you will start to seep,
Into the sleep in which you weep.
Then in your dream,
There will be things that scream.
And you will see,
Scary things that freak you and me.
The longer you sleep,
The more it becomes real.
It makes you think,
You can reach out and feel.
Then you wake up,
And find out it was only a nightmare.
And now you can't go to sleep,
So you sit and stare.

Josh Beck, Grade 7
Fairfield Middle School, OH

Summer, Come Quickly!

Summer is very close by.
School is entirely too long.
Just look at that bright blue sky.
The smell of homemade apple pie,
And birds chirping their happy song.
Summer is very close by.
In the blink of an eye,
Over was dawn.
Just look at that bright blue sky.
To everyone I pass, I say hi!
And then, another day was gone.
Summer is very close by.
I don't want to lie.
But, school makes me yawn.
Just look at that bright blue sky.
On the last day of school, I wave bye.
I cried, "I'll miss you when I'm gone!"
Summer is very close by.
Just look at that bright blue sky.

Lucy Wang, Grade 7
Lusher Charter School, LA

Life

Life is a gift
That passes like a drift
Time flies
Don't waste it and let it go by.
Through the good times and the bad
Through the bad times and the good
Life is a gift
That passes like a drift
Life is the most wonderful gift
you could ever receive
and it's like a cool winter breeze

Samara Reid, Grade 7
Macdonald High School, QC

My Neighborhood

(I see) huge lovely houses, green grass
With wild flowers and jumping bugs
(I hear) yelping dogs, screaming children
Running carefree
(I smell) fresh cut lawns, mouth watering chocolate chip cookies
Made just for the screeching, playful, friendly kids
(I taste) yummy cookies, tasty sweets
That over spill on my taste buds like a roller coaster
(I touch) the lost, fluffy, beautiful, sandy colored cat
who is a lion that runs from the hard volleyball boldly bouncing
(I feel) incredibly safe as I walk with the sun wrapping
around me in warmth like a blanket

Casey Kelly, Grade 9
Southwest Jr High School, AR

Football

Football is power
It lasts for about an hour
When people score the crowd gets louder and louder
When you get tackled your face turns sour
And you just want to go to the locker room and take a cold shower
The cheerleaders cheer
And the crowds get so excited they jump out of their chair
Practice seems like forever
And you practice in any weather
Some players are light as a feather
Some players are as heavy as a lion
But no matter what they kept tryin'

Jaguar Sturdivant, Grade 9
Hazelwood West Jr-Sr High School, MO

Finger Hopscotch

I sit down and gaze at the black and white keys,
calling out to me.
Asking me what sound they will make.
The smell of cooking from only a room away drifts to my nose.
I open my book and take in the new paper and fresh ink,
telling me to share a story without words, without pictures.
Five lines, four spaces, all filled with notes.
Sharps, flats, they all give it a personality you can hear.
I begin to play the first beat, first chord, first rhythm, first note.
My foot cautiously rests on the pedal,
shaking in anticipation of letting the sound mix like a baby's first cry.
Gentle vibrations go through my fingers,
tiny earthquakes painting a dream for ears everywhere to hear.
Like an artist's rainbow, the scales are my colors.
My fingers dance along the board, their own game of hopscotch.
I hear in my mind what sound will be heard,
before I press on to the aged ivory.
A world of sound,
an international language.
Different cultures all understand,
a hopscotch game for all to play.

Mieley Conrad, Grade 7
New Albany Middle School, OH

Through the Water

My family is all gathered,
But no one is talking.
They are all standing still.
It looks as if they are doing nothing,
But inside thoughts and feelings
Are racing around.

Their minds are overflowing with questions,
Who caused this?
How did it happen?
Why him?

We have gathered here for him,
It was his favorite place.
The sound of the crashing water,
Falling off the edge of the mountain
Always relaxed him.

Standing here,
The water speaks to me,
It comforts me.
I know that he is gone,
But I can always hear his voice
Through the water.

Megan Markey, Grade 8
Sandusky Middle School, MI

I See

(I See) That guy
Leaning on his car
(I Hear) Loud, singing birds happily flying over my head
My best friend telling me to say something, say anything
(I Smell) His strong cologne
Sweet flowers covering the ground like a blanket
(I Taste) Cinnamon gum practically melting in my mouth
As I walk in the direction of that guy
(I Touch) His soft, curly hair
My hand moving slowly moving toward his
(I Feel) Like a giddy child
With candy all around me
Suddenly sound invades my slumber
Oh
It was only a dream
Only a dream

Chloe Farley, Grade 9
Southwest Jr High School, AR

Love

Love is red, bright and passionate
It tastes like dark chocolate, sometimes bitter, but mostly sweet
It smells like beautiful roses
And reminds me of home, warm and comforting
It sounds like a heavenly symphony
Love makes me feel alive

Jacqueline Vaillancourt, Grade 8
Wainwright High School, AB

Life and Death

Life, everyone has their opinion on life
And how they view it
Me, my opinion on life is
That nobody takes it seriously
They just live for the moment
And try to do as much as they can
But that's only at that time
They never focus on how much time we have
Some people don't have a lot of time
And nobody takes life seriously until then
Death, the word most are afraid of
Only when death faces them or people they know
They look at life from a different point of view
And wish they have or had more time
Because when you look at death
You look at life and how valuable it really is
So if you are one of those people
You need to stop being selfish and take in life
And all of its joys and pains
Because you might not be lucky
And have then time to say goodbye to the ones you love

John Butterfield, Grade 9
Prairie Lakes School, MN

The Spell of Melancholy

Frozen in a world,
Where nothing changes
And time becomes motionless,
The new moon is set,
No light can seep through
And bring warmth upon my skin,
Instead the gloom spreads all through my being
Letting the monsters come out,
Forcing me into a secluded place
Where loneliness and fear take over,
The symbiote morphing my essence
Into an imitation of euphoria,
Making this frozen world
Appear even more ominous than before,
Fear and apprehension on my mind
While waiting for the sun to shine

Mahala Berry, Grade 8
New Glarus Middle/High School, WI

The Wings

The wings of sorrow
Lifting and pulling me
Making my life dark
No more light is shining through
No more glow around me
Just a dark aurora
Guiding me in the wrong directions
All I want to do is rip off these wings of death

Kent Poirier, Grade 9
Saint-Norbert Collegiate, MB

Young Dreamer

Dream on young dreamer.
Dream far, dream high.
You have no limits but the sky.
Your dream can take you here to there,
Or on a mountain with grizzly bears,
Or in the ocean filled with fish,
Or in the sky if that's your wish.
So dream on young dreamer.
Dream far, dream high.
Your limit is beyond the sky.

Lizzie Benzik, Grade 8
St Joseph Catholic Middle School, MI

Cedar Point!

About to leave
After the sun rose
Outside we go
We are leaving to go to a park.

Inside the car
On the roads
Through the gates
We are almost in for fun.

Within the time
Toward adventure
Beside my family
We end up at Cedar Point.

Ashlen Ortega, Grade 7
Algonquin Middle School, MI

Orange

Orange is the color of flames
That leap at the sky
The flying sparks they spit out.

The brilliant warmth
Of the setting sun
The tiger
Silently stalking its prey

The bright flaring of power
And destruction
The hog hedge of smoldering ashes
Ambition is orange
But without the soft edge
Of the orange wildflowers.

Pumpkins carved into fearful faces
Glow orange on Halloween night

Orange is the calm feeling of autumn
But also feelings of recklessness
And power.

Hannah Cella, Grade 7
Paw Paw Middle School, MI

Horse History

The sound of horse's hooves on the arena ground,
Kids playing outside, running around jumping with the dogs,
Colorful jumps and people having fun.

Everyone is a giant family and help each other out.
Riding a bunch of horses on hot days and playing by the pond.
Memorizing courses, competing in shows,
Winning championships, money, and prizes.

Water fights and staying up late at the hotels,
Late night runs to the gas station for candy and watching movies.
Hanging out with my barn friends at shows is the best part of the summer.

Going to Kentucky, Delaware, Wilmington, Florida, Michigan, Illinois, Indiana
And places around the United States to show.
Pony hunters to the EQ, to tight turns in the jumpers,
The best sport ever.

Michaella Gerlacher, Grade 7
New Albany Middle School, OH

Pretending

We pretend to hate, when all we want to do is love.
We pretend to turn away, when all we want to do is listen.
We pretend not to care, when all we want to do is help.

We pretend so much when we do want to love, and all we can do is hate.
We pretend so much when we do listen, and other people turn away.
We pretend so much when we want to help, and people tend not to care.

If we could stop pretending, and just be who we are.
We wouldn't have to worry about everything falling apart.

Kiara Haygood, Grade 7
Fairfield Middle School, OH

10k

The large mass moved forward as one. The race has just begun!
While the wind slapped my face, and wrapped itself around me,
The cold stung my eyes
Endurance soon kicked in, as my legs went numb
Rounding the first corner, I was striding down the hill.
My arms were pumping in a steady rhythm,
As my legs were pounding against the cement.
Eventually came mile four, and I was gasping for air.
I yanked the cup of water, and let it rush down my throat.
Pain soon triggered through my body,
For I couldn't wait to be done.
Jogging around the bend, the race was soon to end!
Encouraging words filled the air.
The crowd was cheering; I knew the finish was nearing.
Faster, faster, faster, my legs soon ignited.
Reaching for the finish, it was almost in my grasp.
Crossing that line was my final task.
As I jerked my head to the clock,
My greatest accomplishment was done.

Tayler Bruns, Grade 8
Emmetsburg Middle School, IA

Alone

You're gone now,
But I still feel the pain.
I could leave now,
I could finally get away.
Or I could stay here,
In this place you call a home.
I could get up now,
But I'd still be alone.
I see it in your eyes,
Every day's a lie,
You're never satisfied.
I know I'm to blame,
Because tomorrow,
It'll all be the same.

Jillian Gonneau, Grade 8
Monsignor Michael O'Leary Separate School, ON

I Am

I am shattered glass and the past
I wonder how many pieces have scattered
I hear the shards collide with the linoleum floor
I see my past in the pieces as they fall
I want the demons of the past to leave me
I am shattered glass and the past.

I pretend to be apathetic
I feel the shattered glass that is my life
I touch the jagged, arduous pieces
I worry as my hand begins to bleed
I cry for all the things that went wrong
I am shattered glass and the past.

I understand my transgressions
I say that I am sorry
I dream of the glass being whole
I try to forget that the glass has shattered
I hope that the pieces will not harm anyone
I am shattered glass and the past.

Na'Tyra D. Green, Grade 9
Jackson High School, OH

Early Spring

My flip-flops click down the sandy beach
As I toss the Frisbee to my dog.
She effortlessly flows down shore,
Leaping to catch the red disk
While my rainbow painted toenails tingle
In the too-cold-to-swim water.
She carries the drool-covered Frisbee back, wanting more.
I release the Frisbee, and it glides over the water line.
She races for the red blur,
Pouncing into the calming waves of Lake Michigan
As my footprints wash away behind me.

Jill Hascall, Grade 7
Otsego Middle School, MI

Shy

A crippling, cold shiver rushes through my body,
as cold as a blizzard in the middle of winter.
I want to blend in with the rest of the colourful crowd,
like a lizard blending into the wall.
Too numb to move.
Too scared to talk.
I wish I could disappear.
All those new faces.
That huge crowd.
Is there a place to hide?
Staring at the blurring ground,
like a pitiful, guilty, puppy.
I spring through my speech way too fast to understand.
Clap, clap, clap, clap…
It's over.
Done…

Leah Baxter, Grade 7
Linwood Public School, ON

Siblings

brother
mean, weird
working, bossing, teasing
humongous, mechanical, worker, mother
caring, fostering, providing
affectionate, determined
sister

Dakota Washburn, Grade 7
North Crawford High School, WI

A One Man Stand

Bullies
One on one or seven man gangs
Jumping me, pounding me, making me miserable
Blood boiling, veins popping
Flashbacks of being beaten to the ground
My life a joke to them; my body their punching bag
Not sure if I can do it

One against many
Thinking and believing in myself
It's my moment
I stand against what I hate; I stand tall
Feeling the pressure
Wanting to explode
Ready to fight

I feel strength flow from within me
My anger drives me
I need to let them taste their own medicine
But I can't do it
I won't do it
I'll stay mad for all eternity
But I will not turn into one of them.

Richard Ward, Grade 8
Virgil I Grissom Middle School, IL

Summer

Flip flops, sunscreen, and the sun
I know I'm going to have fun
Picnics, parties, and the pool
I don't ever want to go back to school

Lauren Thomas, Grade 7
St Gerald Elementary School, IL

Who Am I?

I am a human,
    Like a fragile vase.
I am a girl,
    As pretty as can be.
I am a leader,
    As if I was a captain.
I am friendly,
    Just like an innocent baby.
I am funny,
    As if I was a comedian.
I am silent,
    Silent as a mouse.
I am proud,
    Proud to be who I am.
That is who I am.

Andeka Vuong, Grade 8
Beverley Heights Middle School, ON

The Poet's Failure

I'll never be a poet
That's something I can't ever do
I'll keep making clichés,
Everything old and nothing new

I'm not clever with kinds of words
(I've never claimed to be)
I can't put rhymes in sentence forms
Let alone metaphors and similes

Poems of love, truth, and righteousness
I'll never learn to write
I will never see my finished work
On the shelf in spotlight

I can't do it!
It's impossible, you see,
Anyone could be a poet;
Anyone but ME!

Hannah Cline, Grade 8
Nine Oaks Academy, IA

Trees

Trees in a forest,
Standing so sincere,
Every year they shed their coat,
Because of winter fear.

Eric Burden, Grade 7
Fairfield Middle School, OH

Jews

Come my children and I will tell you a story of the good old days,
I was about eight years old when this all happened, way back then,
I knew a girl as pretty as the moon, who shown so brightly like the sun,
We had not one thing in common, except our hiding spot
Which was soon given away about ten o'clock
We were hiding as usual upstairs in the attic
Behind the book shelf and there was a knock on the door as we all fell silent
Our next-door neighbor ran over to our hiding spot with her son the pilot
She told us how they were coming for us now to go away to camp
But then the lamp went out, and you could hear footsteps about
They got some nerve our neighbor shouted
Not soon after we were out
I had a bad feeling of going off; I got lifted, onto a truck
Then soon got out to jump into muck
There was the camp surrounded by barbed wire fence like a prison cell
I could hear a far off bell and that's when I knew I had to run out of that hell
I grabbed some friends and family and a doll, to keep me company
That night we made a run for it
It is quite zany, we ran like crazy
In order to save our Jewish soul

Maggie Wanecke, Grade 7
St Monica School, IN

Love Promise

I met you in a place that involved a lot of other people.
When we looked each other in the eyes,
I could feel the connection between us.
People could notice the sparks flying when we were together.
You had to leave and you had no choice
And I don't think we'll see each other again,
But if hope shines on me maybe one day you will be here to stay.
Forever and for always.
It may be a strong word but I think I'll feel the love
I have never felt before and you know what?
I think you will be the only one in my heart.
For now, I will cry once in a while but remember
That no one can feel what we have felt together.
Promise me one thing, never forget me.

Jennifer Griffin, Grade 7
Weledeh Catholic School, NT

My Mom

My mom gave birth to me at 11:17 A.M. on 11-13-1993.
And on that day was a start of a beautiful friendship
From that day on we were best friends. And we are still to this day.
My mom is cool, my mom is pretty, my mom is my mom
My mom has helped me with my homework, problems,
Or just helps me pick out my clothes.
My mom can do anything in my eyes,
She can save the world and still have dinner done by five.
My mom loves me even when I do bad things
My mom has been there when I felt alone
There are no more words left to say to let you know I love her very much.

Brandi Greathouse, Grade 7
Fairfield Middle School, OH

Grown

See, look how hard I'm trying
But you're just not listening.
I'm trying to write something happy
That's about you and me,
But, see, here's the thing,
Happiness never stays with me.
So screw happiness.
I'm sad and that's the way I'll always be.
Oh, my, just look at how we've grown.
I'm one half and you're my whole.
I don't want anyone else.
Don't try to tell me
What I need, because I know this myself.
And just to let you know
"Stop calling yourself ugly."
To me you're as pretty as sparkling snow.
But I can't tell you what to do.
And I think that you have known
I still love you but, my, look at how we've grown.

Alex Chastain, Grade 7
Jefferson Middle School, IL

Love Is Like…

Love is like a never ending roller coaster.
It's like a bunch of twists and turns, ups and downs.
People that don't have it,
will do anything to find it.
People that do have it,
will do anything to keep it.
It's something that many people want
and feel they need.
Love is like a necessity of life.
Sometimes there's problems,
and sometimes there isn't.
For some people, love works out.
For others, it doesn't.
But for those others that feel like they can't find it,
keep in mind that love conquers all.
Love is like a journey,
and finding it is the best part.

Brianna Cook, Grade 8
Trotwood-Madison Middle School, OH

My Grandma

I miss my grandma I really do
there's no person to run to and hug
her house which is now non-empty
with my uncle living in
The farm is now dead
no pumpkins growing in the fields
no pigs no horses
no cows no nothing
I wish my grandma was still alive
so then I'd still have a person to run to and hug

Jessica Rodriguez, Grade 8
Goshen Middle School, IN

Who Am I?

I am

The bodacious browser of books
Maker   of stories
Keeper   of tales
A   harmonious starling
And a   dauntless darling
The inspirer   and the inspired
An   unfathomable adventurer
Fantasy   fiend
A hidden   prodigy
The master   of melody
The maestro   of euphony
Over-comer   of the impossible
The unseen   philosopher
The music   maker
The dreamer of the dreams

Because I am a dreamer,
Many dreams don't come true.
But it doesn't mean I stop dreaming,
Each day I dream anew.

Rebekah Montgomery, Grade 8
Little Miami Jr High School, OH

Up North

When I go up north I feel like I'm free from the world.
I can't wait for the weekend so I can get out of town.
When I go up north my mind clears of my problems.
I feel as if the tranquility calms me down.
When I go up north I hate that I have to come home.
When I'm up north the time flies.
When I go up north I feel like I'm free from the world.

Tyler VanEss, Grade 8
Edison Middle School, WI

Mrs. Wilson

This teacher always starts her class with a hello.
If not some funny acknowledging words.
For one example, she might say, "Jell-O"
If she could, she would even say hi to the birds.

Speeches are always the nerve-racking part of the class.
She will answer any question you think of,
Listening will definitely help you pass.
If you don't listen, she can resort to tough love.

Friday Family Time is always a different game,
As long as you follow her simple rule.
Her easygoingness and yet skill puts us to shame.
She can make Fridays the best day of school.

Oral Communication would not be the same,
Without Mrs. Wilson, the class would be lame.

Zach Nordin, Grade 9
Southwest Jr High School, AR

Forgotten Lore

A baby born on a future day,
Someone who lives in a modern way,
Never hearing about long lost war,
For war is now forgotten lore.

Ryan Moran, Grade 8
Stephen Mack Middle School, IL

Soccer

When I woke up it was all clear,
I can't believe I am here.
I sit down, and look around,
and notice all the cheers.
I take a quick glance and I see Lance,
one of the soccer stars back in the day.
I asked what am I doing here,
he said it's your turn to show us today.

Shayda Ashraf, Grade 7
Fairfield Middle School, OH

Kaylee Otterbacher

Outgoing, not shy
Used to be shy
Learning life lessons
Living each day as it comes
True to who you are

Kaylee Otterbacher, Grade 8
Whitewater Middle School, WI

Fishing

Down the hill,
Past the lake,
Towards the playground
You can find the best fishing spot.
In the lake,
Beneath the water,
Near the fallen, rotting logs,
You can catch largemouth bass.
Beyond the fallen logs,
Among the dark green weeds,
Until the hungry fish leaves,
Tiny fish swarm around,
Since I felt a tug,
Upon my hook,
In place of my worm,
There is a large, green catfish.

Owen Shaw, Grade 7
Algonquin Middle School, MI

Molly Elaine Griep

Goofy and loud,
Had a few surgeries,
Having fun with friends,
Maybe going to college,
A lady of humor!

Molly Elaine Griep, Grade 8
Whitewater Middle School, WI

I Am Free

I feel free,
like a bird flying.
Doing what I want to do
and going where I want to go.
I am free
like I am walking on air
nothing in my way to bother me.

Destany Martin, Grade 7
Weledeh Catholic School, NT

As the Wind Blows

As the wind blows,
The candle flame flickers,
And everyone knows,
That he's getting sicker.

As the wind keeps on blowing,
The flame's getting weaker,
And everyone knows,
He's not going to make it.

The wind blew its hardest,
Till the flame was blown out,
And everyone knows,
He's not coming back.

Alana Spalding, Grade 8
Southwestern High School, IN

I*

I am lost in a pink satin dress.
I am lost in life.
I am lost in my fairy tale.
I am lost, lost, lost, I fear.

I am lost in your arms.
I am lost in your eyes.
I am lost in your touch.
I am lost, lost, lost, I fear.
I was lost in a pink satin dress.
I was lost in life.
I was lost in my fairy tale.
I was lost, lost, lost, I feared.

Then you found me, for I am not lost.
Found is my new word.

You found me in a pink satin dress.
You found me in life.
You found me in my fairy tale.
You found me and saved me.

Jennica Mann, Grade 7
Carlisle Elementary/Jr High School, IN
*Dedicated to everyone who is lost,
for there will come a time
that you are found.

Cross

This is
a cross,
our faith
in which
we believe.
Jesus died for us and saved our lives.
He is amazing in every way. He has
so much meaning in our religion.
He is the
reason that
we are alive
today, He
saves us
and He
loves us.
So this is
the meaning
of the cross.

Alex Fernholz, Grade 8
Shakopee Area Catholic School, MN

Hurt

When I get hurt
I feel like shattered glass.
The shattered glass poking
upon my feet like a porcupine
attacking its predator.
It makes me determined
to give the person revenge.
I hate being pushed
out of the way of everything
I'm let down.
I'm being laughed at
I'm being bullied
Everyone else is being nice to me.
I feel thankful
for supporting friends.
At the end everything
is going to be okay.

John Unger, Grade 7
Linwood Public School, ON

I Am There

In the midst of all the busyness,
I am there.
You may not see me,
you may not care.
But, I am there.

I was there when you were crying.
I was there when you were smiling.
And I'll be there the day you are dying.
I am always there.

Danielle Osborne, Grade 8
Rahn Jr High School, IL

I Am From

I am from a little town,
where who you are doesn't matter.
I am from an immensely vast space,
where eagles soar through the sky.

I am from a native land,
where totem poles stand tall.
I am from a woodland forest,
where waterfalls cascade down.

I am from an infinite sea,
where waves lap against the shore.
I am from a mild island,
where lightning crackles and thunder roars.

I am from a beautiful vista,
where mountains stand petrified in the distance.
I am from the rocky cliffs,
where animals lay dormant in hiding.
I am from an incredible fantasy,
where dreams are realized.

Brena Dea, Grade 8
Weledeh Catholic School, NT

The Hunt

Shooting a deer is like making a buzzer beater shot.
When I'm in the woods I feel like a wild wolf ready to attack.
As I wait for a deer my senses become keen.
I feel anxious like a raging bull.
I smell fear in the animals.
I see the fright in the deer's eyes.
I hear the bang of the gunshot.
I can taste the venison on my tongue.

Brett Ledvina, Grade 8
Edison Middle School, WI

I Am From

I am from sharing gummy bears on my back deck,
  playing hide-n-go seek in the corn fields at dinner time.
I am from the chocolate drizzle on my ice cream cone,
  not forgetting to give a little to my mom.
I am from being one of the guys,
  football all day, and Sunday night football at 6.
I am from riding my bike,
  dodging oncoming pirates.

I am from American Idol,
  David Archuleta all the way.
I am from lacrosse,
  Chelsea and I exchanging glances of joy!

I am the same person that I was,
  but more improved.
Don't forget the girl that I used to be,
  she is still here,
But in my memories.

Elaina Enich, Grade 7
New Albany Middle School, OH

Basketball

When I hear the basketball bouncing down the court.
I feel like my body is going up and down.
I can see the ball ricochet off the rim.
I feel like a superstar when the crowd goes wild.
I feel the sweat rolling down my back,
As I run down the court.
Win or lose,
I know I played a great game
And gave my best effort.

Holly Lenss, Grade 8
Edison Middle School, WI

Love

Love is sweet,
Love is something you keep.
Love is kind,
Love is something you have in mind.
Love is in your heart,
Together or apart.
Love is not proud,
Love is quiet and love is loud.
Love is not easily angered,
But sometimes is endangered.
Love is patient,
And will forever be ancient.
Love is here, love is there,
Love is with you anywhere.
Love does not boast,
Love comes through the most.
Christ shows the best kind of love,
When God sacrificed His Son from the heavens above.

Kaycee Fahlen, Grade 7
Grant Christian School, MI

Band Room

Do you know that place,
Where flutes sing like a high wind,
Where bassoons emit its wave of lowness,
And where clarinets mutter out its clear middle range?

Do you know that place,
Where trumpets blow out like typhoons,
Where oboes vibrate with its unique sound,
And where horns pour its melody out of the bell?

Do you know that place,
Where saxophones cry with a manly voice,
Where percussions make bouncy dance that jumps off the wall,
And where vague rumble of low brasses explode?

Do you know the band room,
Where different instruments, various importance,
Each with their own beauty and colour,
Meet together and create one song?

Lutan Liu, Grade 9
Elboya Elementary and Jr High School, AB

If

If you can keep your head up after you missed the shot without your teammates getting on you,
You know they're good.
If you can shake it off after you got the ball stolen,
And your teammates just say, "You're fine, get it next time."
You know they're golden.

If you get upset after you strike out,
And your teammates say, "It's okay, you'll hit a homer next time."
You know they're forever.
If you drop the ball and don't pout,
And your teammates yell out to you, "You're fine, no worries."
You know they're keepers.

If you get discouraged after getting hit
And your teammates come out to help you up,
You know they can stay.
If you made the winning touchdown,
And your teammates don't get jealous;
You know they're one of a kind.

Trey Miller, Grade 7
New Albany Middle School, OH

Alone

This girl who is very quiet and really has nothing to say, has many friends,
but never depends on them to do things her way. Except when help is needed she fully listens to reason and never disobedient.
Confidence is scheduled later on in her life to come after all her accomplishments then see who she's become. Closed in a box
all by herself studious and remarkable is her first step, to become somebody to all the ones who doubted her, supported her,
or just didn't plain like her for who she was, but others' opinions shouldn't matter to her in all this because the only things that
matter are the things that are seen in the eyes of the beholder which is her, which is true because that is what her father has
told her. This girl is me, even though my self-esteem has changed who I have turned into I am still through listening to others
who seem to be untrue. This is me and I am proud of who I have become.

DeJahnna Crockett, Grade 8
University Academy, MO

Paper and Scissors

Patterned paper, stickers, and glue, an addiction I cannot control.
Swiping paper cutter though the picture…OMG! It looks so nice.
The aroma of fresh paper quickly fills my nose.

Working at my desk, quiet and calm.
I am so free spinning in my chair.
Just listening to my radio.

Lying on my bed reading a book.
I get zoned out and I take a look, and I stare at my desk quiet as can be.
Then I hear it say, "Get your paper and scissors and come over here and work with me."

When I'm lost and out of whack.
All I need to do is grab a seat, and pull up to my desk.
Get some paper and scissors, and what do you know, I'm back on Earth sitting at my desk.

If you can't find me just come to my room.
And there I will be spinning in my chair.
Spinning in my chair and so peaceful and carefree.

Amy Steckman, Grade 7
New Albany Middle School, OH

What a Smile Hides

She hides so much behind a smile
pain
suffering
dread
She grins to hide the facts
words
hatred
sadness
She lets it all out in a walk
mad
sad
tears
She holds in what shouldn't be heard
scared
sobbing
scars of memories
But she still knows people who'll be there
God
Jesus
Holy Spirit

Abigail Bax, Grade 8
Lewis and Clark Middle School, MO

Dancing in the Rain

Running through the street,
dancing in bare feet,
feeling no pain,
yes, this is how I imagine dancing in the rain.

Feeling the drops on your head,
laughing 'til your face turns red,
nothing to lose, nothing to gain,
yes, this is how I imagine dancing in the rain.

Going crazy, acting like a maniac,
no matter who, prep, jock, or brainiac,
from this, happiness, you can only attain,
yes, this is how I imagine dancing in the rain.

On your face a smile not a frown,
no one can break you down,
so take time, skip and prance,
and go in the rain and dance.

Rachel Roberts, Grade 8
St Monica School, IN

Love's Gate

The love within the heart cannot break.
But on the outside love is at stake,
My heart wants to tell you,
But my mouth is shut tight.
You're in my dreams all through the night.
The day will come and we'll be soul mates;
Not wind nor fire could break our love gate.

Chelsea Rabbermann, Grade 8
Red Bud Elementary School, IL

I Am From

I am from a tiny town,
where we can enjoy the beach.
I am from a tiny town,
where there are desolate roads.

I am from a family,
where we believe in the Northern Lights.
I am from a family,
where we can enjoy eating caribou meat.

I am from a mother,
who believes in my hopes and dreams.
I am from a father,
who teaches me grammar and lifelong advice.

I am from a cold place,
where we say "Eh!"
I am from a cold place,
where the maple leaf trees grow.

I am from Canada.

Charlene Sayine, Grade 8
Weledeh Catholic School, NT

Ode to Thee

Brilliant is not what you are,
And you are not horrible;
Between the two.

I love thee, I hate thee.
Thy life and thy soul make thee.
Neither kind or mean, nor polite or rude.

Thy face; a brilliant smile or a sorrowful frown.
Speak your words and hear mine.

Taste the air that surrounds you.
Time grows short as you grow tall.

I ode to thee,
For you are human, just like me.

Sadie Brown, Grade 8
Hadley Jr High School, QC

Ode to Erin

Oh, you're my best friend.
We will be friends forever.
You and I will stick together.

No other friend could take the place of you.
You're funny, smart, and you care a lot.
I will never doubt that you love me a lot.

The bond we have will never be broken.
It is a friendship that is beyond compare.
It is a friendship we share.

Amber Dean, Grade 7
Trinity Lutheran School, MI

Poems

Some poems have a rhyme
Others go by the beat of time
One, two, three, or four
You can always add more

Limerick or Haiku
How about you make two
There's quatrain
Or cinquain
I hope this poem inspired you

Tala Akkawi, Grade 7
St Gerald Elementary School, IL

My Parents

My parents make me special.
My parents make me whole.
Without them here to guide me,
the world would take its toll.

From when I was a baby,
till only seconds ago,
my parents take good care of me.
And teach me all they know.

Without them here beside me,
my heart would have an empty space.
A place where they belong,
but today, that's not the case.

Every day they teach me,
getting me stronger, stronger yet.
Until I'm ready to face the world,
without a hint of threat.

Even more than I know myself,
my parents know me.
And I know that they complete me,
and that it's meant to be.

Marissa Roper, Grade 7
Thompson Middle School, IL

The Joker

Eternal darkness,
Never to see the light.
Blind and unforgiven,
I am alone.
Ridiculed and laughed at,
I am the joker and the world is my king.
But with that comes pity,
The worst torture of all.
Me, I am the judge of heart.
For people are best seen blind.
Yet still, I am the joker,
And the world is my king.

Melissa Reid, Grade 8
Red Wing School, SK

One Voice of Many Thousands

I am one of many thousands just like me!
And just like you, I was a working family man.
Never knew that one day the race I was born to would be discriminated against.
No trial by jury, just judged by one inhuman, sick, twisted man!
His orders were to kill all the Jews!
There were no limits to the way the Germans carried out these orders!
We were hunted down like a social disease.
Few of us got out, but thousands had no chance!
The Germans took us by the train loads to death camps,
Where unheard things were done to us!
It didn't matter if you were a man, woman, or child.
The torture, the beatings, the rape, the firing squads and even gas chambers.
Then our dead bodies were thrown into huge man made holes in the ground,
And just one at a time but by thousands at a time!
Yet no one seemed to care about the fact this one sick, twisted man,
Was half Jew, half German until it was almost too late for us
The Jews!! Please don't' forget me for I am one voice;
Of many thousands just like me that have died in vain, in the Holocaust.

Justin Slavin, Grade 8
Parkway Middle School, OH

I too, Sing America

Here I am sitting in this chair
The same chair that I've been basically sitting in for my entire life
As I stroll pass one and another
All they do is stare at me and my mother
I sit and try to think every day
Wishing that I could walk
Wishing that I could talk
Wishing that I can eat with no one else's help
Wishing that my parents didn't smoke crap
But were considerate of their future baby's trap
All I can do is try to think
Hmmm…
Sitting and wondering
Why
Why me
Trying to think why couldn't I've been a regular blessed child
What did I do
Is it my fault
Am I to blame
I, too, am America

Rahimah Gaither, Grade 9
Gwendolyn Brooks College Preparatory Academy, IL

Friends

Friends are ones who love.
Friends are ones who care.
Friends are ones that always forgive the sins that you have made.
Friends are ones who stand by you.
Friends are ones who never leave.
Friends are ones who never let you down.
But most importantly,
Friends are ones who make our lives even more unique.

Sara Hughes, Grade 8
Dassel-Cokato Middle School, MN

Dear Mommy

"How would you describe your mother?"
Someone asked me one day;
"There are not enough words to describe,
How much she is perfect in every way;"
A special type of person that I am blessed with,
I thank God every day;
Always there to talk to,
And always that will stay;
Always there to comfort me,
And always knows the right words to say;
That one-of-a-kind mother,
Her love for me she always conveys;
To pay her back for all she has done,
Would be a price I could not pay;
The family you've built is strong;
We will stick together and never sway;
Your love and inspiration will be with me forever,
Not just for today;
There are not enough words to describe,
How much I love my mommy this Mother's Day.

Petina Benigno, Grade 9
Cor Jesu Academy, MO

My Best Friend

Distance between you and me
Is only a heartbeat away,
For you and I dwell in each other's heart —
There forever we will stay.

You know all my emotions,
Many they may be.
You know when to be gentle,
when to chastise me.

Two gentle souls deeply connected,
Thoughts not spoken,
There is no need —
For the other knows what he is thinking
Even before he speaks.

So with all the love I have
In my heart today,
I want to express to you
These feelings I want to stay.

Demarcus Curole, Grade 9
McKinley Sr High School, LA

Love

Loving you is like cuddling with you,
Loving you is like spending time with you,
Loving you is like getting to know you,
Loving you is like partying with you,
Loving you is like…
     "Just being with you"

Toni Steward, Grade 9
Saginaw High School, MI

His Daughter

A beautiful child of God is born today.
A child who will like to play at the bay as the days grow cooler.
A child with the cutest little accent.
A child who is meant to be God's follower.
She will not be hollow.
She will be loved.
She will dance like the butterflies.
She sings like the birds.
Her beauty will make the guys come running.
But her father is also cunning.
She is FOREVER in his eyes a little angel.

Amber Metrejean, Grade 9
Borne's Home School, LA

Meadow Love*

Edward stone cold,
Like a marble Greek god.
Bella warm brown eyes,
An angel from heaven
Sent for his personal hell
In their meadow, evil lurks.
The buzzing bees,
To the crawling ants,
To the beat of a heart.
The couple knows, that their pixie sister, Alice watching
Laying under the sun,
Edward the vampire sparkles.
Bella the human watches
In amazement
So as the story is told
The lion fell in love,
With the breakable lamb.
Prey and Hunter, caught in emotions,
Love
Only thing that, can never be Forgotten!

Megan Creen, Grade 9
Clintonville High School, WI
*Dedicated to "Twilight"

Going to Albania

Above the clouds
Through the jet stream
Nearing the airport
We are going to Albania.

Outside we are
Beside my cousins
At Grandpa's house
My cousins and I are playing soccer.

Again up high
Below is Albania
Toward home
I am sad, because it is time, and we have to go.

Juliano Pjetrushi, Grade 7
Algonquin Middle School, MI

Nothing to Replace

When I look at her,
she has no different face.
She is a normal teenage girl
that no one could replace.
But when she speaks
I realize how special
she really is.

I feel the warmth
welcoming me while saying,
"Lou Lou"
and rushing towards me
for the great big bear hug
I have been waiting for
for months.

The long drive
is always worth it
when going to visit
the cousin
I will always
remember.
Rachel.

Sarah Rasmussen, Grade 7
Humboldt Middle School, IA

Running Free

Wind on my face
Running fast in the darkness
Smile on my face
Getting away from this place
Many different thoughts in my head
Where am I going?
Long, silent steps
Soon I will be FREE!!

Ashleey McCarthy, Grade 8
Wainwright High School, AB

Lily Leaves

Fluttering lightly in the breeze
are the bright yellow lily leaves
bold in life but small in bud
it sticks out in the dark brown mud

As the raindrops run down my face
I look at that lily and have more faith
As I see the contrast of color
it reminds me of the difference
between me and my brother

Lily leaves stand alone
no matter how much they've grown
Lily petals speak of a song
though it is not very long

Casey Humphreys, Grade 8
Owensville Community School, IN

Summer

Summer is a bright yellow, the color of sun rays.
It feels like water at a pool or sprinkler.
Birds chirping, kids playing, and ice cream trucks surround your ear.
Baseball, sand, popsicles, and chlorine fill the air.
Juicy watermelon, fruits, and BBQs are the tastes of summer.
Summer is the best time to play and hang out!

Selvio DeAngeles, Grade 7
Hamlin Upper Grade Center, IL

Day Dreaming

Staring.
Thinking
Looking at one single spot.
Staring, but can't see what is in front of you.
Not knowing what your mind is going to produce.

It starts off with one single idea.
One idea leads to another,
all linked together like a chain that grasps your mind
skyrocketing to the clouds.
Back down at Earth, your body is motionless.
Everything is so peaceful and worry free,
thinking you're someplace better than where you are.
And then…

BAM!!! Something snaps in your brain like someone stepping on a branch
your head parachutes down from the clouds,
your eyes come back to focus,
and you're back in history class…ugh…learning.

Mackenzie Van Bargen, Grade 7
Linwood Public School, ON

Anna Jean Grolle

I am someone who has fun and cares about life around me
I wonder how and why people you care about have to leave
I hear spontaneous laughs all around the world
I see a great world coming together piece by piece
I want to be able to live my life to the fullest
I am someone who has fun and cares about life around me

I pretend that life is perfect — never has a flaw
I feel you should have fun when you can and be serious when needed
I touch emotions that surround me in my life
I worry that when I speak no one can hear me
I cry when life has to end for the people close to me
I am someone who has fun and cares about life around me

I understand at times things get carried away
I say "We need to care about the surroundings and appearance of life"
I dream about life around us that lasts forever with great twists and turns
I try to make my family approve of what I want my life to become
I hope lives of others and mine will keep going great
I am someone who has fun and cares about life around me

Anna Jean Grolle, Grade 8
Otsego Middle School, OH

School for Fish*

Well, granddaughter, I'll tell you:
School for me was never like
The crystal-clear-beach waters of the Caribbean Sea.
It was infested with jellyfish
And stingrays that stung you
And hammerhead sharks,
And even crabs that bit my toes when I was not looking,
But through the years
I kept on swimming
And riding the waves,
And sometimes even treading water,
Trying not to drift out too far into the sea
Where the waters got dangerous.
So don't stop swimming now,
And don't stop kicking your legs
And paddling through the water
Because school gets better,
For I made it through myself.
And school for me was never like
The crystal-clear-beach waters of the Caribbean Sea.

Blaire Guidry, Grade 9
Destrehan High School, LA
*With apologies to Langston Hughes

Astronomy

astronomy is fun
spending time with grandpa
we'll have a great time just don't stare at the sun

we sit and we watch Miser 43
as the stars quickly fade
just my grandpa and me

Daniel Sprague, Grade 7
Tripoli Middle/Senior High School, IA

Drift Away

How could you forget about what we had?
I loved you with all my heart and you couldn't see it
I cried every night just to let the pain drift away
But, when I see you at school it feels like a new day
I forget about why I was mad at you
Walking in the halls holding your hand
I feel so comfortable just with you nobody else but you
But, when lunch comes it's a new you
You leave me by myself
Flirting with this one and that one
And as the end of the day comes you run and hug me
I just walk away and say nothing
I cried that night just to let the pain drift away
I guess I will never get a chance to tell you how I feel
When I do tell you it seems like you don't care
So, as I put my fingers through my hair
Stressed from all these things you did to me
Hey, I guess me and you was just not meant to be

Osheanya Jones, Grade 9
Springfield Boys and Girls Club ABC Unit, IL

My Dumb Dog Is Stupid

My dumb dog is stupid and can't do a thing,
He can't howl or hunt or do a doggy sing.
He can't tell the difference,
From a rock and a bone.
And he chases his tail,
When he is alone.
You let him outside,
He runs all around.
If you let him go,
He might tear up the ground.
My dumb dog is stupid and doesn't know nothin'!
When you give him a toy,
He'll tear out the stuffin'.
He has a sideways run,
And a lousy sense of direction.
Though he don't know it,
He's far from perfection.
My dumb dog is stupid,
He can't howl, hunt or sing.
Now that I think of it,
He can't do anything!

Danielle Breeden, Grade 7
Jefferson Area Jr-Sr High School, OH

Farming

The soft cows and calves lay and moo in the pasture,
Eating green grass inside the electric fence.
The red barn doors open,
And the cows come galloping in.
Big cows lose some weight,
Leaving behind their soupy manure for others to step in.
White and black cattle go into their stalls,
Eating the yellow corn.
Chores are done,
As the cattle get milked.
Fluffy annoying cats meow around,
Waiting to be pet.
After the morning chores,
Men hit the rocky fields,
With their dusty tractors and machinery.
The clock ticks all day,
And the same process is done the next day.

Aaron Pingel, Grade 9
Clintonville High School, WI

Love

My love for you is strong and solid
Passionate and beautiful
Full of inspiration, wisdom, and faith
You make me laugh and smile all the time
Deep inside me your love will stay
And will never end
I love you forever my Martina, my love

Aaron L. Gartner, Grade 8
Prairie Lakes School, MN

Falling Star

I've finally made it to the top, now I am falling. Tailing the best was hard at first easy, but than I lost myself. I became selfish
and jealous.
I've finally made it to the top, now I am falling. I don't want to feel the cold harsh ground. I want to scream I don't want to be
grounded, even though I can't.
I've finally made it to the top, now I am falling. My glow that held me up is now fading faster than the light came. I wish it
would stop. The blinking starts to act like a migraine. The pain nails you like a shooting star falling out of place.
I am raising again, but now I'm known as a "falling star" to always rise again.

Erin Lomasney, Grade 9
East High School, WI

Young Love

A gorgeous, magnificent young love with tender silky skin
running through the surface of her gentle body

Soft, gentle voice of an angel talking a soft melody to the ear of the listener's stroke of sound,
soothing the soul and transporting the spirit to a tranquil place

The fragrance of the aroma that her body emits
leaves a sweet scent to remember and never forget

Those delectable stolen kisses from her delicious lips that have a golden savor,
their fruity taste that leaves a mouth wanting for more

The warmth of her body emitting a known heat as a burning fire lit for comfort,
ready for the release of warmth within an affectionate embrace

The forever enriched love of a girl.

Alejandro Angeles, Grade 9
Southwest Jr High School, AR

The Inevitable

It's really unpredictable how it will happen.
Anytime, anywhere, to anyone.
I think about this even though I don't want to.
Paranoid and worried thoughts enter into my mind.

Many questions fill my thoughts: will it happen in my sleep?
Underwater or in a fire? In my car or even at my house?
Will I fight for my life or not have the chance? Am I going to be alone or surrounded by others?

Some believe there is another life afterwards: some believe otherwise.
Nobody lives to prove the truth. Theories are all anyone has.
Where will I go? Heaven or Hell?
Among the stars? These questions are impossible to answer.

In the end, I want to have lived my life to its fullest.
Will I have accomplished what I had wanted to accomplish?
I want to have left my mark on those I met.
Was everything a good investment or a waste of time?

It is all so unpredictable. Tomorrow, in a few weeks, in a few years;
It could all end in an instant. I will never know.
All I can do is stop fearing the inevitable, live my life to its fullest,
And most of all, have faith.

Taylor Irvine, Grade 8
Gilbert Middle School, IA

Sacrifice

Nails in hands, limp body, pale face,
All to save the human race.
Persecuted, whipped, pierced in the side,
Hanging from a cross He died.
A crown of thorns placed upon His head,
Who knew the next day He'd be dead.
He shed His blood to save our sins,
The least we could do is live our life for Him.
Yet we push our limits, cross the line,
When He deserves all of our time.
We say we have to time to spare,
Yet we can paint our face and fix our hair.
Just give it all up, take a chance,
He's the music, our lives are the dance.
Glorify Him, find your purpose,
Praise Him and lift up worship.
The greatness is beyond imaginable,
So give it up, take a chance,
The music's loud, begin your dance.

Kelsey Lucas, Grade 8
Oakland Christian School, MI

The Revolution

I stand right here today free and equal
Because of the war my fathers bled for
If one stole my rights, they'd get a sequel
So high does the American Flag soar
Through the roar of cannon and musket shots
Of so many hard fought bloody battles
Against the rule of the British despot
King George the 3rd loud incessant prattle
From Bunker Hill in the freezing north
To the Battle of Cowpens in the south
The American Militia drove forth
Patriotism spread by word of mouth
Because of our nation's revolution
We have an evolving constitution

Jacob House, Grade 9
Southwest Jr High School, AR

My Greatest Dream

Basketball is the sport for me.
When the game's on the line, I'm there.
I will do what I need to do.
I'll be Dwight with the 0.8 seconds left.
You can guarantee that I will make the shot,
I may not be tall, but I will fight for victory.
Becoming the greatest player is what motivates me.
Day in and day out, I will work out every day.
Whatever it takes I will do it.
I don't care what team I go to.
If I make it to the NBA.
I would love to go to Orlando
But I don't care.
I play for pleasure.
That is my dream.

Blaze Carr, Grade 7
St Pauls Lutheran School, IL

Furious

Possession, pain, power
Crumpled fists ready to explode like a canon
People stutter
You're like a tornado trying desperately
To spin the anger off
Stomping
You stomp as loud as
An earthquake
Stopping at nothing
Waiting
You've waited all you can
You're ready to explode
Like a volcano
Anger surrounds you
Like a burning flame
It's loud, it hurts
Furious

Kristen Fisher, Grade 7
Linwood Public School, ON

I Am a Shadow of My Heart

I am a shadow of my heart
I wonder what's behind the door,
I hear about all the good things on the other side
I see golden light shining through the gaps
I want to wash away my darkness in that light
I am a shadow of my heart

I pretend that nothing is wrong, but
I feel all the darkness coursing though my veins, but when
I touch the golden floor, my fingers begin to burn
I worry that I'll never get to go through that door
I cry when I think that my heart will never be golden
I am a shadow of my heart

I understand that it'll hurt to change, yet
I say dark things when all I want is change
I dream of walking through that door one day, so
I try to do what other good people do,
I hope one day that I will be something new, because now
I am a shadow of my heart

Andy Waugh, Grade 9
Jackson High School, OH

September 11

S eptember
E leventh
P eople were
T errified
E ntire
M emory
B ut
E verlasting
R estrength of the U.S.A.

Mason Masters, Grade 7
Fairfield Middle School, OH

Not a Love Letter or a Good Thing

I give you my heart,
It is hard, broken because of you,
It promises pain,
Like the tiny prick of a thorn,
Here
It will be always hurting,
Like a broken bone that won't heal,
It will make me realize,
You were never good for me,
I am trying to be strong.
Not a lover or a girlfriend,
I give you my heart
Its breaking will not even hurt you
No remorse, no guilt
It's all for you to take,
If you like,
Hurting,
Its scent will cling to your heart,
Cling to your soul.

Baylee Moulder, Grade 9
Leeton Middle and High School, MO

Happiness

Happiness is soft yellow
It tastes like an apple
It smells like flowers
It reminds me of dancing crickets
It sounds like a million love songs
Happiness makes me feel so light

Edda Sturm, Grade 8
Wainwright High School, AB

Seasons Change

Bright sunny days and
Brilliant green grass
To cloudy skies and
Colorful leaves
Then to snow days
And snowmen.

Warm days and
Outside play to
School work and
Jackets on all day.

The day comes when
You must leave, and
Language arts
Won't ever be the same.

Good luck for you
In the future,
So farewell, toodloo and
Hope to see you soon!

Hannah Louvier, Grade 7
Highland Middle School, IL

You Bring Out the Teenage Daughter in Me

You bring out the Gemini in me
One day I'm happy one day I'm sad
With you I can never be sure
You bring out the inquisitive side in me
I question over and over again
If you really do love me
And I have yet to find an answer
You bring out the teenage daughter in me
Why won't you just listen?
Do you want to ruin my life?
You bring out the anger in me
The I hate you and I wish you weren't my mother in me
It kills me to say that sometimes…
I wish it was you instead of him
You bring out the sadness in me
You make me cry myself asleep time and time again
Wishing that he were here to go through it with me
But somehow you bring out the Christian in me
The I know God is always there in me
I pray, and then I know that he will not put more on me than I can bear.
And for that, I thank you, Mom.

Wylisa McIntosh, Grade 9
Gwendolyn Brooks College Preparatory Academy, IL

Garrett

I, Garrett
Funny, creative, thoughtful, playful
Sibling of Damon and Cole
Lover of pets, family, Brittany
Who feels joyful, fantastic, heroic
Who needs family, friends, love
Who fears some movies, death, and nightmare
Who would like to see Disneyland again, my old dog Buddy, Brittany
Am a resident of Yellowknife, Northwest Territories

Garrett Benoit, Grade 8
Weledeh Catholic School, NT

You Can't Change Me

You can't change me, you won't change me.
I'm me whether you like it or not. There's nothing you can do,
I'm me.
You may hate me, you may love me,
But you can't change me. You can try, but it won't work.
God made me like this, whether you like it or not,
I'm me.
You can't do anything to stop me, you can try to tell me no,
But it's not going to work. I'm going to do things God's way.
Not yours, not mine, nobody's else's. You're never going to change it,
So get over trying to change me, cause it's not going to work.
I'm sticking to what I believe in,
    That's it!
There's no more to it. You are not going to change me,
You cannot change me, you will not change me.
Cause I am me.

Kendra Nobava, Grade 7
Ireton Christian School, IA

Who...

Paige, a girl who loves to live.
Who feels she needs to make the world a better place.
Who needs a good joke every once in a while.
Who gives love to everyone.
Who fears war and death of people close to her.
Who would like world peace.

Paige Kovach, Grade 7
New Albany Middle School, OH

Late Night War

Boom!
      Debris flying, people running,
        an antiaircraft shell
          exploded. There is a
smell of gunpowder
      throughout the air.
        Running, fighting, hiding,
          a machine gun goes off
in the distance,
        a sharp pain in your right arm
          as a bullet pierces your skin.
          The enemy hiding,
troops crawling,
      in the dense forest.
        "Grenade" someone yells
          just as everyone gets out
of that area.
      Over in the distance,
        the sun goes down in the horizon.
          Peace comes back until
the next day of war.

Alek Arnsman, Grade 8
Otsego Middle School, MI

What Is My Name?

They call me the great sensation,
Glorious, gorgeous combination
When I'm around it's a celebration
On top of the game, best there is
Look at me with admiration
Champion and achiever,
They know my name across the nation
I'm the star of all the TV stations
Girls consider me the competition
Boys look at me and they start wishin'
Princess is what you should call me
Superb, smart, sassy and style
I make the day worthwhile.
To hang with me you need an invitation,
Make me mad and you'll pay so I suggest
Never getting yourself into that situation.
...Okay so maybe it's a lie, an exaggeration.
But I sound so much cooler when
You use your imagination.

Kailey Adams, Grade 8
Little Miami Jr High School, OH

Julie's Happiness

I am Julie's happiness.
I am very bright, usually pink or orange.
I take up a lot of Julie's life.
I have surrounded her with great memories,
    And give her many wonderful times.
I am very good friends with joy,
But I am not too fond of anger or jealousy,
    Because they make my job a lot harder.
I am Julie's happiness
    And because I make her happy,
    She is able to cheer others up,
      And make their day a little brighter.

Julie Hurst, Grade 8
Blanchester Middle School, OH

Romantic Stranger

I saw you walking down the street
Almost hidden by the dark.

Your black dress follows behind you.
Mysterious?

I see you again walking down the same street
This time with red roses.

You look beautiful, stunning...
Perfect.

You look independent, but fragile
You are very quiet, but noticeable

She is a bliss
Everything I could wish for.

If only I knew that
Romantic Stranger.

Eliza Reid-Webster, Grade 7
Menno Simons Christian School, AB

Anger

My body boils like a pot of hot water.
My legs turn into armies in an important battle.
My heart rages as if flames are curling around it.
I keep my mouth SHUT! Wishing not to offend anyone.
My fists become talons trying to show my true emotions.
I keep a steady stare making sure to protect my back.
I breathe harder now as if a bomb
      was ticking inside me.
My mind races with terrible thoughts.
I want to scream, but
      pride is keeping,
      me back.
The more my mind rages, the more my anger turns to...
¡HATRED!

Angela Guest, Grade 7
Linwood Public School, ON

Midnight Sky

Boom bang boom bang boom
Flashes light the midnight sky
I watch silently
Annie Penning, Grade 8
Shakopee Area Catholic School, MN

The Crow

The poor old crow
Never left his nest.
He just sat there,
Looking at the sky.
No one cared
Even when he cried.
If you ask,
He will sing.
"Oh, I lack
A pair of good wings.
I cannot fly
I cannot try."
There will be tears
On his cheeks
When no one hears
The song from his beaks.
With a little sigh,
He stopped and lay.
It is because
He is made out of clay.
Tong Yu, Grade 8
Northwest Jr High School, IA

Luau Green

Backyard days of years ago
Many monumental moments
Joy, passion, nonchalance, pure
Acres of memories
Birthdays on the deck

Endless summer time
Soaring shady trees
Congruency with the mind
Times things feelings
Melange

Cops and robbers in pursuit
Sand box truck filled
Dreams of young
Fresh cut grass remains
As dense as the bliss

Aroma of chestnuts in summer
Hot sun descends from horizon
Beautiful backyard sunsets
Cool night liberates from stifling day
History is present in becoming the past
Matthew Boelter, Grade 8
South Middle School, WI

The Shores

a glaring, warm sun
echoed by the raging waves of the lovely shores, gone, then back again

smiling people, loud with laughter and movement, some crying
the people were jokers. a wicked wind lost in the crisp, bright air.
the wind was like a hurricane.

the smell of fruity pineapples picked properly at market
salty water rushing to shore

a combo of wild fruit juice
and spicy shrimp

rough sand between your toes
the wet lotion soaking in

and the feeling of the calm, gently moving wind in your face.
Morgan Bradley, Grade 9
Southwest Jr High School, AR

The River

The cracked dry riverbed thirsts as the black ominous clouds roll in.
The rain begins to sprinkle the Earth like a baker carefully decorates his cake.
Flowers sing cheerfully as the water flows from the threatening clouds.
Wonderfully wet water is beginning to quench the parched river's thirst.

Harder still the rain falls like a hammer pounding a nail.
The river is now flooding, submerging the land in the treacherous water.
The flowers that sang cheerfully are now crying frightfully.
Water is covering them but they can't go anywhere.

Just when the swift, flooding water covers the flowers, the clouds break.
The flowers are now breathing easily because the water is receding back to the river.
The river is now a gentle mother relaxing and nurturing the flowers.
Peaceful and serene the river flows until next time when the clouds return.
Ciarra Davis, Grade 7
New Castle Middle School, IN

The Bad News

I was playing outside. I was with my friends. I was having fun.
Everything was "A-ok" until my mom got the call.
My grandfather was sick. He wasn't breathing well.
We drove up to Michigan and took him to the hospital to treat him.
My mom came out and said, "I have some bad news."
"Papa has cancer." I let that sink in a minute and asked "What is cancer?"
She said, "Bad news." They said it would be ok.
He started to walk. Then turned yellow and got sick from chemotherapy.
We took him back to the hospital and he was put on an IV and an oxygen tank.
My mom came out and said that I could say hi and I followed.
I went back and sat down. My grandma came out crying.
My dad came out to tell me the bad news. Frank Hunsberger died in old age.
Friends and family shall always remember him.
It was not about how he died, but more of how he lived.
Brett Jones, Grade 7
New Albany Middle School, OH

The Mission

Soaring, gliding, dipping, diving,
Sending an array of burning spray.
Havoc in wake behind,
Out of the distance flies.

Moving slowly looking lowly,
The squire of the king approaches.
Sword held high, catching light
Off hilt and blade alike.

He squares off with dragon black.
With hiss and bellow,
Brute strikes with blazes.
Which consume but air.

Pointing sword skyward, he cries out,
"For my king my master my lord I charge
In his name I slay you fowl beast."
With a mighty yell he stormed forth.

The fiend was dead and gone.
Service done, to king he returned,
And his king his master his lord rewarded him,
Thanking him, he put him in charge of many things.

Chase Sutter, Grade 8
Grant Christian School, MI

What's My Name?

They call me the Gatekeeper
Playing sweeper
And helping everyone, especially the keeper
I stop the madness
When the player popping past my team heads to score
STOP! I reverse the direction
Up the field…SCORE!!!
My team is the best!
Losing always makes us better,
I sometimes get breakthroughs
And there I go…UNSTOPPABLE,
But that's not my fame,
Keeping the line is.
We don't stop playing
Till the whistle is blown
Then we know we WON!

Madison Reiman, Grade 8
Little Miami Jr High School, OH

Horses

We have people that love and care for us.
We run like the wind with our beautiful hair blowing.
We love to run and play all day.
We love to be brushed, cared for, and loved.
We go to places with our owners and do our best in shows.
But we also love to come back to our own home.

Taylor Haese, Grade 8
St John Lutheran School, WI

If

If you are proud of yourself,
And confident, strong, brave and a man.
If you treat women with respect,
And act like a gentleman,
As every boy and man should.
The world would be a better place.

If you persevere and always keep trying,
You will go somewhere in life.
If you don't give up,
You will be a success.
If you are a true gentleman,
You show it through your qualities and your actions.

Albert Miller, Grade 7
New Albany Middle School, OH

What Family Is For

Family is kind and loving,
Everyone's family is rare,
Even though they get on your nerves,
They are happy to share,

Like colorful patches in a quilt,
Each person's story is richly built,
Into a family story that is mine and ours alone,
Each gives our kind, caring family its special tone,

Family is kind and loving,
Brothers and sisters, aunts and uncles,
Parents and grandparents too,
Always there to share their love with you.

Rachael Yoho, Grade 7
New Albany Middle School, OH

Rock & Roll

My instrument is calling to me
I put on my strap and plug in the cord
My amp buzzing behind me
I play the song on my radio

I see frets beneath my fingers
And memorized tabs on the floor
I feel as if I'm no longer in my room
But playing for an audience

I start to perform
Feeling the smooth metal strings under my fingers
The music surging through me
My parents telling me to turn it down

The amp roars like a lion
Music is surrounding me
AC/DC and Black Sabbath booming behind me
Unfortunately the song must end

Logan Bush, Grade 7
New Albany Middle School, OH

Dreams

I fly in the sky,
And no one can stop me.
I fly in the sky,
And believe me, I'm free.

I'm deep in the jungle,
With nothing to fear.
I'm deep in the jungle,
With all my friends near.

I'm under the sea,
And swim far from the shore.
I'm under the sea,
And my tail touches the floor.

I'm ruler of the land
That's inside my head.
I'm ruler of the land
When I go to bed.

Rebecca Ganow, Grade 7
Van Buren Middle School, OH

Never

I wish upon my lucky star
For everyone to hear
And even though you're far
I feel you're very near
When I see your eyes
There's nothing I can do
You are a big surprise
That's how I feel about you
This feeling will never change
It will last forever
I will never rearrange
Never, ever
Never

Abigail Nelson, Grade 8
Rahn Jr High School, IL

Music

Music moves me
It sways me
When I listen,
I absorb the beauty
The magnificence
The lyrics with their secret meaning
The beat that stays constant and true
The voice with its calling to me
My foot taps
My head shakes
My fingers drum
My dance and the music are one
Music moves me
It sways me

Mariah Clark, Grade 9
Blair-Taylor High School, WI

I Am From...

I am from a busy place, where kids talk and play.
I am from the soccer fields, where we love playing soccer.
I am from a place, where people work a lot.
I am from a snowy town, where the winters are warm.

I am from an unpermissive town, where schools are short and hard.
I am from the light environment, where the town is small and bright.
I am from a friendly place, where all my friends are around me.
I am from a place, where my family is loving.

I am from a town, where everyone is loved and cared for.
I am from a beautiful town, where the seas are blue and bright.
I am from a place, where Noah's Arc landed in.

Narek Khachatryan, Grade 8
Weledeh Catholic School, NT

It's Good

I hear the crowd cheering our names! EAGLES! EAGLES! EAGLES!
The vibration from the crowd jumping up in the air.
As we come running in we hear the crowd cheering even louder.
I pick up the ball and shoot. IT'S GOOD!!

I shake hands with the other team.
Jump in the air and receive the ball.
I dribble down the court.
I pass. He shoots! IT'S GOOD.

The opponent has the ball. I sneak up behind him.
I steal the ball.
Start running for the other hoop.
I do a lay-up and IT'S GOOD.

We have 10 seconds left in the game.
I see someone open. I pass the ball to him.
I run to the basket. He passes.
I do a lay-up and SWOOSH!
We just won a 22-20.

Junaid Tariq, Grade 7
New Albany Middle School, OH

War on Terror

W eeping mothers like rain pouring from the skies
A bandoned wives
R equiems for the dead like a forgotten parade

O il For Blood. Ka Boom
N o one left unchanged.

T he government's betrayal
E veryone is expendable
R ich man's war encouraged in shiny office buildings
R esponsibility falls to the poor to fight their sweat and blood not the suits
O ur countdown to Apocalypse is now like a stopwatch to a deadly race
R ise together or divided we fall

Jerry Bay, Grade 9
Hazelwood West Jr-Sr High School, MO

Sadness

He was running fast like a cheetah with all his might
He is my knight in shining armour,
My tears were running down my cheeks like a waterfall
Trying to hold them in,
Sad,
Upset,
Wistful,
I try to smile but my lips are icicles,
Hanging from a roof,
People who come to remember, laying down wreathes,
Like grieving families leaving flowers at a grave
Coldness,
Damp,
Shivers,
The pipes cry songs of remembrance as we hear names
Of lives lost,
SADNESS.

Ali Hergott, Grade 7
Linwood Public School, ON

In My Dream

In my dream I feel so small
In my dream they feel so tall
But in my dream I know we are all equal
In my dream I hear yelling
In my dream I hear moans
In my dream I hear gunshots like thunder is thrown
In my dream I see ashes in the sky
It is as if I try to grab one
But I have no energy to do so
In my dream I taste ashes on my lips
In my dream I taste dust
In my dream I taste rotten soup
As if it were a must
In my dream I smell dead bodies
In my dream I smell rotten food
In my dream I smell a gas
I wish I would wake up and
This would be the end but
Is this a dream is this a dream

Claude Coffman, Grade 8
Parkway Middle School, OH

David the Boy

Childhood remembrances are always exciting
If you're a boy
You always get into mischief
You don't have to take baths
Stay out 'til you can't see your hand
In front of your face
You wrestle with your brother
Play sports
You fish and pick up frogs
And scare all the girls with them

David Pusateri, Grade 9
Runnels School, LA

Remember

Always remember that every night has its dawn,
That every star has its glitter,
Every person has a heart.

Always remember people can hope,
And people can pray,
God can give and take people away.

Always remember everyone has a memory,
And I will remember you,
Never forget me, and I will see you soon!

I love you Granny!!!

Ashley Moffett, Grade 8
Carlisle Elementary/Jr High School, IN

The Battle of the Sky

As I lay in a lush green meadow, I look up at the sky
and see 100 white horses galloping from the south
and into the clear blue sky.
They're on their way to a battle with the North.
After about 3 hours the sky turns dark
and I retreated to the safety of my bedroom.
You can hear the guns firing,
and you can see the glow of the cannons as they are being fired.
The war has begun.
One by one millions of soldiers start to fall from the sky,
and soak into the ground.
As I watch from my room,
I begin to see the war coming to an end.
The soldiers have stopped falling to the ground
and there are no more sounds of guns or cannons firing.
Peace has been restored, until the next thunderstorm.

Rebecca Owens, Grade 8
Mount Vernon Middle School, MO

That Is Me

Look and what do you see;
    Smart, brilliant and beyond the extraordinary
That Is Me.

Helpful, kind, strong and brave
    Is that what you see?
Guess what? That Is Me.

Accelerate in school;
highly satisfied with life and almost winning everything.
We're a team! Somebody got to lead the team.
    This Is Me.

See we'er living in a new society;
    Be what all you can be.
And one day you be Better than Me.

Da'Montae Quincy, Grade 7
North Dayton School of Discovery, OH

I Am

I am Ashley Mietzner.
I hear horses galloping across the hard, green ground.
I see horses running freely through the bluebell meadows.
I touch horses with rough and soft hair rubbing against my blue jeans.
I say whatever is on my strong willed mind.
I cry when someone or something I love is lost or gone.
I am a down to earth, caring horse lover.

I am a very opinionated teenage girl.
I feel happiness, excitement, hurt, sadness, and my heart beating several times per minute.
I try to improve everything I can because you can always improve on something.
I dream to be a successful person in life.
I live in a small town where I can live life to the fullest.
I try to achieve my goals in life.
I am Ashley Mietzner.

Ashley Mietzner, Grade 8
Stewartville Middle School, MN

Is This Really Happening?

We're the only ones left trying to survive,
Hunger calls to me, "Feed me to stay alive!"
But just as I lose all hope,
I make out a figure of a vehicle coming down the slope.
SCREECH!
The trucks come to a halt
Just as the bodies stop screaming in the fiery vault.
Their ashes come down as a hazy image comes into the camp without a sound.
Everyone is screaming and running for their lives
One man asks me, "Do you think these men will help us survive?"
I worked up the courage to run my fingers along the men
As the zoo behind me closes in on them.
The salty tears fill my mouth
Along with the blood and dirt from the day before.
The aroma of the odors stretching from dead bodies to grungy, alive skeletons
Mix with the beautiful scent of the rescuer's flesh.
With everyone's crying out, I sit there to think to myself.
A wave of relief crashes over me like a wave on a beach.
Seems like I've been here forever, anything's better than this, even blood getting sucked by a leech.
But here before me is a present from the Holy Father to take away my pain,
I'm praying for my rescuer to help me so I don't go insane.

Rachel Miller, Grade 8
Parkway Middle School, OH

Reflection of a Star

Look through your window and you will see me.
I am the lone star staring back at you.
I am not the silvered coloured car passing through the bridge, nor am I the man who hurries past.
I can be stirred like the wind, but the wind is not me.
The lamplight on the weary road only encourages the reverse image of me.
The building across the street shuts out my image.
The ever-changing stop light has no relation with me, nor does that lone tower peaking above me.
You might think I am the flashing plane across the sky, accepting I am not.
You are like the rest of humankind — you look too far.
Yes, look closer — not at the world outside but at the reflection — the reflection of me.

Moustafa Abdalla, Grade 9
Don Mills Collegiate Institute, ON

Silence the Butterflies

Butterflies hammer my stomach out wide,
Nothing to do but run, or hide.
Stuck in the middle, mere scraps of hope
Nothing to do, can't hardly cope.

Can't hardly breathe, can't hardly see
Nothing to do, someone save me.
No light in the tunnel, not even fresh air
Nothing to do, my options: not there.

Screaming whispers into cries,
Someone sound the lullabies.
And sound the sorrys, laughs, and all
Anything to prevent my fall.

But suddenly, I catch a glimpse of light
Nothing to do, but I can try to fight.
To fight through the hurricanes, minus the strength
I'll silence those butterflies, bring hope to arms' length.

Jessica White, Grade 8
Highland Middle School, IL

Robin Hood

There he goes with all his glory
All power and mighty
His arrowhead, which is so gory
You thought he was all white and tidy
He robbed from the rich and gave to the poor
Greedy Prince John taxed people of Nottingham
He lived in the forest with branches as his door
Greedy Prince John sure did put a bam on Nottingham
But roguish Hood and Lil' John didn't give up
Robin went to win the archery contest to win Maid Marian
But instead almost got killed, but never gave up
After his entire struggle he married that fox Maid Marian
And they lived happily ever after
That fox Maid Marian and roguish Robin Hood.

Celia Gardner, Grade 9
Southwest Jr High School, AR

Dream Factory

Over the clouds and into the breeze
is a place we all know called the dream factory
This little place can be big, can be small
can be colorful, can be creative, no limits, no walls
This factory is a wondrous, magical place
imagination powered, it's a pollutionless space
but how do you get there?
Close your eyes and believe
just give it a try, it's easy to dream
While the art is at work and the brains start to storm
inside your soul is a dream being formed
a dash of happiness and sprinkled with pride
can you feel that rush of excitement inside?
Here is your dream, now it's all up to you
go back to reality and make it come true

Olivia Pei, Grade 8
College Avenue Public School, ON

Totally Bugged

I am so frustrated, irritated, annoyed!
My eyes become spinning wheels on their axles
The gardens' weeds wind wordlessly
around my frustrated feelings —
I talk under my breath
as hoarse and quiet
as the whispering wind
A significant sigh seeps out between my lips.
Ticked off.
Mom's rushing rage renews my anger all over
again,
again,
and again.
Suddenly my whole body is an enormous erupting volcano
but Mom's magical meter stick,
instantly closes any possible mourning.
Totally annoyed!

Elsie Hoover, Grade 7
Linwood Public School, ON

My Grandma

She was everything to me,
Her sweet smile was like the bright sun shining on everyone,
Even though she was only with me for a couple of years
I will always love her forever,
Sitting in an old chair singing a song,
She was a wonderful sister, grandmother, and wonderful mom,
She helped everyone who needed help,
I don't know why she had to leave my side
Because I loved her very much.

Lourdes Castro, Grade 9
Leeton Middle and High School, MO

Nobody Cares

I looked at the world, in its state of disrepair,
It occurred to me that nobody cares.
For all of our fuss, no one takes much action,
Preferring to seek their own satisfaction.
While there are those who truly do care,
I must admit that those people are rare.
The rest of the world still voice their distaste
But no one seems to help in the race.
So humanity continues on, destroying each other,
While we make the rest of the world lie and suffer.
Now the dilemma I pose might appear to be small,
But in fact, it isn't at all.
Because if we can so easily destroy one another,
Then maybe we could band and help each other,
In this quest to save our home,
It would be much better if one was not alone.
But humanity is unwilling to swallow its pride,
And instead they push this problem aside,
And I don't see how they can help when,
Saving their home isn't important to them.

Zac Hill, Grade 9
Southwest Jr High School, AR

What Did I Do?

Your voice is deep
Your belly big
Your smile is a grin
We used to get along
And now it's impossible
You eat everything
Drink everything
But you're my brother
What did I do?
To get stuck with you

Sohbat Badesha, Grade 8
Wainwright High School, AB

Two People on My Shoulder

Two people sit upon my shoulder,
Much smaller than me and you.
They are always there no matter what,
And they tell me what to do.
One tells me to do my homework,
Then go out and play.
The other is a little different;
This is what he will say.
What does your homework do for you?
You're missing out on the fun.
When your playing gets boring,
Then you can get your homework done.
One has definitely taught me a lesson.
It's as simple as night and day.
Before I do my homework,
I always go out and play.

Adam Reece, Grade 7
Fairfield Middle School, OH

R.I.P. — Sparky

Without you Sparky,
What should I do?

Go catch the bone,
That I just threw.

Please come back,
Nothing can replace you.

We'll always be friends,
And that's very true.

And now that you're gone,
I'll really miss you.

You the best dog,
I ever knew.

Sparky, Sparky where are you?
Sparky, Sparky, where are you?!

Sahiban Katari, Grade 7
Pleasantville Public School, ON

Spring Has Come

Spring,
A time of many beautiful sights.
Roses, daisies, and daffodils sprouting in a large, clear meadow,
Wind blowing in gentle breezes,
Birds singing high in a cloudless sky,
Water flowing in a tiny creek or a large river,
Trees swaying in the wind,
Sunrises and sunsets coming in a variety of mystic colors,
People chatting joyfully, no worries on their minds,
Children playing cheerfully everywhere you look,
Animals scurrying about in forests or woods,
Families spending vacations in places around the world,
All this on my mind as I wait for spring to come.
I then feel a gentle breeze blow by.
Spring has come.

Nathaniel Wisniewski, Grade 7
Linton-Stockton Jr High School, IN

See You Later

I am a girl who misses you greatly
I wonder if you're all right
I hear your sweet voice in my heart
I see that you are missed so much by the ones who loved you
I want you back!
I am a girl who misses you greatly

I pretend that I'm all right, but in reality I'm not
I feel that things will never be the same
I touch the things you left behind, like that old teddy bear you loved so much
I worry the world will forget how amazing you were
I cry my selfish tears not thinking that you're in a better place
I am a girl who misses you greatly

I understand you're gone
I say it won't be long until I'm with you once again
I dream about you every single night
I try to be strong to those around me
I hope you hear me
I am a girl who misses you greatly

Caitlin VanKoughnett, Grade 8
Wainwright High School, AB

Accepted

Why can't a person be accepted?
Why can't a person just be apart?
Why do I judge you and why do you judge me?
Why do you make fun of someone for what they wear or look like?
Why is there cool kids and not so cool kids?
Why does it matter what color our skin is?
Why does it matter how much money so and so has?
Why do these things matter we should accept a person for who they are
   and not what you think you know…
Just…why can't a person be accepted?

Emilee Byrne, Grade 9
Ottoville High School, OH

My Cousin

My baby cousin was born premature
She was very small and weighed very little
She had tubes coming out every which way
Her tiny little face told us the story.
That she didn't like it
She wanted to leave, go to home, to be with her family
She would open her tiny little blue amazing eyes
and with our own adore her and shower our love upon her.
She had visitors every day
She had love and care and hope from everyone
She was very tender and sweet
She fought and overcame the obstacle
She is now stronger and healthier
She now had no tubes to worry about
She can play with her brother
She is finally home where she belongs
Welcome home, Scarlett Rose.

Samantha Hamlin, Grade 9
LeRoy-Ostrander High School, MN

Drawing

Sure, free strokes
A distinctive style
Lighthearted and fun
Innocent but purposeful

I watch her
Effortless, original and creative
She laughs at herself
Something she draws amuses her

I smile, hoping to one day know her secret

Jhana Valentine, Grade 9
Maharishi School of the Age of Enlightenment, IA

A Soldier's Breath

When you rest down your gun
You have a split second to run
And even when you are far away
You can't enjoy the rest of the day
But you can take that breath
Unless you don't have one left.
Knowing that you have a family at home
Probably brushing their hair with a comb
Waiting to say "Hi"
But they might just say "Bye"
Cause you might not go home today
So you can't exactly say "Yay."
When the war is finished
And the men who were demolished
Now lay in the ground
Where dinosaur bones were once found
And you have to think
Who is going to write about this in ink.

David Prokupek, Grade 7
Sir Ernest MacMillan Public School, ON

My Personal Best

Bunched up in starter's position,
I desperately pray that I will not fall,
Just keeping my eyes on the track,
I barely see anything else.
The finish line ahead calls out to me.
So far away, but will I reach it.
Quick as lightning I'm ahead,
I feel good and I tell myself to push,
As I beg my body to go faster,
The question plays at the back of my mind —
Will I make it?
As I turn the corner people cheer.
Purposefully picking up the pace I see the finish line.
"Run to me" it begs.
A quick look around me,
The stadium is buzzing with excitement.
Friends are yelling encouraging words,
As I cross the finish line.
I don't care if I get first.
I don't care about people saying I was fast,
All I will ever need is with me — my feet and shoes.

Mina Shahbodaghi, Grade 7
New Albany Middle School, OH

Scared

They turn the corner as I sit there in fear
all I can ponder are their thoughts.
As they stare me down like hawks
my palms start raining with sweat,
and my scalp becomes cold.
My heart now a beating drum quickening at every step
I wish I could disappear,
like a mistake under whiteout.
Vulnerable,
terrified,
unwanted.
Loud, lashing words
cut into my barren body.
My knees shake
but all my feet can do is stay anchored to the ground
I'm the mouse to a lion's catch
what can I do?
I'm powerless.

Jenny Norris, Grade 7
Linwood Public School, ON

Sounds of the Game

Swish! The shot falls through the net
Boing, Boing! They bring the ball up the court
Clang! The shot bricks off the rim
Smack! He grabs the rebound
Bang! He slams the ball through the hoop
Whoo! The crowd goes wild

Josh Vermillion, Grade 7
Logan Hocking Middle School, OH

The Beat of the Baby's Heart

So much depends upon
The beat of the baby's heart
Forced to be born early
To keep it from stopping

Covered in stitches and scars
Caused by surgeries done
To comfort his life

Waving goodbye to the angels
Because he refuses to leave with them…
No he won't…
Not this time…
Because this time…
Ethan goes home.
Kayla Hyndman, Grade 8
Goshen Middle School, IN

Dreams

Eyes closed shut in place
As the soul drifts through a silver gate
To a made up space
Full of laughter, joy, or hate
A place you wish to stay
Or a place that you
Desperately need to get away
But then you wake up
To a dark familiar room
And your dream waits for you
Chad Loomis, Grade 8
Emmetsburg Middle School, IA

No Regrets

There was once a time
When I was complete
Whenever my heart
Always skipped a beat
You were my prince
I was your flower
We could talk and talk
For countless hours
You used to tell me
In such a carefree way
Those three little words
That are the hardest to say
It was so obvious
The way that I felt
Even when you blinked
I felt my heart melt
This may not mean much
And I know it's hard to get
But I love you so much
And I have no regrets
Pua Lee, Grade 9
Farmington High School, AR

Anger Taking Hold

The serpent tightens,
Its muscles tense.
The constricting body,
Squeezes mine.
My anger takes hold on me
And contracts.
Until the end,
When I can throw
Off the serpent,
And finally find peace.
Zack Vrana, Grade 8
Pilgrim Park Middle School, WI

What Are Stars?

A
Star
is a light
in the dark
A star is a flame of hope
in the sea of darkness
that is night.
A man might wish upon a star
A wish for anything at all…
Kevin Donoghue, Grade 8
St Peter Catholic High School, ON

Heartache

One night
you left my life,
gone forever.
You enriched my life
until you left.
You tried to battle it
now I must suffer
without you.
I miss you,
a lot.
Goodbye,
for now.
Carly Cairns, Grade 7
Weledeh Catholic School, NT

Beautiful Stranger

She is very uncommon.
She has a strange giggle.
Like a piece of silver
Dropped on the ground.
She is very beautiful.
I have never seen a stranger
Like her.
People look at her
With soft shimmering eyes.
She is a stranger.
Jacky Hong, Grade 7
Menno Simons Christian School, AB

Infinite

Every day
I look out my window
the early morning
still painted in the horizon
like a canvas not yet dry
It stretches for miles
and seconds and lifetimes
infinite.
A vast expansion
of hope.
Blue,
calm,
hope.
With serene waves;
an added reward.
How did I end up here
in this beautiful place
with this magnificent life
on this dazzling Earth
I give thanks
and start my day.
Lauren Detweiler, Grade 8
Goshen Middle School, IN

The Millipede

His legs move like the waves
in an ocean.

The soft moss beneath him
helps him find his way.

His long, black body
travels across the land.
Anthony Jesmok, Grade 8
Pilgrim Park Middle School, WI

Loving Memory

Since the day I met you,
everything has been,
from loving to break up,
from one thing to another,
from this to that…
When I walk past you,
I feel the sorrow,
I feel the sadness,
and I feel your love…
Anna Wu, Grade 8
Holden Elementary School, IL

Hamlet

Hamlet a nice guy,
But blinded by some revenge,
Got revenge but died.
Joseph Saldivar, Grade 7
Hamlin Upper Grade Center, IL

You

You never know when your time is up.
Always try and never give up.
Live life to its fullest every day.
Never stop talking if you have something to say.
When life knocks you down, get back up.
Always think water is half full in your cup.

Lindsey Dreyer, Grade 9
LeRoy-Ostrander High School, MN

Angry

You feel as if you want to scream
like a child who just got grounded
your rage is on a risky level
your hands are shaking with terror
and your eyes are like swords piercing through an enemy.
You feel negative.
You feel alone.
You feel positively pained by your own miserable self.
Your heart is like a rusty chain
dirty and forgotten.
You have withdrawn from a war
of honourable happiness and horrible hostility.
You are lost and miserable.
Guilty and disgusted.
Your stubborn stupidity has ended you.
All hope is lost.
But we are all alienated
and so we shall continue to be for all eternity.
I am guessing, that there is no turning back now.

Rebeca Costisor, Grade 7
Linwood Public School, ON

What If?

What if I wasn't born?
Would the world be different?
What if that lady never got across the street?
Would all her cats go hungry?
What if there were no clothes?
Would everyone still be ashamed?
What if there was no skin tone?
Would there still be a race?
What if everyone was blind?
Would there still be truth in what we believe?
What if people didn't have an opinion?
Would some still think highly of others?
What if there was no school?
Would some still think they're geniuses?
What if there were no standards?
Would everyone be the same?
What if there was no one reading this poem?
Would my words still have meaning?
What if I wasn't born?
Would the world still be the same?

Sheanisse Hughes, Grade 9
Gwendolyn Brooks College Preparatory Academy, IL

Kindness

Pick up the pencil
your neighbor has dropped.
Give support when others have stopped.
Food is a blessing
to those in need,
nothing brings joy like doing a good deed.
When you see someone struggling,
help them out,
because seeing someone smile is what it's all about.
Generosity is like a boomerang,
it always comes back to you.
So caring is what you need to do.
So no matter how big,
no matter how small,
a little help says it all.

Eric Poycker, Grade 8
Stephen Mack Middle School, IL

That's What Makes a Best Friend

Sharing memories there's a million and one
The fun times are never done.
Parties, boys, and the always-late nights
Sleepovers, summer days, and don't forget the fights.

Yelling and screaming over the phone
A soft cry that turns into a moan
No one wants to apologize, but in the end it turns out right
And once again our friendship ignites.

Summer days that bright up our year
A new school year, no need to fear.
We'll be together through it all
Everything means big and small.

Bringing laughs into my pool of pain
You comfort me and there's no need to explain
When you're sad my arms extend
And that's what makes a best friend.

Carly Stewart, Grade 7
Highland Middle School, IL

Martin Luther King

Martin Luther King was a strong black American
He tried to put the whites and black back together
And live life free for everybody
He did it in four words "I have a dream"
He marched with the people that believed in him
All just to stop the racism
He marched for hours he marched for a day
He didn't even care who got in his way
We should all love and worship Martin Luther King
'Cause the day he died he had a great dream
Martin Luther King was strong about his speech
Only thing I can say is REST IN PEACE!

Tommaneka Rashay Wallace, Grade 9
Andover High School, MN

Alone

You see that girl,
She sits alone,
She cries alone,
You walk by her,
You say "Pathetic"

We all start out alone,
Full of nothingness,
And sorrow
We ask ourselves these questions,
Why am I different?
Why am I an exile?

We cry and cry,
It never ends,
It rips you apart,
Judgmental remarks,
They make us cry

They say "Pathetic,"
But they know nothing,
Before you laugh,
Before you point,
Just remember you were alone too.

Madison Klein, Grade 7
New Albany Middle School, OH

Ice Cream

I will never leave you
I will always lick you
I like it when you melt in my mouth
You taste so sweet
You make me jealous
You always put a smile on my face
You're colourful like a rainbow
I love you ice cream.

Annriza Enerio, Grade 7
Weledeh Catholic School, NT

Perfect Setting

I see sparkling water
I smell wet sand
I hear seagulls
I feel wonderful
I taste salty air
I think it is perfect

Robert Stone, Grade 8
Wainwright High School, AB

Spring

Spring
The sun, the flowers
The sweet sound of chirping birds
Spring is really here!

Brittanie Chludzinski, Grade 7
Algonquin Middle School, MI

War

I really hate war, why does it have to happen?
The children suffer. Everyone suffers, just for a cause;
can't you just take a moment and pause?
War destroys everything, from houses to lives,
if the guns are taken away, then people fight with knives.
War is like a disease, going through the ages,
children and women all get locked up in cages.
War is a killer taking lives without a thought
People don't realize what they have wrought
The gun goes "bang!" and the jet goes "whoosh!"
Tanks just step on you till you turn to mush.
People lose their arms and legs just to get out of harm's way,
all the dead people are left to decay, and still living people hide night and day.
War has wrought what God has wished not.
While the children lay dead on the ground,
their mothers mourn without a sound.
War is as dangerous as a tiger ready to kill without mercy
and the prey won't have a chance to flee.
I really hate war, why does it have to happen? Children suffer.
Everyone suffers, just for a cause;
can't you just take a moment and pause?

Simon Lim, Grade 8
Beverley Heights Middle School, ON

Never

Once again losing life never gaining, nothing ever true always lies.
Like a bottomless pit, things dropped in never to be seen again.
Thoughts of love, but lost to the pit, attempts for actions but also, lost.
Letters written but still laying on the floor, gifts bought but never given.
Forced to stay at the pulling pit never to understand the unique.
Never to feel the unusual. Clothes lost to the pit and dates never met.
Dances never danced, trapped in the pit never to escape from my lowly hole.
The only time I did live was to see death.

Sara Shafer, Grade 7
Knoxville Middle School, IA

Ecstatic

Fizzing with excitement I act all jumpy!
I squeal like a pig running from the Christmas' butcher!
My anticipation bubbles over. I need to meet her!
My feelings are scattered by my exhilaration
I fantasize my vivacious, vibrant voyage of jubilant bliss with her.
Like a leaf lingering down, I wander throughout the house.
They're still at the hospital!
Why do they get more time with her?
She's my sister too!
As swiftly as possible, my dad drives me to see her.
My new baby sister, I cuddle her close,
I am way too ecstatic to let go.
I absorb our moment,
as my mom takes her away
My heart pounds like a tasseled drum.
Craving our next meeting.
Driving home with my family I know I'm ecstatic.

Brianna Bowman, Grade 7
Linwood Public School, ON

If I Were...

If I were in a story,
I wonder...
Would I be the brave heroine who saves the day
Or the meek companion who guides her way?
If I were in a tale,
I wonder...
Would I be a pretty sight
Or a monster who causes fright?
If I were in a novel,
I wonder...
Would I be the shining star
Or the character they pity from afar?
If I were in a book,
I wonder...
Would I be a high and noble lady
Or the ringleader of something shady?

Cayla Etter, Grade 7
Hadley E Watts Middle School, OH

I Don't Remember

I don't remember having feelings of joy.
The pleasure of achievement, the pride of triumph.
I don't remember what it feels like for someone to be kind.
For someone to thank me, to be polite.
I don't remember what it feels like to be appreciated.
To be treated as an equal.
I don't remember ever being loved.
To be held with soft hands, to be kissed on the cheek.
I don't remember what it feels like to have some freedom.
I feel the pain of slavery on my shoulders.
I don't remember when my hunger was satisfied.
The shelves are filled, but beyond my reach.
I don't remember belonging to someone.
Billions of people, but no one for me.
I don't remember how to live life anymore.
Why they believe there is a reason to live.
I don't remember.

Farah Khan, Grade 7
Islamic Foundation School, ON

Girl World

Gossip, rumors, and lies
There's always one girl you despise
As you walk down the hallway people stare
But do they really care
It's just you against the world
Who really knows who you are?
Not even knowing your place
Picking out that perfect outfit
Will they notice?
Is today your big break?
You hear them whisper
But why should you care
Just be you because they don't deserve you as a friend

Emily Hake, Grade 7
New Albany Middle School, OH

Dare to Dream

Dare to dream of never losing a game,
Dream of playing college ball.
Dreaming of the perfect aim,
Dreaming that you will never fall.

Training to become faster,
Putting your heart and soul into focus.
Your coach seems like your big sister,
Yelling and cheering, it almost sounds like a circus.

Thinking that the net isn't there,
All the players on this side are my team.
Jumping, spiking in the air,
While the team is building up steam.

Dare to dream of beating out all the rest.
Dare to dream of being the best.

Lauren Hickson, Grade 7
Bristol Elementary School, WI

Words

The people say that rain falls out of the sky
But tonight it pours from my eyes
Some say it's foolish to cry
But I know everyone cries inside
You always get mad at me for the smallest of things
You cause me pain, not by action but by word
It's said that sticks and stones may break my bones
But words will never hurt me, and I say that's wrong
Words can be a curse
Words can be a blessing
Words can build a nation as high as the stars
Words can strike it down like lightning in a violent storm
Our words define who we are
Don't let the next words you say
Be the last ones you say
To someone you love
Words can be a curse
Words can be a blessing
Words can build a nation as high as the stars
Words can strike it down like lightning in a violent storm
Words mean everything

Fallon Wright, Grade 9
Southwest Jr High School, AR

Tree Stump

Gravestone of what used to stand
Slain by a jagged hand
Scars run deep
Rings capture time
Layers added line after line
New life; the wreckage past
Translucent petals bury the corpse at last

Dodie Paige Thiel, Grade 9
Maharishi School of the Age of Enlightenment, IA

I Am From

I am from popsicles that melt and make my fingers sticky. From French braids and pigtails with long, pink ribbons. I am form summers finding sand dollars at Saint Simon's Island and bicycles that have sparkly streamers. From playing with Polly Pockets and watching *Out of the Box* every morning.

I am from visiting the waters where Nessie the Lochness Monster lives and making the British guards laugh. From boring ballet classes, broken legs, and being levitated at magic shows in Vegas. I am from singing "Super Alley" in the subway and watching my dad's soccer games.

I am from dogs that watch *Peter Pan* with me and eating Miss Tish's peanut butter cookies. From silver lockets and playing with the hats form Nana's hat shop. I am from running down the hill in my backyard to meet Daddy on number eight on the golf course.

I am from blue fish named Goldy, Girl Scouts and thirteen hour drives to Florida. From "calm down girls and stop screaming!" and "patience is a virtue." From tumbling classes and tennis lessons. I am from being a lefty, growing up, and having fun.

Brittany Mayo, Grade 7
New Albany Middle School, OH

The Snow Keeps Falling

I can hear the whistles blowing and all around it keeps on snowing.
It's like an eternal rain, bringing more hurt and pain.
I see the sadness all around, feeling my head and heart pound.
Most people go in for morning showers and will never come out for the rest of their hours.
They use this thing called Zyklon B. I just hope they don't use it on me.
When do we get out? No one can know. We just hope not to be part of the snow.
The others around me are just like ghosts, remembering the things that they miss most.
The fire is roaring louder than ever. Will we be free? Most say never.
I taste the smoke and smell the fire. We are trapped in all this wire.
I hear the screams and see people dying. I taste the tears and see people crying.
I hate the taste of the moldy bread. With the pain I feel, I'd rather be dead.
I can still smell the fire and I can see the flames rising up higher.
This camp is just like a grave and everyone here is just its slave.
There is a smell of fear from the Nazis to everyone here.
They are worried about what they have heard. Keeping this secret is not easy as preferred.
The Allies' canon comes with a bang as the bells of freedom rang.
I am now afraid of what will happen to me. Why am I afraid now that I am free?

Haley Roehm, Grade 8
Parkway Middle School, OH

Abortion Is a Crime

Abortion is a crime and you're taking your child's lifetime
So think about it first and don't make the mistake this ain't a lie this ain't fake
Don't let him die, open up your heart and don't tell him "no" because it's so great to see them grow
So I beg you please don't let him die because someday that child might fly
Don't make that error because it can turn into a terror
Don't let him die because you haven't seen his face yet
Don't let him die because he hasn't felt warmth yet
Don't let him die because you haven't met him yet
Why are you doing this, he needs to know why don't you give him a chance to grow
You were the one that made the mistake letting your passion go wild (is his life easy to take?)
Abortion is like shooting someone on the street abortion is like throwing a dead body on a creek
Your child cries boo hoo and when you find the error you did you'll cry too
If you keep him then you are strong for if you murder him his life won't be long
Then you can't teach him the lessons that brought him along
Abortion is a crime!

Walter Argueta, Grade 8
Beverley Heights Middle School, ON

Last Day of School

Here it is; it's finally here.
We've been waiting for this all year.
Students are edgy, waiting for it to come.
They are waiting to get out and have fun.
The suspense in the air is a weight in the room.
It is hot and stuffy in their classroom.
RING! RING! RING!
At last it has come!
The great golden sun lifts its huge flaming head
To listen to the long awaited toll of that most beloved bell.
Cheers ring out
'Round the world today.
They run out
Breathing in the fresh, summer air.
No more cares, no more worries;
They are free!
The first day of summer
Is finally here!

Ryan Grant, Grade 8
Holy Savior Menard Central High School, LA

I Am From…

I am from the country that has suffered,
but the citizens are rebuilding hope.
I am from the pearly, saltwater ocean,
always warm and overflowing with tanned locals.

I am from the land of only two seasons,
with the monsoon that brings rain to flood houses
and summer that welcomes flocks of tourists.
I am from wise, experienced grandparents,
who never shy away from God in times of trouble.

I am from clever, unpredictable sisters,
who are just plain old fun and laughter.
I am from a generous mother and stepfather,
very relaxed and trusting.

I am from an overachieving school,
where students are free and one of a kind.
I am from bedtime prayers to God,
He is one of my connections to my father.
I am from novel ideas,
The Lord inspires me to think passionately.

Nha Ly, Grade 8
Weledeh Catholic School, NT

A Boy Named Zach

A boy named Zach played basketball every day
He loved to shoot each and every way
Zach shot the ball
At the hoop on the wall
And soon could make each shot every time he would play

Zach Roose, Grade 7
Trinity Lutheran School, MI

Soldier

I fight to protect and never forget,
what fears I met on that warm winter night.

The booms and bangs that never really end,
the pain of others,
and the antagonizing fear,
that we all know will never end.

This is our job as soldiers,
to fight not only for our lives,
but for all the people of America.

If we were not here,
all of our families, friends, and people never met,
would all be dead.

This is why I fight to protect and never forget,
what I saw on that warm winter night.

Samuel De Cero, Grade 7
St John the Baptist Elementary School, IN

Ode to the Chalk

Ode to chalk moving and hitting
Against your old buddy chalkboard.
Always fighting with chalkboard
Hitting and scratching it and sometimes
Breaking your point for hitting it so much.
Students use you to write their names on the board
But teacher uses you to write information down.
But I'll remember you as a great warrior
Trying to destroy your foe the chalkboard.

Christopher Avalos, Grade 7
Hamlin Upper Grade Center, IL

The Bat Not Taken*

Two bats hanging on a spinning rack,
And sorry I could not buy both,
And be one shopper. Long I stood
And practice swung as long as I could.
But bought the other as just as good,
And having perhaps the better claim,
Because it was longer and easier to swing.
Though as for swinging them,
They really were the same.
And both that morning equally long,
I took the first for another day!
Yet knowing how way leads to way,
I doubted if I shall ever come back
I shall be telling this with just a sigh.
Somewhere ages and ages hence.
Two bats hanging on a rack,
And I took the one that didn't look cool.
And that has made all the difference.

Ryan Cassell, Grade 7
Hamlin Upper Grade Center, IL
*Based on "The Road Not Taken" by Robert Frost.

Grass Meets Lawn Mower

My luscious lawn,
So fresh, so green.
You will soon meet the jaws
Of a frightful machine.

You proudly reach up,
To touch the sky
But you must be cut down,
At this, I cry!

The mower has come,
It whirs, whines, and cuts.
With shiny metal blades
And wheels that leave ruts.

Right now you feel angry,
Man is so vain!
But don't worry, you'll see,
You will grow tall again.

Kelly Johnson, Grade 9
Hazelwood West Jr-Sr High School, MO

Wintertime

I always liked winter
Best
You can drink hot chocolate
By the fire
And eat roasted marshmallows
And drink cider
And homemade gumbo and soup
At the campgrounds
With friends
And listen to
Country music by the fire
In the morning
And standing
Out in the sun
Fishing
And never getting
Overheated
And at least being able to sit back
By the fire
Late at night
To keep warm

Dylan Hammond, Grade 9
Runnels School, LA

Race to the Goal

Soccer is like racing down a speedway
Your heart races faster and faster
When you kick the ball it feels like
An engine roaring
When I shoot a goal
It's like getting a checkered flag.

Brianna Barth, Grade 8
Edison Middle School, WI

My Dad

My dad is like my hero. He can pick me up when I am down.
He will listen and show how much he cares.
He knows that I have made mistakes, but he tells me that's all right
And don't worry about little things.

And as I have been growing up, he has stood patiently behind me,
And when I needed him, he was right there beside me.
I know someday that I will have to spread my wings and fly,
And when I get in hard times, I will be fine.

I know that I have made him upset by many things,
And by saying those hurtful things.
I hope you know I don't mean those things.
Thank you Dad for supporting me in the choices that I have made.

Brittany Eastvold, Grade 9
LeRoy-Ostrander High School, MN

The Summit

Celestial clouds reaching to infinity and beyond,
the mountaintops, overflowing in an aura of majesty.

The howling wind, a quiet drone whispering with the wilderness,
softly fades into a spellbinding silence.

The light breeze bears the aroma of the good outdoors,
soft pines illuminate the senses with Mother Nature's perfume.

My ski poles, the scepters that authorize my reign over the world,
crunch through fresh snow.

The empowerment of a god rushes through my veins.

Cassidy Green, Grade 9
Southwest Jr High School, AR

The Magnificent Morning Glory

Oh! the morning glory, he blooms in the morning,
He retreats in the evening, but is always beautiful.

He loves the sun, and the rain,
But he hates the snow, and the cold.

He's open, he's closed, he dances with the breeze,
He sprouts, he dies, and he does it with ease.

As I watch him, with pure astonishment,
I begin to think, how he does it all.

For spring turns to summer, and summer rolls into fall,
With darkness creeping, closer and closer.

The morning glory is no more, replaced by cold, hard, ice,
But he will be back again, to put on his spectacular performance.

Danielle Rodrigues, Grade 7
Nativity of Our Lord Catholic School, ON

Moment

Laying on the warm sand,
Admiring the stars above.

I look back in amazement,
As my eyes stumble upon the Big Dipper.

The way this moment is shared with others.

Laying on the cold grass,
Admiring the stars above.

I look back in amazement,
As my mind wonders…

Are we sharing the same moment?

Shelby Downing, Grade 8
Goshen Middle School, IN

Ways to Drive Elizabeth Crazy

Untie my bows
Poke my tummy; I may giggle
Barge into my room; I scream and shout
Rearrange my magnets
Push me into a puddle; I may be befuddled
Mess up my room; I'll give you a broom
There may be many more but all I ask is for my sister
To knock on my door

Elizabeth Eversole, Grade 7
St Monica School, IN

Storm's Insight

I am outside on a sunny day
when I hear my sister scuffling on the front porch.
I suddenly see an ominous black cloud on the horizon
that is growing by the minute.
I head to the porch to see what she knows.
"We're under a severe thunderstorm warning!" she exclaims.
So I head into the house to watch the weather reports.

The house is darkening and the sky is going blue-green.
Suddenly it starts to rain, and as I am looking out the window,
I see a bright flash of light followed by a loud "CRAACK."
That makes everyone even more excited.

My mom and sister are outside
taking pictures of the storm.
The rain is coming down harder,
the thunder and lightning are closing in,
my house is darker and my sister is freaking out.

It suddenly clears up.
The rain subsides and the thunder and lightning grow faint.
The sky is still dark but I know it is over with…
for now.

Elizabeth Fredrickson, Grade 9
Central Montcalm High School, MI

Cottage Night Sounds

At night I hear this music in my ear.
Nature's orchestra has begun to play.
A symphony of sounds from far and near.
Lost to our senses in the din of day.

The haunting calls in the dark from the loon.
Echo across the lake like an oboe.
The eerie hoots of the owl 'neath the moon.
Like a bow on the strings of a cello

With a gentle percussion that wings beat.
Waves like a thousand tongues lap the shoreline.
Bugs click-clack like castanets at my feet.
Hear the lullabies of whispering pines.

This mosaic of night sounds bring deep sleep.
Memories of them in my heart I keep.

Daniel Cropley, Grade 7
Nativity of Our Lord Catholic School, ON

I Am

Morgan Elizabeth Hanthorn
I am energetic and fun to hang around.
I wonder if people are thinking of me right now.
I hear the laughter of my friends and I goofing around.
I see the smile on people's faces, and I smile back.
I desire people to get along and be friends.
I am energetic and fun to hang around.

I pretend I don't hear mean things people say.
I feel I can change how I treat other people.
I worry that people don't like me for who I really am.
I cry when people start rumors that aren't true.
I am energetic and fun to hang around.

I understand why people make fun of other people
I say "Who can stop them?"
I dream people will love and the world will come to peace.
I try to make the difference.
I hope everyone can just be friends no matter what.
I am energetic and fun to hang around.

Morgan Elizabeth Hanthorn, Grade 8
Otsego Middle School, OH

An Ode to Dogs

Dogs, always there for you
Always faithful, always true
Forever, always loving you

Dogs always know when to care
Always knowing you are there
Greeting you with the love you share

When you're sad they come to you
Letting you know they're there for you through and through
Dogs are always there for you

Samantha Banaszak, Grade 7
Trinity Lutheran School, MI

Yellow "Rugrats" Blanket

So much depends upon
my yellow *Rugrats* blanket

Long and warm
folded on my bed
with the characters
playing on a slide
my yellow *Rugrats* blanket

There to remind me
that my daddy loves me
my yellow *Rugrats* blanket

That blanket my daddy bought me
when he left to Mexico
my yellow *Rugrats* blanket

There to keep me warm
when my daddy isn't there
my yellow *Rugrats* blanket

The one with my favorite show
when I was little
my yellow *Rugrats* blanket

Ana Rosa Marin, Grade 8
Goshen Middle School, IN

Spring

Springtime is great
In 2008
And is filled with fun
Out in the sun
The flowers are out and smelling sweet
Like raspberries you'd love to eat
There's always time for shopping
Just come and get it popping
Springtime is here and looking great
Let's get out and celebrate

Ashunti Coleman, Grade 7
Magnate Academy School, LA

Spring

Today's the day the flowers
Trees and plants regrow
The time of year the weather is luxurious
Spring is like a sunset
That always looks beautiful
Green, pink, yellow
So many colors of spring
The blue sky full of birds
When the animals come
Out from hibernation
Babies are born
Spring is the rebirth of Mother Earth

Melanie Harper, Grade 7
Paw Paw Middle School, MI

Pretty Face

You don't know what it's like to break a pretty face with runny mascara eyes.
You're not the one facing it like I am through the mirror.
If you adjust it just right in the light you can clearly see agony flush the cheeks
instead of blushing bright pink.
This is the time when you don't see a pretty face break
since it refuses to drop a hint of sorrow from the flashing silver lining eyes.
You'll never understand the coal black tears streaking the cheeks like war paint.
This pretty face had been stricken with puppy love while you possibly didn't,
uncertain if you honestly did adore such a pretty face.
It seemed like a trick upon the heart.

Kristyn Childers, Grade 9
Tippecanoe Valley High School, IN

Death and Survival

I remember these images as if it was yesterday
Smoke mixing with the clouds from burning pits full of bodies
People being dragged to the pits or standing in line to meet death
Soldiers shooting their guns and laughing like they were mad
People falling to their knees, dead before they hit the ground
This is the Holocaust
I remember the guards dragging dead bodies to burning pits
People being shot because they had to use the restroom
I recall having to sleep with five older men at night
Captain's orders being passed to their squadrons
The trees waving at us as if saying goodbye
As I get closer to the branches, a heavy cloud of gunpowder hangs in the air
As I walk past the guards, boxes of white bread and meaty soup can be seen
We walk past the "burial grounds" and instantly throw up because of decay
I hid for awhile in the back of a warehouse
All of a sudden, a guard crumples over, holding his chest
The people who were once scared, now take the offensive
Shots are fired everywhere
People were famished, looking very aggressive and mean
I remember the memory of the white flag when it was raised in surrender
We were saved

Kean Butler, Grade 8
Parkway Middle School, OH

One Less

If there was one less bullet, and one less gun
There could be one less terrorist, and one more nun
If there was one less minute with the moon, and one more with the sun
One less moment of terror, and one more of fun
Only if we knew the power of One
If there was one less death
One less tear, there could be one more breath
One less bad, one more change
One less city, one more range
One less racist, one more King
One less death the news will bring
One less person depressed
One less person trying to rule the rest
One less thing to get off my chest
Only if there was One less

Cullen Lyons, Grade 8
Oak View Middle School, MN

A Mother's Love

You are there through the good times and the bad
Although, you my not wear the latest fad
You are my best friend
and I'll love you until the very end

You always lend me a helping hand
I tend to make you listen to my favourite band
You always kiss my booboo's away
and you are there for me each and every day

When I look into your eyes
My love for you never dies
Your love and beauty is all I can see
and I know you will always be there for me

Have a great Mother's Day
A perfect mother you do portray
I want you to know, I miss you when we are apart
and that I love you with all of my heart

Stephanie Pacheco, Grade 8
Villa Maria High School, QC

I Am From

I am from the back land,
where the bugs are everywhere.

I am from the snowy ground,
where Skidoos hurdle over snow.

I am from the Mackenzie River,
where you see kids leaping into the river.

I am from the ski hill,
where kids explode with excitement while sliding.

I am from an island,
where people are entertained by our stories.

I am from the ginormous house,
where you can enjoy dinner with eighteen friends.

I am from a loved island,
where everyone is welcome.

Victoria Nirlungayuk, Grade 8
Weledeh Catholic School, NT

Loneliness

Loneliness is gray
It sounds like rain against a window pane
It smells like an autumn breeze
It tastes like ice
It looks like an unlit house
Loneliness feels like there is nothing to gain

Hayley Davis, Grade 8
Taft Middle School, IA

Where I'm From

I am from screams,
From yelling and hollering.
I am from the screeching of tires.
I am from the manual labor
Hands on fixing and do it myself.

I'm from mac and cheese,
From fruit salad and back porches.
I'm from sprinters to turtle walkers
And the All-Americans,
From stovetops to backyard grills
I'm from they saved me with their wishes
And savor their kisses
To telling me what to do I don't care about you.

I'm from throttle twisters
To bike mechanics
I'm from safety hazards to loose cannons
To elbow pads and training wheels
I'm from campfires to cold winter nights.

Justin Hill, Grade 8
Little Miami Jr High School, OH

Nervous

Oh! Here come the butterflies bouncing through my body
My eyes are burning like a blazing fire
Uneasy
Unnatural
Unrelaxed
As restless as the leaves blowing in the wind
The stiff, strained feeling is holding on tight
Jittery
Jumpy body
My hands are sweaty and looking for something to do
As worried as a mouse with a narrow escape from a cat

Salinda Martin, Grade 7
Linwood Public School, ON

If

If you can be kind,
And help your friends through hard times.
If you can be truthful to a friend,
By keeping their secret.

If you can give
To those who need it most.
If you can help others,
Like a boy finding his dog.

If you can be thankful
For what you have been given.
If you can do the right thing,
When no one is watching.
Then you will be successful

Corey Mulvey, Grade 7
New Albany Middle School, OH

The Fly

Sitting here at the table
Concentration am not able.
This constant buzz about my head
This pesky fly, I wish were dead.
I study for a graded test
I really want to do my best.
With jerky flight and then it lands
I missed again with swat of hand.
My next swing, it was lame
It missed its mark and was off aim.
This constant buzzing is causing pain.
Concentration NO, I'll go insane.
I can't believe it's on my book
I roll my eyes with a dirty look
With one last swat, one last swing,
I smiled for victory now it brings!
This victory does not seem so sweet
Sudden quietness is no treat.
I miss that buzzing I miss that sound
I miss that little bugger around.

Blake Biederstedt, Grade 8
Napoleon Middle School, OH

Barking Mark

There once was a dog name Mark,
Very loudly, he liked to bark,
Sitting all day,
Barking away,
Until he went to the park.

Megan Russell, Grade 7
Buckeye Valley Middle School, OH

Invisible

Walking so slow as
They walk right by
Staring as though
I wasn't even there
Hoping people don't talk
As they walk by
I think…I am invisible
I see myself
As the way I am
How do they see me?
Do I even matter?
Am I, is the question
Am I invisible?

Hayley Anderson, Grade 9
Cannon Falls Sr High School, MN

Tests

Stressful, intense
Nerve-racking, intimidating, nail-biting
A student's worst nightmare
Devastation

Andres Moncebaiz, Grade 7
St Gerald Elementary School, IL

Fear

Fear is the color of a dark cold night that cast a shadow over the land;
It sounds like fierce wind whipping through an abandoned house
And tastes like stale dry bread.
Smells like sweat;
Looks like a breathtaking roller coaster.
It makes me feel nervous.

Fear is the color of a pitch black room with no lights;
It sounds like a howling madman laughing
And tastes like cotton.
Smells like a small enclosure;
Looks like a mad gothic clown.
It makes me feel isolated.

Fear is the color of a gloomy, dark morning;
It sounds like a twig tapping the glass window
It tastes like tears that roll down your face.
And smells like a dusty scary book.
Fear makes me feel afraid.

Fear is the separation between reality and imagining.

Courtney Curran, Grade 8
Little Miami Jr High School, OH

Tanzanian Children

There they stand at the gate,
We look at them with such hate,
It's not their fault they have a disease,
We should treat them as they please,
If some people would just take the time,
To maybe talk to them or get to know them, it's not a crime,
They really do love it and we should care,
They are just like us, and how they're treated, it's not really fair,
Everybody always thinks that they need more,
But they are so happy with what they have, even though they are poor,
If people would stop caring about only their clothes and purse,
I believe we could really make a change in this universe.

Aarika Spalding, Grade 8
Kewaskum Middle School, WI

Successful

If you can go back for more, if you keep losing,
If you can keep going, even if your body says to stop,
If you can ignore what other people think of you,
If you could accept the truth in what you don't believe,
If you can have the will power to push yourself beyond what you've done before,

If you can help a friend when they need someone,
If you can hold back a smile just to please your friend for a little while,
If you can look back at your past and say that you would do it all over again,
You would be confident, great role model for your kids and family,
And not to mention, you would feel great about yourself.

Brandon Nixon, Grade 7
New Albany Middle School, OH

Former Best Friend

Today I sit here at my desk.
Jumbled thoughts all in my head.
  She says now she wants to be friends.
But that bond came to an end.
  She's got her friends and I've got mine.
Not to worry she'll be just fine.
  She looks over here and gives a smile.
I give one back, but it takes a while.
  If only she had known how much it had hurt.
Then she would be sorry and feel even worse.
  Now I know what I must do.
Forgive her and be friends with you.
  Now I sit here at my desk.
The jumbled thoughts, now a mess.
  She ropes me in and I can't get out.
I pull away and scream and shout.
  I want to be her friend, but at the same time I don't.
I will NEVER go back, no, no, I won't!
  Now this story comes to an end.
Just like my bond with my former best friend.

Rachel Pittman, Grade 8
Vivian Elementary/Middle School, LA

Forever and Always

My boyfriend's a dork, but a cute one at that.
His eyes have depth like the deep blue sea,
That I get lost in as I gaze for a while you'll see.
He dances like a goof,
I even have proof,
but he's better when he's a goof
which I love to see
because there's so much more that you don't see.
That's why he's special and perfect in every single way.
I love him, I love him and that will never change!
Because we're forever and always
and he's here to stay.
In my heart he'll stay forever and always.
and I think that's beautiful in so many different ways!

Elena Parker, Grade 9
William Kelley High and Elementary School, MN

The Dream

We daze on summer nights,
  Thinking of all the times,
Wishful thinking here and there,
  Never-ending memories to share,
  Morning and evening,
  With evening the best
Amazing thoughts come through your head,
There are some good, and some bad,
  Good brings great joy,
  Waking up is a fear,
  Remembering…
  The tremendous dream!

Morgan Thompson, Grade 8
Little Miami Jr High School, OH

Love

Love is red
It sounds like wedding bells
It feels like hugs and kisses
It smells like roses
It tastes like chocolate covered strawberries
It looks like one big happy family

Shannon Love, Grade 7
Algonquin Middle School, MI

Concerto

I reached out and grabbed the beast by the neck,
And grabbed my bow and applied some rosin.
It locked onto the string and played a chord.
I felt the vibrations like a rumbling train.

As my fingers fly, I can imagine Mark O'Connor
Playing in his Bluegrass Trio
And the syncopation and accents of the sound,
I can imagine myself beating the devil, just like in the song.

Then I slow it down a notch to something more baroque style.
I can see Vivaldi's bright, red hair shaking his head no
I know the bottom half of the chord was flat.
I try again, for I am as stubborn as a mule.

Brahms, Bach, and Beethoven would be proud,
But Mozart still is my musical idol
I have to keep practicing
So I can be able to perform to my highest.

David Stanislav, Grade 7
New Albany Middle School, OH

Clay

A nondescript lump transforms
  Into the classic snake.
  It squirms, and slithers,
    But then —
    Silence.
  Frozen in place,
    It's a pretzel,
    Ready to bake.
Oh, the sweet, doughy aroma,
  The large crystals of salt,
  What a tantalizing treat!
    But wait.
    Wrong color.
The green mass is squashed,
Returned to its former state.
  Lumpy, lackluster clay
  Is all that remains,
Complete with all of its endless possibilities
  Ready to be imagined away.

Jennifer Chuang, Grade 9
Troy High School, MI

Where I'm From

I'm from the barn, the sweet smell of hay and the soft nicker of horses.
I am from the soft, squishy mud outside in the tree covered backyard.
The crystal clear creek waters on a bright, warm, sunny day;
The sound of logs splitting and the lawnmower being driven up the hilly yard by me.
I'm from the tractor spinning its huge back tires trying to get through all the mud.
Building forts with blankets on a dark, stormy day.
I'm from the steak cooking on an open fire wishing that was how life is.
I'm from that sweet smell of alfalfa cubes and gentle touch of lips taking it off your hand.
I'm from the drama, lies, and tears of all these teenage years.
The fresh-cut grass and my green bare feet.
I'm from walking around barefoot on the grass, dirt, and gravel.
I'm from "Goodbye winter, hello summer and all of your memories!"

Hayley Brown, Grade 8
Little Miami Jr High School, OH

Afraid

I was an outsider when I came to my new school.
I was like a blackbird away from my flock.
I missed my old friends, my old school, my old teachers.
And I was scared. It was harder and harder to breathe, to smell,
or to hear anything other than my heart beating as I approached the school…My mom
whispered, "everything would be all right." But I didn't believe her;
I was in tears. *I was an outsider*
The first day of school, I stood alone,
staring at the big brick wall, 8:00 sharp.
The students were all bright-faced, smiling to meet me.
Yet I was like an unwound watch, waiting to go home, nervous.
I was an outsider
"Hi, come over here." Two guys were especially kind to me!
I felt happy melting into my surroundings for the first time, "Why don't you sit with us?"
That day, I made friends.
Now that I have friends, I look back over the three years, surrounded by many friends.
And now I can say without pain or fear:
I was an outsider
Different in many ways,
But not anymore.

Ryan Geoppinger, Grade 7
Stanley Clark School, IN

Utopia/Dystopia

Utopia

Where everyone is united and no one is left outside.

Where everything is perfect, all ducks are in a row.

Here, all the people grow and love and everywhere is sunny.

In this world everything is great and no one has to pay.

Living in a world that's perfect must be a dream come true.

I think there is where you want to be.

Dystopia

Where everything is chaos and all just want to hide.

Where all are dazed and confused and life is very low.

Here, all people hate and die and it's all about money.

Is this any place for young children to play?

For them the hating hurting, it's all that they can do.

Not over here screaming to be free.

Chris Perry, Grade 8
Otsego Middle School, OH

Broken

'Cause I'm so sick of making the same wrong,
Saying I'll stay strong, saying I'll move on.
I'm ready to put my words to work,
'Cause I'm sick of all the hurt,
Ending up with a face full of dirt.
Knuckles bloody ready, with a mind so cold,
And a heart so dead,
But then with a soul so bold.
I'm not going to give in no more,
I'm not going to fold,
I'm closing the door.
So much anger, it's just a whole load.
Tired of the restless nights, and the painful games.
I just wanted to be in sight,
And for you to remember my name.
Carve it on your arm, or tat it on your heart,
I'd tat it on mine, but it's broken apart.
You were the glue,
And you were the tape.
How did something so true,
Just have to break?

Jason Tang, Grade 8
North Kirkwood Middle School, MO

A Sea Called Stress

N ever ever leaving
A t a stormy sea
T he waves crash down
H arder, harder, harder than ever
A t a chaotic, stormy sea
N ever ever can I seem to leave this abyss of stress

H ow I really wish I could
O ver and
O ver the waves crash down harder!
D own in my little boat in a stormy, chaotic, wave filled sea

Nathan Hood, Grade 7
New Albany Middle School, OH

Crushes and Love

Crushes, we all have them
At some point in life.
Whether it be at twelve
Or forty years old if you like.
Crushes, what a hurtful thing
We all have felt that kind of pain.

Love, we see the definition.
You will find you have an intense affection.
Love, it does cause real problems.
For we all at sometimes feel solemn.

Love and crushes, they can be compared.
Love and crushes, they have no affair.
Love and crushes, they aren't alike.
Love and crushes, just sit tight for a rollercoaster ride,

Michelle Byers, Grade 7
Brittany Hill Middle School, MO

A Light

The feeling of sadness,
Runs through your veins,
Swelling your heart,
Eating away at your soul.
The very reason of this emotion,
Becomes lost inside yourself.
Your doubt in justice,
Or your lack of forgiveness,
Overwhelms you.
And ends up together in the pit of your stomach.
Sometimes so much gathers,
That it is too painful to keep it all down.
Why go through the pain,
When all you need is a touch.
A touch of light in a dark room,
A touch of freedom in a locked cage,
And a touch from someone who cares about you
Telling you it's okay.
Okay to forgive and okay to forget,
Okay to live life and cherish what you have
And not dwell on what you don't.

Meghan Jayes, Grade 7
New Albany Middle School, OH

Snowmobiling

When I go snowmobiling,
I enjoy spending time with my dad and brother.
The fresh cold air smells clean,
and it bites at any skin left exposed.
My orange Arctic Cat Firecat 700,
which is outrageously fast.
The big brown whitetail deer,
running and jumping in front of us in the fields.
The fast feeling I get when I take a fast sweeping corner.
The smell of gas and oil burning makes me happy.
Snow dust pelts on my helmet's shield.
Stopping at gas stations for gas,
and a Little Debbie Star Crunch.
These are the things I think about,
going snowmobiling.

Chase Kriewaldt, Grade 9
Clintonville High School, WI

Golden Opportunity

This is my golden opportunity
To help them see
All the great things they miss
When they smoke weed
I am not here to pretend
This is so important on a level you can't comprehend
That stuff you been doing isn't helping you
It is just one stupid thing to do
Live above the influence I encourage you
Live above weed

Amy Schnupp, Grade 7
BOSS Buckeye On-Line School for Success, OH

Save the Wetlands

Wetland, wetlands
How wonderful you are.
Your water glistens
Beautifully from afar.

Your water eroding the sand
away,
leaves us all in
dismay.

Wetlands, wetlands
What a great place to be.
If only you would not go away
So everyone could see your beauty.

So if you like to dig your
toes in the sand,
help in the fight to
SAVE THE WETLANDS!
Heather Underwood, Grade 9
Mount Carmel Academy, LA

Love

Love is red
It sounds like birds in the springtime
It feels like a kiss on the cheek
It smells like carnations
It tastes like chocolate
It looks like the sunset on the beach
Dana Zube, Grade 7
Algonquin Middle School, MI

Blossoming

Spring has blossomed,
Laughter returns to the air
Along with pollen
And the bright, hot, sun.
Spring has blossomed,
Children now play outside
Every afternoon
Once school gets out.
Spring has blossomed,
The snow is melting
Icy winds moving aside
Making room for
The warm summer breeze.
Spring has blossomed,
Outside it just rained
The air now cool and moist
Fresh and clean.
Spring has blossomed,
Rains green the grass,
Paint the flowers,
And bring back the birds.
Hannah Phelps, Grade 9
Cannon Falls Sr High School, MN

Confused

Confused is the color of day with lots of clouds where the sun peeks through.
It sounds like a squeaky car horn.
It tastes like lemonade without sugar.
It looks like a man with one eyebrow up and the other down.
It feels like a bumpy lemon.

Confused is bright green.
It sounds like a big crack of thunder.
It tastes like dirt.
It smells like an old rotten shoe.
It looks like dust.
It feels like sand paper.

Confused is darkness with a hint of light.
It sounds like a glass shattering.
It tastes like salt.
It smells like ear wax.
It looks like a question mark.
It feels like holes in a box.

Confused is like a deer
in the middle of the road,
right or left.

Madi Trulock, Grade 8
Little Miami Jr High School, OH

Thinking of a Topic

Trying to find a topic, but nothing comes to mind.
The uncomfortable pain of not knowing, just comes and goes each line.
I can't expose my mind enough, to come up with the words to show my feelings.
It's too hard to tame myself to write what I am truly thinking.
Robert Sasseville, Grade 8
Weledeh Catholic School, NT

Warmth and Comfort

After long worthless hours of doing nothing,
I make my way down the dark steps to the basement,
As usual, my golden instrument is sitting, and just waiting for me to play it.

I picked it up and cradled it in my tired arms,
Feeling the warmth and comfort in every second,
The black and white page in front of me dares me to play it,
The song starts off slow.

Every note twisting and twirling in the air,
Crisp and clear as ever,
Then the song speeds up, and my fingers break into a quick dance across the keys,
I feel powerful and victorious of the battle that is being conquered,
The song ends with a soft low note.

Making my tongue tickle with pleasure,
Then I put my instrument down,
Like a departure from a magical world,
I turned and walked up the now brighter steps.

Julia Huff, Grade 7
New Albany Middle School, OH

Drugs and You

Drugs are like killing machines
They take you all the way to ruin
Drugs consume you slowly
And then make your life filled with doom
Drugs could give you some pleasure
But then will put you under pressure
You might think you'll never fall
But you can't make any prediction
Drugs will find your weakness
And you will fall in addiction
Youth is a gift of life
Drugs will take it away from you
By making you feel good
And then will kill you with its knife
Drugs dare you to die
They might make you a phony king
But in real world is a lie
They take you away from good thinking
Drug is an evil tool
If you don't use it right
It will turn you into a fool so you better see the light.

Cecilia Alvarez, Grade 8
Beverley Heights Middle School, ON

What Dr. King Believed

Long ago, in the past,
The 1950's, to be exact,
Dr. King had a dream,
That black people would be treated differently,
Respectfully,
Equally.
And that dream would come true.
It's not the same,
As yesterday,
But for the better, things have changed.
And now there is peace and friends,
Like it should have been,
No matter what color or race.
But in the end,
There still are racists,
That judge others' appearance,
And they don't care to believe,
What Dr. King believed.

Courtney Bougie, Grade 8
Freedom Middle School, WI

Flying

Flying is something that you can only imagine.
Flying is a wonderful feeling:
you can throw your arms out and run.
With the wind in your face
nobody can stop you.
You're soaring through the clouds.
Nothing can stop you but yourself.

Faye Engels, Grade 8
Owensville Community School, IN

Names

Brianna
The name represents
kindness and sadness
It is the color of sisterhood.
Her name is Brianna Raylynn Long
and her name represents sadness and kindness.

Tori
The name represents
Love and happiness.
It sounds like the never ending sun.
Her name is Tori Jade Long
And her name represents love and happiness.

Alisha Long, Grade 7
Hamersville Elementary and Middle School, OH

Me Tree

C arefully planted seed
A new tree is born
R ooted firmly in the ground and
O ver time
L ifts its branches and spreads
I ts wings to a new world
N urtured and loved all the while
E volving and changing daily

M aking its way through the seasons
O pen and
O ptimistic
R eaching for the stars to
E ventually become who I am meant to be
H opeful for the future, yet enjoying
E ach
A nd every
D ay!

Caroline Moorehead, Grade 7
New Albany Middle School, OH

Breaking Free

Feelings kept locked away,
never acknowledged,
never revealed.
Always there,
hoping to one day be set free.
As if in a prison,
begging innocence,
yet never believed.
The heart is afraid,
afraid to reveal its innermost secret.
With age comes strength,
with strength the heart gains courage.
At last it tastes the sweet bliss of freedom,
entwining itself with the one it loves.
Never a bond so strong,
never to be broken.

Evan Carpenter, Grade 9
Cannon Falls Sr High School, MN

May

May burst in
With a sudden warmth
It works its magic
Changing everything
For spring
Then without a sound
Disappears
Letting June
Slide in and take over

Jenifer Macdonald, Grade 8
Wainwright High School, AB

Forever Beautiful

You are forever beautiful
Your eyes gleam in the night

You are forever beautiful
Your voice a soul warming song

You are forever beautiful
Your face lights up the sky

You are forever beautiful
Your smile wiping away misery

You are forever beautiful
I am caught in your web

You are forever beautiful

Nathan Jack, Grade 7
Menno Simons Christian School, AB

Turn Around a Goodbye

As tears stream down
A wistful face
A body embraces its open heart.
When this moment comes
You must be ready
To face what you must do.
One last embrace
Gives one more chance
To tell the way you feel.
The truth spills out
A hopeful mouth
To the one you love.
A stunned response,
A relief-filled sigh
Gives them a chance to see.
You take the hand
Offered to you
With love and compassion alone.
This goodbye
Was once permanent.
No longer is it a goodbye.

Alexandra Kuntz, Grade 9
Simley Sr High School, MN

Do You See What I See?

I look out the window, but what do I see?
birds, trees, grass, flowers, leaves.
No, that's not what I see.
That's only half of what I see.
I see beautiful creations, created by the one, the only, Creator
who is the source of all beauty, wonder, and mystery.
What I see is the brilliant colors of the leaves,
with their veins that branch out in an amazing way.
I see the soft, moist soil
that hundreds of great people have walked on.
I see the clouds that reach up to the heavens above
and look as if to be the edible, magnificent cotton candy.
I see the birds that fly, such joy and awe in their eyes.
But, then I look again,
I see love.
The love that the Creator must have for us to give us such wonderful gifts.
The love that makes up this world, which is now so filled of sin and hatred.
The love that created the marvelous wonders we have
and that we take for granted each and every day.
Do you see it?
Do you see what I see?

Emmi Abel-Rutter, Grade 7
St Gertrude School, OH

Nighttime Carnival

flashing and blinking lights, transforming themselves into an electric rainbow.
quickly moving roller coasters with their never-ending clicks.
high pitched laughter from small children having the time of their lives.
a scared scream coming from the slide and the soothing voice of a parent.
fried food from the corn dog stand, dripping with grease.
sweet and crunchy funnel cakes buried under a mountain of sugar.
humid summer air, sticky as glue, clinging to everything in sight.
fresh-squeezed lemonade, a welcome relief from the heat.
ice cold metal of the Tilt-A-Whirl
the ratted seat cushions, torn from years of abuse.
the rushed pace of the carnival never slows, never stops.

Teagan Piazza, Grade 9
Southwest Jr High School, AR

The Garden

In a serene garden, many things were happening that us humans were not aware of
The lazy dirt slumbers, and watches everything going on in the garden
The girlie flowers giggle with each other when the boys are around
The vegetable leaves wave gently as the wind blows softly across the Earth
As the insects buzz through the garden, they demolish plants in their path
The steaks, always the best, monopolize everything in the garden
The fertilizer shoots down and tickles the roots of the plants
The drizzling rain parachutes onto the tops of everything in sight
The worms — in a mad scramble — arise to the surface
The mellow rocks lay back and supervise this well-constructed city
Suddenly…the ghastly rake comes around and ransacks the garden!
…I guess this wasn't such a serene garden after all…

Alexa White, Grade 7
Paw Paw Middle School, MI

Chocolate Chunk Cake

Chocolate covered cupcakes and chocolate chunk cake,
it's all so sweet and tasty but rather hard to make.
It started with some flour and then some eggs and milk,
you stir it up real quickly, so that it's smooth as silk.
Next goes in the chocolate, the heart of our sweet treat,
then we popped it in the oven, and made the kitchen neat.
When it finally came time to eat our chocolaty surprise,
it turned out that our stomachs were smaller than our eyes!
And now we are more chocolate covered than the cake,
I hope that next time we don't make the same mistake!

Melanie Tobias, Grade 9
Home School, MI

My Ithaca

They tell you your whole life "you can't"
"You're not good enough"
"You'll never make it"
But deep inside
the little boy
inside you wants to.
You want to keep trying
but you are too scared
of what others think.
All the odds are against you.
John Wayne was tough
he played football all his life
but he wanted to act.
He once said,
"Courage is saddling up even when you're scared"
I want to be like John
I want to do the impossible
travel the world, climb a mountain
I want to have courage.
I want to live.

Isaiah Sutt, Grade 9
Edinburgh Community High School, IN

Just Different

I walk through the malls with my friends
Looking at every person, as they walk by

I see one person
Who has a completely different face from the rest of us
They are holding another person's hand

I feel everybody's eyes staring right at her
It's not her fault that she is unusual, not liked, retarded

I feel bad for her
No one understands
How she is just human
She has the same feelings

My friends start to point and whisper
But I just block them out and forget

They just don't understand.

Sammie Harkless, Grade 7
New Albany Middle School, OH

Panicky Dismay!!!

Crash! Boom! Bang!
Threatening clouds swallow up the navy sky
as a heavy rainstorm pounds powerfully on the roof
spitting iron nails
lightning split the sky in half
like a knife jamming across a pizza
thunder clapped around my head
like a booming drum representing terror!!!
My head darts under the covers
like a mouse scampering to its hole, away from enemies
angry fists surround my heart charging against me!
I am as spooked as a bear
who found two girls in its den!
My insides churn and shudder
my heart hammers and thuds against my stiff body
my hair stands on end
like a hydropole oscillating in the sky!!!
I cry cantering and colliding with horror
I seem to shrink wibbling and wobbling with fear
finally I shake out of an alarming dream!

Rachel Bauman, Grade 7
Linwood Public School, ON

What Is Change?

What is change?
Is it thirteen? Not adult, not child?
Is it fourteen? Not moody or mild?
Is it the leaves? First green, then brown?
Is it a person's face? A smile, then a frown?
Is it fifteen? Confused and afraid?
Is it sixteen? Bad or good grades?
Is it a flower? A bud, then a bloom?
Is it a thread? That is fabric on a loom?
Is it seventeen? A seat belt or not?
Is it eighteen? Sober or have a shot?
Is it transition? Gradually getting older?
Is it a teen? Getting stronger and bolder?
Is it a baby? Learning to eat?
Is it a toddler? Learning to speak?
Is it a job? And making money?
Is it a girl? Who thinks everything's funny?
Is it a child? Always eager to find?
Is it a boy? With a rather sick mind?
What is change?

Laura McKay, Grade 9
Carberry Collegiate, MB

I

I am the past and the present
I wonder if cats go blind
I hear all sounds outside
I see everything inside
I want to be an artist
I am the past and the present

Takia Brewer, Grade 8
Springfield Boys and Girls Club ABC Unit, IL

Heart Crash

I can hear
her crystal voice
imagining through my mind.

Following her smell through the air
trapping me
she saves me when I am alone.

I get shy when I see her;
my heart stops.

When it comes back
it is too late;
I have to start all over.

Jung-Jae Kim, Grade 7
Menno Simons Christian School, AB

Love

Love is calm like the sea
Love is high like in space
Love is hot like a flame
That would burn in your face

Love is cool like a glacier
Love is smooth like a rock
Or like an old bumpy parking lot

Because love is a thing
That we all share
Because love is always
In the air

Antonio Brown, Grade 7
Lakeside Jr High School, OH

Rainy Day

On this rainy day
Outside where the trees sway
Sky dark as a cave
For a nice day I do crave

Green grass
Raindrops look like clear glass
Falling on the green grass
The rain was such a mass

The brown tree
With birds of three
Chirping birds sing notes by the moat

Children playing in the rain
None can complain
Animals all wet
Like they're trapped in a rain net

David Grosso, Grade 8
Sandusky Middle School, MI

Doomsday

When everyone runs in fear,
then you know doomsday is here.

To see the fear in their eyes,
you then know justice won't rise,

For time has stopped and started again,
in a place with no when.

The curls of time have straightened out
will we die, I have no doubt.

In the end…
the fear is here, all eyes rise,
when will there be another again,
we won't get out, I have no doubt.

Baylee Durbin, Grade 7
Raymore-Peculiar Middle School, MO

Scared

It scares me when you never talk.
It scares me when you walk away.
It scares me when you say you're fine
When we know you're not okay.

It scares me when you never eat.
It scares me when you sit and stare.
It scares me when you're always tired
And always think that we don't care.

It scares me when you exercise.
It scares me when you lose weight.
It scares me when I have to watch you
To catch you when you start to faint.

It scares me when you lie on the floor.
We worry for your sake.
It scares me to think that one day
You will never wake.

It scares me when you're not yourself.
It scares me that you feel poor.
It scares me when you lie to us.
Please don't scare me anymore.

Hannah Schroeder, Grade 8
North Rockford Middle School, MI

Anger Is Red

It sounds like a yelling coach
It feels like a rug burn
It smells like car exhaust
It tastes like saltwater
It looks like a Halloween mask

Pam Schmidlin, Grade 7
Algonquin Middle School, MI

A Flame

The beauty
Of a fire is
Misunderstood
The complexity
Of the design
Is very unique,
Yet we attribute
Nothing to this
Masterful flame.
The mix of red,
Orange, yellow, and
Blue is unusual.
In the heart of
The flame exists
All life, such as
The core of our
Earth.

Melissa Marcum, Grade 7
Otsego Middle School, MI

Heart Break

Heart break is purple.
It sounds like a tear in a book.
It feels like a stab in the heart.
It smells like a burning rose.
It tastes like poison.
It looks like a burning forest.

Vincent Franze, Grade 7
Algonquin Middle School, MI

Impossible

Chills
run down my spine.
My heart beats faster and faster.
My palms get sweaty,
knees start shaking.
All thoughts leave my mind
when I'm with you.

Slow dancing there on the floor,
everything is gone.
The two of us there
alone
forever.
After what seems like only a moment
the song is over.
Our song is
over.

I can't stop thinking of you
but I know I should give up.
Everything runs through my mind again,
and it's impossible to let you go.

Pippa Kennedy, Grade 7
Weledeh Catholic School, NT

But I Know

My painful wounds are just beginning to heal,
But still, the memories run through my head.
A flood of tears stream down my scarred face,
The stench still burns my nose,
The taste of blood still sits in my bitter throat,
My heart feels as empty as my stomach once had.
But I know.
The truth is the scars on my body,
The truth is the cracks in my bones,
The truth is the nightmares in my mind,
The truth is the numbers on my arm.
But I know.
If they could have only been there to see the flames,
To taste the hunger, to smell the death, to hear the cries,
To hear all they said and to see all we were put through.
For one day,
For a picture is worth a thousand words.
To recognize the reason behind the hate.
But for once, I don't know.

Peyton Heitkamp, Grade 8
Parkway Middle School, OH

To My Mom

To my mom the one who hasn't been there for me,
You probably cry on the inside wanting to know me,
But yet you still don't come around,
Even though I still wish you did,
I know you can't take all this back,
But I sit and think of you,
And wish it didn't have to be like this,
Now I see that someday you'll be there for me.
Soon maybe you will apologize and explain, why,
Because that will maybe wash all my questions away.
But I love you Mom!!!

Crystal Straisinger, Grade 9
Leeton Middle and High School, MO

The Most Beautiful Time of the Year

Fall is a beautiful time of the year
The colours of the leaves all change
Harvest time is here
I like to ride horses in an open range
The colours of the leaves all change
The farmers work long hours in the field
I like to ride horses in an open range
It is nice to have a tinted windshield
The farmers work long hours in the field
Kids go back to school
It is nice to have a tinted windshield
The air starts to get cool
Kids go back to school
Harvest time is here
The air starts to get cool
Fall is a beautiful time of the year.

Michelle Hale, Grade 9
Worsley Central School, AB

The Winner Is...

When winning is,
All that matters,
The bond that's between us,
Like glass it shatters.
And all the loose pieces,
Fly off and amiss,
Target my eyes,
And all that exists.
The cheating and hurting,
And yelling and whining.
Punching and slapping,
There's no need for shining.
And all this conforming,
It breaks my heart,
Ripping the canvas,
Killing the art...

That keeps us alive.

Danielle Moore, Grade 9
Francis Libermann Catholic High School, ON

A True Feeling

Life can be full of pain and sorrow
Miserable and sad
Happiness isn't something you can borrow
Just to make you glad

People keep their true feelings inside
Not showing who they truly are
No one knows that everyone has lied
About being who they say they are

People shouldn't be happy for what they do
Everyone should have a voice
Be real and others will too
That's the only choice

So listen to the advice I have just said
Be proud and always use your head

Ashlyn Sawyer, Grade 8
Wainwright High School, AB

Portal to Immortal

Can you open the portal to immortal
Can you seize control of those wondering eyes that I despise
What's worse than here
Fire can't harm me if it harms the same way you do
Leave
You're nothing
Worth little am I
Well woops that's no surprise
Don't be mad be sad
You just lost what you once had

Sara E. Morgan, Grade 8
LaSalle Middle School, IA

Tina Lorek

T he roller coaster started off straight with no hills or knowledge
I n what felt like seconds
N ever thinking of my future, we start
A ccumulating more, and more, and more height,
    and with every inch higher we get, the more I become unsure, I start

L eaking adrenaline, and my face feels like it is going to fly
O ff, and I think to myself, Wow, I
R eally just conquered another humongous roller coaster hill
E ventually, when I stepped off the coaster, a more challenging coaster was ahead of me, I
K new I had to do it, I had to conquer this one too

Valentina Lorek, Grade 7
New Albany Middle School, OH

Joan of Arc

Joan of Arc had a special spark, destined to lead others out of the dark
Between the English and the French a war was starting to see who was the strongest, a new light was shining
Joan had been dreaming of fighting in a war. She decided it was time to make her score.
An armour she got, a sword she fashioned, she was ready to fight; no time for compassion
Dressed like a soldier, in an armour of red and black coal. Her lovely mane no longer there,
the courage of a lion instilled in her soul.
She fought for her people, and led them to victory, the war was almost over, she could change history!
While fighting her last battle her reign came to an end, for she was captured by the enemy with no chance to defend.
They accused her of witchcraft, they accused her of fraud, she was threatened to death, and she prayed to God
Please help me, she cried, how can I carry on? My life is over; the road must go on
Kill her, they yelled, burn her at the stake, she dresses like a man, she is nothing but a fake!
The stick was placed, her body bound to it, they laughed and snickered, as the fire was lit
Everything was spinning, the pain was indescribable, she was losing strength, and the heat was unbearable.
Reminders of the war seemed nearby, the crackling of the fire like gunshots piercing the land.
For God is with me, I fear nothing, she exclaimed. Then she died, taking all the blame
To commemorate Joan's bravery her ashes were scattered, still, many people wonder how her heart never shattered
One girl made a change; one battle was more than enough. She only needed one chance, to prove that she was tough!

Sarah Tomaszewski, Sandra Konji, Meagan Leduc, and Sarah Chippior, Grade 8
St Peter Catholic High School, ON

I Am from Good Times on the Softball Field

I am from
dirty cleats, and sweaty helmets, with bloodstains on my socks, and dirt in my eyes.
I am from
a coach who inspires me, on the field and off, who teaches me, and helps me, who is strict but very kind.
She is the best coach that I ever had. A dream coach that is what I would say.
She will push me, and push me, only so I will get better.
I am from
softball fields, cold, rainy, warm, sunny, softball fields
I am from
a team, the best team, a team that I would like to be with for a long time.
I am from
running ten laps at the beginning of practice, that soon turns into twenty.
I am from
winning and losing, but with a team I will never forget.
I am from
softball, an inspiring coach, and the best teammates.
I am from good times
good times on the softball field.

Adara Mistovich-Perez, Grade 7
New Albany Middle School, OH

Racism

Different faces…all sorts of places…
But what amazes, is that we don't even have enough grace
to tell the people to their face…

Instead we hide…

We should have abided, by the laws that we provided.
Instead of listening to those tiny voices that chided.
("Be racist…Be racist…Be racist…")

Yes the voices that rang in our ears,
Until they made us switch our gears.

Why can't we be kind to others?
Why must we count all the colours?

(Yet this is us, we are the racist.)

Why this trend of hate?
I'm sure there's much more in life to appreciate…
Let us make amends,
a vow to stop these awful hate trends…

Let's be friends…

Holly Swinimer, Grade 8
Chester Area Middle School, NS

Complete

I hope I'm the one
That brings a smile to your face.
I hope I'm the one
That makes you always feel in place.

I hope that it's me
Who you call any time of day.
I hope that it's me
Who makes your cold months feel like May.

I hope you don't mind
That I wrote this just for you.
I hope you don't mind
That it's to you whom I'll stay true.

I hope that you know
That you'll always be in my heart
I hope that you know
That I'll love you even when we part.

I want you to know
That I'm glad we got to meet.
I want you to know
That you make my life complete.

Stephanie Veech, Grade 9
Mount Carmel Academy, LA

A Lost Friend

What happened to the friend I used to know?
The one I could talk to when I was sad.
I never left you so why did you go.
I had to change my having you to had.

I thought that friendships lasted forever.
But when I lost you my thoughts were wrong.
You lied to me many times, whatever.
I can't get over this I am not strong.

I bawled my eyes out when I saw you flee.
All I ever needed was a good friend.
No one can heal the scars you're given me.
Now it's too late because it's now the end.

I don't think you know I am in huge stress.
If only I could change all of this mess.

Marie-Paule Pietrangelo, Grade 7
Nativity of Our Lord Catholic School, ON

The Story of My Life

Playing *Guitar Hero III* is fun.
Hanging with friends can never go wrong.
Cleaning your room is very boring.
Communicating with family and friends is a necessity.
Shrinking pants are a problem.
Balling it up in baseball is amazing.
Chilling at home is cool too.
Finding…Looking…Wanting…

James Petro, Grade 8
St Monica School, IN

Love

Love can hurt
Love can confuse
Love can remain
Love can spite
Maybe even start fights
It can prevail
Or bite you in the tail
It can die
Or maybe survive
You can fake it
Or you can make it
Love can persevere
And sometimes it's not real
Love can be great
Sometimes even fate
It can be grand
Maybe even expand
If you're really bright
And do things right
With the right people
Love can last a lifetime.

Kayla Antoine, Grade 7
Haynes Academy for Advanced Studies, LA

Zoo

Past the entrance
Outside in the zoo
Behind the metal bars
Animals lay on the rocks.

During the sites
After a while
Without a doubt
Soon, we become hungry.

From tigers to lions
To bears and monkeys
On we kept walking
There were so many animals to see!

Kaitlyn Novak, Grade 7
Algonquin Middle School, MI

Destroyed Dreams

You destroyed my every dream
The words you said were vile
You hurt me so deep
That I forgot how to smile
I try to survive the day
Your name causes me great pain
Your face, your eyes, your smile
Drives the hurt in me insane
I try to bury all my fears
All that is ripping up my heart
I try not to think of you
But even that tears me apart
At night I lay awake
Trying to keep myself together
All those painful memories
Will be with me forever
Now as the time is ending
I try hard not to cry
To every hope and dream
I sadly say goodbye

Tatiana Kopchuk, Grade 8
St Kevin Jr High School, AB

Arizona

Up very early
Into the car
Toward the airport
I'm going to Arizona!
On the big plane
By myself
Except for my bags
The trip has just begun!
Off the plane
Through the doors
Outside I see my mother
She's standing there so proud.

Ashley Salsbery, Grade 7
Algonquin Middle School, MI

Why?

Why is the world so complicated?
Why do people die?
Why do people get hurt, and then they will hurt others?
Why can't you ever get what you want?
Why is it the person who does the right thing is the one who gets looked down on,
    and the person who does the wrong thing become popular?
Why do people put on a show and never show their real self — deep inside?
Why do people give up on their dreams because of obstacles?
Why does a bad guy always come out looking better than the good guy?
Why can't everyone get along?
Why isn't there enough time in a day?
Why does the time zoom on by?
Why won't I ever know the answers to any of these questions?
WHY?

Julie Schmersal, Grade 9
Ottoville High School, OH

Matthew

Introduced with a smile.
It started with a shared style.
But soon it was all laughs, trouble was our names,
Just Gobiec and Ames.

They said "joined at the hip"
We shared everything, every last corn chip.
Best friends forever,
Soul mates if you want to get clever.

As time passed, we were having such a blast.
But when the call was made, we knew it couldn't last.

Together forever wasn't in the company's plan.
It seem like we had just began.
This can't be the end.

Finally they day came.
It seemed so normal, like every other game.
Until the clock struck nine,
He was always supposed to be mine.
With a tear in our eyes, we hugged our goodbye, for the very last time.

Heidi Ames, Grade 8
Little Miami Jr High School, OH

Me

Travis
Brother of Chelsea
Lover of a dog, laugher, and fun
Who feels happiness from love, lonely by myself, and nervous when sitting
Who needs friends, family, and love
Who gives love, joy, and happiness
Who fears mice, loneliness, and the end of love
Who would like to see him leave Prairie Lakes, changes and never come back
Who lives in a house on Pearl Lake
Parton

Travis Parton, Grade 9
Prairie Lakes School, MN

Art Set

My family is an art set
Full of the supplies to make
A beautiful piece of art.
Dad is the beginning pencil,
Creating the structuring lines
To hold us all together.
Mom is the bright, colorful paint.
Filling the lines with beauty and love.
My brother, Steven, is the color pallet
Making everything wild and exciting.
Noelle, my older sister, is the blending pen,
Helping everything flow together.
Kyra, my little sister, is the paper
That everyone affects and helps turn into
Something magnificent.
And I, I am the painter's audience,
Watching it all
Come to life.
My family is a fully equipped art set.

Alillie Brady, Grade 7
Paw Paw Middle School, MI

Oh Cold, Soft Cotton!

It lies from the meadow to the road,
This whole place is covered, oh what a sight!

The thin ball of cotton,
   — Oh, cold soft cotton —
That falls from the sky
   — Oh clear, blue skies! —

The children love to play in it…
With the air like the ice,
And the sounds of the wind are a ghost,
And yet nothing will stop them from making an angel,
Or even creating a man.

The sun's looking down on us,
Although it does not heat.
But we do not need the warmth,
   Just our clear blue skies
      — With the sprinkling white snow.

Ashley Weeks, Grade 8
St Peter Catholic High School, ON

Basketball

Two seconds left, I'm past half court
and my teammate passed the ball from afar.
I catch the ball and quickly shoot it in
And awkward silence fills the room
Then I hear a faint swish
Loud roars and applause fill the gym.
After the game with a trophy in our hands
we go outside to get in the vans to go home.

Brandon Castillo, Grade 8
Weledeh Catholic School, NT

Missing You*

Adel! Adel! Adel!
How I miss you!
Wishing you can come back…
For me to have someone to talk to or call
The list goes on and on…
Oh! How I wish I can see your face
I'll give anything to see it one last time
Or to even hear your voice
But I'm scared if I do
I may not let you go…
Now I cry…
When I think about you, see your pictures
Or even look at my friends…
Cause I know you're not there
Now I wait by the phone
Waiting for you to call
But knowing you never will
Adel! Adel! Adel!
How I miss you!

Michelle Thomas, Grade 9
Beebe High School, AR
*In loving memory of Adel Mahmoud!

My Sanctuary

I wish to be in a sanctuary.
Where I do not have to be wary.
Where I will not fear death,
and I can just take a deep breath.

Filled with peace.
Where I will cease my thirst for justice.
For all will be fair,
and nothing will snare or suffocate me.

No one and nothing will have to protect me,
and it is impossible to feel sickly.
From either disease or words spoken.
I won't feel broken.

Geena Lardino, Grade 7
St Eugene Elementary School, IL

Fall of Society

Trample down
The majority
Thinking only with technology
We are the children of the future
Of a world gone insane
Crushing honesty and electing the dead
Kneeling to greater officials, higher powers
Who keep secrets and start wars
Behind our backs
This is not real democracy
Bring the giants down
Rebuild society
Turn your face toward
A new dawn of civilization

Sarah Brady, Grade 8
Haynes Academy for Advanced Studies, LA

The Outsiders

Under the streetlight
Dally lies smiling, dying
Now all is silent
Vivian Diaz, Grade 7
Hamlin Upper Grade Center, IL

To Grow

April 28th, 1995
The ground was cracking,
the snow was melting into the ground.
The tender plants were breaking through
the thawed ground.
I broke through too.
My parents named me Allison,
Allison Johnson.
My name was supposed to be Lilly,
but I was late,
too late for Easter.
Late like the spring.

I broke through.
Tender like the new growth,
just waiting to grow.
Just waiting to get somewhere.
Just like a tender plant.
Allison Johnson, Grade 7
Silverbrook Middle School, WI

Darker Than the Brightest Star

Darker than the brightest star,
Darker than the lights of a car,
Darker than the moon itself,
Or darker than an actor's spotlight.
Darker than my dad's work light,
Darker than the doctor's flashlight,
Darker than the shine of my TV,
Darker than a glow stick, shining by me.

Darker than a room closed off,
Or even darker than a room at night,
Darker than a movie theatre,
Darker than the middle of the night.
Darker than Alaska in winter,
Darker than the tip of the ocean,
Darker than the mines of gold,
Darker than the bottom of the sea,
That's how dark my tragedies can be.
Olivia Ganser, Grade 7
St Monica School, IN

Disaster

The storm breaks silence
and rips through the wilderness,
calmed nothing left.
Zach Wolfe, Grade 8
Lowell Middle School, IN

I Have Learned...

I have learned that love is often mistaken.
I have learned that respect should be given and taken.
I have learned that the best love comes from the heart.
I have learned that families shouldn't be broken apart.
I have learned that love doesn't always guarantee happiness.
I have learned that what you sometimes think is light really might be darkness.
I have learned that love could be everlasting.
I have learned that going overboard can be drastic.
I have learned that sometimes love could be magical.
I have learned that with certain people you have to be practical.
I have learned that love can be achieved.
I have learned that sometimes all you have to do is believe.
I have learned that life can't be replaced.
I have learned that some memories just can't be erased.
I have learned many of life's lessons.
I have learned about all of my blessings.
Miya Ward, Grade 9
Gwendolyn Brooks College Preparatory Academy, IL

Annoyance

Every day I see Annoyance at school.
He charges through the front entrance
wearing the same wind pants as yesterday.
I can hear those orange wind pants skidding together
as he stomps his feet on the ground,
making me want to rip my ears off.
He yells across the hall to me
as he chomps on a strawberry piece of gum,
demanding the answers to the next hour's assignment.
Annoyance always has a pen to click and a pencil to tap.
He lives next door to me,
has a small house with thin walls and two small siblings that scream.
At times it seems like Annoyance is gone,
but in a matter of seconds his screechy voice
and bright red hair storms back again.

Steven Davies, Grade 9
Clintonville High School, WI

Sun

The summer sun beats down while the winter sun sneaks around
It warms our baby faces and makes us dream of tropical places
We sure do miss it when it's gone
But too much sun is not that fun
The sun gives us shadows that follow us around
They're our close friends that never make a sound
We wish the sun was here to stay
But sometimes the clouds want to play
Bam! Bang! Boom! The clouds sing that tune
But when they're done, there's our friend the sun
We say goodnight and dream of all the fun that will happen in the morning
Because when it's sunny, it's never boring

Madeline Falash, Grade 7
St Philip the Apostle School, IL

Grandma to Granddaughter

I remember the days in Trinidad,
Walking up the hills in the morning
To watch the sun rise,
Bright.
Wandering to the beach with the children,
The beady, damp sand stuck in my sandals.

Waking up again to see the sun
Blazing into the room like a large furnace,
Then completing daily jobs to keep the house clean.

Only cleaning until the light from outside dims,
Later awaiting the creatures of the night
To emerge
And the island breeze blowing harder,
Fierce.
The day ends with a view of the island sun.

Karlene Woods, Grade 9
Destrehan High School, LA

The Porch

Birds chirp their sweet music
as they glide across the still road
Orange orioles,
tan sparrows,
plump robins,
tiny hummingbirds
All grace the air with their presence.
A slight breeze cools the beating earth
With a thin country fragrance;
If you were to breathe,
you'd feel awake when an inch from slumber.
A flat, rolling field lies just across the highway
from the five step porch.
life-less stones set flat,
prop my body, and make comfort right.
As time passes,
Its speed increases,
And life goes at a blink of an eye
Calm, and peaceful,
The porch gives all who come
Peace of mind.

Derrick Ronald VanDeraa, Grade 9
Clintonville High School, WI

Alone

being alone can deepen your mind,
it can enhance your thoughts,
and occupy your time.

being alone, can help you focus on the land,
the trees and the dirt,
but being alone can also make you question your self- worth.

if you are strong enough to withstand being alone,
you will soon understand,
that being alone is a lot to withstand.

Marissa Price, Grade 9
Fort Zumwalt East High School, MO

Time Travels

I used to be a rebel
Then I saw the light,
and now I no longer live like a devil.
It used to bring me down,
but now I have God,
and it's amazing how much I've come around.

Carlos Gonzalez, Grade 9
Prairie Lakes School, MN

The Opera Ghost*

A grotesque romance,
Not happening by chance.
In the midst of a strange masquerade,
He thought he had pulled off the charade.

As he sat in his lair
All he had was despair.
She, being his only love,
Thought that he was sent from above.

In him she saw nothing but light,
But in truth he was as dark as the night.
His obsession
Leading to aggression.

Friend or foe
We shall never know
But the tale we shall miss the most,
The tale of the Opera's Ghost.

Sarah Craig, Grade 8
Sandusky Middle School, MI
*Inspired by "The Phantom of the Opera"

I Love You

I see you but you don't see me anymore
I wave and you smile but not at me
We used to be close, really close
Like paper combined in a notebook
Until the day I made a BIG mistake
And now you barely even look at me
You told me you loved me
And I said nothing but
I wished I did
Because I feel the same way
And my heart goes Thump, Thump, Thump against my chest
And I had to tell you the truth
So I tried to tell you in a note
But you threw it away without reading it
So I tried to tell you in person but
There SHE came your new girlfriend
WHY? I thought you loved me
But I guess I ran out of time because
Now I'm sitting here all alone wiping my tears away
While you go out and laugh at the funny things

Stephanie McGuirk, Grade 9
Hazelwood West Jr-Sr High School, MO

Raphael the Rooster

Raphael the rooster
King of the farmyard
Looked down from his roost
Atop the stockyard
With his chest puffed out
And his head to the sky
He let out a call
That echoes from stall to sty
There is commotion and clutter
As the animals stir
The farm tosses and turns
The cat lets out a purr
Raphael the rooster
Has lost track of time
He is not calling the sunrise
But to the moonlight so fine
Raphael the rooster
Is no longer called king
He must step down
So night peace over the barnyard
Can once again ring

Hannah Pagel, Grade 9
Runnels School, LA

Fly High

Look at the sky,
It looks very high,
I wish I was a kite,
I would fly in the night,
Without a single care,
With the night sky bare,
I would look up at the stars,
Or look down at the cars,
I would fly on cloud nine,
I would say this one's mine!
Look up at the sky,
How very, very high,
It's time to go to sleep,
As my slumber becomes deep,
I drift away to a place,
But no ordinary place,
A place where I can fly,
High in the sky.

Cailea Jones, Grade 8
Maple River East Middle School, MN

A Veteran Is…

A veteran is brave,
A veteran is determined,
A veteran is fearless,
A veteran is bold,
A veteran is daring,
A veteran is decisive,
A veteran is a hero.

Kristian R. Bess, Grade 8
Blanchester Middle School, OH

Journey to the American Dream

We began a journey, knowing that it could cost our lives
but we risked everything for the American Dream…
We left our family behind, for now a new life we will start,
this is a hard journey, as every second I confront my fears,
children cry of starvation but like warriors they won't give up,
following the example of their peers…
We are almost to the border only a few miles to go,
As we get closer to the border, from far behind we hear a big Bang!!!
My heart is replete with fear, for my friend has got shot but I can't do anything,
all I got to do is sprint to the land of dreams…
The American Dream is here, I can sense it next to me,
As I cross the border, freely, I imagine a new world full of happiness and luxuries,
now I find myself unhappy here, I want another atmosphere
but I don't want my folks to die so, I'm here sacrificing my life for their living,
My opinion is not valid nor counts here…
we take insults and work from dusk 'til dawn every day
Why?? Because we are the phantoms of this country, who are seen and not heard
It seems to me as if every day I question myself, is this the price I'll pay??

Cynthia Molina, Grade 8
Goshen Middle School, IN

Marcus Ward

M y personality is like massive bomb sounds
A nyone can hear from one mile every direction.
R acing through the dark sky
C reating energetic winds,
U seless trash dancing around in its power.
S urging through city by city, combining with ground breaking thunder,

W ith blinding flashes of lightning.
A ngry clouds rumble and tumble into
R aging waves of fury
D ampened by the blinding rays of sun.

Marcus Ward, Grade 7
New Albany Middle School, OH

The Twister

Here's a little story about a twister, per say, it can hit anyone, anywhere, or any day.
It's as cold as the pole and as dark as the night, as it makes swishing noises and turns
every day and every night. The inside is a dusty Sahara as the sand tickles you
in the face. The inside is as damp as the sea. Once sucked in, you are now
trapped in the never ending black hole. The grey of the twister
is the house burning down, as it screams in your face.
Kansas, Missouri, Kentucky, all very dangerous.
But the most dangerous is the twister valley
of Kansas, Oklahoma, and Texas,
which is where the most
twisters in the world happen.
So be careful, I must indeed say,
because like I said,
it can hit
ANYONE,
ANYWHERE,
OR ANY DAY!

Alexander Cosenza, Grade 8
St Peter Catholic High School, ON

Where I'm From

I am from potatoes and homemade pizza,
From the monkey puppet that would squeak,
And beanie babies. I am from Skittles (lots of color)
To Alexander Ovechkin of the Washington Capitals
From "beastly" and "Dream On."

I am from SportsCenter early in the morning
From all 13 books in the *Series of Unfortunate Events*
To playing catch, in the backyard.
I am from the scar on my leg
From exercising and being a professional hockey player
To listening to Akon and T. Pain on the radio.
I am from practicing hockey to b-ball
From being an agent or sports commentator
And waiting to score the touchdown in football.

I am from sushi to traveling
From sports and school.
I'm from yearbooks found in boxes
Everybody smiling and having a great time
The tears roll down your cheeks with so many memories.

Kiefer Sherwood, Grade 7
New Albany Middle School, OH

A Broadway Audition…

Waiting for years for my big break.
My name up in lights on Broadway.
New York is where the chance is to take.
It's hard to think of what to say,
Bullets of sweat fall down my face.
I'm so nervous, can't bear the wait.
All I can think to do is pace,
The casting director controls my fate.
I stayed up all night rehearsing my script.
I sang and I sang till I could no more.
I'm pacing so fast I almost trip.
This is it, I'm broke, I'm poor,
They call out my name and down drops my heart.
I just hope I get the part…

Ami Arnold, Grade 8
Pilgrim Park Middle School, WI

The Sunset

You can look; or you can stare,
But it will always take your breath away.
The sun, the sand,
Even the wind and the water,
Such a sight.
So vivid, so clear,
A sunset over the calming waters.
You notice it's leaving and the moon creeps in,
A sigh or a whimper as you count down
The last rays of light to reach your eyes.
And then it is gone.

Ehrick George, Grade 9
Clintonville High School, WI

My Little Brother

His face is so hypnotizing when he looks at me
I look in his eyes I feel his pain I wish it was me and not him
I see him struggle and struggle and then some more
Then everything stops it's done it's over he's free
He's out of his pain and now he's up and playing ready to go
And that's when I know God is watching over him
That God is real and he's my little brother's guardian angel
The brother is mine forever
My little brother

Carissa Urquieta, Grade 7
Lawton Middle School, MI

What Is Summer?

Summer is a burst of water when you jump in a pool
Summer is a breeze, swift and cool
Summer is the pain of getting a splinter
Summer is a heat wave right after winter
Summer is sleeping late every day
Summer is watching a bee buzz away
Summer is licking an ice-cream cone
Summer is going fishing alone
Summer is getting too many mosquito bites
Summer is sleeping outside on starry nights
Summer is like reaching the top of the tree
Summer is kites flying as far as the eye can see
Summer is fireworks on the Fourth of July
Summer is falling off your bike and trying not to cry
Summer is like dancing in the rain
Summer is doing something insane
Summer is great, summer is grand
Summer is a beach full of sand
Take a nap or take a hike
Read a book or ride a bike
This is what summer is like

Ellen Cluxton, Grade 8
Hillsboro Christian Academy, OH

Mami Don't Cry

It's exactly one year since he's been away
I know she feels the absence every single day
I try to be the strong one, so that way she won't cry
'Cause I don't like to see tears coming out of her eyes
She works so hard day and night
And when I see her cry I hold it with all my might
The tears and the pain I hold it inside
Just so I won't see my mami cry one more time
Sometimes I wonder how much of him does she miss
But by now I've learned she yearns for it all, even just a kiss
She loves him so much she'd never let him go
They've been together sixteen years, that's how I know
Through the bad and the good, through the good and the bad
They'll always be together, if they're happy or they're sad
She's ready to see him or just hear his voice
Just a phone call or a letter makes her rejoice
She wants him so bad I see it in her eyes
But all that I ask is Mami don't cry

Liz Garcia, Grade 9
Holland High School, MI

I Am From…

I am from Teddy Grahams and milk in the early mornings, and playing outside all day.
From little sundresses and sand in my shoes.
From singing along with the Wiggles, and waiting for the bus to roll by,
Knowing my big brother and sister would be home soon.

I am from soccer in the morning on weekends, and tee ball in the evenings.
From sleepovers with my friends, and tagging along to my brother's baseball games.
From playing with all the other younger siblings,
And swinging on the swing sets.

I am from bedtime stories and waiting to be tucked in at night.
From "Don't make me count to three!"
And running around barefoot and having to wash my feet off.

I am from family gatherings and craving grandma's cooking
From making up Christmas plays with my cousins,
And playing a bunch of card games waiting for dinner to be served.

I am from chalk-filled, happy go lucky days and waking up for the very first day of kindergarten.
From my favorite kid-filled neighborhood
And never wanting the summer days to end.

Erica Blankemeyer, Grade 7
New Albany Middle School, OH

The Ups and Downs

My mind is racing no time for pacing
Decisions and questions running through my head what is love and is it something we dread?
Forgive and forget a little white lie heartbreaking heart wrenching breakdown and cry
A sweet embrace a smiling face
Lost in your eyes my wondrous surprise
The rights the wrongs that one perfect song
A longing for affection being led in the wrong direction
Lost in my dreaming a powerless meaning
Screaming and yelling
Kicking shouting
Making up
Breaking up
Stupid lies your disguise
Meaningless tears realizing fears
Sweet words and romantic times
Wanting to turn back the clock live for a moment make the time stop
My mind is racing push and shove those are the ups and downs to love

Allie Fischer, Grade 8
Wayzata Central Middle School, MN

Love Is When

I used to think I didn't love, but now it's all I could ever want. I see couples walking down the street holding hands and I wish I were them. It kind of makes me jealous.

I imagine myself with him and how happy I would be. My friends, who are dating, tell me that relationships are confusing and that I'm lucky I'm not in one, but to me it feels like they're lying.

I dream at night that I'm with him and that I'm the happiest girl in the world. The alarm clock rings and I realize that is was all just a dream.

Sometimes I wonder if I will ever meet the right guy. Then I wonder if I will be alone forever, but you never know. Until then I will wait and stay strong.

Brittney Stickdorn, Grade 8
Logan Hocking Middle School, OH

The Thunderstorms

The sky is a blanket of darkness,
Silky black for as far as the eye can see,
Droplets of rain scatter all around,
The sound of "pitpat" echoes through the air,
A beautiful, vibrant light beams down out of the sky
Followed by the sound of a crash in the distance,
The cold bitter air bites at the night,
The stars are hidden by the storm,
The rain creates a beautiful pattern over the landscape,
The ground enjoys the soft mist soaking up all it can,
The sky is releasing emotions of all sorts,
The storm is sad, for it is very misunderstood,
It cries tears of sadness, for no one will ever see,
The emotions deep within that no one will ever know,
Unless they take the time to get to know the storm,
It gives off comfort in the night,
And sings a lullaby on the windowsill,
It seeks attention, for the storm is desperate,
So next time there is a storm,
Take time and listen.

Matt Heflinger, Grade 8
Little Miami Jr High School, OH

Bright Shining January

January is beautiful, bright, and romantic
but as the fireworks shoot
up into the still black night
it becomes something else.
It becomes something important.
It becomes a symbol of a new beginning.
A symbol that life will go on
even when it's difficult.
It is just like the sun
as it sets into the night.
We always know that
even though darkness comes,
it will come tomorrow
and shine again.

Sabrina Berry, Grade 7
Nativity of Our Lord Catholic School, ON

He Calls to Me

He calls to me,
On a warm afternoon,
The sun shining down on me,
He calls to me when coach says,
"First team defense on the field."
He calls to me when the ball is snapped
The quarterback drops back to look for an open man,
And throws a Hail Mary to my receiver,
He calls to me when he comes spiraling,
Towards my face,
He calls to when I put my hands up,
And catch him,
He calls to me when I toss him to the ref in the end zone.
He calls to me.

Jake Gigliotti, Grade 7
New Albany Middle School, OH

A Unique Soul

My soul is like a pink and black kite
Always up and down
To match my moods
The pink symbolizes a nice beautiful baby girl
So cute and peaceful
However the black symbolizes a loud crashing storm
Booming in the middle of the dark night
My soul moves like a rubber band
If you stretch it too far it will snap
It dreams of old memories
Recreating the images in my head
Makes me feel like a fluttering butterfly
My soul had been known to change lives
My soul is like a bipolar monkey
You never know what to expect next

Amber Thorn, Grade 9
Clintonville High School, WI

Guilt

My stomach feels empty
like an old, hollow, tree.
I look at the floor,
and try my hardest not to make eye contact.
My knees lock and they feel like
they will never unlock until this is over.
I rock from foot…to foot…
like a rocking chair rocking back and forth.
Great, guilt gawks at me.
I feel like a slave
being whipped over and over
I cannot take it anymore
so I…
spill…
the…
beans…

Brandon Wagler, Grade 7
Linwood Public School, ON

Surrender

Here I lay stuck on the frozen ground.
I am warm but I am not melting the heart of the ice.
Wanting to break free from this day's black fate
But He will not let me freeze.
Fighting against the cold that bites my skin
With my sword of righteousness.
At the moments I have triumph
Mutiny breaks my back
And cuts me down by the knees.
Not getting back at the chide of one's want for gold
But shining a light so they can see the day of today
Opportunity blinds them and exhales the truth
Because we are not listening to what God will say.
Do not be bankrupt but wealthy in His love
Or one will have heaven on Earth and not in heaven.

Cody Lowe, Grade 9
Discovery Middle School, MN

Death

As my family drives I cry,
I cry for everyone.
When I arrive all I see is more,
More crying and talking about her.
That is all I hear anymore!
As I take a seat they talk about her life
We all sit for an hour or so,
Then we all have to leave.
We drive for what seems like forever,
Then we arrive at the grave.
I watch them lower her.
I don't want them to,
But I have to let her go.
Then again, all I see is sadness.
Sadness whispers in my ear,
It's telling me to cry, but I don't.
As I look down, I see something.
It's dangling from my neck.
It's the last thing I have to remember.
I hold it; everything feels okay now,
I can move on.

Danielle Hartel, Grade 8
Sandusky Middle School, MI

Blue

Blue is water, shirts, and blueberries.
Blue is the taste of Kool-Aid.
Water and markers smell blue.
Sadness makes me feel blue.
Blue is the sound of water, and fish.
Blue is blue jeans and a blue rose.
Cars are blue.
The sky is also blue.
Blueberries are blue.

Cassie Lickman, Grade 7
Algonquin Middle School, MI

Free Verse

Free Verse doesn't have to
Rhyme, so I'll have a
Very hard time figuring
Out how to write
A free verse poem tonight.

About what should I write?
The story of my life?
How to hold a knife?
About the first day of school,
Or soccer rules?

So since this night
I cannot write
A non-rhyming poem.
I won't!

TJ Roth, Grade 7
Thomas Jefferson Jr High School, IL

Stop Sweating

Sweatshops steal sweet children's souls, making them sew certain clothing,
giving them small salary, in a small scary space.
Somehow our society should start saving some of these sorry innocent souls.

Kiyah Morocco, Grade 8
Mary Ward Catholic School, ON

Vali

I know a dog, her name is Vali and she is very sweet.
She loves it when I walk her as her wonderful treat.

Two days a week I do my job
through wind, and rain, and sleet.

She's not really my dog, she's my neighbor's,
although I get paid it is still like a favor.

She's by herself in the pen just waiting for me to come.
When I open the door she pounces and squeals, and knocks me on my bum.

We have a plan when we go on a walk,
she doesn't speak English so we just don't talk.

She fetches all the toys I throw,
and brings them back in a neat little row.

I put her collar down, and make her lay…
Oh my gosh wait, I was supposed to walk her today!

Chloe Antrobus, Grade 7
Ballard Brady Middle School, OH

I Am

I am wild, yet full of questions
I wonder why people worry about their social image
I hear my past reminding me of my mistakes
I see the world around me, in all its sorrow and destruction
I want my descendants to live in a world without war and conflict
I am wild, yet full of questions

I pretend that I am not disturbed by the fact that my skin color is different from others
I feel afraid that our country is slowly falling apart
I believe in a completely free world
I worry that I will not be successful later in life
I cry when I see "nerds" being picked on
I am wild, yet full of questions

I understand that everyone is special in his or her own special way
I say be yourself
I dream about flying unassisted
I try to be the best that I can be
I hope to get into a good college
I am wild, yet full of questions

Evan Nelson, Grade 7
New Albany Middle School, OH

Love

Don't let it swallow your innocent soul
Don't look in its eyes or you'll disappear
It leaves you lost in a very dark hole
Taking your heart, it dies, leaving you here
You might want it close, for its scent is sweet
It is simply romantic, attractive
When it speaks, it sweeps you off of your feet
But in the end it's what you'll never forgive
I simply warn, for I've felt its strong hold
It stole my heart, but I still have not learned
For it has me trapped, but yet to feel cold
Maybe the sorrow that I felt was earned
For love can be good if it's meant to be
If not, it hurts, that's what happened to me

Emily Sparks, Grade 9
Greendale High School, WI

Don't Give Up

You're looking but not seeing
You're listening but not hearing
You're touching but not feeling
You won't pay attention
You're cold but not shivering
You're hurt but show no pain
You're crying but where are the tears
You shouldn't keep it held
Your friends try to help but you turn away
Your blood runs dry but you still breathe
Your heart is crushed but you still love
Thoughts of death are found
Questions of why to carry on
Just whatever you do…
Don't give up

Steele Milligan, Grade 9
Salem High School, AR

Me

Who am I…
I really don't know.
Some people say I'm Mexican
and some say I'm American.
But where do I fit.
  I'm not fully Mexican
but I still think it's my country.
  My life
American?
Yeah I was born in Chicago.
I'm fine by that but I don't remember how it was.
But it's still
  my life.
  For me it's fine being both…
but do people think I'm both.
  Who am I…
Mexican or American.

Dolores Reyes, Grade 9
Sennett Middle School, WI

Global Warming

Our lights, our phones, our cars
Are all a part of the problem
At night I can't even see the stars
Because every fake light robs them
The way we shower an hour each day
The words we always constantly say
Are all part of the problem

Sending our garbage into the air
Being greedy and star-struck for money
Littering and ruining without a care
That's the reason the Earth is too sunny
Why the ice keeps on melting
Why the summer rains are pelting
It all ties in with the problem

Why shouldn't we care
Or try, fail and decide to quit
This is why people stare
This is why we all wonder
This is how we're falling under
This is the problem that I keep warning
This problem's name is Global Warming.

Natasha Young, Grade 7
Our Lady of Fatima Separate School, ON

Sunrise

Everyone has a novel.
A book they write themselves
that encompasses all that they are,
all they have been, all they will be.

They say this book has no beginning.
They say it can't be started anew.
They say that no matter how hard you try,
the pages are already filled.

But there is a sunrise in the east.
A new hope shining on the world;
an inspiration in its own right
that inspires you to start over again.

So have no fear of starting anew.
There is no script to follow.
After all you write your own
so change the ink from black to gold.

Mimic all the colours you see,
that come with the rising sun;
colour your life a sunrise,
and erase the monotone.

Fiona Brough, Grade 9
Mulgrave School, BC

WNBA

The basketball court,
like a large, square fort.
The basketball ball,
cold and warm like fall.
The basketball hoop,
has small, little loops.
My career
will start right here.

Jessica Stapleton, Grade 7
Fairfield Middle School, OH

The Senses of Baseball

The swing of the bat
The roar of the crowd
The smell of the grass
The cheering so loud

The crack of the bat hitting the ball
The smell of the hot dogs in the air
Feeling the ball hit my glove
There's no feeling like this anywhere

The salt of the seeds
The heat of the sun
The texture of the ball
These are the things that make it so fun

These are the senses I enjoy most of all
When in the summer, playing baseball

Brady Gross, Grade 8
Stewartville Middle School, MN

I'm Sorry Mother

I'm sorry that
I couldn't be
the daughter that,
you wanted me to be.
I'm sorry that,
I made mistakes
that made you hate,
the things I say.
I'm sorry that,
I ruined your life,
that I laughed,
and that I cried.
I'm sorry for,
the things I said,
that made you go,
out of your head.
I'm sorry that,
I cared so much,
that I acted,
like I loved.
Mother, I'm sorry.

Danna Gardner, Grade 9
Lincoln High School, AR

If

If you can tell the truth when you know it could get you in trouble,
If you can do the right thing when no one is watching,
If you can stand up for someone when you know they might pick on you instead,
Or help one of your friends when someone hurts them,
Even when you're having a bad day.

If you can do your chores when your parents aren't home,
When you'd rather be watching TV,
If you can tell the teacher the truth when you haven't done your homework,
Even when you know that if you do you're going to get a working lunch,
If you can try your best in all you do,
You will always succeed.

George Miller, Grade 7
New Albany Middle School, OH

A Long September's Day

Life went on like a Shakespearean play
Skipping and playing with friends at school
But behold on that long September's day
Everyone would be terribly afflicted by the actions of a fool

We watched in terror as the Twins were struck by planes
Our teachers scream and our parents cry
Families of the workers in the Twins were taken over by pain
As we all saw the Twins be swallowed by the ground and people die

We cried out in horror and were overcome with grief
What culture, what people would do such a thing?
What people thought killing as part of their core belief?
What satisfaction or pleasure would this to them bring?

But whatever those people who killed us may say
Our lives as Americans were changed on that long September's Day.

Enoch Graham, Grade 9
Southwest Jr High School, AR

The Mountains

Fidgety squirrels,
Played with by the agile deer masked by the tall trees above.

Quiet footsteps of stealthy animals sneaking around in the leaves
And echoing calls of the hunter finding his prey.

The chilled mountain air as it blows through the window.
The thick bug spray on my jacket hits my nose as I slowly breathe.

Savory dried-fruit
The mouth watering jerky as I eat to keep my stomach from sounding like a bear.

My knife, shiny, but swift, as it slides out of its sheath
So I can whittle on a spruce branch. My aged bow strong as an ox.

Adrenaline as it courses through my veins.
I AM THE HUNTER!!!!

Chris Quick, Grade 9
Southwest Jr High School, AR

A One-Way Street

Life is a one-way street
The green lights mean you live on
The yellow lights mean something bad happens
The red lights mean your stop is here
Some people stop so soon
Still others stop later
Some hit all green lights
Some hit many yellows
Some hit none at all
And live in only mother's womb

Mitchel Huttema, Grade 9
Credo Christian Schools, BC

A Family Meant to Be

I once knew a girl, whose mother had died,
When that girl found out, she cried and cried.
She had an older sister and a younger brother,
They no longer would have what they called a mother.

Their father told them "don't be scared,
You knew your mother really cared."
This girl I knew had just turned eleven,
When she told me that she'd see her mom in heaven.

I told this girl that she'll always have me,
And she told me "thanks, that's just what I need."
So I would call this girl almost every day,
Reminding her that I'll be her friend till our hair turns grey.

She told me that I was a truly good friend
We'd always laugh and never pretend.
We knew that we were meant to be,
You could even say we were family!

Yara Hanna, Grade 7
Nativity of Our Lord Catholic School, ON

I Am From

I am from a cold frigid place,
where our hair freezes in -30 weather.

I am from the yellow sand pits in the summer,
where I ride freely on my dirt bike.

I am from the indoor gym,
where I stop balls from going in the net.

I am from WCS,
where I can hang with my friends after school.

I am from the concrete ground,
where I like to skateboard around.

I am from the movie theatre,
where I like to go to the show.

I am from the N.W.T.
where the capital city is Yellowknife.

Evan Gathercole, Grade 8
Weledeh Catholic School, NT

My Room

My room
My world
My chamber of everything
In a peaceful state

My room
My haven of jerseys
That have been through many tough games
Of what were mostly battles on the turf and the hardwood

My room
My sanctuary of thoughts
Joe's mind: your room is pretty organized for a guy
Joe: hey, that's just the kind of a guy I am

My room
My world
My haven of jerseys
My sanctuary of thoughts
My chamber of everything
In a peaceful state

Joseph Siegenthaler, Grade 7
New Albany Middle School, OH

This Crayon Had Worked Its Magic

It's time to color.
I had just finished my drawing but it needs color,
Lots of it.
I picked up the waxy, light green crayon.
That reminded me of school and I colored.
Once my hand touched the paper,
The crayon swiftly brushed across my page.
The different shades and textures made my drawing realistic.
I needed more, so I go many different colors,
So my paper had all the colors of the rainbow.
Done.
Beautiful.
This crayon has worked its magic.

Liza Nunner, Grade 7
New Albany Middle School, OH

You're Leaving Me

I know you like her,
but what about me?
She's moving in and I may be gone,
is that how you want it to be?
She ruined so much for you and your family,
I can't believe you'd pick her and lose so many like me.
We all love you so much,
now you're leaving us for her touch.
She's not nice, sweet, or pretty,
you should get a dog or maybe a kitty.
I can't believe you'd ever do this,
leave me behind just for a kiss.

Jessica Jones, Grade 9
Northeastern High School, OH

The Glass Death

It's raining today
Raining atmosphere
The sky is cracking
Shards falling from the heavens

Slicing through the air
Shattering on the porcelain world
A glass world falling apart
Glass buildings crashing to the ground

Glass people and
Glass cars
Glass cities
Coming apart

This is the end
Of a fragile world
A fragile industry
The glass death

Aryell Grist, Grade 7
New Albany Middle School, OH

Summer

School is out
learning's over!
Go to the beach
or just lay in clover

There's something to do
or something to say
we can help the world
or just have fun today

Not going to waste it
have to make this summer last
we can do whatever we want
no matter the price of gas!

We may just be kids
but that's no bummer
we know how to have fun
and that's perfect for summer!

Meara McNitt, Grade 8
Boyet Jr High School, LA

You Took It

You took it and you didn't even ask.
You didn't even wear a mask.
I didn't even know it was gone.
Not even for how long.
You took it in such a short time.
It must have been a perfect crime.
No one else took part.
Little do you know you took my heart.

Ivette Quintero, Grade 8
Columbia Middle School, IN

My Wedding Day

Bouquet in hand, hair done up tight,
Every curl in place, bearing to see the light.

Linked at the elbows, we stand here and wait.
Thoughts running through our heads, were we connected by fate?

I eye the carpet, laid out just for me.
We begin to walk slowly and I tremble at the knee.

My dress fitted tightly, not a tear in the seam.
It sparkles like crystals, yes beautiful I may be.

When we reach the altar, don't shed a tear,
I'm still your little girl, my love is always near.

I know you loved me first, I'll remember that forever.
But me and him, we chose to be together.

I'm going into good hands, ones I can cherish and hold.
Take care of Mom, and make sure she stays bold.

Today my heart goes to him, open your wings and set me free.
And remember your little girl, will always be me.

Kelcey Stauffer, Grade 8
Sandusky Middle School, MI

Luscious

Standing in the alluring aisle,
My two loves rest before me,
Begging me to crave for them,
Their similar individuality makes me baffled.

One soft, fine, and heart melting,
Slicked up in fire red apparel,
The other firm, tough and manly,
Stylish in caramel gold attire.

The two abolish my woes,
I long to be with them eternally,
Though that is surely unattainable,
Therefore a verdict is mandatory.

I examine my beloved's,
Snag the champion, and stroll home,
Relaxed on my couch, I unwrap the cover,
The paper crunching makes me feel inflamed.

The smooth, naked body of the delicacy makes my body tremble,
I pop it in my mouth, and the outer shell begins to melt,
Putting warmth inside me,
I tell myself I have chosen the superior one.

Jennifer Li, Grade 9
Elboya Elementary and Jr High School, AB

The Swirly

These fierce swirling monsters will demolish you
in an instant, these thunderous beasts of nature
will destroy in an instant
these giant swirling objects
pick up cows and houses
and even a school
or two, you better
be careful,
you might
be
next.

Russell Conway, Grade 8
St Peter Catholic High School, ON

Too Many

The smell of burnt flesh and hair fills my nostrils.
Guns firing in the background along with screams
of terror and joy from our arrival.
The smell of death fills the air
as if the reaper was there himself.
the scene of bodies is everywhere,
what I think are people look more like skin covering bones.
They touch my skin, the fingers feel so rough and cold
as if life is barely worth living anymore.
Too many go in but so few come out,
too many have gone above into heaven.
While the devil and his minions remain in the middle
instead of in their rightful place in hell.
The Jews look at us as if we were angels killing demons
that have held them prisoner for too long.
Too many are not coming out alive because of a simple man
possessed by the devil himself.

Alix Strobel, Grade 8
Parkway Middle School, OH

Today's World

How can the Lord put up with all this?
The killing, the violence, the cruelty.
How does one man cope with a loss?
The heartbreak, the last look.
How can a person never care?
The hurt, the teasing, the pain.
How does a person sleep at night not knowing?
What happens next, what's happening now.
How can one be truly happy without?
Love, safety, knowledge.
How does everyone smile when?
The world will end, millions are dying.
How can every boy and girl
How does everyone in the world
How come every time I cry
How come every time someone dies
We lose, we win, we call it a tie?
The answer is that we're lost

Megan Meisner, Grade 7
Hantsport School, NS

It's Not Called Gym-Nice-Sticks

Calluses and rips all over my hand
Blisters and scraped shins they proudly stand
I eagerly put my grips on my hand

When I hear the first beat of my music
I know everyone is watching me
My music makes butterflies jump in my stomach
I have to smile so big that the sun gets jealous
Present and flip are my thoughts

I see the chalk as it floats down on the vault
I am going for the flip
READY,
SET,
GO!
FLIP IT!

Four and a half inches of pure beam
I am ready to go
Salute as if I am the letter "Y"
All my thought are to dance like a pretty ribbon
Be the beam!

Lauren Livingstone, Grade 7
New Albany Middle School, OH

The Street Race

While cruisin' downtown late Saturday night,
I met a '48 Buick who pulled up on the right.
He rolled down his window and yelled, "How 'bout a drag?"
I said, "You're on, but I don't want to brag.

My Deuce Coupe is rumblin', the engine is purrin',
And when I get her into fourth, she'll really be roarin'."
We lined up at a bright red stoplight,
And I could tell I was in for a fight.

As the light turned green, we started to race,
Down the street we drove at a deadly pace.
Then I heard it, the ear-splitting bang.
I swerved hard to the left and my tires sang.

The Buick was engulfed like Dante's Inferno,
Flames leaping out of places internal.
I watched in shock as the car exploded,
And the siren of an ambulance, through the air it floated.

I think back to that horror-filled night,
With a corpse of a car still in my sight.
There is still one thought that cuts me like a knife,
Was a race really worth a young man's life?

Nicholas Morton, Grade 9
Grimsby Secondary School, ON

Life Without Love

Life without love
Is like featherless doves
Like waterless oceans
And meaningless motions
Like music void of any sound
And falling when you're on the ground

Life without love
Is like no rain from above
Like cold summers alone
And winters chilled to the bone
Like no warmth in your heart
Or feeling like there's a missing part

Life without love
Is like sadness you can't get rid of
Like an emptiness that doesn't feel right
Or days that seem darker than night
Something that you don't want to think of
Is life without love

Michell Kim, Grade 9
Eppler Jr High School, MI

Sports

Sports are great,
But you cannot be late.
There are a lot to choose from
So you better come.
So pick a sport
And meet me on the court.

Melissa Fox, Grade 7
St Gerald Elementary School, IL

Sorrow Forevermore!

You say it's my fault, 'cause you tried.
You say it's our fault, that you cried.
You say it's his fault, 'cause he died.
I'm dying on the inside!

I don't even know who to trust anymore,
Sorrow, forevermore!

I don't even know, what to do.
I don't even know, anything about you.
I don't even know, who to trust.
My whole life, is starting to rust!
I don't know who to believe in more,
Sorrow, forevermore!

I am hopeless, as I start another day.
I never even knew, what to say.
I don't know my friends anymore,
Sorrow, forevermore!

Ryan Plumadore, Grade 8
St Peter Catholic High School, ON

Future Occupation

To be an x-ray technician,
you have to know about technology.
Although it's very easy,
you have to study radiology.

Ashli Tanner, Grade 7
Fairfield Middle School, OH

You

I can't find the words to say this
and I know I'll never be able
to share with you.
All I want to say is
I love you
and
I miss you.
I wish you could come back.
I know that it's never going to happen
and each and every day
I'm praying and wishing
that one day we will meet again.

Allison McIsaac, Grade 7
Weledeh Catholic School, NT

Water

The water is a blue endless road
Water is an ant kingdom
Water is a rainforest filled with life
Water is a flood without any end

Josh Espiritu, Grade 7
St Monica School, IN

Save Our Earth

Will there be sunlight?
Will we have streams so broad and long?
Will the deer roam on our lawn?
Will there be trees,
Or how about the bees?
Is the Earth dying anytime soon?
Will the caterpillars still spin cocoons?
Will there be no more bears?
Some people don't even care.
Will we still breathe fresh air?
Save our Earth
Or what's left.
I know we can.
Let's keep it going,
And keep the wind blowing.
Don't regret things we have been given
Such as the blessing to live
Or the joy we have to give.
Keep it clean with all of our power
But remember we have each other
This may be our last hour.

Emma Brown, Grade 8
Center Middle School, OH

A Teardrop

As a teardrop falls,
An icon of sorrow,
No will comes to think
Of what joy holds tomorrow.

Whether a heart that is broken,
Or a spirit is crushed,
No one seems to think
After that teardrop is brushed.

Yes, the heart, it will mend,
And the spirit will strengthen,
But to you, right now
The scars seem to lengthen.

As the teardrop falls,
That icon of sorrow,
Stop, and think
Of what joy holds tomorrow.

Jennifer Penkov, Grade 9
Aurora Charter School, AB

Why?

We used to ask why all the time…
Why is the sky blue?
Why is the grass green?
Why are some people so mean?
Why does she look different than you?
Why don't you do it like I do?
Why are you tall?
Why do we fall?
Why is it cold?
Why do I get old?
Why is it bright?
Why do you have to fight?
Why does it matter?
Why is it called Saturn?
But our parents used to always say,
Because God made it or them that way.

Madison Craft, Grade 9
Genesee Jr/Sr High School, MI

Basketball

B ouncing the ball back and forth
A iming at the basket to make a shot in
S hooting the ball in a hoop
K eep running back and forth
E ncouraging your teammates
T ipping the ball to start the game
B reathing heavily from running
A ll the fans cheering
L ooking for a good pass
L earning to be a good sport

Nicolette Vanderwarren, Grade 7
St Gerald Elementary School, IL

In the Summer…

In the summer,
wind is fresh,
spring succeeded by warm, soft flesh
of mountains, groves, and sycamore trees,
the birds, the bees, caress with ease,
the sun soaked flowers of early morning
grow by night of earth and glowing
stars; the street as warm as fire,
the cars, swaying past, grind their tires
as deer and squirrels parade down the street,
what more than animals dancing with loose feet!
Go away! I say, as they move about,
for summer, short, is timed about.

Nathan Deeprose, Grade 9
John Paul II Catholic Secondary School, ON

My Dirty Room

My house, an elegant place,
Until you hit my room,
Just take one step into my room
and you are engulfed in a foul stench,
It is low, dark, cold, and damp,
It has an immense pile of clothes
piled to my ceiling in the corner,
Boxers,
Old smelly T-shirts,
Gym shorts,
And putrid smelling socks,
Under my bed is a ginormous clutter
of various artifacts from old broken toys to clothes,
Then my bed, it hasn't been made or washed in a year,
My garbage can has more garbage next to it than in it,
My stereo speaker bashed in with a baseball inside it,
My parents try to get me to clean it,
But they wouldn't dare venture into *my dirty room!*

Blake Persha, Grade 9
Clintonville High School, WI

Beautiful Stranger

That stranger sitting across the room
Gets tangled up in my mind

He is a treasure
Valuable and precious

He is a rainbow
Beautiful and radiant

He sits there without a clue, not knowing that I am here
Forgetting about all the surroundings around him

He notices other girls
Doesn't give me a chance

Only if I knew that
Beautiful Stranger

Tiana Yu, Grade 7
Menno Simons Christian School, AB

Awaiting

I'm in pain and sadness
Broken up inside
My wings have shattered like my life
Going crazy by the minute
Those tears I shed and hide
Waiting for you by the window side
I'm letting myself go now
As I fall from height
I see you standing there crying in my sight

Havi Nguyen, Grade 7
Fallingbrook Public School, ON

In the Old Home

Inside the house the floorboards squeak
The house groans please don't stomp on me
As you pound against the door
I think please don't do this anymore
When you decide to gut me out
This surgery hurts me all about
Then you hide my pretty floor
As your junk grows more and more
But when I hear the children cry
All I can do is sigh
Yes you think I'm just a house
But inside I care for every mouse
I love them when they come to stay
And I miss them when they go away
I might get a little battered
But that's why being a house ever mattered
I try to make myself a home
Even for the garden gnome
I remember every creature that stayed in my walls
And welcome others into my glorious halls

Katie McMillen, Grade 7
St Monica School, IN

When I Closed My Eyes

When I close my eyes,
And open them you are gone.
What happened we seemed like a good couple
What went wrong
Everything went black when I closed my eyes
All I see is what used to be,
I thought that everything was okay
And nothing could go wrong,
But when I closed my eyes
You were gone,
So now when I close my eyes
The biggest smile appears on my face,
When I closed my eyes there we were
Happy as can be,
When I closed my eyes I think of what used to be,
When I closed my eyes for the last time
I said goodbye and I love you to the end of time.

Brandy Mooney, Grade 9
Delta C 7 High School, MO

The Uncle I Never Knew?*

Robert Leo Eickholt, the uncle I never knew?
Robert Leo Eickholt born in 1947.
All too soon found his place in heaven.
A door gunner in a Huey helicopter never asked to be in the Army.
He no longer will be able to spend another day on God's beautiful green Earth.
Just three more weeks to serve this fine country, that he died for and he would have returned to Fort Carson.
He never made it to Fort Carson Colorado alive, only a body bag.
October 16th was his last day to write to his loved ones back in the States.
He never again will be in the midst of Jerome, Anna Marie, and his ten other siblings.
PFC Robert Leo Eickholt killed in Vietnam.
Helicopter crash…was what the Eickholt family read in 1947.
Even though it's been over 40 years.
Still today, thinking back there are many tears.
Robert Leo Eickholt the uncle I never knew?

Brad Eickholt, Grade 9
Ottoville High School, OH
*Dedicated to Robert Leo Eickholt.

Kara

Eyes like the morning sun, skin smoother than a baby's. Hair like silk blankets or flowers burning in the night, trees in the day blowing in the wind, lips like strawberries ripest of the season, teeth white as the snow is cold. A heart bigger than the world, her personality is so divine, perfect in every way, every angle, every inch, every ounce, she is perfect.

Orlando Guerra, Grade 7
River Forest Jr High School, IN

Sabrina and Silicon

There lived a girl, there lived an element; Sabrina and Silicon
When one would rise the other would set.
The rings of the silicon atoms represented a meal
Each one was a course in Sabrina's life to which she could not return after leaving it.
Silicon was a road in Sabrina's life, which she traveled.
Both the road and the traveler had high boiling points.
Silicon's strong bond to Oxygen was like Sabrina's love and devotion to her family.
Sabrina was useful and used for much just as Silicon was present amongst many things.
As Silicon was made of neutrons, protons, and electrons, Sabrina was made of a heart, a mind, and a body.
These were three essential things in each case but yet, it was enough.
The colors in which Sabrina perceived the world were as varied as the colors of Silicon.
Just as sodium silicate preserved eggs, Sabrina preserved happiness in the life of others.
Silicon's surface at times, was as smooth as Sabrina's life was.
The smell that each would shed, was like a sweet smelling rose.
Both the element and the girl worked hard
The element and the girl had been so close.
They were sisters; Sabrina was the sun and Silicon, the moon.
It was Silicon and Sabrina; it was S and S who had lived side by side without knowing it.

Sabrina Nolan, Grade 7
The Study School, QC

These Tears I Shed Are for You

These tears I shed, are for you. These tears remind me of how much you hurt me! Sometimes when I cry I think "Are you worth the pain and suffering I'm going through! Are you worth all these tears?" You hurt me like no other has before! These tears I shed, are for you. Thinking of the memories, thinking of you and all the good times…I can't explain how much I miss you and wish you were still mine, but its too late, alone I stay trying to shine…I just want you to be happy and not hurt, just know you'll always be my biggest flirt. I love you today, tomorrow, and always, I will always be here never leaving you alone, or lost. These tears I shed, are for you!

Tiffany Allore, Grade 7
Holy Trinity School, OH

Ode to an Apple

An apple
O' little red fruit falling from a tree
As juicy and crunchy as can be
You can be green, yellow, or even red
And you're a good snack to have before bed
Covered in caramel is such a treat
You can be delicious whether tart or sweet
Baked in a pie or poured in a glass
Your taste is something I won't pass
O' apple you are as red as a fire truck
If I eat you once a day, with the doctor I'll have luck
Round, robust, and ruby red
"You're good for me" my mother always said
I can bob for you on Halloween
And it is still fun even if you're a teen
The apple is red like an embarrassed face
I love you so much, I could eat you by the case
You can be used as an expression such as "the apple of my eye"
I'm sure that this expression will never die
An apple
Danny Winterrose, Grade 7
St Philip the Apostle School, IL

Sky

Sky has a face full of cloudy acne
that the wind cleanses as a daily routine.
When her best friend, Sun, goes to bed,
she dresses in her navy blue
and gold polka dotted pajamas
and stays up all night with Moon.
Does Sky ever sleep?

Katie Higginson, Grade 8
Fallingbrook Community Elementary School, ON

Hopeless War

Staring up at the dark night sky
I can't help it so I start to cry
This place is so beautiful
Or at least it once was
Before they came
And we had to fight for a cause
Now my city, once my home,
Is on fire and can't be helped
While I'm all alone
And will never be able to describe the things I've felt
Death is all around me
I keep trying to hold on
But I know I won't make it until the next dawn
I just want to let go
I can't stay here and watch anymore
For this fighting is endless and may never be resolved
My heart is slowing, my body is so very sore
Please, I'm begging
Someone please end this hopeless war.
Lauryn Woodyard, Grade 7
New Albany Middle School, OH

The Plunge

As I stand on the board, the world around me goes silent
The smell of chlorine
The hunger for fresh water
I gather my concentration

I feel the adrenaline coursing through me
My chest tight as I take a deep breath
I wait for the hovering feeling as I leave the board head first

I jump
I dive
The water rises up to meet me
I want to greet it like an old, well-known friend

The world spins rapidly as I flip
I spin around and around, as fast as a cheetah
I am in the air
I slice through the water like a knife

I jump
I flip
I hover
I dive

Jenna Metcalf, Grade 7
New Albany Middle School, OH

50 Stars, 13 Stripes

America, 50 stars, 13 stripes
America, Constitution, Civil Rights
Red, the blood we gave
White, the good of our brave
Blue, the love of our stars
This flag is ours

Christopher Columbus sailed the ocean blue in 1492
On October 12th, the crew spotted land
Oh, how they thought this was grand
George Washington, first in office
The one who led us all
Abraham Lincoln, our 16th leader
Who never told a lie
He was such an amazing guy

We have Founding Fathers
A lot to be exact
If you want to be like them
This is how you act
Be nice and kind, always use your mind
Be brave and wise, and heal other's cries
America, 50 stars, 13 stripes
Brittany Kessler, Grade 7
Owensville Community School, IN

The Motor City

Detroit
Polluted, crowded
Standing, growing, shining
Jazz-filled streets galore
Downtown

Ava Selke, Grade 7
Trinity Lutheran School, MI

Remember

First walk slowly,
Then start to run,
Focus on the burning
Of your lungs.
Feel the beating
Of your broken heart.
Try to escape
From the dark.
You're so close
And yet so far.
Mend your wounds
And cover your scars.
Try to hide,
And then you're lost.
For all your choices,
Consider the cost.

Hayley Steele, Grade 8
Boulan Park Middle School, MI

The Fierce Tiger

The fierce
Dangerous, even fast
Sprinting towards its prey
Quick
Tiger

Reily Hundley, Grade 8
Little Miami Jr High School, OH

Fall

Fall is orange,
Like the leaves on the ground,
It feels like falling in love,
It sounds really windy,
It smells like the year is passing by,
It tastes like orange pie,
Fall…it's always in my mind.

Monserrat Cabrales, Grade 7
Hamlin Upper Grade Center, IL

Flutists

F lutists play this every day
L ulling people to sleep
U sing their fingers to play
T hey could be a boy or a girl
E ither way, they always play

Alexandria Schoon, Grade 8
Mount Carmel Middle School, IL

I Once Loved You

I once loved you, but you broke my heart.
You said you loved me, but if you did you wouldn't have left me like this.
I once loved you, but you broke my heart.
You said I was your everything, but if I was you would be here with me.
I once loved you, but you broke my heart.
You said we were meant for each other, but if you meant it you wouldn't have left.

I once loved you, but I have to say you're going to miss this.

Heather Davis, Grade 8
Houston High School, OH

The Setting Sun

I stop, and gaze at you,
Taking in all of your magnificent touch of beauty.
I gaze at you,
Seeing millions of rays, creating millions of colors.
I gaze at you,
Observing how you appear to be an orange goblet of fire.
I gaze at you,
Knowing how hard you worked the day,
Wondering how you can look so peaceful now.
I gaze at you,
Enveloped with passion, thanks, and love for the nature you are able to create.
I gaze at you,
Pondering the thought of what it is like to see the world, with your big eyes.
I gaze at you,
Hoping that you will always stay golden.
I gaze at you,
Questioning how many others are able to see the lust and bliss that you give to us.
I gaze at you,
The Setting Sun.

Hannah Schlacter, Grade 8
Daniel Wright Jr High School, IL

A Dream

Maybe there's more to life, than just what meets the eye.
There's a dream inside of all of us, if we open up our eyes.
There's a whole new world around us, and the limit is the sky.
All you have to do is let your dreams begin to fly.

A dream is a voice unheard,
A silent song that speaks to the world.
A dream alone, has the power,
To guide us through our darkest hour.

But a dream is just a dream.
It's nothing more than it seems to be.
We think of it as a brand new creation.
It's just a figment of our imagination.

Maybe there's something greater, than just the two of us.
It's something greater we may never know, but it creates a bond of trust.
So come with me and together, we're more than we seem;
Our hearts are true for me and you, and it begins with a dream.

Umar Farooq, Grade 7
Gilbert Middle School, IA

Cyclone

A peaceful day in Myanmar,
No one knew a storm would befall.

Going about as they would have been,
No one knew of the danger that would begin.

A speck of black in the twilight sky,
All for those who knew no alibi,

Storm that came, just that fast,
No one came out of the aftermath.

Bodies thrown and strewn away,
People screamed, thinking this could be their last day.

No help came,
Their government wouldn't let them,

So no one would guess,
That on that fateful day,

Thousands would die,
And their spirits wouldn't roll away.

Mikayla Vogel, Grade 8
Sandusky Middle School, MI

I Am From

I am from an island,
Where the sun shines so bright.

I am from an island,
Where the ocean is calm.

I am from an island,
Where the people are kind.

I am from an island,
Where the day just passes by.

I am from an island,
Where the sugarcanes grow day by day.

I am from an island,
Where the field of grass makes you melt away.

I am from an island,
Where the birds fly free.

I am from an island,
Where the citizens call it paradise.

Ashini Nunkoo, Grade 8
Weledeh Catholic School, NT

Summer With My Family

My cousins and brothers eat ice cream cones,
As my sisters turn off their cell phones.
All are sporting swim suits,
Where we used to play in our snow boots.
Our brand new swimming pool,
That is oh so cool.
I feel so warm from my calloused toes,
To my sun-kissed nose.
All ten toes are painted pink,
As I think,
What a wonderful time this will be,
To spend time with my family.
This beautiful season,
Full of the bright, yellow sun,
Gives us a reason,
To play and have some fun.
My family looks forward to summer.
We enjoy each and every day.
What a bummer,
That it will soon go away.

Alexis McDowell, Grade 7
Danby Rush Tower Middle School, MO

Animals on a Colored Day!

A **b** eautiful **c** olored **d** ay!
E nthusiastic **f** rogs **g** reatly **h** opping,
i guanas **j** umping, **k** angaroos **l** aughing.
M any **n** umerous **o** ctopus **p** laying **q** uietly.
R abbits **s** earching **t** ogether **u** nderneath **v** ines
w ith e **x** cellent **y** ellow **z** ebras.

Tiffany Swanson, Grade 8
Shakopee Area Catholic School, MN

Anne Frank

I am happy with my friends.
I hear the birds and laughter.
I see blue skies.
I say good morning to everyone!
I cry when Hello isn't around.
I am free!

I am scared.
I want to play.
I need fresh air.
I hope the war will be over soon.
I fear what will happen to us if we are found.
I am still hopeful.

I am moving on a train.
I feel tired.
I try to keep a smile.
I wonder if Daddy will be okay.
I dream of freedom, and what it once felt like.
I am Anne Frank!

Mariah Andersen, Grade 8
Boulan Park Middle School, MI

Frustration

It
Starts out
small
Then gets bigger
Every
Little
thing
Adding on
It
Feels like
I'm
About
To explode
The
Ever growing
Bubble
About to pop
School, Home, Friends, Work
Building up inside
About to burst

Jessica Vaughn, Grade 9
West Jr High School, MO

Candy

Chocolate, chips and cookies
three delicious things.
The taste and the flavour is irresistible.
Once I start I can't stop.
As it melts in my mouth
only I matter.
I feel so vulnerable when I eat you
because you make me happy
and make me laugh.
When I share you with my friends
we savour you
and make you last.
I love these three special things
named chocolate, chips and cookies.

Sarah Black, Grade 7
Weledeh Catholic School, NT

why me?

why…why…why is it always me…
why do i have to do it all
i…me…why me?
stop why? this is me…
that is you why can't i be you…?
if i were you and you were me…
things would be different
i would not be me anymore
and i would no longer be alone
but wait i would rather be me than you
because i can do things that you can't do
so it's much better to be me than you

Jake Konyha, Grade 8
Central Middle School, MI

A Normal Day at a Death Camp

This morning I wake up, weaker than the day before.
There is screaming all around, moaning galore.
I walk out into the coldness, stumbling as I go.
Looking up in the sky, I see lovely snow.
Sticking my tongue out to taste it, but snow isn't there.
For it is ashes I see, floating in the air.
The ashes are snow falling from the sky.
They come from the crematoria, where the smoke rises high.
The smokestacks are like mountains, a mile high in the air.
Bodies burnt there daily, and the Nazis just don't care.
I go to eat my breakfast, which is hardly nothing.
How I wish to be home eating Mother's stuffing. "Yum!"
But now all I taste is bitter coffee and stale bread.
None of the prisoners are even close to being well fed.
I go off to work now, but a Nazi stops me.
He takes me off to the crematoria with many others, where I can't see.
He pushes me in line with his cold hard hands.
The stench of rotting bodies, I cannot hardly stand.
The smoke burns my nose, while I catch a glimpse of the fire dancing.
I can smell the burnt bodies and hear the fire sizzling.
I feel the heat of the fire, the end is almost near.

Jamie Dicke, Grade 8
Parkway Middle School, OH

Nursery Rhyme

Just because I am a child
It doesn't mean I don't know war,
And all the daily struggles that lie outside my door;
It doesn't mean I go to school to learn to read and write,
Or have a mom and dad who will always hold me tight.

Just because I am a child
It doesn't mean I've time to play,
And listen to silly fairy tales to brighten up my day;
It doesn't mean I get tucked into bed, when night is close at hand,
No, I care for all my siblings or work the barren land.
It doesn't mean I've clothes to wear,
And have someone to talk to, like a fuzzy teddy bear;
It doesn't mean I brush my teeth or even wash my face,
For I haven't got the time to leave my hiding place.

Just because I am a child
It doesn't mean I'm free from all disease,
And can smile anytime I'd like or get when I say please;
It doesn't mean I've got a home or even got a name,
Still I wake up every morning and play life's little game.

Just because I am a child…please listen when I speak out
And save me some trouble so I do not have to shout.

Hannah Fisher, Grade 9
Olds Jr/Sr High School, AB

Live or Die

Up or down, left or right,
You be strong now
Put up a good fight.
Stop or go, leave or stay,
Life's nothing but a game
So get out there and play.
Walk or run, swim or fly,
Keep your chin up
Don't you dare cry.
Jump or crawl, whisper or scream,
Reality check
This is not a dream.
More like a nightmare,
That we all call life.
Spending each and every day,
Just trying to get by.
Trying to fool people
By keeping everything inside.
The only real choice you have
Is to live or die.

Chelsea Vancleave, Grade 9
Southwest Jr High School, AR

My "Sister"

Long distance is free
But, love pays the price.
Miles and miles away from this place
Thinking of you, thinking of me
Imagining us together
Hand in hand
Heart with heart
Sharing our secrets
And laughs from when we were apart.

Sarah Nagel, Grade 8
Prairie View Middle School, IL

A Child's Song*

So much depends on
    A short, little lady.
        Struck with her beauty
        Standing by my bed.
She tucks me in
    With a sweet little song
        Then kisses my head
        As I dream along.
As I wake in the morning
    My breakfast is waiting
        Her soft song just soaring
        All through my head
Just thinking of her now
    So much depends on
        A short, little lady.

Justine Richardson, Grade 8
Goshen Middle School, IN
*Inspired by William Carlos Williams

Immortal Burn

You
have left me to endure
with myself
alone.

How dreadful and cruel
could you be?

Your love
ever distant
has created a disaster
in my heart.

You
are the reason
why I
mourn.

James Vandergraaf, Grade 7
Menno Simons Christian School, AB

That Night

In the dark sky,
The moon is bright.
I let out a sigh,
I can see the stars in sight.

I hear the animals roar
While I watch the Northern Lights dance.
I see the birds soar,
And the wild horses prance.

I lay on the ground,
In my backyard,
Enjoying everything around.
How can anyone say that life is hard?

My world is filled with treasure,
That I'll need a lifetime to measure.

Alexa Valleau, Grade 8
Wainwright High School, AB

Baseball

Baseball is like the best restaurant.
You can smell the popcorn.
The cotton candy.
I can hear the vendor,
"Get your ice cold drinks!"
The great players.
The hard seats,
Like cement.
Watch out!
The balls come out of nowhere,
Might be a strike out.

Cody Small, Grade 7
Paw Paw Middle School, MI

My Own Worst Enemy

Those wicked eyes pierce through me
Like a million daggers
She cackles
Obviously taking pleasure
In my sense of defeat

She doesn't know me
And I'm unfamiliar with her
She's living on the edge
I prefer to play by the rules
In a way, I think we complete each other

Sometimes I'm jealous of her
She doesn't fear the world
She's something I wish I could be,
Powerful
But I'll never be like her

She's so intimidating
It takes all my living breath
Like a candle in a hurricane
Just to look away
To pretend I didn't see her
Looking back at me in the mirror

Alexa Bien, Grade 8
South Middle School, WI

The Rose in Hand

The rose in hand
Its thorn is sharp
It cuts a hole within your finger
and blood may linger

The rose in hand
It is so beautiful
It's like a baby being born,
but do not forlorn

The rose in hand
It will not be forever
It dies so fast
and will not last

The rose in hand
You feel that you love him so
He loves you with much love
from up above

The rose in hand
You'll see it's true
You'll face the hard hitting blows
You'll find the meaning of the rose

Autumn Callender, Grade 7
Washington Middle School, OH

Where I'm From

I'm from here, there, everywhere
I'm from a place where being polite and treating your elders with respect is a must, and should be first
I'm from a place where friends and family are valued the most.
Where partying comes before everything else
I am from a place where being weird and dumb is the normal thing to do.
Where girls gave up on guys a long, long time ago.
Where we hide out behind bushes because we don't want to go home
And we make s'mores in the microwave
Where dancing in the rain is a normal ritual
You drop what you're doing to help someone else
Where you always think of others before yourself.
And you never disobey your elders
Where a sisterly bond is held onto tight
Where I was born is just like everywhere else
We just choose to spend our time differently than yours
And I'm ok with being different or not being from the same place as you
Just because we have different backgrounds doesn't mean we can't have the same future of friendship together.

Alexa Brandalik, Grade 8
Little Miami Jr High School, OH

Remembering You

Sittin' at the hospital,
Listening to the clock tick,
I watch you in the bed worryingly.
Memories of me and you rush through my head;
Memories of when we still ran from cooties,
Times we thought it was the world's end as our parents tried to hook us up,
Memories of our nervous hands holding on to one another,
Times you ran behind me just to make me jump,
Memories of you coming behind me chanting, "ummmm," as I tried to meditate before a big game,
Thoughts of the first time our lips touched,
And hoping you would just wake up
Remembering me as I remember you.

Jennie Caswell, Grade 8
Poplar Bluff Jr High School, MO

Critical Times

There is no way but one way out of life…
critical times, teens committing crimes and kids getting caught in a drive by,
So why then must we fight?
No!
Why then must we suffer?
To prove to the next person that he or she is tougher?
In every step you take,
In every move you make,
There is always someone seeking to devour you!
And with each second and minute that goes around, you catch a gang banger
on the curb about to commit a murder and joke about it like a clown.
We Are Living in Critical Times!
And I'm not just saying this because I wrote down a couple lines,
and a couple rhymes.
I'm saying this because once you're on that hospital bed and those doctors yelling "Clear!"
Your family is at home, in tears…because of fear.

Dequandre Williams, Grade 8
Cuffe Math-Science Tech Elementary Academy, IL

Civil War — Antietam

The shots were being fired all over the place
People dropping all around
He bolted towards the camouflage shelter
Not able to hear a sound

His friend was in the small shelter
Shot twice in the arm
He didn't have time to stop and help
The enemy had set off the alarm

He ran outside just to see
Bodies soaked in blood
The few men left fired away
Hidden in the mud

As the enemy got so much closer
Out of there he scrammed
For he didn't want to be yet another
Casualty in Antietam

Maegan Clark, Grade 9
Southwest Jr High School, AR

Peace

The sand betwixt my toes with peace,
The tides go on in rows,
Waves crashing in a cadence
Like a metronome in beat,
Sitting in the tepid sand,
The lavish breeze in coconut trees,
The extreme is pure,
The sunset is immaculate,
The placid roll up my feet
Leaving sand betwixt my toes with peace,
Leaving sand betwixt my toes with peace.

Shanna Kim, Grade 8
Little Miami Jr High School, OH

Spring

When I see the white blankets of snow turn to muddy brown,
I know it's spring.
When I hear the drip, drip of melting snow,
I know it's spring.
When I smell the fresh crisp air,
I know it's spring.
When I hear the crack of a baseball bat,
I know it's spring.
When I hear chirps of singing birds in the morning,
I know it's spring.
When I see the buds pop out,
I know it's spring.
When I see the green sea of grass,
I know it's spring.
When I see the rainbow flowers blossoming,
I know it's spring.

Blake Singewald, Grade 9
Cannon Falls Sr High School, MN

Family

My family comes together,
As perfect as can be,
Where everyone is loving,
And I can just be me.

My family comes together,
No matter color, shape, or size,
You will always see,
Love in each other's eyes.

My family comes together,
By happiness, peace, and love,
No matter if they're here,
Or ever up above.

My family comes together,
With exciting and fun times,
We never know what's next,
(Because I can't think of anything that rhymes)

My family comes together,
It is always so much fun,
With lots of joys and laughter,
We'll always be as one.

Ginny Fielhauer, Grade 7
Holy Cross Elementary School, MI

Anger

Anger is the color of the fierce tiger's blood
It sounds like the rage of a lion
And it tastes like the spicy salsa of the south
It smells like the steam coming from an engine
It looks like the wild animal guarding its cubs
It makes me feel enraged

Anger is the color of the blazing orange fire
It sounds like the screaming of a train quickly stopping
And it tastes like the bitterness of a lemon
It smells like a candle that has been blown out
Anger looks like the faces of the provoked
It makes me feel curious

Anger is the color of the somber gale sky
It sounds like the silence of thoughts
And it tastes like red peppers chilled through the night
It smells like the dying trees
It looks like a strike of lightning hitting the surface
It makes me feel dangerous

Anger is what breaks apart the good and bad.

Kaitlin Silver, Grade 8
Little Miami Jr High School, OH

Camaro

C orvette's little brother
A nother great machine
M ore and more popular
A nd I think they're the best
R espected car at its best
O nly car I want to drive

Logen Bonnema, Grade 8
Ireton Christian School, IA

Calm as an Open Pond

C alm as an
O pen pond on a hot summer
D ay
Y oung

A nd quiet
N o one thinks I am wild or loud until…
K ERPLUNK
E xcited, free, and fresh when a
R ock falls into the pond
M aking wild ripples without
A nybody to say
N o

Cody Ankerman, Grade 7
New Albany Middle School, OH

Years

The years pass by
Time flew by
You've been you've gone
So quickly you barely knew it
You're surprised
Hearing all the things you've done
In those short years

Delanie Allen, Grade 8
Wainwright High School, AB

Summer's Here!

Summer is here, it's time to play!
Go outside and shout hooray!
Let's make it last,
it goes by too fast
we'll play while it's here
with laughter and cheer,
until next year!

Jenna Reno, Grade 7
Ponchatoula Jr High School, LA

My iPod

I have an iPod I call Mo,
I take her wherever I go,
She plays pop and classical,
Her rap's fantastical,
Mo's a music diva, fo sho!

Alexa Del Riesgo, Grade 7
Buckeye Valley Middle School, OH

Seasons Change

Blue sky, birds fly, warm breeze, summer ease.
Talking friends, school ends.
Mosquito bites here and there. Bees buzzing in the air.
Trees grow tall, orange leaves come, green ones fall.
Grassy "Race you to the bottom" hills.
Oh, look, finally here's autumn. Pumpkins, candy, costumes galore,
Looks like Halloween's at my door.
Snow, snow everywhere. Look, there's an old hare.
Don't be so loud, you might give him a scare.
Christmas time. Oh, what a joyous time! For family fun and toys.
All the snow has melted away. We can now go out and play.
Flowers got big and brighter. No more heavy coats, much lighter.
School is coming to an end. Oh, what a bummer, but cheer up,
Because it looks like again
Here's summer!

Athena Sheehan, Grade 7
St Pauls Lutheran School, IL

The Rays of the Sun

Upon the water its light is blinding and bewitching —
The enchanting rays of the sun.
The ungraspable golden glow wraps me up in warmth —
The tender rays of the sun.
Its illumination comes and goes as melancholy clouds roll by —
The unforgettable rays of the sun.
A beam of hope and peace cast from the heavens —
The blessed rays of the sun.
A radiance not to be possessed yet cannot be relinquished —
The perplexing rays of the sun.

Julie Zhang, Grade 8
Fern Avenue Jr/Sr Public School, ON

The Finish Line

The gun signals the start,
People spring to life,
They look as fast as cheetahs compared to those standing on the sidelines.
I make sure that no one can pass me.

I feels like it's 100 degrees, as hot as the desert.
Parents are cheering from the side,
Screaming for you to speed up.
We start to get tired.

Trying not to trip over the orange cones marking the course,
The only sound is our feet hitting the ground.
There's the mile mark,
Volunteers call out our times.
We keep going, knowing that it's only half over.

Everyone's tired and wants to quit,
The disgusting smell of sweat hangs in the air.
I get to the track, only 100 yards to go.
My heart is beating quickly,
The finish line is calling my name.

Elissa Burack, Grade 7
New Albany Middle School, OH

Something Wonderful

Everything is a blur, rushing by,
Just trying to focus on what's next.
Birds chirping, squirrels climbing.

The smell of the newly grown grass
Seeping into my nose. Smells like freedom,
Almost like you're untouchable.

I can hear the motor roaring like a lion.
I feel my wrist start to ache from turning the throttle,
But I don't care.

On the straight dirt path, you go as fast as lightning.
Seeing so many great things in the woods,
Such amazing things.
Even when you stop, or slow down,
Things become so clear, so wonderful.

Can't imagine it coming to an end,
But when it does, you feel this sensation.
Like you have conquered the world.
It was, something wonderful.

Sean Conley, Grade 7
New Albany Middle School, OH

Cloe

My puppy Cloe is cute
My puppy Cloe is small
My puppy Cloe is the greatest
Of them all

She is white and brown
She has a twinkle
In her eyes

She loves to play
She loves to run
She loves to sleep
Under the sun

She makes me happy
Never sad and
When I come home
She makes me glad

My puppy is my best friend
She will always be
And when it's time to play
She will always make
Me happy

Jenna Wozniak, Grade 7
St John the Baptist Elementary School, IN

Frustrated

I stomp my feet like an angry giant,
My hand clenches like a pair of pliers.
I feel like screaming,
Like a little kid not getting his own way.
I am a bear searching for food,
Not able to find it.
I groan like I have a pop quiz.
Grumpy,
Mad,
Frustrated.
I try to leave but something is holding me back.
Then I start to think to myself,
Why keep going on about it?

Tiffany Shantz, Grade 7
Linwood Public School, ON

September

I guess God got many angels that day.
Why? Why? Why!! Does it have to be this way?
Why were so many taken that fateful September?
Why were so many families forced only to remember?
Loved ones lost at their hands.
Innocent civilians murdered by their plans.
As we watch the towers fall and fall that September.
We should remember the families that have to remember.
Loved ones lost that day.
In an event that rocks the world to this day.

Bailey Akers, Grade 7
Bedford Community Middle School, IA

Fly*

Fly into the sky
Like a balloon
you're sure to make it to the top
Heaven
It's where you belong
With her forever
Go up and say goodbye to us
We will meet again someday
Don't worry
For we'll grieve your loss
But we can get through it
By sticking together as one
You'll be watching us
We will always remember that
The world will change without you
But I'm sure we'll find a new path
The road you led was wonderful
Your memories you leave us with will never be forgotten
You have been called upon by God
Take the journey and eventually we'll be sure to catch up

I love you Great Grandpa Stoffel.

Tori Twohig, Grade 9
Campbellsport High School, WI
*Dedicated to Jerome Stoffel, who was my great grandpa

Days

Days are long, brutal, but sweet
Days are short, sweet, but brutal
Days are different, up and down
Days are crazy all around
When you wake up every day
You will get up and say
Oh just another ordinary day

Ashley Wilson, Grade 7
Thomasboro Grade School, IL

Goodbye

I lay on the floor
Teddy bear in hand
I think of my dad
Who died from a heart attack!
I wish I could have said goodbye
When does your mouth,
Say goodbye to your heart?
Now I feel apart,
Away from his love
I wish to fly away
Like a little white dove
Because I couldn't say…
Goodbye
When does your mouth,
Say goodbye to your heart?

Stephanie Amundson, Grade 8
Smyser Elementary School, IL

Home to My Heart

Outside is foggy
with mist,
I'm in my bed
staring out my
big square windows
into it
thinking,

How could I
give my heart
the right home?

Where meals are always hot
and where water does not
get thirsty —

An idea struck me;
but just a
single one…

I think
that in this world
nobody can make it
through alone.

Kalyn Reinardy, Grade 9
Cannon Falls Sr High School, MN

Hope

Hope is the color of never-ending sky, that contains all of the dreams of the world.
It sounds like the gentle breeze whispering through the rolling hills.
Hope tastes like cool ice cream on a hot summer day,
It smells like blooming honeysuckle and lilac flowers in the early spring,
Hope looks like the sunrise with all its brilliant colors.
Hope makes me feel peaceful.

Hope is the brightest color you can imagine,
It sounds like baby chirping birds,
It tastes like sweet, fresh picked cherries.
Hope smells like the fresh morning air,
It looks like beautiful, calm waves.
Hope makes me feel at ease.

Hope is the color of a beautiful red rose,
It sounds like the gentle beat of rain,
Hope tastes like a ripe watermelon,
It smells like the ocean.
Hope looks like a beautiful airless cloud,
Hope makes me feel confident.

Hope is what makes the world go 'round.

Heather Stern, Grade 8
Little Miami Jr High School, OH

Life

Life is like an ice cream; enjoy it before it's gone
Until it's totally done with, have fun from dusk to dawn

Life is like sour Skittles; sweet, sour, and bitter all inside
With tasteless and tasteful memories; full of both hurt and pride

Life isn't like a story; you won't know the end till it's done
There really is no guide book on how to live for fun

Life's sweet and fun and bitter; you'll meet people fun and nice
You'll also meet some people whose hearts are cold as ice

So when you go out in the real world, life can be a game to win
It can also be a drama that will rise above the din

So even when you're a child, enjoy life to its best
Don't bother getting so worried; don't waste time being stressed

Just have a lot of fun and make your life worthwhile
And don't be afraid to let people in; always save for everyone a smile

That's how to live life well; good luck to you, I say
Enjoy life to its fullest and do something special every day

Rachel Bromberg, Grade 8
Pleasantville Public School, ON

Untitled

I dribble, dribble, and dribble down the field
But suddenly I come to a yield

I look ahead, the defense all around
My feet steadily planted in the ground

Dribbling, now running, concentrating
Thinking, it's all worth it in the end

Determination fills my soul,
Especially when I make the GOAL!!!

Nicolette Beeken, Grade 8
Mater Dei School-Nativity Center, IA

The Time of My Life

Watching the team before us hit everything,
My nerves get even more tense;
As the team walks off wishing us luck,
I hear our fans going crazy in the crowd.

The announcer says our name,
We skip on stage happily smiling
As we walk out on the fuzzy floor,
I tell myself that I will not mess up.

We stand at our starting positions,
Music starts blasting and the crowd roars,
Judges are just a few feet away
Watching your every move like a hawk on its prey.

We hit our last stunt and the music tops,
Our coaches run over to hug us,
They say we did spectacular!

I was so happy we did great.
My life is right here on this big, blue spring floor.
It didn't even matter if we won or lost.
I was proud of us anyway.

Sam Guirlinger, Grade 7
New Albany Middle School, OH

I Love You

You're my one and only
I never want to be lonely
When I close my eyes I see your face
Your eyes shine just like a red ace
I want to be with you until the end of days
Even though our love is like a maze
I love you more than anything
I wish I could tell you everything
I want to grow old with you
I hope you never say we are through
I love you without regret
I haven't found anyone like you yet.

Halei Carl, Grade 7
Triopia Jr/Sr High School, IL

Ode to Shoes

High heels, flats, and wedges,
you're the best,
you're stylish everywhere I go.

Jimmy Choo, Versace, or Prada,
doesn't matter what designer label you are,
you're still the best in my mind.

Black, silver, or red,
doesn't matter what color you are,
you still add spice to any outfit.

Anna Gasperetti, Grade 8
Whitewater Middle School, WI

I Love You

Tears went down my face
When I picked up the phone
They told me you were gone.
I didn't know what to do or say but just cry.
I
Miss
You
Words can't express what you meant to me,
You meant the WHOLE WORLD to me.
I
Love
You
You're in my heart, in my everyday life,
I think of you every day,
You were and still are
My GRANDPA!

Lilit Harutyunyan, Grade 7
Weledeh Catholic School, NT

Auschwitz

The bitter taste of death in the air.
The scent of rotting corpses all around,
and the skeletons walking by.
The pain from the hunger hurts way too bad,
like an axe in the back.
The wood from the shovel splinters my hand as I work.
The same pain as before.
We eat only bitter soup,
while we smell the food from the S.S. quarters.
The sight of the smoke,
makes me want to be sick.
The burnt stench of human flesh drifts across the camp.
The guards scream at me to get to work.
Boom! Then gun shots all around.
The dying sounds of people crying out.
The flash and the bang.
Then all is black.
Now all is peaceful, no more screams, no more fear.
No more pain and suffering.
Finally I can rest in peace.

Gage Regedanz, Grade 8
Parkway Middle School, OH

Blackbeard

There once was a pirate,
Who people called Blackbeard.
Who sailed across oceans
Stealing treasure he adhered.

He and his crew,
Sailed on the Queen Anne's Revenge.
Working for the British
Who sought to avenge.

One day up ahead
He saw a big ship.
With many treasures aboard.
That would soon be held in his grip.

Their crew was exhausted,
And could barely defend
Blackbeard captured the treasure.
And let them sink to their end.

Not wanting anyone else
To have this great treasure
He buried it all.
Where it shall stay forever.

Kaitlyn Foote, Grade 8
Sandusky Middle School, MI

Babies to Elders

Babies
Loud, playful
Cry, eat, sleep
Pacifier, diapers, dentures, clothes
Funny, loving, smelly
Wrinkly, old
Elders

Carah Poffenbarger, Grade 7
Fairfield Middle School, OH

One Window Is All I Need

One window is all I need
To know what could have happened
To know what I would have done
For me to finally rest
To see who I could have became
To know if I could change the world

Robert Steele, Grade 8
Wainwright High School, AB

Elyse Walton

Crazy and fun
Had a weird heart
Living for the day
Living on right now!
Going out for life

Elyse Walton, Grade 8
Whitewater Middle School, WI

welcome to my world

Welcome to my world. Sometimes it stinks, sometimes it doesn't.
It may be harsh but I can make it through.
At the end of the day I know it's true that I have a great life.

Ryan Rahlf, Grade 8
Kewaskum Middle School, WI

I, too, Sing America

I too, sing America
America, I'm the one that mows your lawn.
No, I'm the one that sells your hair at 12 at night.
Wait I'm the one that doesn't have an education.
But I'm the one that is "trailer trash."
You all know that I'm in the mafia.

America
I'm black and blue.
I'm yellow and red.
I'm pink and orange.
I'm white and green.

America
Don't stereotype me. Don't write me off.
Don't look down on me. Don't segregate yourself from me.

America
I'm Mexican.
I'm Korean.
I'm African American.
I'm Caucasian.
I'm Italian.

America, without me there is no America.

Taja Silverman, Grade 9
Gwendolyn Brooks College Preparatory Academy, IL

Track

My nerves are shaking,
My legs are twitching,
My heart is pounding rapidly,
There is nothing I want more than to come in first.

I am at the starting line trembling with fear,
I feel the bounce of the rubber track,
I am ready to take off,
POW! The starter shoots the pistol.

I take off thinking of nothing but victory,
All I can feel is the beat of my heart,
I hear the roaring fans in the distance,
I try to stay focused.

Suddenly someone passes me, I build up all my might to run faster,
I am beside her trying to keep up,
My legs want to quit, but I keep going,
I can feel victory in my hands.

I spread my arms out and leap across the finish line,
I AM THE WINNER!

Stephanie Tari, Grade 7
St Clare Catholic Elementary School, ON

A Familiar Feeling

I feel this *familiar feeling*,
quite often:
at many times, in many places.

On a blizzardy snow day
I bounce, like a ball in a wild game.
My grins are large, odd coloured bananas.
On Friday afternoons, just as the final bell rings,
anticipation of fun flows out from me.
At Christmas,
my super smiles spring from every wall,
like the sun on the open ocean.
When I win a great prize
my smiles are brighter than the sun overhead.
At birthdays
our laughs overflow from us like
150 gallons of water in a 100 gallon tub.
Just before music class
silly smiles and gigantic grins cover my face.

I couldn't feel more…more…
What *do* I feel?

Michaelah Robinson, Grade 7
Linwood Public School, ON

I Have Learned

I have learned things aren't always as they seem
I have learned the nicest people turn out mean
I have learned never to trust people with my secrets
I have learned only to tell people stuff that I know can keep it

I have learned not to depend on anyone but myself
I have learned how to take care of me and preserve my health
I have learned to think before I talk
I have learned what it means to crawl before you walk

I have learned the true definition of love
I have learned to strive high and aim to be above
I have learned not saying anything can gain me respect
I have learned that silence gives off a lasting effect

I have learned how to improve my own self-esteem
I have learned that it's more than normal to dream
I have learned when it's time for something to come to an end
I have learned when a friend is not truly a friend

I have learned mistakes will always be made
I have learned that love never fades
I have learned that promises are meant to be broken
I have learned to treasure life like a precious token

Shawntha Penro, Grade 9
Gwendolyn Brooks College Preparatory Academy, IL

Soccer

Soccer is fun for everyone to play and enjoy
Kick the ball hard, kick the ball soft
Rolling across the grass, maybe a goal
Many players, coach, line judges
Friends and family cheering on
Watching out for offsides
Head the ball
Kick hard
GOAL
Fans cheer, players line up
Start again, kick hard
Coach is coaching, moms yelling
Up the field, down the field
Score again, pats on back, fans cheering
Soccer is fun for everyone to play and enjoy

Elsie Lang, Grade 8
Shakopee Area Catholic School, MN

Who Am I?

I am a dancer who loves to dance all night long.
I like to dance alone in the studio,
I feel the pounding of my heart
When I work really hard.
I hear the music so loud it makes me sway,
I see the grin on my face,
And the determination in my eyes,
When I glance in at the mirror.
I am a dancer who loves to dance all night long.

I wonder how others feel when they watch me.
I know they are jealous,
When they see my moves.
I care about their feelings and try not to brag.
I wish everyone could watch me.
I am a dancer who loves to dance all night long.

Sydney Cunningham, Grade 7
Paw Paw Middle School, MI

Ecstatic

I explode with happy things to say
my heart pounds like a drum
twitching, twirling like a clown
jumping, joyfully up and around
I'm fizzing like excitement
   I'm happy
   delighted
   overjoyed
My hands are eager like a hungry bear with lots of food
frantically, fighting around
jumping for pleasure and glee
I'm as wild as a rock band playing loudly
My heart races like a train on a railway track
I am stirred up with excitement
   I am ecstatic

Martha Martin, Grade 7
Linwood Public School, ON

To Love

In many years ago,
The battles between us were fought high and low.
We declared to see each other dimly,
And cover the sorrow of thou changing faces.

For we knew of a shameful past,
Both filled with crimes despised by ourselves.
For the beginning of the end is here and a sign of new hope and love to follow.

Sought revenge by her persecutors for the memories to despise,
Sought revenge by his persecutors for the sorrowed depressed memories to deny.

Of many who wiser than we, predicted the prophecy of love.
Love in which would break the spell of internal sadness.

In the triumphant times in which we hear the horns call the depressed, sad,
and sorrowed ones shall be free from their sepulcher and will find revenge sought for so many years.
The blind will see, the deaf hear, the ill cured, and unloved loved, and this is their tribute — to love.

Tanner Jones, Grade 7
Chillicothe Middle School, MO

I

I am calm and collected.
I wonder why there are so many questions in the world, as if life was meant to be a perpetual mystery.
I hear life calling to me, telling me to help repair our shattered world.
I see concealed decrepitude everywhere I go.
I want peace to be my country's chief export; I'd care for nothing else.
I am calm and collected.

I pretend that we all play set roles in the grand scheme of things, and that I know it will end happily.
I feel that we could all do our part to save the world; no one does more damage than he who knew he could do something, and
        yet did nothing.
I believe that if we all work together, we can solve any problem.
I worry that the people of today will be seen as the generation that did nothing because they restrained themselves to thinking
        they couldn't do anything.
I cry when I think of the world we will have created for our grandchildren.
I am calm and collected.

I understand that my idealism will almost always leave me disappointed.
I say that life is a right of those who spend their lives working for the greater good.
I dream of a world in which there is no violence and no malignance, no plague and no destruction.
I try to make the world a better place each day.
I hope that we will one day find living in peace with everything around us is the only solution.
I am calm and collected.

Arman Odabas, Grade 7
New Albany Middle School, OH

Winter

W is for weather that's like vanilla ice cream in the winter
I is for the ice that sleeps through the night
N is for the whistling night that is filled with pure darkness
T is for the trembling of the body when in the cold
E is for the extra snow that feels so fun to play in and good to eat when falling
R is for the reindeer that Santa has on his sleigh with the gifts crackle-popping back and forth

LaDonna Jones, Grade 9
Hazelwood West Jr-Sr High School, MO

Monopolized

The undescribable
feeling of pain and neglect,
the thoughts of it
being all inside me
I've been so generous
giving these species everything I have,
and what do I get in return
hatred, bombs, and war
I want it to stop
all right now
just give these sentimental things,
freedom and peace
With these two things, my countries,
would be free and loved,
the neglect would be lifted
and the pain shall be healed
I feel like I've been hijacked
I've given them signs of what they've done,
the hatred of one another is tearing me apart,
as the years have passed,
I felt the control leave me, the Earth.

Kyle Magill and Rachel Van Erdewyk, Grade 9
Carroll High School, IA

The Dreamer

"Mommy mommy," the little boy cried,
"Someone in the woods is trying to hide.
He ran and ran till he didn't know where
He doesn't know how to get back to the fair."
"Tommy Tommy that person was where?
Oh no, you just woke from a dream of being there."

Alex Thien, Grade 7
Fort Recovery Middle School, OH

In Memory of Tuffy Lee Lamb

Inside two stories of wood and metal siding,
Come some of the memories of the good and bad
Things growing and things that are dying,
And one of my memories that make me sad,

Last month I lost a dearest friend,
A friend that can never be forgotten,
Tuffy fought for his life till the bitter end,
On an orange quilt filled with cotton,

I cried when I heard the horrifying news,
My favorite four legged family member,
That we thought we could never lose,
Had gone to heaven and left me forever

Our dog was most unique of his kind,
Now God has him and he probably still does not mind.

I WILL ALWAYS LOVE YOU TUFFY!

Danielle Lamb, Grade 8
Otsego Middle School, OH

Just Once

I see it there sitting on the grass
It's dark, black, and little
Yet somehow it always wins
It's almost as if it's mocking me
Since I've failed so many times before

I beat every other one except for this one
This little demon can never let me win
I can beat seventeen others of these,
But not number eighteen
I never stand a chance

But not today
Today is the day I will win
I have practiced long and hard for this moment
All those long, endless hours will be worth it
If I succeed

As I stand on the eighteenth green looking down at the hole
I try to remember it's only a seven foot putt
I pull back steady, and stroke through clean and gracefully
It breaks right into the little devil as if to kill him
I no longer shall carry the heavy burden of defeat

Nick Karzmer, Grade 7
New Albany Middle School, OH

Where I'm From

I am from the artist inside
From my conscience speaking in my mind
I'm from where you picture me to be
I'm from where I picture myself to be
I'm from the wind in my hair
I'm from where you breathe fresh air

I'm from where you are confused
From a place of dreams
I'm from the glowing moonbeams
I'm from the band within
And from the music playing in
From the orchestra of my mind
I hope to one day find

I am from the stars in the sky
And from missing the past
Trying hard to love the new
I'm from moments that make a memory
Although there are few
I am from all the bliss
From things you didn't know you would miss
I believe I am from here

Maddy Grossl, Grade 8
Little Miami Jr High School, OH

Smile

S miley faces
M ake everyone
I n our world
L ove and care for
E ach other.

Kari Monnens, Grade 8
Shakopee Area Catholic School, MN

Truth

Lost and confused.
Broken and bruised.
Don't have a clue what to do.
You keep breaking me,
As if you didn't know.
Didn't know how much it hurts
Or all the truth I behold.
I need someone to care.
Someone to always be there.
You are my prince charming.
My knight in shining armor.
So, why am I not being rescued?
Why does this pain never go away?
You can set me free.
You can make this easy.
I am so much in love with you.
And I want you to feel the same way too.
I will never let you go.
And I will never say goodbye.

Tiara Hill, Grade 8
Genesee Jr/Sr High School, MI

Left Out

I sit there with my chin in my hands
Like a dog without a playmate
The world closes around me
Leaving only a thick brick wall
　With no way to get out
The shouts and laughter around me
Become a lion roaring after its prey
　I'm lost
　Lonely
　Left out
I try to paint a smile on my face
But my lips are as dry as a desert
　Baking in the sun
My stinging eyes become thousands
Of bees mad at an intruder.
My longing for a faithful friend
Is as sharp as a needle pricking
Into my finger blood oozing down
Then the question comes to mind
　"What have I done?"

Veronica Hoover, Grade 7
Linwood Public School, ON

Writer's Block

Laying awake
Page blank
Writer's block

Almost asleep
Page empty
Idea sparked

Sitting awake
Page filling
Words flowing

Soundly sleeping
Page filled
Everything said.

Ellen Schneider, Grade 9
Big Rapids High School, MI

Pain

As the rain descends upon the earth
Thunder and lightning
Light the night sky,
Oceans rise up
Strong winds blow
As I stand oblivious
To the chaos,
Soaked to the bone
I walk towards
The eye of the storm,
Nothing will stop me
Not until I find
The source of my pain,
These chains that bind me
Hurt so much
But not as much
As when you left,
The source of my pain
Is you.

Jessica Kruger, Grade 7
Weledeh Catholic School, NT

Baby Boy

My baby boy.
At first I hear his cry and then,
I saw his head,
his cute face,
and his little bitty hands.
I looked at him with tears in my eyes
and joy in my face,
and I think of that time every time
I look at my baby boy
and smile!

Jenn Nolet-Massé, Grade 8
St Peter Catholic High School, ON

I Am From...

I am from the red forests,
where the trees are enormous.
I am from the clean rivers,
where the salmon swim upstream.

I am from the mystical forest,
where the black bears are white.
I am from the Rockies,
where they stretch in the U.S.

I am from the moonlit night,
where nature can be heard.
I am from the ocean,
where the water is warm.

I am from the rough beaches,
where you can find shells in 7 colours.
I am from the coast,
where the totem poles can be found.

I am from an island,
where a city is named after a queen.
I am from British Columbia,
where it seems like paradise.

Keanan Campbell, Grade 8
Weledeh Catholic School, NT

Horrible Holocaust

As I watched them get thrown
Off the train
I felt their fear grow stronger
Into sudden pain

I saw the mamas holding
Their babies real tight
I heard them whisper in their ears
Everything's all right

Then the families
Were split in two
Not knowing
What the commanders would do

Men off to one side
Women and children to the other
The little ones cried
Holding tightly to one another

About a month or between
The inmates grew pale
As pale as a ghost
On the night of Halloween

Tabitha Biederman, Grade 8
Parkway Middle School, OH

Letting Go

I always feel so much alone,
I have to live my life on my own.
You always told me never to fear,
And that you would always be right here.

I can't believe that you would lie,
Why in the world did you have to die?
You were the best friend that I ever had,
And now, I am always so sad.

I try to imagine you in a better place,
But all I need is to see your face.
I hope that you are in Heaven with the angels above,
And never forget that you always have my love.

I can hear you telling me to move on with my life,
But how can I do that with all of this strife?
I realize that this is the way things have to be,
And in my heart I know that you will always be with me.

I pray for your soul every night,
And pray to God that you see the light.
Knowing that God will protect you from all fear,
Is enough to wipe away my very last tear.

Maria Lewis, Grade 9
LeRoy-Ostrander High School, MN

I Am From…

I am from a place,
where there is snow.
I am from a place,
where they drum and dance.

I am from a place,
where we love to stay up.
I am from a place,
where we love to play soccer.

I am from a place,
where we like to go hunting.
I am from a place,
where we fix Skidoos.

I am from a place,
with fifteen hundred people to comfort me.
I am from a place,
where fish bit and jump.
I am from a place,
where stress becomes death.

Bryce Burles, Grade 8
Weledeh Catholic School, NT

Sweet Summertime

The most amazing season of the year,
The sweet summertime sun shines in the sky,
No more snow and no more cold ever to fear,
Blue jays soaring and flying very high.

Kids are excited to be out of school,
There is no more work all kids do is shout,
People are swimming like fish in the pool,
We're all having fun because school is out.

Kids play soccer, baseball, and basketball,
People are having a good time outside,
All day the flowers are dancing tall,
During summertime kids have joy and pride.

Summertime is the best season ever,
We all wish it could last forever.

Melissa Mukhti, Grade 7
Nativity of Our Lord Catholic School, ON

The Time of Night

The time of night, the color of night,
The part of the day which is never bright.
It can be the most beautiful thing you have ever seen,
Or something as dark as the color of black itself.
Where things unknown seem to happen.
And drunk drivers for some reason don't strap in.
The stars are as bright as ever.
And people of the planet Earth gather together.
The time of night is a time of celebration,
Sadly is also a time of rest.

James Anderson, Grade 8
Haynes Academy for Advanced Studies, LA

Graduation

This is our last day
Many things I want to say
But I cannot express
The sorrow that I suppress

Everyone separating this fall
No more walking around or playing ball
Going to all different schools
Meeting new people; wouldn't that be cool?

But it's different without you
Won't walk around looking at shoes
Hours turn to days as our time is short
At this last dinner, staring at our forks

Thinking about our days in core
And finally, we walk out those doors
One last look back and I will see
How much everyone here means to me

Jessica Luong, Grade 8
Beverley Heights Middle School, ON

The Undying Struggle

Darkness surrounds me;
There's nowhere to go.
I seem to be trapped
In the nightmare I know.
A beginning, an end,
I cannot escape it.
A second goes by,
Another one wasted.
The power of this monster
Affects all that I know,
But I have to be stronger,
And take every blow.
My battle with this creature
Seems to never end.
How do I surmount a fiend
That's here now and back then?
Neither light nor dark
Can leave a mark
On the creature I despise.
It's always there, everywhere,
Just open up your eyes.

Joseph Metzger, Grade 8
Gilbert Middle School, IA

A House

Caring, loving people,
Fill the house,
Soft furniture,
A beautiful sight,
Taste of love,
Fills the air,
Dinner runs to the table,
For everybody to taste,
Kids playing in the basement,
TV's trying to cover up the sound,
Safety is the first priority,
Freedom is the best,
Clean laundry,
Like the new air,
Smell of newly baked cookies,
After dinner,
The best house,
My house.

Brandon Ling, Grade 7
Paw Paw Middle School, MI

Black*

Death is black
It sounds like funeral music
It feels like a broken heart
It smells like old socks
It tastes like burnt popcorn
It looks like a family crying

Jessica Fullingim, Grade 7
Algonquin Middle School, MI
*Dedicated to my grandma Meme RIP

I Am From

I am from hair clips and Disney movies,
From things making me laugh.
I am from the little swimming pool in my back yard,
From trampolines and little playgrounds.
I am from a place with tennis balls everywhere,
From the open field behind my house.

I am from my Aunt Monica and Uncle Brian when they come over,
From Beanie Baby wars in the hallway with my brother.
I am from bowling in the house with plastic cups,
From watching *Dragon Tales* and *Teletubbies*.

I am from where everybody holds me,
From going to the zoo so many times.
I am from tee ball with my brother
From where we have a good time.
I am from where spending the night at my grandparents' house,
From playing soccer every night.

I am from a girl who wears braids every day in elementary school,
From practicing swimming class
I am from a blue house in New Albany
From fighting with my brother.

Kendall Linnabary, Grade 7
New Albany Middle School, OH

The Flight of My Feet

As I walk onto the track
The starting point only meters away
Years pass as I slowly walk to my position.

All eyes begin to fall on me,
The ref's hands go up and there is dead silence,
"On your marks, get set," the gun fires, and the silence is broken.

"Bang" I hear the clump of feet running like lions,
I start to run, my feet then transform into eagles, and I have no control over them,
The sprinters ahead, like lightning, never seem to stop.

While they pass me on the bleachers, the visitors and my own team,
I keep my eye on all my surroundings
Just as I speed up the pain hits.
Like 1000 bullets hitting me I also feel tired,
As I see the other team pass the finish line
I sprint like never before.

As I finish the race, gasping for air,
I start to walk and feel the sweat down my face,
I can still hear the other team cheering for their victory.

Jared Abramowitz, Grade 7
New Albany Middle School, OH

The Pain I Feel

Why?
Why does it have to happen?
It makes me feel so angry.
Angry at him, why does he make me feel this way.
Does he find joy in it?
Joy in hurting me, making me so furious.
It makes me so frustrated.
Frustrated in not knowing what's going to happen next.
I do not know how much more pain I can handle.

Kylie Burbidge, Grade 7
Weledeh Catholic School, NT

Confused

Sitting in the background, afraid and alone
Nobody's there, nobody's home
Every day is the same
Nothing new, nobody to blame
Fear, caution, anger, hope are the four things I live by
What it all comes down to is a life blank and dry
It's like no one else's, it's sad and hard and cold
There sometimes is a light side, that to me, never gets old
My life is full of sadness, resentment, and plainness
My life is also full of love, joy, and happiness
I'm not the coolest kid in town
But I've got the best friends around
This life of mine is nothing special, normal is more like it
Ups and downs and turn arounds, sometimes I can't hike it
But there are good parts too
Fun parts, sad parts, silly parts, one or a few
I'll take this life by the hand
And show it that I'm still in command
No matter how bad things can get
I still love my life, it's the best

Savannah Gabel, Grade 7
Jefferson Jr High School, IA

Away from Home

Many children watch television
Surfing through the channels
Alive and free
They watch the news
Learning about the soldiers
Fighting in the war
Fighting for peace
Of our nation
They are far
Away from home
First they must train
To be ready for battle
So they can come home
And hear the baby's rattle
And the cry of their wives and mothers
Giving big hugs and celebrating
Their homesickness, love, and heartaches

Myleka Jefferson, Grade 7
Alexandria Middle Magnet School, LA

Blind

Who is the man that's truly blind?
The one with the cane who can't look behind
Or the one shut out from the world and mankind?
He that will walk by a flower not staring
Or feel a sea breeze and continue without caring?
He is the one with the burden now bearing

Many will say that the eye's most significant
But without a heart nothing's magnificent
And nothing meaningful is placed in it
He is the blind

A helping hand could be outwardly stretched
And the blind's imagination being too farfetched
Would reel in too early, missing the catch
The world is too wonderful to set aside
But those that can't see will be caught in high tide
Pushing away because of their pride

So is it the one who reads from the Braille
Or the hard exterior and the heart oh so frail?
We are left with a choice to end our tale
Who is the blind?

Madison Dennis, Grade 9
Hazelwood West Jr-Sr High School, MO

The Boy Not Taken*

Two boys both like me, but I only have to choose one.
And sorry I could not be with both.
And be one girl, long I stood
And looked at them as long as I could
Then I told the other, as just as sorry
I was for hurting his feelings.
And having perhaps the better claim,
Because it was difficult, to choose
Though as for the boys' feelings.
I had realized that they both looked
Really about the same,
And both that morning equally dressed up
With the same T-shirts.
Oh, I kept the first for another date!
Yet knowing how way leads to way,
I doubted if I ever had a boyfriend.
I shall be telling this with a sigh
Somewhere ages and ages hence:
Two boys fighting over me, and I —
I took the one best for me,
And that has made all the difference.

Lizette Castaneda, Grade 7
Hamlin Upper Grade Center, IL
*Based on "The Road Not Taken" by Robert Frost.

The Incredible Race
We all strive to get ahead of others,
To stand out from the crowd,
To get our five minutes of glory,
To gain the respect that we all desire.
So when you look at others, those shining in front of you, what else would you feel
Other than the frustrated will to seize that position in which you know you can prevail?
Such a race! Such a race!
Everyone striving to get ahead and no one stopping to consider
The lost time spent in fighting through such a race.
But who would mind, losing half their life in chasing after the first place?
The position is certainly worthwhile dedicating one's life to, is it not?
It is the highest throne one can be seen on,
It is the rank of great respect,
It is the placement of pride and happiness!
But is it not also the status that is the most quickly forgotten with the following successor?
Must we all rush to get ahead?
Must we hurry past the roses as we go through the garden?
Many of our society think so, and as those competitors continue on the race track,
Others choose to stay on the sidelines as they enjoy as much of the race as they can,
The race that is more commonly known, as life.

William Lee, Grade 9
West Jr High School, MO

Chasing Stars
A dreamer,
Leaping in and out of whispering shadows
Searches for a long-lost wish
Scattered amongst a stormy sea of dreams dangling from the sky,
So brightly, hopefully awaiting the return of their creators
He loses himself in this great, sparkling maze
So many thoughts and hopes rush to him, tickling his ear, beckoning for his hand
Yet he pushes forward, his outstretched arms longing to embrace this wish, this dream once more
His hope is his wings, his heart is the wind beneath them
And at long last, his soul is reunited with the love he remembers
And it is with this that he is drawn into sheer bliss.

Joanne Dynak, Grade 9
Ridgewood Community High School, IL

Where the Birds Sing
Smoke plumes in the air
The crystal clear water has waves softly eroding the shore
Cicadas sing and birds chirp merrily
Problems disappear
But only for a little while
Soon the rest of the world violently pulls you into the damage and death like a thrashing current
Where in the world is there peace?
Now all is consumed by the panic, fright, and devastation
Is there any place for peace and serenity left?
Any place where birds chirp and cicadas sing?
We can only wish
For the smoke pluming in the air
And the crystal waves softly eroding the shore…

Britta Thinguldstad, Grade 7
New Albany Middle School, OH

Friends

A scorching summer is finally here.
Friends I have are always near.
With friends close by,
We create lasting ties.

The intense heat of the sun
Doesn't ruin our fun.
Through the sprinklers we leap,
'Til through our clothes water seeps.

We're hand in hand and together for now,
To survive without friends I wouldn't know how.
Even when we're apart,
Our friendship is an art.

Together many strong bonds we create,
Each person contributes with their own special traits.
Like a chain linked together,
All are equal and not one is nether.
Smiling and laughing, we are friends
Forever and always to the end.

Tarah Thompson, Grade 8
Boulan Park Middle School, MI

I Am from the World of My Own Thoughts

I am from the love of my parents,
I am from parents, whose life as children was tough for them,
I am from a family that has hope for me,
I am from parents who have an assistive soul.

I am from a life filled with difficulty,
Sometimes I wonder if I seem alien to others,
But I know that I am only different in the mind of thoughts,
I am from the thoughts of my mind.

I am from the world of thoughts,
This place is far away but still very close,
I always take the train of thought,
I never know where my thoughts take me.

I am from the sands of my own nightmares,
I am from the house of my dread,
I am from the desert where hope is nowhere to be seen,
I always try to find a way out of this dreadful place.

I will find the hope that I lost,
I will move on,
I will keep on going,
For life is not what you're from, but how you carry on.

Robert Harris, Grade 7
New Albany Middle School, OH

Victory

She takes a sideways glance at first base.
She pauses for a moment, winds up, and whoosh!
Right past the batter into the glove. Strike one.
She can feel the batter standing nervously
with sweat trickling down their face.
She touches her cap, winds up, throw it, and splat!
Into the catcher's glove. Strike two.
She can smell the victory.
She winds up one last time, throws it, and…strike three!
She breathes a sigh of relief.

Lindsey Broek, Grade 7
Ireton Christian School, IA

Bye Grandma

from 6:00 p.m. i watched,
i watched my grandma die,
the pain and suffering i will never forget
everyone in the room with her, the tension and feeling,
are no words to describe
she was leaving, the angels were coming,
it was a struggle to keep her alive
she was breathing hard, we had her hooked on a machine,
we knew it was time, her love no longer existed
my eyes full of tears with none left to cry, i keep asking God…
why? why her? and i still do till this day
i just don't understand,
her love and comfort, and support were
out of this world…
if only…i can hold her and see her;
again…or maybe just to hear her voice
to tell me that she loves me!
but now i know she's resting and the pain is all gone.
and now she's in a better place
r.i.p. ama a.k.a. grandma i love you!!

Denise Flores, Grade 8
Oaklawn Jr High School, LA

Life in a Holocaust Camp

In a Holocaust Camp you are barely lucky enough to eat.
You work all day in the extreme heat,
I wonder why we get beat?
Nazis are as mean as snakes,
I wish I had some cupcakes!
You can taste death in your throat,
It tastes so bad you choke.
The people are so skinny,
It's a wonder that we eat.
I just wish I didn't get beat.
The smell of dead bodies I could not bear,
And my heart would only tear.
The soup is like water, goes down real smooth,
They also took my gold cap off my tooth.
The Allies are coming in,
The battle will soon begin!

Sean Mendez, Grade 8
Parkway Middle School, OH

My Fish

Fishing on a Minnesota lake
not getting any fish to take
It is only me, my mom and dad
all starting to get mad
All we can do is wait, wait, wait
for the fish to take the tasty bait
I just want that one wish
only one or two big fish
waiting here on this summer day
might just pay.
The red and white bobber went under
the reel sounded like thunder
the fish jerks to the left, then to the right
Man! This fish is putting up a fight
Finally, I reel the fish in
I put it in the gray bin
After a long hot day on the lake
It is time for a yummy fish bake.

Sara Meyers, Grade 9
Cannon Falls Sr High School, MN

Uproaring Sky

U nbound light cracks the sky,
P ounding thunder whooshes by!
R ocketed water splatters madly,
O ver the hills, dirt mushes sadly.
A n arch penetrates the clouds,
R evealing virtuous colors.
I nside the distant haze,
N ow the angered god withers.
G reat clouds shift aside,

S unlight raids the hills.
K eys unlock your bolted door,
Y ou step into the world.

Alex Robinson, Grade 9
Hazelwood West Jr-Sr High School, MO

Pain

Pain
emotions I've never had.
Feelings I've never felt.
Pressure that I've never
been under.
Thoughts going through my head,
stuff I've never really thought about.
Things that I'm trying to see
when there ain't nothin' in sight.
I've just got to relax,
take it easy
and let
the good things flow.
I need to make like simple
and let the bad stuff go.

Narlie C. Dapilos, Grade 8
Weledeh Catholic School, NT

Joan of Arc

There was Joan of Arc who left one big mark
In the country of France she was their chance

To fight the English oppression and the French depression
But the English were quite mean and killed her at nineteen.

She dressed as a boy when the English broke Troy
She was as strong as most men but couldn't use a pen

God sent her visions to defeat the English divisions
With her sword she would perch ready by the side of the church

She was wounded in battle and was trapped like cattle
There was no denial, she was guilty before trial

A witch she was named, on her death they aimed
She burned on the wood right where she stood.

Although she is dead the motion is still lead
St Joan of Arc has left her mark.

Joel Dorion, Mackenzie Rack, Kevin Tessier, and Jordan Gibbons, Grade 8
St Peter Catholic High School, ON

Friendship

It smells like chocolate-chip cookies baking in the oven.
It feels like the warm, soft, fuzzy feeling you get when you hug a teddy bear.
It sounds like the beautiful, familiar voice of a person you care about deeply.
It tastes like a cupcake, fresh from the oven.
It looks like the twinkle of a star in the moonlit sky.

Lauryn Bettag, Grade 7
Fairfield Middle School, OH

Forever, Left to Die

Deeper than the despair in your eyes
Deeper than the grave I dig
Stronger than your hatred more powerful than your stare my pain you cannot feel
Vibrant as the sunlight blind as love can be
The game you play is cruelty winners meant to kill
Colored with emotions vividly my own
Feelings have been washed away black and white is what remains
Too harsh too feel it coldness I can't grasp
Numb to compassion crazed by disgust
Bound for disappointment I can only hurt so much
Nameless among the rest wanting all the same
We've sunk low enough at your hands we ask Mercy
Nothing left to live for struggling to gain what's lost
Surrendering my soul giving up my heart one day you'll be avenged
You'll think about me with no regrets
In your doings you see no wrong
My faith is strong my word is useless
I'll never hate you I've seen what comes from hate
I've seen a rainbow after a storm
I've heard the chirp of birds at dawn
I've also seen the way hate can make you forget those things

Katie Hilgedick, Grade 8
South Middle School, WI

Massacre

Slavery
They head north to freedom mostly at night.
They hide in the bushes till no one's in sight.
You may want to ask, "Why didn't they stay?"
Their master treated them as animals, as many might say.
Their tired legs and tired eyes,
Their broken thoughts and broken hearts,
They kept moving.
Their friends and family gone,
After crying and screaming
Praying and bleeding,
They kept moving. They never stopped.
They hid in the trees as the dogs barked.
They proceeded on. Alone in the dark.
Slavery
Why can't they be free?

Tori Davis, Grade 8
Stewartville Middle School, MN

If You Can…

If you can like yourself when others don't,
And offer comfort to those in need.
If you can be strong when others won't,
And be a crutch for those who bleed.

If you can tolerate to lose,
And do it with pride.
If you can stand to choose,
But not to take sides.

If you can look past what other can't,
You'll do the things that others don't.
Then you can be what others shan't,
And you'll go the places others can't.

Grace Meilen, Grade 7
New Albany Middle School, OH

Black Snowflake

A few moments ago it was snowing,
now the ground is covered.
I look up to see one single snowflake fall from the sky,
it's black though?
But why? Snowflakes are white.
As I look closer it appears to be moving,
in a spiral motion.
It falls, on the white ground.
I look down at the snowflake,
and can see the beautiful crystallized pattern.
I pick it up. It is hard, but cold.
It's hasn't melted?
How beautiful, such a beautiful snowflake,
a black snowflake.
Black snowflake.
Pure beauty.

Damon J. Fry, Grade 8
Columbia Middle School, IN

The Big Dipper

This is the end,
this is the way I wanted it all along.
I understand to most,
it would be considered wrong.
Though the pain's unbearable,
I'm at peace.
I get to die by your side,
and our fighting has ceased.
Chargin' in across the river,
I remember seeing your face.
Who knew we'd meet again,
in such a horrible place.
I couldn't have imagined a better way to die,
in this pointless war.
Brother vs brother, North vs South,
the hatred growing more and more.
I've missed you, brother,
as we've fought this way.
"I hope God gave us a place in the Big Dipper."
That's the last thing I had to say.

Courtney Schaal, Grade 9
Southwest Jr High School, AR

I Am From

I am from the busy city,
Where there are people bustling.

I am from the snowy land,
Where the ground is white and fluffy.

I am from the bumpy, white hills,
Where there are people sliding all weekend long.

I am from the beautiful territory,
Where there are flowers and trees surrounding the land.

I am from the flowing river,
Where there are families joyfully swimming.

I am from a loving family,
Where nobody is alone and by themselves.

I am from a caring family,
Where we always celebrate events together.

I am from a proud family,
Where everything can change in one minute.

I am from Yellowknife.

Shelby Benoit, Grade 8
Weledeh Catholic School, NT

Alone

As Ariel walks down the corridors of the school building with friends feeling so superior over those who walk alone with no one to talk and laugh with. While they are walking they pass a girl with a look of such sadness upon her face but, they pass her without even giving the slightest smile to the young girl because Ariel is so sure she will never be like her, but as the years pass Ariel's friends begin to fade away one by one until she has none. Now Ariel walks the corridors alone with no one but her shadow beside her as she walks she passes the girl that she had seen years back the one that had the look of sorrow upon her face but that look was not there anymore it was replaced with a broad smile and she was walking and chatting with friends but not just any friends Ariel's old friends and they breezed right past her without a single glance like she was a bug on the wall, or just a single leaf in the forest. As she made her way to class she realized that the simplest smile could have changed her whole life and now she would walk the corridors alone forevermore.

Antionette Portillo, Grade 8
Homer Jr High School, IL

Where I'm From

I am from South Hale, where the idea of me was conceived, and so was I.
I am from South Artesian in a townhouse painted green
Where I had Barney and ponies in my backyard on my first birthday.
I am from South Emerald, where I ate homegrown, sliced fruit directly from my Grandma's hands,
While my cousin and I sat under an umbrella-equipped table
I am from South Phillips and technically I still am, because my Daddy still resides there.
I am from 89th Street where I spent my tenth birthday
Without my father living with me, where I learned to do my own hair,
Where Mommy wasn't always there anymore, where I first gave a boy my phone number (and regretted it later),
Where I lived in walking distance from several shopping centers, two parks, and my cousins' residence
I'm from there too.
I'm from South Vincennes, where I learned to take public transit to school every morning, by myself.
Where I found out that it didn't matter where I lived,
Cause I made it my home.
Where I learned that I don't always have to do everything on my own.

Mariah Janese Robinson, Grade 9
Gwendolyn Brooks College Preparatory Academy, IL

In the Dirt

Standing on the light brown, with white chalk softball diamond,
I feel at home.
The glaring glow of the sun is shining down on me,
And my bat shimmers at the brightness of the sun.
I watch the pitcher wind up, and throw a pitch as fast as the speed of light,
And I know that I feel at home.

I stand here smelling the fresh, crisp smell of the soft, light brown dirt
Mixed with the smell of new, fresh leather on my glove and the smell of the freshly cut grass,
It is an irresistible scent.
Home plate calls to me, urging me to come home, but I resist, until it is time.

I feel the dirt blowing on my face, and the warmth of the sun beating down on my silky, tanned skin.
The excitement rises as I slide into home plate, scoring the final run.
When I crush the ball deep into the healthy, green outfield,
I get a rush of energy that makes me run faster every time.

I hear the crack of the thick, metal bat,
And the crowd cheering, stomping their feet on the bleachers.
I hear the howling, frustrating wind
Through the holes in the side of my deep blue helmet.
In the dirt filled diamond, I feel at home.

Karly Medich, Grade 7
New Albany Middle School, OH

War Is...

War is a battle between life and death.
Where people fight for their rights.
Where people stand up and get up
and won't give up the fight.

Sneaky as a fox.
Death can be as bloody as Lundy's lane.
War is like a bomb that is unexpected.

Where people fight for their life.
Where they won't give up the fight.
People suffering in pain.
The tears will drop as rain.

The goodbyes can be everlasting.
War is that feeling of death.
Where they can't wait much longer.

A war is like thousands of horses running by.
It's like their heart is in their hands.
War can be so dreadful or so painful.
As the guns around them go bang, bang, bang.

As their heart beats like a million drums.

Zulma Ramirez, Grade 8
Beverley Heights Middle School, ON

Lightning

You sit in the darkness
during the storm
and suddenly a bright light strikes the sky.
It is bright for only a moment,
then darkness finds its way back to us.
CRACK! BANG!
The sound of thunder follows shortly after.
It is like a light flickering
on and off in a dark room.
But what is this mysterious light
you may ask?
This is
  l
    i
      g
        h
          t
            n
          i
            n
              g!

Jessica Franklin, Grade 8
St Peter Catholic High School, ON

Promises

I told you that I would never leave you.
I told you that you would never get hurt.
I told you that no one can hurt you.
Those were my promises to you.
I don't want to leave you.
But I have to.
I didn't want anyone to hurt you.
But I didn't know that I would be the one to hurt you.
I didn't mean to break your heart.
But I really need to leave you even though I don't want to.

Jeff Yuvienco, Grade 8
Weledeh Catholic School, NT

Jackie Robinson

Basketball is a sport Jackie played.
He could run up and down the court.
He was the best in his day.
He was on the local sports report.

Football was his favorite sport.
He could kick, catch, and run,
However football is not played on a court.
He was better than everyone.

Baseball was Jackie's worst sport,
But it is definitely what he is remembered for.
He played it on neither a field nor a court.
Every time he got up to bat, he was ready to score.

Jackie changed the way baseball was played,
And that is why he is in the Baseball Hall of Fame today.

Dalton Galloway, Grade 9
Southwest Jr High School, AR

My Stay at the Beach

As I enter its territory,
It greets me,
With a warm sensation under my feet.
And as I make my way up the sandy cliff,
My eyes are amazed,
With the blueness of the ocean
And the sky colliding together.
As I hear a wave approaching,
It crashes against
The jagged face of the cliff.
A mist of sea water hits me in the face,
I see a rainbow from the mist.
Then I flop back on the warm sand,
And just lying there
Thinking while sunbathing, in the warm sun,
I just drift away,
As all of my problems are just blown away,
In the gentle wind,
I'm just drifting away.

James F. Smith, Grade 8
Sandusky Middle School, MI

Ode to Soccer

Soccer is a sport and
A glorious game
In Europe it's known
By another name.

It takes talent to play
So you better obey
This glorious sport
That you will love someday.

You play as a team
To achieve your fame
Because soccer is the only
Sport that is not lame.

Dardan Agushi, Grade 8
Whitewater Middle School, WI

Hawaiian Paradise

A glance out the window
Turns my good day bad.
The sky is a threatening gray
And rain consumes the city.

It pounds the streets
And soaks the locals.
With a thunderous cry,
It makes the skyscrapers shake.

My finger traces a palm tree
Onto the foggy window.
I can feel my mind drift away
To a land I well know.

Breathtaking sunsets
And sand between my toes.
Sun-kissed cheeks,
And frosty lemonade glasses.

Luaus and hula dancers,
Pineapples and piña coladas,
Oh, beautiful Hawaiian paradise —
Take me there.

Erin Coburn, Grade 7
Highland Middle School, IL

Global Warming

Global warming makes me sad
Global warming makes me mad

We need to plan on the double
Or else our world will run into trouble

So please show what you're worth
Stand up for Mother Earth

Jonathan Eskra, Grade 7
St Gerald Elementary School, IL

Contrast

Black, white, white, black
Line, line, oval, line
Notes flying through my mind
Fingers dashing through the melody
Nothing is around me, nobody can distract me

Dinner's cooking, smells like spaghetti
The musty smell of old music books smells even better
All around me, Beethoven, Bach, Chopin, Mozart
Debussy, Mendelssohn, Schumann, Grieg, are telling me how to play my pieces
The music screams its notes inside my head,
The rush, the thrill
The sweet, sweet sounds that are music
Fingers against keys, feet against the cool pedals
Mind racing

I am in my comfort zone,
This is what I do,
This is what I was made for
Everything is clear, a thick black line showing me the way

Everything is black and white,
Such contrast between the two, but they go together so well,
Like an old photo, a preserved memory.

Emily Sproule, Grade 7
New Albany Middle School, OH

Shell Shocked

All our eyes have wandered slowly, slowly, up towards the sky above.
All our eyes have filled with fear, and then we see the devil's gull.

That's what we call it as sirens ring, that's what we shout, our voices hoarse,
as we dive into muddy trenches, waiting for the deafening fall.

"It's our seventh today!" someone shouts, though I had lost my count.
"They're getting closer" I hear again, though my hands on my ears are pressing tight.

Beside me I could see my buddy shake, his upward eyes glazed with fear,
I wouldn't watch it, not again, but felt it, I regrettably did,
BANG!
It hit the ground like an earthquake, I could imagine the crater deep,
the mud on the walls around me slid, my buddy screamed, screamed, shook.

I crawled to him, I had to, as quickly as I could I held him close
but he just shook, shook,
shook his teeth clacking, the tears poured down his dirty cheeks.

"Come on," I whisper, "Gotta move," but move he surely does not,
"Someone's down," I yell with tears, "Another's been shell shocked."

Amber Kortekaas, Grade 8
St Peter Catholic High School, ON

Where I've Lived

I've lived in more than one neighborhood.
There's Rossford, Perrysburg, and some BG.
I have some memories, both bad and good.
It's hard moving from city to city.

My parents got divorced when I was two;
My dad moved to Rossford my mom to BG,
But, I still got to see them both, phew;
Knowing whose house I was at confused me.

I moved to Perrysburg when I was eight,
I met some new friends the first day;
I spent most my life there and it was great;
I live in Grand Rapids up to today.

My dad just bought a house in Michigan,
But I'll stay here; I'm not moving again.

Jacob Keene, Grade 8
Otsego Middle School, OH

Absence of Water

Nobody ever said that pools had to be full of water,
Grab your skateboard and shred like a cheese grater.
Carve every wall of the light blue kidney shaped pool.
Grinning with feelings, trying to be cool.
The fumes of pungent spray paint, on the inside it lay.
Ride up the walls like a tiger stalking its prey,
And grinding the coping, slightly like a kiss on the cheek,
The sound that it makes, the pool screams "EEK."
The smooth surface of the pool is much like a baby's face,
"Whoosh" smooth and round, easy to keep up the pace.
Hours and hours off in the deep end,
Until day turns to night, you'll always be my friend.

Alex Ramsey, Grade 9
Hazelwood West Jr-Sr High School, MO

White and Black

Some days I feel black
Alone in the darkness of it all
Showing no emotion
Showing no existence
Lost and trapped
Between two worlds of darkness and light
Lonely and scared
Other times I feel white
So alive and bright
It makes me feel secure and safe
From all the darkness of black
When I feel white
I am a good person
When I am black I am a good person
With bad emotions
Black and white are part of me
What am I today

Jason Stone, Grade 9
Prairie Lakes School, MN

What Do You See?

When you wake up in the morning
And look out through your window,
What do you see: the sun, the birds?
I see something even more.

I see a new day where everyone
Can laugh and play and enjoy life.
I see the time people spend together
And the lives people bring together.

I see friends telling secrets
And people sending gifts and packages.
I see people learning and teaching
And changing lives with feeling and compassion.

What do you see in a day?
You could see another day of fun;
You could see opportunities come.
Even more you could see progress.

When you wake up in the morning
And look out through your window,
What do you see: the sun, the birds?
I see something even more.

Sarah Baker, Grade 8
Gilbert Middle School, IA

I Am From

I am from a place,
Where the sun is luminous.
I am from the tallest trees,
Where the blossoms bloom brightly.

I am from the long green fields,
Where the leaves are crisp and orange.
I am from the yard,
Where the birds chirp nonstop.

I am from the city,
Where children play and joke in the streets.
I am from the lakes and oceans,
Where I can swim and splash.

I am from a green country,
Where more than enough people are garrulous.
I am from a place,
Where the rain drops heavily.
I am from a beautiful house,
Where I am loved.

Mackenzie Hobbs-McLean, Grade 8
Weledeh Catholic School, NT

Violence

Why must we fight?
Why must we shout?
What is this VIOLENCE really about?
From pushing to punching,
To shooting with a gun.
People must think,
It is quite fun.
But all it is,
Is a fight to be cool,
Whether they do it,
At home or at school.
Don't fight!

Jordan Swingle, Grade 7
Philo Jr High School, OH

I Am...

I am a puddle
I wonder when I'll be happy
I hear a tear splash
I see a ripple in my surface
I want a companion
I am a puddle

I pretend to be deep
I feel incredibly empty
I touch a tear
I worry about my happiness
I cry for a companion
I am a puddle

I understand I am not deep
I say I should be happy
I dream of a bright future
I try not to cry anymore
I hope for a companion
I am a puddle

Cheyenne Hunter, Grade 9
Jackson High School, OH

Wind

I tickle the trees' leaves
When I whistle my lovely song.
You cannot see me
You only realize me when I am strong.

When I come strong
You better run.
For things may go wrong.
I'm not always fun.

But I am helpful
In the beautiful spring.
In summer I feel nice and cool.
For I am the real thing.

Elizabeth Schultz, Grade 8
St John Lutheran School, WI

The Meaning of Poetry

Poetry to me is the key to my life that has many doors still left unopened.
Poetry to me is the thoughts and opinions still left unsaid from my heart.
Poetry to me is the connection between life and death.
Poetry to me is my feelings still left unfelt.
Poetry to me is the cure to many of the unhealed illnesses.
Poetry to me is the limited amount of love trying to escape from my heart.
Poetry to me is unlimited amount of knowledge trying to escape from my brain.
Poetry to me is the expression of truth told from the expression of lies.
Poetry to me is the connection of many different ethnicities coming together as one.
Poetry to me is the difference from right and wrong.
Poetry to me is the true language from my inner-self.
Poetry to me is the time still left unlived.
Poetry to me is a clock of unending happiness.
Poetry to me is the music that our voices sing on or off note.
Poetry to me is my voice in the still emptiness of nothing.
Poetry to me is nothing but a rap song told from the beating of my heart.
Poetry to me is the unending love I have for my family.
Poetry to me is the story of my life.
Poetry to me is everything.

Kyle Snider, Grade 9
Franklin-Monroe High School, OH

The Crocodile Hunter

The Crocodile Hunter's name is Steve,
He makes his job look so easy; it isn't hard to believe,
That if there was something he needed to do,
You can be sure Steve will follow through.
He loves animals and is a great person as well.
When it comes to croc catching, Steve is really swell,
He's made best mates and is a hero.
Now there's millions of people 'round the world shouting "Go, Steve! Go!"

Katherine Welling, Grade 7
Home School, IN

I Am Haylee Rose Keel

I am the simplest rose; black and red.
I wonder what mermaids sound like when they sing
I hear the silence that laughs and cries
I see vivid colors through a blind man's eyes
I want to fly in the diamond waters
I am the simplest rose; black and red

I pretend to dance in fire with the grace and beauty of Aphrodite
I feel the pain of others' sorrow in the wind
I touch the spirits' cold, blue hands of death
I worry the water nymphs will fly away and drown in the deep
I cry without tears, but with a puma's scream of pain
I am the simplest rose; black and red

I understand I'm the only one that's found the gold at the end of the rainbow
I say pain creates love with silky gaunt fingers
I try to show how a dead rose bush will grow
I hope people will soon see a dead flower blossom,
For I am the simplest rose; black and red

Haylee Rose Keel, Grade 8
Otsego Middle School, OH

Summer Sunset

In a field of flowers,
I sat and watched
A sunset.
Even though you're gone
I know you're always near,
Like a guardian angel
On my shoulders.
You're with me always,
Like this sunset,
You'll never leave me,
But I'll never hear your
Voice again.
Though my tears will
Come and go like this
Sunset, nothing will
Bring you back but memories.
So sitting here
Under the sunset
I feel you're beside me
Because in my heart
You never left.

Amanda Michkowski, Grade 7
Nativity of Our Lord Catholic School, ON

Heartache

As I stood there
In the rain as cold as ice;
A chill ran down my spine.

All the while
I think of you;
The life you lived,
Dreams you had.

The memory of you
Lingers all around me,
Like a bad feeling.
One day you're here,
The next you're not.

You were always there,
Someone to talk with.
Now you're gone and
I'm left alone in mist.

Rain falls down, faster as if in a rage.
There is nothing, I can do now besides cry.
Cold and alone,
I leave in a fog as thick as the rain itself.

Tina Foote, Grade 8
Sandusky Middle School, MI

Love

No matter what happens
For some reason I can't stop loving him
No matter how hard I try
I can't forget how much I truly do love him
Even when I say I don't
He's my true love
Even though we went our own ways
I still feel the same way
And I always will

Sara Booth, Grade 9
Thomas A Edison Jr/Sr High School, IN

Twilight

If Darkness were a man he would be a knight
He would be
Strong
Brave
Honorable and
Mysterious
He would be a quiet winter night

If Light were a woman she would be a princess
She would be
Smart
Kind
Trustworthy and
Bright
She would be a warm summer day

The knight and princess would never die
Live forever
Caring for each other 'til
They would meet for a second and be Twilight

Brad Bergeron, Grade 8
Prairie View Middle School, IL

Everything Changes

My life is horrible as you can see
I've lived my life through misery
My dad has hurt my family
He's hurt us all emotionally
I'm glad he's gone
And my life's turned on
Now there's this guy
What a great dad is he
He picks up his kids every week
Now I can see a future for me
And I can't see the past from my x-family
He turned us all around in a good sort of way
And I'm positive that he's going to stay
He'll set everything right
So in our house, there won't be another fight
He's a great dad and a good friend
And every day I pray to God that this will never end

Tabitha Morehouse, Grade 7
Carlisle Elementary/Jr High School, IN

My Imaginary Friend

There was always someone beside me
when I was sad.
Someone to laugh with,
when I made a mistake.
They make me enjoy life,
to the fullest.
Someone to help me,
when I really needed it.
This person has been in my life
since I was 2.
That person is
my imaginary friend.

Lynnell Potyok, Grade 7
Weledeh Catholic School, NT

Holocaust

One day
A family was sleeping
And awoke by a big bang
And a bright light
The soldiers come in
The family wants out
The soldiers asked for
The whereabouts
Of Mr. and Mrs. Pout
The family says no
The soldiers beat
The family down
With a loud *Boom*
People still
Sleep in the town

Kimmie Robertson, Grade 8
Sandusky Middle School, MI

Like a Wave

Life is like a rolling wave
Sometimes short and sweet.
But others come crashing down
Leaving it incomplete.

The foam is the after affect
Of the things we've done.
Sometimes just needing to look
Towards the setting sun.

Tides are the rising falling actions
That make us think about
What life is worth here
What secret is sought out.

The inside is the peaceful place
Where all our hearts should be.
'Cause after life is done here
Heaven we will see.

Emily Davidson, Grade 8
Sandusky Middle School, MI

Bursting Balloon

The ego is a balloon that inflates with every compliment that goes to your head,
Over confidence, one's pride, one's self.

First believed the Earth is the centre of the universe,
We now think it's the Sun.
But in the eyes of every egocentric person — they're the centre;
And everything revolves around them.

Their actions are what dictate the many,
After all in your eyes everyone lives to serve you.
In your eyes the Earth spins because you tell it to,
In your eyes the moon only rises because you like its glow,
In your eyes you are the god who sees over everything
And you will not want to let that power go.

But one day it will dawn on you that
You are not the only savior,
And in fact you are quite insignificant on the grand scale of things.
Fronting an image to try and belong,
But really you are distancing yourself.

You will learn that the Sun will rise in the East
And set in the West without your bidding,
And the tides will always ebb and flow.

Hannah Borland, Grade 9
Mulgrave School, BC

Rainbow Pride

Everyone's heard of a little something called "Rainbow Pride."
Red, yellow, blue, pink, purple, brown, orange, green
The colors of the rainbow.
The colors of the people that stick together in this world.
United they stand, divided they fall.
I don't' know if you caught it or not,
But out of the colors I mentioned that get along with each other,
The only two that I did not write…are black and white.
Together, they can't seem to get it right
And overlook the differences between dark and light.
We hate them, the former despises the latter
But if we're trying to move ahead in this world, should it matter?
All blacks have a little bit of white in them anyway
And they become more and more like us every day
And we often find members of our kind dying their hair blonde and buying
Green contacts, when they know that they see perfectly.
While, I don't really care, I find races to be
Who they are intended to be, flawless imperfectly
We might as well get over it and just let it ride,
Take care of our business, and embrace this Rainbow Pride
'Cause this world is Technicolor, and not just black and white.

Tionna N. Alderson, Grade 9
Gwendolyn Brooks College Preparatory Academy, IL

Clouds

Clouds can be so many things,
So many stories hidden in the clouds
Ducks
and beautiful butterflies
fly around
while a whale and a fish
play tag
A couple dances
A pharaoh rules
Angels water-ski,
leaving a wake of icy white clouds behind in the rolling waves
for a crippled giant to walk on
While a grandpa snowboards,
an evil, warty witch and a two headed snake
plot against the cloud cities
Then,
rain bursts from within
and everything smears and disappears
But when the sun returns,
clouds will be restored.

Carolina VonKampen, Grade 8
Trinity Lutheran School, IA

Missing You

I walk in silence listening to my heart beat.
I wish I could hear you talk to me
And tell me how much you care.

I want the past to be the present
And the future to be in our hands,
So our dreams could come true.

I wish and want everything,
But only want you.
I look into the sky
And see a face looking back at me.

I see a face that has no doubts, no fears, and no regrets.
I feel relief because I realize you never left me.
You've been there all along
And for a moment I feel like you never left.

Kathleen Wallain, Grade 9
Gordon Technical High School, IL

Silence

I wish I could help him but he won't listen to me.
I wish he would listen he just wants me to let him be.
He does not see how it hurts us.
He says it sets him free
And that it helps because people almost never let him be.
I wish he could feel how much it hurts me.
To see him this way but maybe one day he will snap out of it.
Right now I just hope.
Also for now I can't look at you, I'm just going to mope.

Nicole Peterson, Grade 8
Edison Middle School, WI

When Opposites Attract

A boy and girl are always different,
But sometimes they attract,
A boy is like a muddy dog who loves to go and play,
Play in the summer, play all day.

A boy and a girl are always different,
But sometimes they attract,
A girl is like a flower, different in many ways,
She stands loyal and free, night and day.

A boy and girl are always different,
But sometimes they attract,
A boy is like a dunce,
He can be smart and dumb at once.

A boy and girl are always different,
But sometimes they attract,
A girl is like Hollister, precious and expensive,
If you act the wrong way, she might become defensive.

A boy and girl are always different,
But sometimes they attract,
Like what's happening now somewhere,
Where love is all that's there, in the air!

Heidi Martin, Grade 7
Sherman Middle School, MI

Happy

Happy…
Smiling like the sun,
You feel fantastic.
Your dreams come true,
You don't even feel blue.
High, happy, hills,
Where Jack and Jill…
Go tumbling down.
You feel like a clown,
Smiling and singing silly songs.
Happy…
Your birthday is coming up,
You are full of energy.
You get tons of presents,
That start a new life.
You got a first in shoe kick.
Thundering, thirsty, thorns,
That tickle down your throat.
Just like a boat,
That stays in one spot on the middle of the water.
Smiling, super, smiles.

Edna Martin, Grade 7
Linwood Public School, ON

Nobility

The noble race, what does that mean? That we are better than all others?
Or that we can keep ourselves clean?
Is it our ability to love, represented by fair Aphrodite and her doves?
Or is it our brain power, represented by the wise Athena and her owl?
Our distance from the world, and nature? Kept safe from savage species by our houses.
But of course! It must be, our ability, to hold things in our hands.
The Noble Race of Opposable Thumbs, how clever we must seem.

But how can you judge what's better than others,
Or who has more love for their mother, or who can think faster than others,
Or who holds things better?

Well, we aren't so clean I'm sorry to say, and our relatives,
The apes and monkeys, can learn just as we do.
Baby chimpanzees can make the same distinctions as a child, and do just fine out in the "wild."
"These relatives of ours are making trouble"
Our leaders sulkily mumble. But, aha! We are saved!
Our opposable thumbs will clear our way!
Again the Noble Race is back on top, because we can hold a mop.

But alas, woe is us, so can our relatives the chimpanzees, koalas too,
Oh what to do? Has my plan to advocate for our noble race failed?
Our egos are draining, I feel frail.
Funny how the word naive can be so easily switched with nobility.

Kalin Malouf, Grade 8
Ballard Brady Middle School, OH

Let's Just Be Friends (Racism)

As every day passes by there are thousands upon thousands of people being discriminated.
You don't know what insults you are going to run into today.
Whether you are poor, tall, short, from a different country or origin
you can hear the laughter of people making fun of you from a distance.
People despise you because you took their jobs away
or we hate them because they get all the glory while we work our butts away.

Why can't we forget about the racism and get along?
Most importantly, why can't we just be friends?

People don't want change.
They don't want people changing the rules of the game.
That's why they want a bigger border so nobody can get out or come in.
People have stereotypes against you
like gangsters, lazy bums, liars, cheaters, tax evaders, and killers.
But treating people like they don't belong here, isn't that a sin?

To me there is no such thing as black, white, brown, or yellow.
We were made by the same God. Let's just be friends.

If someone insults you, offer the other cheek
and don't give up on your dreams no matter how hard it seems.

To me no human being is illegal. Why can't we just be friends?

Rolando Herrera, Grade 9
Southwest Jr High School, AR

I Am Paige; Hear Me Roar

There's this ache in my chest,
A "hole" if you will,
Where my heart used to be.
But now it's lying on the floor, the heartbeat fading
All because I left it in the wrong hands
There's this ache in my chest.

There's a boy I love, my hero, my idol
His name? Harry James Potter
He's so brave and chivalrous!
He's the boy, the only boy I love,
The only one I can trust with my heart
There's a boy I love, my hero, my idol.

I have best friends, whom I love to death
They're always there with me and for me.
Whenever I have a bad day, They're always there.
They'll always take my side.
Sure, we fight, we're only human, but we make up.
I have best friends, whom I love to death.

I am Paige; hear me roar!

Paige Pobocik, Grade 8
Goshen Middle School, IN

If I Dare

Here I sit and stare,
Wondering if I dare.
If I dare say
What I feel for you.
If I dare hope
You feel this way too.
If I dare dream
Of what we could be.

Here now, I stand.
Now I am daring
My heart is racing
As I realize what I'm facing.
The rain falls,
My heart stalls,
And I dare, I dare to tell you that I care.

Here I lie
Trying desperately not to cry.
The feelings I had for you still reside,
Yet I am jumbled up inside.
For there is another, who has caught my sight.
And where this will lead, I cannot shed light.

Corina Fischer, Grade 8
Gordon Head Middle School, BC

My Life

Just sitting here, with no one to love
Metal bars keeping me
From getting out.
Just sitting here
On the cold hard concrete floor.
It's loud with dogs barking.
When the door opens
Everything gets calm and quiet.
A family of four walks in
With a little boy and a little girl.
They stopped in front of me
And they said that they
Liked me and that I was cute.
They filled out the forms,
Put me in their car and took me home.
Now I have a home that I can call my own.
No more metal bars to keep me in.
Now I get a second chance
At a good life.
And I get someone to
LOVE.

Mitchell Hartwig, Grade 8
Francis Granger Middle School, IL

Coast Guard

The waves, toss, turn and roar
the rain pounds, soaks, and pours
the engine of the boat hums, spins and moves us through.
The blinding towers of the waves gives us a hint, a clue
screeches of people flow in the air,
the wind moves through my hair.
Now I know what I want to be
a helping hand, at the wondering sea.

Meg Finke, Grade 7
Fairfield Middle School, OH

Under the Sea

Beauty outstretched,
farther than the eye can see
colours everywhere,
shadowing over the light, blue water
life stirring, in every colour
nothing inactive.
A marvel, a wonder
yet still, predators loom,
hunting the unexpected
still yet,
the seaweed dances,
the corals sing in the soft current
Still,
the sand sparkles,
and life outstretched
For life, under the sea,
never ends.

Lareinaa Aloysious, Grade 7
Nativity of Our Lord Catholic School, ON

Poetry Makes Me Mad

As I sit in my seat,
I stare down at my feet.
My mind has gone blank.
All my ideas have sank.

I couldn't think of something funny,
Even if you paid me money.
Not a thought crossed my mind,
As I sat there and whined.

I go home sad.
Poetry makes me mad.
Now there isn't much time,
I need to think of a rhyme.

Please Mrs. B.,
Poetry is too hard for me.
I'm trying my best,
But I'd rather take a test.

Then an idea came.
Even though it's kind of lame.
My spirit is diminished,
But my poem is finally finished.

Michael Stone, Grade 8
Sandusky Middle School, MI

Children

They laugh, they play,
They smile for you.
They don't know what to say.
They don't know what to do.

Have a doll,
Or a Tonka toy,
Funny girls,
And silly boys.

School is fun
Nap time — the enemy
They scream and run,
"The monster is out to get me!"

See the doctor — get a lolli,
Grandma is the cookie queen.
The leader at the center's jolly.
The daycare food is turning green.

Cousin Sarah took the last cookie.
Uncle John is making fun of Josh.
The TV said Barney's taking a snoozie.
Boots in winter slosh.

Addison Mumm, Grade 7
St Mary School, WI

Beautiful Is What You Are

Beautiful is what you are,
When you walk down the stairs,
You shine like the North Star.

Beautiful is what you are,
When you comb your hair,
I can't help but to stare.

Beautiful is what you are,
Just look at you beautiful woman,
My love for you is something to bear.

Beautiful is what you are,
You're my shining angel from above,
Just for you I'll prove my love.

Beautiful is what you are,
So don't ever change,
Because beautiful is what you are,
You beautiful woman of mine.

Timothy Ashley, Grade 8
Cottage Grove Upper Grade Center, IL

To Win

I want to hear the swish of the net.
To hear the crack of the bat as I swing,
To feel the rush of adrenaline as I play,
To hear the crowd chant our name.

I want to drive down the middle,
To steal a base while he's pitching,
To run faster than before,
To hit the quarterback harder this time.

I want to make the last second shot,
To score the winning run,
To catch the Hail Mary touchdown.
I want to win.

Ralph Laux, Grade 8
St Monica School, IN

Lexi, My Special Person

Lexi loves to make me laugh,
Leaping in the air.
She is black, brown,
And I love her very much.
Hyper, energetic
Loves to run.
Her age of one.
Acts like she's younger.
Lexi the dog,
Loves me very much.

Jason Waller, Grade 7
Paw Paw Middle School, MI

The Candy Drawer

They call to me.
Each of them asking me to indulge
Taunting me as I refuse.
Jumping up and down begging.
I yell no, they yell back yes!
Laying in the dark, closed drawer,
They sit and wait for their next victim.

Molly Somerville, Grade 7
New Albany Middle School, OH

Courage Within

She was brave
She was smart
He was weak
He was ignorant
She was optimistic
She was kind
He was pessimistic
He was cruel
Comparing all day
Wondering who just may
Believe and agree with him
I dare not say
That I ever make someone's life so dim
Anne Frank had courage within
I just wish that Hitler had been learning
From what was going on around him.

Sydney Griffin, Grade 8
St Pauls Lutheran School, IL

If Only

If only time would slow down
    If only time would stop.
If only we could have a chance
    To heal a loved one's heart.

If only there was refuge
    For the weary and trembling soul.
If only there was a place to rest
    For beings, young and old.

If only there really was a friend
    Who would never fail.
If only time would never end
    Against life's roaring gales.

If only there really was a way
    To stop all of life's sufferings.
If only, if only today was the day
    When love could be revealed.

If only

Beau Deal, Grade 8
Little Miami Jr High School, OH

Clouds

They do appear when it is bright.
They are hard to see when it is night.
They are bulky and black when it must rain.
You see them when you're in a plane.
You gaze at their different shapes.
You can even see them from up in space.
They creep silently across the sky
And some days they do not come by.
When it is stormy they move fast.
When it is snowy they are vast.
To where they go, you do not know
But some will go by very slow.
But when you stare upon a cloud
You will know that more will come around.

David Fritz, Grade 8
St Paul's Lutheran School, IL

Writing

Trying to write,
Can't find the words.
Can't get it quite right
Can't mock what I've heard.

The bluebird sits on the fence and sings
No words come to mind
Only the tune it brings
Still searching for the words I cannot find.

What's wrong is the place I've tried to find
The words are to come from my heart,
Not from my mind.
Slowly but surely the writing starts.

We all have the capability to write
It's just the flame beneath us, we need to ignite.

Delaney Miller, Grade 7
Alexandria Middle Magnet School, LA

The Willabee Witch

The Willabee Witch flew high in the sky
looking down at the ground for birds flying by,
because of a dare that the other witches despised,
so she had to turn a goose into a duck, mid-fly.
The Willabee Witch looked all around,
but no goose mid-fly had she ever found,
though strangely enough she saw a great big hound,
higher than 10 kilometers from the ground.
In amazement the Willabee Witch saw
the goose she was looking for, in awe,
and shouted out in a cry, "Hoorah!"
and rummaged in her pack for her special claw.
The Witch turned in a frightful U-Bend,
and told the spell that could lend
her a helping hand in succeeding, which she recommends.

Brigit Tronrud, Grade 7
Gordon Head Middle School, BC

Martin Luther King Jr.

I am captain of the clouds
soaring high, being heard everywhere
fighting, for the civil rights
of African Americans throughout my world

What I do is tough
I know I could get killed
but it's worth it for my sons and daughters
so they can all be free

They treat us like we're trash
they don't care if we die
we're treated like a bad disease
but they're the ones who are sick

I had a dream one day
and I fulfilled that dream
because the times we're in now
we all have equal rights
and that is the way it should be
because I am captain of the clouds

Logan Garthe, Grade 8
Highland Middle School, IL

Australia

Up in the air
Toward Australia we go
Above the clouds
We fly on our way.

Through the glass door
Among all Australians
To the limo we go
We are on our way to the Drum's household.

Beyond their house
Out in the open
Beside the hills
The Blue Mountains are there.

On the road we went
Inside the wooden gates
From there we saw them
The beautiful kangaroos and koalas.

During the trip we saw so much
After the five week vacation
Without the Australian air
It's sad to say it is over.

Samantha Gray, Grade 7
Algonquin Middle School, MI

Sun

Lighting up the Earth
A boiling hot ball of gas
Rising in the east
Center of the universe
Giving heat to creation

Jessica Buice, Grade 7
Trinity Lutheran School, MI

Telescope

The stars shine so bright,
Up in the desolate sky.
Planets so visible,
With my telescope eye.

Andrea Hecker, Grade 7
Fairfield Middle School, OH

My Soul

My soul is like a heart
Always pumping
Sometimes faster
Sometimes slower
It never stops
Even through hard times
It keeps on beating
Beating like a drum cadence
As I go through life

Dylan Netzel, Grade 9
Clintonville High School, WI

Voices Unheard

Voices unheard
In the world all around
Pleading for help
But not ever found

Always ignored
And never heeded
It was someone's help
That these voices needed

But now it is too late
The stage has been set
Their fate is decided
And destiny met

If only we listened
To what they had said
We could have saved them
But look where this led

Lives are destroyed
Families are broken
With violence as
Our eminent token

Kelly Clare, Grade 8
Grand Traverse Academy, MI

What Did I Do?

What did I do?
I broke so many hearts
I really don't care about more than one special one
She gave me life I showed her the door
She gave me more than I could ever ask for
She loved me when I felt alone and never asked for something in return
What had I done — she gave me everything and loved me all the same
What did I do?

Shannon Foster, Grade 8
Wainwright High School, AB

Fantasy

In a little house on top of the hill
Where Cinderella sings to Jack and Jill

Where Humpty Dumpty sat on a wall
And the one main season is the beginning of fall

Where dragons and unicorns laugh, play, and run
And flowers bloom in the winter sun

Where Tinkerbell cast a spell on the frog
And the main character in this poem is a talking dog

Where you look out your window and you swear you're in space
Then you look back again and you're in a whole new place

A place where your wishing all your hopes and dreams can come true
And obviously mine have because standing right in front of me is still you.

Kole Brodigan, Grade 7
Tripoli Middle/Senior High School, IA

I Am the Holocaust

I am a Jew.
There is lice on my head and filth on my body.
The pain I feel is unbearable.
Every day the camp grins at us getting pleasure off our misery.
I am a Nazi.
The reek of death and body odor fills my nostrils.
The stench of smoke fills me.
We are monsters.
I am a concentration camp.
Bodies litter the ground.
People walk everywhere through the ash.
Ashes float toward the sky like little lives floating towards heaven.
I am Hitler.
Music and laughter fill the streets.
People cheer my name.
The whole world bows down at my feet.
I am an Allied Force.
Sweat and grime cake on my lips.
Smoke makes its way to my mouth.
I feel enormously small as I roam through the camp.
I am the Holocaust.

Megan Fisher, Grade 8
Parkway Middle School, OH

Baseball

Gorgeous green grass
Summers in the sand
Baseball with my friends
It is a blast

No matter what time of day
Morning, noon, or night
We'll all get together and play
Even if I have to put up a fight

Those memories are what I cherish the most
My team is the best
I mean not to boast

State is the greatest
4 hour rides
Staying up late
With all of the guys

Baseball means the world to me
Fills me up with lots of glee

Hope this season goes real well
That would be super swell

Peter Elton, Grade 8
Stewartville Middle School, MN

Nathan

Low bass explodes as I open the door to our own little world
Something to take us as far away as possible.
He is erupting with life
Knowing that his days won't last forever
So living as if nothing mattered.
Pink flows from his skin, like a forever blush
Telling the world that there isn't time to rest.
Loud, outspoken
Showing everyone this is the way to live.
His hair shines in the sun, making even that look dim
Awkward in shape, not round, not skinny, indescribable
Being the source of talk in this little town
With slowly ending streets to nowhere
That come to life as we race down them
Faster than I can say stop.
Endless sounds of laughter and giggles
It never stops here.
Everyone envies this
Everyone wonders what happens when we're here
But no one knows until they fall into it
And never want to come out.

Laura Onasch-Vera, Grade 9
Maharishi School of the Age of Enlightenment, IA

Ode to Frogs

O, Frogs,
You hop very high.
Catching bugs,
As fast as can be.

You swim through water,
And hop on rocks.
Jumping wherever you desire,
Or sitting as still as stone.

Mr. Frog,
You're the nicest of greens.
Your croak is so deep,
It wakes me up with a smile.

Summer flies by quickly,
And fall is out the door.
It is getting colder,
Day and day.

O, Mr. Frog you must go too,
To hibernate and find a hole.
But you'll be back in spring,
With a hop and a croak.

Francine Neander, Grade 7
Nativity of Our Lord Catholic School, ON

Amen

Dreams can guide my life.
My hopes can be my light.
These are from my soul,
Not the books nor the mind.
Happiness can pull in
All the love I will give
To the one that I have and hold.
Then the spirits will take me,
When God told,
Go and take her for me.
It is her time to go.
In the after life,
I will guide
Those who are still here,
Who stood by my side.
Then, when they see me once again,
I will recite this poem and end with Amen.

Nycole Janes, Grade 8
River Forest Jr High School, IN

Rain

Rain slips in like a cuddly kitten,
But it drenches everything it can see.
Quietly it comes, then BANG! There it is,
Pouring down on my bedroom floor.
Like a tired cat, it slowly, gently slips away.

Carleen Yntema, Grade 9
King's Christian School, BC

I Am From

I am from the Rocky Mountains,
Where horned-sheep travel.

I am from the hot springs,
Where fresh water flows.

I am from the ice fields,
Where the aging water drifts.

I am from the stampede,
Where people yell and shout.

I am from the fort,
Where old buildings live.

I am from the hoodoos,
Where they lay for years and years.

I am from the prairies,
Where the hay is rolled.

I am from the land,
Where champions are…Alberta.

Kristal Church, Grade 8
Weledeh Catholic School, NT

Soccer

Forward
Fast, good
Kicking, shooting, scoring
Outdoor, swiftly, strongly, indoor
Blocking, running, saving
Black, white
Football

Jake Roush, Grade 7
Algonquin Middle School, MI

Loveless

When I think about you,
my heart will feel weird.
Love is a strong word.
I never use it until you say it.
Every time you are beside me,
my heart will feel funny.
All around you,
you will be protecting me.
I'll never feel pain,
unless you will be protecting me.
Someday, somehow.
You'll be gone.
Not being beside me.
Sometimes I'll cry.
You are gone.
Love is a strong word.

Alex Crapeau, Grade 7
Weledeh Catholic School, NT

Thai Deli Owners

Always working
Always busy
Slightly bland Thai food sits on my flowered plastic plate,
Smiling back at me
They rush from cash register to customers
Her dainty hands not cut out for this work
She scoops enormous helpings of Thai tofu vegetables
More than you want
Their once bright eyes wear a cloak of weariness
Six years ago
A smile and friendly conversation every time
Tray in hand we splurge on key lime pie
Luminescent smiles cast a golden glow on their faces
Troubles left behind in Thailand
Our bulky arms embrace their delicate frames
As we thank them for the lovely Thai dresses, stowaways in their suitcases
Things are different now
Wrinkles are permanent residents of their foreheads
No time for conversation barely a hello escapes their pursed lips
Now the only thing that smiles
Are the vegetables

Lila Cutter, Grade 9
Maharishi School of the Age of Enlightenment, IA

Lake Superior

The peaceful lake waves
To swimmers at its shore,
Beckoning them to take an unknowing
Dive into its mysterious depths.

The narcissistic sun
Struts through the endless blue sky,
Showing off its vibrant rays,
While keeping watch over the world,
Like a lion guarding its prey.

The old, decrepit cliffs
That line the shore,
Stare out over the water, longingly. Waiting,
For the water to brush up
Against its cheeks as the tide comes in,
Then cries, as it melts away.

Weary seagulls spy on the younger children,
With their beady black eyes,
Watching for helpless crumbs
Scattered on the trodden pathway to be devoured.
And as the day moves on, the tired sun abandons its post,
And slowly slumbers into the lake, not to be seen again until morning.

Leah Bolin, Grade 9
Wayzata High School, MN

Friendship

Everybody needs a close friend to give them love
Friends are there for you no matter what
True friends don't judge and always care
They don't care how you look
Friends can cheer you up
They always love you
Friends are truthful
Share secrets
Priceless
Have sleepovers
Friends share stories
Friends go shopping together
Friends like to be together
Friends spend lots of time together
They come over just about any day
They will catch you every time you fall
Everybody needs a close friend to give them love.

Sarah Rodriguez, Grade 8
Shakopee Area Catholic School, MN

Crisis

I'm writing something down that's burning in my heart.
Day by day the world is falling apart.
It's hard to watch the people dying,
And the screaming of the children crying.
Getting shot in the leg, or maybe an arm.
Why are we all causing harm?
Murder is not the way to play,
Nobody should have the price to pay.
Life is too short, this I found.
Life is worth living, so don't mess around!

Ryan Schomer, Grade 7
Hannah Beardsley Middle School, IL

Mom

Always there when I need her,
Comforting me even without words.
Whenever I am sick, she can always find a cure.

If I call her in the night,
Darkened as it may be,
She will stay, until it is light.

Driving all around the town,
She takes to practices and such.
Every day she does this, without even a frown.

Cooking dinner every day,
She keeps our house running.
She is amazing, I'd have to say.

Without her I don't know what I would do.
Just thought I'd tell you,
Mom I love you!

Mary Chelminiak, Grade 8
St Monica School, IN

Only if When

A little girl once told me,
the one thing she'd never say

"I'll be happy," she said,
"when I die and I'll do many things.

"But only if when the sky is purple,
my little dog can talk, and I can hold onto the wind,

"Only if when I can fight with pirates,
on a huge blue ship, with a hat on my head,

"Only if when I can be a mermaid,
and swim with a whale, maybe ride on its back,

"Only if when I can go to Mars,
and meet green Martians, with a monkey from the zoo,

"Only if when I can soar with an eagle,
over a huge skyscraper, and not even get tired,

"Only if when all these things happen,
will I ever, ever say,
that I like boys."

Nicky DelPrete, Grade 7
St Monica School, IN

On a Swing

I see a pretty white dress
With a ribbon that ties
Those cute little shoes
That help her get by
She laughs as she gazes
Up at that blue, clear sky
That great, green grass below her swifts by her feet
And she feels the sun all through that swings seat
She feels like she's flying
Just in her backyard
She hears those birds singing away
She hears those bees buzzing all through the day
She tastes baked goods from her kitchen inside
Her mommy comes out
"It's dinnertime!"
She laughs and she giggles and leaps off the swing
It seems as though, she has wings
I see a pretty white dress
With a ribbon that ties
Those cute little shoes
That help her get by

Kendel Elliott, Grade 8
Kewaskum Middle School, WI

A Day at the Beach

I smell the greasy French fries coming from the hotel a hundred feet away
I smell meat being cooked in a barbecue and hear my stomach start to contract
I smell the chlorine in the hotel pool which many people think is quite cool

I listen to the seagulls fly above me, and then squawk away
I listen to the waves crash one by one, then listen to the foam bubble away
I listen to the people yelling and screaming, having a good time at least for the meantime

I feel the warm, grainy sand when I rub it in-between my long smooth fingers
I feel the hot, comforting rays of the sun shining all over my body drying away the salty ocean water at midday
I feel small, spiky pieces of once beautiful shells under my feet when I walk over them

I see people tall or short, large or thin, white as a dove above, or dark as chocolate
I see the people running into the large sea hoping they will be seen again
I see the colorful towels and bathing suits absorbing the powerful rays of the blazing sun

Before I leave I turn around to face the glistening sea
Pink, orange, yellow, and purple illuminate the never-ending sky
I pause for a second, turn around, and walk away slowly but when I do I think to myself
Why can't every day be like today?

Tatiana Stevenin, Grade 8
South View Middle School, MN

Amusement Parks

(I see) enormous crowds of people standing, waiting patiently in the endless lines.

(I hear) the shrieking screams from the roller coasters roaring past me like angry lions. While venturing through the park, I glance up at the scaling exciting rides to see them blocking the sun from my eyes.

(I smell) the delicious aroma of the hot sweet kettle corn piping throughout the air. I smell the sweet scent of powdered sugar being sprinkled upon the golden funnel cakes.

(I taste) the cold fizzy soda as it enters my parched throat quenching my desperate thirst. I taste the fruity refreshment of the rainbow domed snow cone.

(I touch) the silver steamy railings while working my way through the crowd to the Wildfire roller coaster. My legs touch the scorching metal of the roller coaster seat after waiting hours in line.

(I feel) boundless joy while blasting up the tracks anticipating the steep drop about to happen next.

Blair Ralston, Grade 9
Southwest Jr High School, AR

Adrenaline

The peaceful pool, like a cool oasis, the motivating coaches,
As loud as bullhorns as soon as swimmers hit the water.
The enthusiastic cheering from my best friends at the end of my lane,
The whistle, piercing through the air giving all swimmers an adrenaline rush.
The sharp, comforting smell of chlorine bringing back so many memories.
The pungent smell of Sharpie on my body reminding me of my races.
The sweet taste of Gatorade as I try to stay hydrated for my race,
The nutty energy bars giving me a quick burst that quick burst of energy I needed.
The water, cool to the touch, as my friend swam swiftly through the shivery water.
I hug my fired-up, laughing teammates in celebration,
The excitement, anxious rush of the tired swimmers as they happily celebrate their victories.

Britanee Russell, Grade 9
Southwest Jr High School, AR

Helping Others Out

Have you ever needed helping out?
Do you feel like you're about to shout?

If only someone would've assisted you,
You wouldn't be feeling blue,

You would not be so frustrated,
Or even a little irritated,

We've all been there; it's such a relief,
They may be in disbelief,

You'll feel good for the rest of the day,
And they may get on their way,

They may have been sad and feeling bad,
After you help they'll be glad

So the next time you see someone who needs a hand,
Help them, they'll understand,

When you need help, you'll get it back,
You'll set their day back on track.

Cade VanRooyen, Grade 7
North Rockford Middle School, MI

A Little Dirt Road

A little dirt road
That's all it will ever be
All it was on my shoulders; just a big load
All my memories of this town to me
Will be left on that little dirt road

All those people I had met
I should be glad
But yet…
Is my heart so bad

Am I able to leave
Am I so cruel
To leave the web I weave

Does this show my weakness
No! My good-byes are said
Good-bye dirt road with you I leave weakness

Now as I look back all I can see
Is a little me
And a little dirt road

Candace Caldwell, Grade 8
Buckeye Jr/Sr High School, LA

Sickness

It's the thing we all get,
makes our friends not want to be with us,
that's what happens when you're sick,

It stays on us like a bloodsucking tick,
it's slowly but surely sucking your life away,
that's what happens when you're sick,

It weighs you down like a cement brick,
you're heart's now black and it's holding you back,
that's what happens when you're sick,

You're bottling in the beast and don't know what to do,
there is one thing you should realize,
Anger is the sickness holding on to you!!!

Hunter Mobley, Grade 8
Holy Savior Menard Central High School, LA

I've Changed

It's this feeling in the depths of my soul
and it's starting to take control
It's controlling my thoughts, actions, and emotions
it's like my life is going in locomotion
All they do is Fuss!!!
and it's starting to make me cantankerous
It hurts so bad
because I was never ill-tempered
I was never always mad
I was the sweetest thing
but life's experiences have given me a different song to sing
my song is related to things so vindictive
I hate being angry!
but now I am addicted
I pray to God for some type of tranquility
someone grant me with the serenity
historically I am happy
but, unfortunately, anger will be my legacy.

Collette Harmon, Grade 8
Jefferson Middle School, IL

The White Flag

The colors of the forest all
The wilderness whispers cold thoughts in my ear
Squirrels chatter all around the distant bait pile:
Bright golden corn scattered across the ground
My head nods from the long day,
When the "snap" of a twig pulls my head alert

Brown dances through the trees
The focus of finding the sweet treat
Bow's gently drawn
When a white flag is lifted
And brown is gone, dancing through the trees
I surrender for today

Adam Mohnen, Grade 9
Clintonville High School, WI

Anger

Anger is red with rage,
It sounds like disagreeing friends
And tastes bitter.
It smells like a smoky fire.
It looks like a tomato.
Anger makes me feel depressed.

Anger is black with emptiness,
It sounds like a harsh storm
And tastes like undercooked steak.
It smells like burning gasoline.
It looks like sharp lightning.
Anger makes me feel sad.

Anger is the color of a stormy night,
It sounds like thunder
And tastes spicy.
It smells rotten.
It looks like a raging forest fire.
Anger makes me feel frustrated.

Anger is the first rung
On the ladder of hatred.

Tyler Lawson, Grade 8
Little Miami Jr High School, OH

Sun, Teach Me

Sun, teach me to shine,
To be a light in other's lives,
To lead them away from the darkness.

Sun, teach me to be strong,
To not give in easily to lies,
To believe with all my heart.

Sun, teach me to grow,
To leave behind me the sorrow,
And to embrace the future.

Adam Wray, Grade 8
Vernon Virtual Education School, BC

The Green Line

Soles kissing the ground
Laces tightly wound
Pulled patiently into perfect bows
Appendage lined up in rows
Spreading for miles
The green line never stops
A steady beat walks out the door
Marching on, off to war
Engines roar in the back
Say good-bye to your country
A knot in your stomach
You know you won't make it back

Elory Hranicka, Grade 9
William Fremd High School, IL

Time Changes Life Re-arranges

Every man should be born equal and free,
To an extent the world disagrees,
Every man is born with his rights,
But none are equal and fair.

Destination and liberation are equal,
Raise your fist and create the realm of freedom,
Liberation is achieved by the weapon of perseverance,
True freedom above all is the most difficult to achieve.

There isn't a mortal weapon that could separate man
From his destiny, his liberation, his joy.
There is no remedy for perseverance,
Liberation presents itself only to those who persevere until the end.

Liberation manifests itself into the wonders
And in the potential of man.
Liberation gives man his rights, his privileges and equality above all.
Liberation only presents itself to those who are willing to sacrifice.

Gagandeep Singh, Grade 9
QC

Love

It sounds like harmony and melody in music working together.
It smells like the sweet warm vanilla scent of a candle.
It feels like the warmth of the blazing fireplace.
It looks like 2 people in love walking on the beach without a care.
It tastes like sweet chocolate melting in your mouth.

Chabre Tucker, Grade 7
Fairfield Middle School, OH

Jealousy

Jealousy is the color of the turbulent flames that eat at the wood lavished forests.
It sounds like the animosity waves of the wretched sea.
It tastes like the bitter knowledge of sinister acts.
And smells like the stench of tobacco smoke.
Jealousy looks like the scornful Arabian sun.
And makes me feel unworthy of extravagance and glory.

Jealousy is green with envy.
It sounds like the thunder claps of a vicious storm.
It tastes like spoiled milk.
And smells of rotten apples.
Jealousy looks like the scorched desert sand.
And makes me feel oblivious to the outside world.

Jealousy is the color of the radiant superior sun.
It sounds like the barbaric Thailand tsunami.
It tastes like treacherous poison.
And smells like deteriorated wood.
Jealousy looks like dried cactus.
And makes me feel immensely troubled.

Jealousy is the element of greed.

Samantha Burton, Grade 8
Little Miami Jr High School, OH

Home

How thy home warms me in deep winter's gaze
Far from all harm when I lay in my room
Nothing to do but watch the dawn's daze
Comfy and cozy just like in a tomb
Under the sky, my house is gray and white
Owned by my family we have great times
Loving every moment with faces bright
Downstairs with the radio plays sweet chimes
Upstairs has many rooms including mine
Another room is where the gamers play
Hundreds of systems in a big line
All of these games just make one dandy day
I love my home and all who live inside
Just makes a good place to go out and hide.

Rachel Wilkerson, Grade 8
Otsego Middle School, OH

Grandpa

It's hard to be without you
but I know I'm not alone.
Missing, loving, caring about you is all gone.
All I have is the memories of you.
When I looked into your eyes
all I could say is I love you.
You are the most precious thing in my life.
When you told me you were leaving,
I didn't know what to do, just to cry in my room.
Doesn't make sense.
To be in your heart,
always, feels like the right thing to do.

Roza Balasanyan, Grade 7
Weledeh Catholic School, NT

Two Slurpies Not Taken*

Two Slurpies
And sorry I could not slurp both
And be one person, long I stood
And looked at both as long as I could
Then slurped the other, and was just as tasty.
And having perhaps the better claim.
Because it was blue and slushy;
Though as for that the coldness
Had made them about the same,
And both that morning equally slushed
Oh, I kept the first another day!
Yet knowing how way leads on the way,
I doubted if I should ever come back.
I shall be telling this with a sigh
Somewhere ages and ages hence:
Two Slurpies in the store and I —
I took the one most colorful,

And that has made all the difference.

Bianca Salamanca, Grade 7
Hamlin Upper Grade Center, IL
*Based on "The Road Not Taken" by Robert Frost.

Constant Battle

I talk; no answer
It's the same old thing
My words to you sound like a say-so
An ongoing noise, plainly annoying

Giving you more than what's deserved
Still there's nothing to concur?
In one ear and out the other
I'd accept that, but I'm not your brother

Tried everything, I have not a clue
Problem's left for me, but right are you?
Your nerves are pushing over mine
Finally, something we both agree is true!

Now I see where I stand
Opposite of you, but in front of the MAN
Been the bigger one, since the start
Don't worry; I'll end with this remark

I used to begin, and you would end
A bond once solid as rock, now just brings dismay
Two peas in a pod left with no choice
Either we disassemble or mesh fast like clay

Abbas Abbas, Grade 8
John English Junior and Middle School, ON

Spring

Spring comes so slowly in Minnesota.
The first warm days are followed by snow.
Spring peeks its head out,
And then hides again.
The robins are the first to announce it.
Then they shiver in the trees.
Were they too early?
Fooled by a sudden warm spell?
The first sights and sounds of spring
Are undeniable to me.
Birds singing, dogs barking, children playing
Sounds I grow tired of by spring's end.
Still, I am impatient for spring.
I long to see the snow gone,
The flowers begin to bloom, and the grass turn green.
I want to place my boots and coat
In the winter locker and close the lid.
But spring won't come until the rain falls
And the earth awakens.
It won't be spring until it smells like rain
Spring…I await you.

Makala Hoot, Grade 8
Stewartville Middle School, MN

Snow Day

Feeling
Awesome
Crazy like a cheetah running
Jumping up and down like a bunny
This is how I feel
On a snow day
Snow's shooting like a bullet coming
Out of a gun.
Snowmobiles rushing
Like the storm's never gonna end
Snowplows rushing as hard as they can
Shoveling the driveway again and again.
Having snowball fights like a kid's dream
Building snow forts this is our dream.
Snowmobiling over snow drifts
Bumping up and down
Flying through the fluff
Like I'm in the clouds
That's a snow day to me.

Josh Schneider, Grade 7
Linwood Public School, ON

Standing Tall

There was a small cherry tree sprout,
In gales it would sway all about,
It grew big and tall,
From the spring to the fall,
And now it stands tall, proud, and stout.

Nicole Smith, Grade 7
Trinity Lutheran School, MI

Frogger

Once there was a frog
All pink and spotty.
Blue spots and green stripes on his back.
Green feet that were really hoppy.
If you haven't guessed
His name is Frogger.
He hops on logs, trees and lilies.
He stays under water until he is safe.
He hops up fast,
Sticks his sticky tongue out,
Catches a fly.
He croaks in joy!
Then Frogger leaps to land
To find a mate
To live his joyful life with.

Rebecca Lutz, Grade 8
Lawton Middle School, MI

A New Season

An old dusty field
Beginning a new season
A purpose; again

Jerrison Barber, Grade 8
Wainwright High School, AB

Sound of Peace

When I feel mad,
I run to my room.
In there is a wooden figure with strings.
The wood seems like a shining sun.

When I pick it up I feel like I'm in another world.
I feel as though nothing matters.
I'm peaceful.
When I strum the strings they are like bell chimes.

They were singing to the world.
The wooden object is like a bird it is plain, but makes a beautiful noise.
I smell the wood and it smells like a grove of new trees.

I'm peaceful and nothing can make me leave.
When I'm done I'm not mad.
When I come back to the world it says hello and I smile back.
I know nothing is bad.

Trevor McInnes, Grade 7
New Albany Middle School, OH

Liberators

We came into the camp
The taste was smoky and air that was dirty and toxic
We came in farther and could see bodies and screaming Jews
The place was a zoo
The Jews were like homeless animals
They were begging for food
They were so hungry they could eat anything
You could hear the screams as gun fire rang in the air
Bang! Bang!
You could hear some Americans were puking at the smell of the place
The smell was unbearable
It was a nasty mix of flesh, smoke, and burning fire
You could see the smoke climbing into the heavy
And at the same time cool morning air
You could see all the Nazis laying down their weapons
The Nazis were just giving up
They knew it was over
They knew that they couldn't take all of us
All of us liberators

Brett Swygart, Grade 8
Parkway Middle School, OH

Daddy

My love for you could not be contained or expressed with a thousand words.
My joy is to think of the sparkly-eyed little toddler to the beautiful lady you are today.
Your beauty and charm is only surpassed by your priceless personality and heart.
I consider myself blessed to be called DADDY!

Mariah Falck, Grade 9
Blair-Taylor High School, WI

5, 6, 7, 8

Front to back, side to side.
The dancing has started; it's no time to hide.
I'm feeling the music, emotions in all.
I see the movements, and the instructor's calls.

Our feet are moving, the music's alive.
We're out on the floor; it's our time to shine.
It's burning up, like a hot summer day.
Then the music goes off, and there's nothing to say.

Off of the floor, going over what we learned.
Then we do it over and over, until class is adjourned.
It's time, class is over, it's off to the next.
I'm cursed with this hobby, but it's no bad hex.

I've done this forever, through good times and bad.
Traveled the country, it's made me happy and sad.
This has been a favorite of mine, since I was just three.
On and on I've done it, it's made me delightfully pleased.

No matter where life takes me, on this road or another.
I will always remember these memories,
And the big impact they had on me.

Ilise Green, Grade 7
New Albany Middle School, OH

Blue

Feels like silk
Tastes like cotton candy ice cream
Looks like the ocean
Sounds like waves crashing against the shore
Smells like thin crisp air
Blue is everything but nothing

Julia Shelbourn, Grade 8
Whitewater Middle School, WI

I Am

I am funny and wild like a cub looking for honey.
I wonder when the world will come to peace.
I hear Blue Jays singing like they're on stage.
I see the sun rise as a new day and a new beginning.
I want to know the theme song to my life.
I am funny and wild like a cub looking for honey.

I pretend to be a kitten wanting to be a lion.
I feel my heart warmth heating a homeless person's house.
I touch the ocean breeze as the memories stay with me.
I worry about the fields becoming offices.
I cry when a relative dies.
I am funny and wild like a cub looking for honey.

I understand how, but don't understand why.
I say, "Love is like the wind. You can feel it, but can't see it."
I dream to be married at sunset on the beach.
I try to be different, so nobody is the same.
I hope everybody's life is a life worth living.
I am funny and wild like a cub looking for honey.

Courtney Schreiber, Grade 8
Otsego Middle School, OH

Unreal

A symbol of love
Of beauty and peace.
A symbol of love
To cherish and keep.
A symbol of love
Presented to the accepted.
But are all flowers beautiful?
Must every present, be something that'll die?
Chocolates and roses,
That fall from the sky?
Do the flowers prove anything?
A symbol of love?
Rooted from its home, and left in a vase,
Waiting to die?
But are all flowers beautiful?
It's like a bullet through a flock of doves
Pain is lost in a myriad of love
A red rose, the color of blood
Dies in a vase, but is seen as love
But it's unreal,
Because not all flowers are beautiful.

Kassondra White, Grade 8
South Milwaukee Middle School, WI

Summer Love

Oh how I love to walk outside and smell the fresh air.
Smells so good, but I couldn't dare.
Smell the roses, touch the thorns, my fingers cannot bare.
When I get a call from him, I think of summer love.
Look out my window, I see two turtle doves.
Look at the sky, wonder what it's like up above.
When I see his face I think of love.
He's never going to break my heart.
He's such a sweetheart.
My summer love has been massively rad.
I think to myself nothing could ever go bad.

Kirsten Hankins, Grade 8
Tuckerman High School, AR

Undefined

Life comforts us with the past because we fear the future;
undefined.

We fear the future, the unknown. We hope;
undefined.

We're trapped in the present feeling our way out;
undefined.

We celebrate life's fulfillment and pray the future is welcoming;
undefined.

We define our lives with the choices we make.
We seek the future, ready for the undefined.

Emily Townsend, Grade 8
Prairie View Middle School, IL

The Real Thing

My screams fill the bitter cold air,
For I do not know if I can ever bear,
This tragedy that has suddenly arrived,
Before my scared and petrified eyes.

I hope he will continue to fight
I'm praying that he will be all right,
I don't know if there's any hope,
How could death lie so very close?

I stay with him till help finally comes,
And by then I am completely numb,
With coldness, dread, and tons of fear,
As I silently start to cry some tears.

Why does it have to end like this,
Where there is no peace or any bliss,
I just wish this was all a dream,
But I know it's the real thing.

MaryAnne Skora, Grade 8
St Jude Elementary School, IN

Ninja

Their silent hand
moves as a cheetah
swift, unstoppable
staring at its prey.
Why do you dare to move?
They'll catch you anyway.

Brittany Barnes, Grade 9
Cabot Jr High School North, AR

Do You Remember When?

Do you remember when,
We believed we could touch the sky,
When we could hardly stand,
To watch the world rush on by?
Do you remember when,
We used to wish on a star,
Shining in the night time sky,
Though it was so far?
Do you remember when,
We left footprints in the sand,
As we walked along the warm beach,
When we could hardly stand?
Do you remember when,
We used to wish we were tall,
Like our moms and dads,
When we were so small?
Do you remember when,
Our childhood was here,
When the monster under our beds,
Was the only thing to fear?
Do you remember when?

Katelynn Smith, Grade 8
Prairie Heights Middle School, IN

My Window

Looking through my window I see everything
I see familiar faces and places I will always remember
I can see my friends, family, and moments I will always treasure
I smell the fresh air from Mother Nature and watch as Father Time flies by
Nothing is more beautiful than the things I can see through my window

Rosie Leuby, Grade 7
New Albany Middle School, OH

I Don't Miss You

We had the best of times living, laughing, smiling all around
Until suddenly it all smashed into the ground.
I didn't smile or even laugh this is all the things I'm hating
Because my vision of you is fading.
Feeling abandoned, lost and confused I need to get strong
By double-checking if you were right or wrong.
One last cry tears rolling down
No more sobbing after my last frown
It's been so long but I'm just over you
Have to move on, got to make it through.
I'm finally happy now in love and right mind
I have a new sweetheart, as you might find.
He makes me smile and calls me beautiful I'm head over heels and you're not there
I'm in love and you don't care
I'm amazed how things have changed I guess what I'm trying to do
Is tell you that I don't miss you.
I have found the apple of my eye I have found my dear
And yes unlike you, he is very near.
This is the first and last time that we speak I hope it's not a shock to you
Just please remember one thing, I don't miss you.

Amber Viles, Grade 8
Paul Hadley Middle School, IN

A Warm Welcome

Excitement and joy
pulse through me as I burst through the front door.
The gentle breeze tickles my cheeks,
and the air smells so fresh and warm.
The sun nearly blinds me with the intensity of its rays:
that trillion-watt bulb
is obviously glad to see me again!
Birds chirp cheerfully above me
in the cloudless sky,
and for one moment it seems like their songs alone
bring on the brand new day.
I carelessly roll around in the grass.
Its needles poke me, and it screams, "Get off! That hurts!"
So I lie there mocking those tiny green needles with my
I'm-not-moving-and-there-is-nothing-you-can-do-about-it attitude.
As I relax, I listen to the hurry of ongoing cars
and the laughter of children that can be heard for miles around.
But all I really notice is that breeze —
playing with my hair, calling my name,
and welcoming me back
to summer.

Miranda Pederson, Grade 8
Humboldt Middle School, IA

Failing

From failure comes something beautiful,
The exaltation of the lost,
Without failure we would be short of everything
Awe-inspiring and astounding,
Not to fail would be to live in nonexistence,
Without failure we would be lost,
Lost for words to fill the empty voids,
Lost of life to draw,
For in our failure a hand reaches out,
So if not for our shortcomings, deficiencies and, falls,
It would be worth nothing at all.

Adrianna Pontalti, Grade 9
Heritage Christian School, BC

Insomnia

I used to dream the rain would stop
a childish dream, of wanting and needing and having
Now, it's a walking hallucination, rejected and retained
I used to dream
of running
so fast
I could
fly
I used to look out my window at night
in inexcusable darkness
I used to dream of living. Ha! A childish dream!
I used to…
I did…
I was…
A past tense dream
of what no longer can be
The rain falls
softly slowly
a hundred whisper heartbeats
and still I cannot
sleep.

Raisa Tolchinsky, Grade 7
Nichols Middle School, IL

Christ's Crucifixion

Christ died for our sins.
He did this so we could all live.
He rose three days later in a cave-like den.
We should praise Him for all He did.
Without Him being nailed to the cross, we wouldn't be here.
Jesus was brave on the cross; the cross was very tall.
He is always near.
To Him we should always call.
He changed the world forever.
Gone today, but soon to come.
We will never forget it, never!
Seeing what He went through makes me numb.
Christ's Crucifixion was good and bad.
Seeing what they did makes me very sad.

Bethanee Russell, Grade 9
Southwest Jr High School, AR

Accessories

A girl can never have enough,
But when selecting it may be tough,
Bangles, clutches, and a big bold ring,
Boys you wouldn't understand, it's a girl thing.

Purses are great,
You just cannot hate,
The way that they shine,
It looks so divine.

Blue, pink, orange and yellow,
Shoes are all great, especially a stiletto
If you cannot decide on just one,
Buy them all, have some fun!

Shopping is fun, you can't disagree
The best brand is Burberry
If you want something special, and something unique,
Try skipping K-Mart, and hit a boutique.

The cost is totally worth it,
The way you look is oh so perfect
The passion for fashion is thriving,
To look great, you need to keep striving.

Carly Mausolf, Grade 8
Sandusky Middle School, MI

Lonely

Invisible,
out of sight.
Lying here alone in the dark
trying to fit in.
Feeling like a tucked away, forgotten toy.
Abandoned in this dusty old place
never to see the light again.
Left behind,
lost.
Where do I go from here,
no friends to go to,
no one to hear my cries.
Where is my role model,
someone to guide me?
Where,
who,
when?
When will I learn my past is behind me?
Afraid to come out of my own shell.
My hands unclench, my emotions drop to the floor.
Loneliness.

Natasha Runstedler, Grade 7
Linwood Public School, ON

I Am

I am a Jew.
I look up and see a tall chimney staring down at me.
Into the heated flames people go, and out from the top falls the warm snow.
The bitterness of death creeps down my spine; I have a feeling it's almost my time.

I am a Nazi.
Cries of the children ring in my ears; these people have shed thousands of salty tears.
I take these people from their places with sorrow and shame all over their faces.
The people do not belong with us, and they cannot be trusted.

I am a train.
Click, clack, I carry these people from place to place; it's like a wild goose chase.
They sit and wait in my cars; they're like prisoners behind bars.
Some may climb in and never back out; others will stand for what's right and shout.

I am a chimney.
Into the heat of my flames go the old and the young; once they go in, what's done is done.
From the top of me come out ashes like snow; they fall to the ground — where else would they go?
These people go in and never come out; why should I give them any doubt?

I am a camp.
Thousands of people come in; they live in corpse smelling shacks of tin.
Most will find their death here, all of them with the taste of fear.
Sounds and fumes of the Allies flying overhead and they will be freed; this is a happy ending indeed.

Alyssa Cochran, Grade 8
Parkway Middle School, OH

Mournful

Mournful is the color of clear tears running down people's cheeks.
It sounds like the deep breathing of people trying to be strong for others:
And tastes like the home cooking of relatives from far away.
It smells like millions of brilliantly colored sweet flowers;
It looks like too much dark brown foundation.
It makes me feel gloomy.

Mournful is the color of eyes as red as cherries;
It sounds like a roaring of people discussing memories and lost time
And tastes like having to much to eat when you weren't hungry to begin with.
It smells like fresh dirt.
Mournful looks like albums filled with pictures of past years.
It makes me feel overwhelmed.

Mournful is the color of dark freshly cleaned dress clothes;
It sounds like the memory of a man whistling to his radio early in the morning.
It tastes like the delicious breakfast he prepares first for everyone else, then for himself.
And smells like a farm house filled with the aroma of biscuits, gravy, and sausage.
It looks like a young man who has no enemy.
Mournful makes me miss old times.

Mournful is a sad feeling but it makes you think back
And remember the happy days you'll never forget.

Lisa Franklin, Grade 8
Little Miami Jr High School, OH

Where I'm From

I am from Ben & Jerry's
chocolate brownie ice cream
that has melted just a little to perfection
I am from Friday nights with my buds
eating popcorn and talking until the sun comes up
I am from Sunday morning eating Cocoa Puffs
while watching a scary movie with my friends

I am from the books I have read
that take me on long journeys to imaginary places
I am from the beach where the water glistens
and the shells collect on the shore
I am from the campfires
where we all sit around singing and playing songs on the guitars

I am from the swings in my backyard
on warm sunny days when the grass has just been cut
I am from the Fourth of July parties
where we take goofy pictures and watch the fireworks
I am from Kings Island with my friends
on the twisting and turning roller coasters

Lauren Bradford, Grade 8
Little Miami Jr High School, OH

Remember

I went to school, just like I've been.
What did I do different that I didn't do then?
I went in my class as the bell rang,
Then this student called Cho came.

I went to school, I haven't forgot.
I still hear them, shot after shot.
We ran and hid so we were out of sight.
Closer the shots came sending us trembling in fright.

I went to school, not expecting so much terror.
Could we have helped him, was it our error?
A teacher I knew survived the Holocaust back then,
And gave his life to protect students and friends.

I went to school to remember those lost.
Thirty-two lives was a devastating cost.
The fright it brought to survivors after,
Will force them to remember college without much laughter.

I came home from school so my parents could see me,
And red-rimmed eyes is what I came to greet.
I'm sorry, my mom said, hugging my neck.
I'll always remember Virginia Tech.

Breanne Durovic, Grade 9
Walter Payton College Preparatory High School, IL

A Reason

People come in your life for a reason.
What we must realize,
That our need has been met,
Our desire fulfilled,
Their work is done.
The prayer you sent up has been answered.
Now time to move on.
We never know what that reason is until
The changing of the season.
Sometimes those people leave
Without questioning.
Sometimes they leave in search of a new someone.
But you'll always know that
They were there for a reason.
They know they have to move on.
Let you be free.
And let you land in the arms of a new
Angel to hold and protect
You for a reason.
People are here for a reason.

Jennifer Salyers, Grade 8
Little Miami Jr High School, OH

Friday

Friday is like hot pink
The color of fun
Friday feels like the weekend
Friday sounds like kids laughing
Friday smells like fast food
Friday tastes like hot dogs, hamburgers, and fries
Friday the beginning of the weekend and the beginning of fun

Katie Condon, Grade 7
Hamlin Upper Grade Center, IL

If You Can

If you can do someone a favor without being asked,
If you can see someone is hurt, and you get help really fast,
If you can see someone is down, and you help them get better,
If you can help a friend if they are struggling in school,
If you can battle a sickness, when you feel like giving up.

If you can volunteer at a charity event, and want to be there,
If you can give old clothing to those who don't have the money,
If you get good grades and study really hard,
If you can do your housework, without being asked,
If you can enjoy spending time with your family,
Instead of just sitting around.

If you can babysit for the neighbors,
Even if your friends asked you to do something else,
If you cannot let what others say about you hurt you,
If you can believe in yourself, all things are possible,
If you can believe that life makes you strong,
You can accomplish something.

Gabi Layne, Grade 7
New Albany Middle School, OH

He Is Always There

The raindrops are God's tears
Thunder is God's protecting shout
Lightning is God's fears for you
The sunshine is God's smile of happiness
The rainbows are here to show
That God is always by your side
God's love for you,
Is shown through every day of your life
You just have to know how to see it
He is always there.

Jaimie Ford, Grade 7
Greenbank Middle School, ON

The Words That I Am Speaking

When I talk
Do you hear
The words that I am speaking?

Or do the transparent words
Go through one ear
And out the other?

Do you remember
My name
Or what I even look like?

Of course you don't!
Because you don't
Listen
To the words that I am speaking.

Margaret Chamberlain, Grade 8
Blanchester Middle School, OH

Happiness

Happiness is the color of bright yellow
It sounds like the birds chirping
It tastes like sweet candy
It smells like fresh food
It looks like a smiley face
It makes me feel joyful

Happiness is bright like a sunny day
It sounds like kids playing
It tastes like milky chocolate
It smells like a rose
It looks like a shiny gem
It makes me feel good

Happiness is the color of a sunflower
It sounds like a beach party
It tastes like fresh and juicy fruit
It smells like an ocean breeze
It looks like a clear blue sky
It makes me feel cheerful

Ryan Braidich, Grade 8
Little Miami Jr High School, OH

Writer

In my career, I'll be a writer.
Pulling my brain restraints, a little tighter.
I will write about happiness, sorrow and greed.
That is my ultimate writer's creed.

Brenden Davis, Grade 7
Fairfield Middle School, OH

What Is Poetry

Poetry…
    It cannot be described as a thing
But as a lifestyle.
    For those who may think otherwise,
They cannot be described as true poets
    They can only be called readers who cannot truly
understand the language poetry speaks.
    Those who really understand poetry don't just read it.
They live it.
    Poetry fills every aspect of a poet's life for no matter where they go,
poetry is there with them
    in the things they see, things they hear, taste, and feel.
They see it everywhere. They hear it whisper its sweet words
    into the depths of their minds.
Poetry is the bridge that connects the heart to the soul.
    It brings together real life and everything
that is truly imaginary.
    The lifestyle of poetry can only bring happiness to those who really understand it
And live a poet's lifestyle.
    Poetry is…the thing that keeps imagination
and dreams alive.

Daria Holston, Grade 9
Gwendolyn Brooks College Preparatory Academy, IL

Monday Morning Music

Once a little girl told me Sunday morning sunshine
Can never be as great as Sunday morning music.

She had blonde hair and blue eyes
She looked as if she did not know what she was speaking about.
I asked her, "You are just a mere child how would you know?"
She looked me deep in my eyes and said,
"You are a true person. You will have to look deep in your heart."
I was confused!

She seemed very wise for a child!
As days went by Sunday morning sunshine was on my porch
I glared deeply into the sun and remembered the little girl
And started to listen to the sounds of Sunday morning music.

I heard chimes and blue birds sing together as if they were a choir.
She was right I was so foolish to look at something so simple
And not hear the sounds of music that make me.
And so I tell all of you Sunday morning music
Is knocking at your door, open up and listen
And to your amazement you will find destiny!

Karen D'souza, Grade 7
Nativity of Our Lord Catholic School, ON

Anonymous Heroes

The ones I turn to for any help needed;
the ones that will always be there for me.
I could not have asked for more, even if I'd pleaded:
they will be my heroes for eternity.

They are the people I look forward to seeing every day;
if my day's gone bad, they fix it with a simple "HEY!"

They are the lamps unto my feet, and lights along the path.
We may have our arguments and disputes,
but in the end they always make me laugh.

Basically, all that I am trying to say,
is I love you Mom and Dad, "all day, every day."

Mason Deville, Grade 8
Holy Savior Menard Central High School, LA

The Hand of Hope

In a time of need
People turned away
Leaving them to die
They called out for help
Yet, no one seemed to come

Many could hear
That death was near
Still, they did nothing
They had fear

The pain, the sorrow
The starvation and disease
Brought many strong men down to weaklings

Many years went by
Then finally someone held out a hand
They held on with all they had left
And they knew
It was the Beginning of the End

Victoria Bordayo, Grade 8
Waverly Middle School, MI

Trees

Swaying, swinging, gliding,
In the breeze they stand.
Reaching out with branching arms,
I'll proudly take their hand.

Stretching, extending, reaching,
Trunks that touch the sky.
Look up to see them towering,
And let out a deep sigh.

Majestically they loom above my head,
Arms and branches are widespread.

Rochelle Allen, Grade 8
Haynes Academy for Advanced Studies, LA

Summer

Every year, during the last day of school,
A sense of happiness fills my heart.
Thinking of what to do over break
Makes me ready for fun to start…

I think of all the possibilities,
Like inviting friends and family,
Turning on the grill in my backyard,
And enjoying fresh food with iced tea.

I think of taking a walk in my neighborhood,
Feeling the wonderful sun and the light breeze,
Seeing the green grass and walking by the sprinklers,
Hearing the ice cream truck and the honeybees.

I think of walking by the coast,
Hearing little children laugh and play,
While savoring some saltwater taffy
And sipping lemonade by the bay.

And when the bell rings and ends the school year,
It hits me: Summer is finally here!

Carmen Lee, Grade 9
Troy High School, MI

I Fell Apart

All that got us together
Was simply a dare,
I never thought,
We would be such a great pair.

Everything was going good.
Wherever we went,
We always went together.
Moonlit nights together, ice-skating,
Going to the movies, and holding hands,
Laughing, joking around, and lying in the sand.

The summer months went by so fast.
Quicker than what we thought,
It was time that could never be bought.
We drifted apart, during that fall,
We each went our own way
And he finally called.

He said 'goodbye,'
And broke my heart,
He found another girl
I never thought we would be apart.

Adrienne Schultz, Grade 8
Sandusky Middle School, MI

Heaven Is Where You Lay

The dark gloomy sky hung over
The mountains stood so strong
The lightning struck with power
While the thunder played its song
But from where I laid it all seemed calm
No worries came to thought
I just laid with my father
While the lightning and thunder fought
The window was left opened
Allowing the breeze to come through
I was being handed back to mother
When our family lost you
One single strike of lightning
And your life was taken away
One single window opened
And Heaven is where you lay
Felicity Burns, Grade 9
Richmond Regional High School, QC

The Beach

The softest ocean breeze
Brushes against both of my cheeks.
My toes in the sand;
My heart belongs to this land.
In peace I sit on the beach.
Danielle Schomaker, Grade 7
Trinity Lutheran School, MI

Silence

Many words
Without meaning
Fill the growing
Silence

Not all
Thoughts
Can be expressed
I stop,
Waiting

For
The setting sun
The falling leaves
Your fading footsteps
To say
What can be said

No words
Without meaning
Fill
The silence
So it speaks
Caitlin O'Connor, Grade 8
St Monica School, IN

Life

Life is a tiger with soft fur
I pet it with my hands and it growl
Happily he licks my hand
He finally lays on my lap and falls asleep
Marco Flores, Grade 9
Prairie Lakes School, MN

Long Journey

Long journey
to some it sounds
like a vacation
to some
a cross country trip
and to others
their lifetime
but to me
it is the meaning
of my name
Rachel TerMarsch, Grade 8
Oakland Christian School, MI

Stories

Sitting around the kitchen table
Listening to stories being told
Not worrying about anything
Just thinking about family
And the good times
Sitting around the kitchen table.
Connor Davis, Grade 8
Little Miami Jr High School, OH

Love (Or Lack Of)

it reaches out with icy fingers
clinging onto whatever it can
and deftly consumes from within,
tearing apart heart, sanity, and soul.
It seeps into every crack and crevice,
coldness spreading across nations.
Frozen tears fall
as the world is corrupted
shattering explosions
filling the night.
Faces turn away from desolation
and ruins of a land once bright.
They fall to the ground,
pleading in vain…
but it's too late.
Trees wither and flowers fade
as the beasts shudder,
then cease.
All because of love…
or lack of.
Gwen Marchel, Grade 9
Clintonville High School, WI

Tennis Shoe

I turn three today,
And I'm really worn out.
I'm tired of these stinky, old feet,
It is putting me in doubt.
I'm tired of walking through the snow,
And running in the mud.
I'm tired of playing in the rain.
I'm tired of being all tied up.
My rubber sole is wearing down,
And I'm sick of eating ground.
Through the years I've taken a beat.
Please get out!
These stinky, old feet!
Chloe Henson, Grade 7
Dunlap Middle School, IL

Where I'm From

I'm from the ball going down the plate
Fast or slow

I'm from my parent

I'm from the ball in the pitcher's hands
Curve ball or slider

I'm from the base stealing in baseball

I'm from the batter's bat
Big barreled or small barrel

I'm from the dirt and dust from the fields

I'm from the cleats on the batter's feet
Metal or plastic
DJ Davis, Grade 8
Little Miami Jr High School, OH

Flaming Eyes

angry
I'm growling viciously like a,
bull dog being teased.
Shaking wildly like an earthquake.
I am blushing with flashing flames
burning in my eyes.
I am stamping and screaming.
My face is gleaming red like,
the sunset.
I am pushing and pounding like
a runaway horse.
My teeth smash together,
and my fists clutch
angry.
Betsy Lahman, Grade 7
Linwood Public School, ON

If I Could Change the World

To change the world
That would be a hard thing to do
I have a wish
But I know it won't come true

I have a wish and only one
That's not a lot…is it?
That there weren't drugs in this world
Then my mom wouldn't need to "visit"

I have no idea where he is
He's supposed to be my dad
Haven't seen him for eight years
He's never come to see me, and I really wish he had

I wish we could all be a family
The way they took was bad
But they chose what they chose
Instead of being mom and dad

So their children suffered the consequences
Because they wanted to be thugs
I live with it every day
All because they chose to do drugs.

Katrina Marsh, Grade 9
Woodbine High School, IA

How to Be Successful

If you can be kind,
even when no one is kind to you
If you can do the right thing,
even when no one is watching
If you can care about the people around you,
even if there is no one to care for you
you will be the one,
that everyone will be listening to

If you can support your friends,
even when no one is there to support you
If you can keep yourself from gossiping,
even when it is buzzing all around you
If you can be that one good friend,
I guarantee you'll have one

If you are listened to and respected
If your friends are envied, for having a friend like you
If you work hard at whatever you do,
then you can be great,
and called successful, too.

Alison Koenig, Grade 7
New Albany Middle School, OH

A Blind Man

Deprived of one's self,
Deprived of one's essence,
Yes, negative attributes,
But a superior man.

One can observe but not see.
A gift — for innocent to the sins of humanity.
Untutored joy — for immune to the burden of seen knowledge,
Unbalanced attributes, positive superior to negative.

His conscious would conjure a plea for possession,
From an ordinary man.
Timid in comparison to a blind's conscious mind
Is that of an ordinary man.

Farhad Yusufali, Grade 7
Woodbine Jr High School, ON

Fly Away

I wish I was a bird,
To have flight and freedom,
Oh what a feeling!
To spread my wings and soar over the clouds
Dipping, diving, floating and flying
All over the world.
I would have no worries about
Jobs or
Work or
Money or
War or
Pollution or
Death or
Disease.
I could live without a care, flying through the air,
With other birds
And discuss with them important things like
Peanut butter and bread crumbs and how to build a nest.
But alas, I am not
A Bird.

Heather McHugh, Grade 9
Newmarket High School, ON

Sky Blue

Sky blue is the wispy air and robins eggs in the spring.
And it feels like it's going to be a great day.
Sky blue is the taste of dew drops
Clouds and rain smell like sky blue
Being able to fly makes me feel sky blue
Sky blue is the sound of birds chirping on a sunny day,
and the sound of people playing happily after every school day.
Sky blue is a sunny day, a beautiful time,
and your very own home.
Playing after school is sky blue.
Playing video games and watching TV is sky blue.
Sky blue is when I'm feeling happier than ever.

Justin Goforth, Grade 7
Algonquin Middle School, MI

I Am From

I am from a town,
Where people are carefree.

I am from a town,
Where the snow christens the ground.

I am from a town,
Where people come and go.

I am from a town,
Where tranquility is but a myth.

I am from a town,
Where friends are always around.

I am from a town,
Where sometimes it seems dull.

I am from a town,
Where it's perfect in my eyes.

I am from a dream and a nightmare,
Where I will never wake.
Whitney Cassoway, Grade 8
Weledeh Catholic School, NT

Forest

F orever safe
O pen for you whenever
R est here my friends
E agerly awaiting your arrival
S atisfied when you arrive
T esting your ability to care
    more about something else other
    than yourself so help save nature
    It only takes 1
Jenna Capper, Grade 7
Tripoli Middle/Senior High School, IA

Dreams

There's a dream in my head
A dream in my mind
I need to wake up
I think it is time
I have the want
I have the desire
This dream in my heart
Is raging like fire
I need to get up
And get in the action
I work for what I want
And get satisfaction
I have the want, I have the dream
I need to start to fulfill what I see.
Alexandra Hnatyshyn, Grade 9
Mount Carmel Academy, LA

Most Important

I think friends are important.
I think a pretty smile is important.
I think a beautiful voice is important.
I think a good education is important.
I think the angels in Heaven are important.
I think an older brother that cares about you is important.
I think being smart because your parents give you a good education is important.
I think playing a sport that you are very good at is important.
I think writing a poem is important.
I think having a mom and a dad is important.
I think laughing is important.
I think having a wonderful family is important.
I think giving my best effort every day is very important.
I think God is the most important.
Abigail Bondi, Grade 7
St John the Baptist Elementary School, IN

If

If you do what's right when right seems not to be a choice.
If you see the other options, then let out your voice.
If you can give back what the world gave to you,
And make good decisions in everything you do.

If you can be a hero to someone who's in need,
Go from being a follower and take the lead.
If you can work with others without becoming mad,
And make someone's day when they're truly sad.

If you can generate happiness where it seems happiness cannot go,
And have kindness when kindness will not show.
If you can take a problem and you can make it right,
You will be successful all throughout your life.
Nathan Scribano, Grade 7
New Albany Middle School, OH

So Small

How small I must be, nothing more than a period in a dictionary.
Printed there with the other six billion marks that define
The Earth.
How small life's planet must be, running with perseverance on its orbit.
Competing against a herd of planets and comets in the marathon around
The sun.
How small this star must be, a solitary needle on the largest of evergreens.
So microscopic, ordinary, and unimportant compared to its mother tree
The Milky Way.
How small our galaxy must be, like a glowing diamond dropped in the ocean.
Lost in the massive sea called the universe.
Falling through the water, lonely in empty space.
Such a tiny piece of matter, you wouldn't even give it a passing glance.
But then you'd have no idea what lived inside that sparkling jewel.
So how can we, specks of dust,
Do anything in the never-ending unknown that has engulfed us?
Start small inside your tiny self, and extend past the barriers of
The Universe.
Sharlo Bayless, Grade 8
St Christopher Elementary School, OH

Unnamed Fame

They said she'd never make it;
Not even if she tries.
All they did was laugh and hit
As they told her tons of lies.

She could never truly believe
Because her mind was always set
On the goals she would achieve
But the real her they never met.

Now as she walks up on that stage
And then she loses all control
Everyone can see she's not afraid,
And that the music's in her soul.

Now every day her dreams come true
And she knows there's nothing they can do.

Rachel Boekhaus, Grade 9
Southwest Jr High School, AR

The Knowing Breeze

Come winter, spring, summer, fall,
Day to day, month to month, and all,
A gentle breeze blows,
Singing as it goes,
And no one knows,
But me.
It sings the song of the past, the present,
And all that's left to come.
It is never wrong.
If you listen you will hear
The song of my friend,
The wind, so dear.
As it blows, and goes, and knows,
What lies in the hands
Of the element of time.

Natalie Mueller, Grade 7
St Elizabeth/St Robert Regional School, MO

Wishing for Better Days

Everyone knows your heart is in your home.
To me I have no home for my own heart.
Feeling oppressed and feeble in my dome,
Hiding and my heart is falling apart.
Day to day I fight for what I believe,
Knowing the fighting will never die away.
Sitting in my room on my knees to grieve,
Wishing tomorrow will be a better day.
On rare occasions I am quite at ease,
Until disaster comes from my front door,
Hoping to escape out into the seas,
But for now I shall stand out on the shore.
For here I will keep wishing for better days,
Sitting out on the shore in a daze.

Cassie Watson, Grade 8
Otsego Middle School, OH

Istanbul Grill

Summer
red and white checkered tablecloths and hi-top shoes
iced tea, french fries
smiles on lips — red cheery tomatoes in salad
five best friends stuck together, sticky layers of baklava

Fall
green plastic booths and cool mint lip-gloss
Cherry Coke, onion rings
secrets on lips — peeling off layers of baklava
two friends alone, glued tight like gum to a table

Winter
cold bitter wind and hot bitter coffee
potato soup, hummus
giggles on lips — loose change tinkling in a purse
tinkling change, life changes, friends scattered

Spring
yellow roasted peppers and dandelion flowers
flip flops, shish kabob
cold smiles on lips — ice in Sprite
the baklava crumbles

Ana Brett, Grade 9
Maharishi School of the Age of Enlightenment, IA

Love Letter

AJ
You are the beat in my heart
The music in my soul
You are my everything

AJ
You are the one I talk about to my girlfriends
The one we laugh about when the stories are told
You are my everything

AJ
You are the very reason I live each day to the fullest
You are the one who taught me to love with my full heart
Myself and others

AJ
You are still my everything
You will be tomorrow
And all my days ahead
Even after the world stops turning
You will still be there in my heart
My everything.

Jenna Reeves, Grade 8
Maquoketa Valley Middle School, IA

Sunshine and Rain

It was an ordinary day so I go outside and think to myself and I say,
"What a peaceful and sunshiny day."
The leaves of the trees are dancing in the wind. The sun is shining brightly in the clear blue sky.
I walk down to the beach and get ready for a show because the white fluffy clouds make me think of snow.
As I get settled in on the warm ground, I listen to the wind play a gentle song. It's a gentle sound.
But wait what's this? It is a different colored cloud. It looks like the sweet sounds are over I now wait for something loud.
As I look up there is another and another, and yet another.
One moment the clouds were as white as snow, and now they are as gray as sadness. Now the beautiful shining sun has hidden itself from my view. Another kind of weather is coming through. The beautiful sky is no longer blue.
The sun is no longer shining. The dark clouds are rising. Higher and higher they rise. My beautiful day is disappearing right before my eyes. Higher and higher up the clouds go, how high will they go I do not know. Will this change in weather ruin my white fluffy cloud show? I tell you I tell you I really do not know. I guess I'll go inside and watch the rain show.

Jordan Stripling, Grade 7
The Calvary Academy, OH

When We Think of War

Men in the field on the run and they are not having fun
Running from Pow! Pow! of the gun
Crush, crunch crumble goes the bush as it sank
Bombs go off left and right lights up the sky like stars at night
Women and children hold each other tight hoping the soldiers will end the fight
The sounds of war will drive you mad like a melody that's gone bad
This makes me feel so very sad everyone feels this way every child, mom and dad
We need to get along today so we no longer have to fight this way
Let us hold each other's hand and sway around the world from bay to bay
Soldiers are walking as slow as snails their backpacks feel like ten gallons of water in a pail
The rain falls down like hail they have a hard time following a trail
I wish war would end I wish peace to all men
I wish a good message we will send I wish we could get along like me and my friend

Gregory Taylor, Grade 8
Beverley Heights Middle School, ON

One Lonely Voice

One lonely voice cries out to me, begs to be let in from the bitter cold
How sorrowful it sounds, it makes the pain in my heart turn from just
a small candle-sized flame to a wildfire
Not even a fake smile can work its way onto my lips, I work hard to keep back the tears that try so hard to reach my skin
My eyes burn with the effort, all is lost
The tears rush down my face and a dark storm surrounds me and darkens my world
It feels as if a raging river has just formed
How? Why? WHY?
There are as many questions running through my head as tears running down my face
When I finally stop the falling tears, my heart burns, I see a light up ahead and hope I can reach it
Suddenly I realize it is coming to me, maybe there is hope
The light becomes clearer, I can now tell it is not just a light
It's a pair of soft gentle looking hands, something about them makes me trust them
The closer they come to me the less hurtful my thoughts become
The hands reach out to me and embrace me, the feeling of the embrace is warm and soothing
My cares are washed away in a sea of love
The hands pick me up like a gentle father comforting his daughter
They carry me back into the world I live in, carry me to the world of hurt,
However I no longer feel the pain
God has saved me from my thoughts, God has saved me from myself
God has saved me from the pain, God has saved me from the pain.

Joelle Swanson, Grade 7
Gilbert Middle School, IA

Who

My friend is there
When I'm down
To push me up
With a
Joke and a smile
A laugh and a tickle
My day will be made
By one simple person
My friend,
My friend
Is the best.

Katya Dvorkin, Grade 7
Nativity of Our Lord Catholic School, ON

Nature's Will

All we see around is nature,
There to help us,
The underbrush waving, saying hello to us,
The luscious green,
Overcoming the gentle,
But hardly innocent blue skies,
It is like a dance,
To wake up the tiresome sun,
From its long night's rest,
To say good-bye to the glittering stars,
And the bright moon,
Morning and night,
The blue softly becomes a darkened purple,
The pink so light it changes to yellow,
A bright sincere yellow,
But nature's force,
Will keep us from going out at night,
For she desires us to stay safe in our beds,
With a hushed good night,
Her dearest friend wakes to morning,
Good night.

Courtney Wilton, Grade 7
Paw Paw Middle School, MI

Back to School

Back to paper and pens,
Back to books and boards.
Back to crowded hallways,
Back to cruel and kind teachers
and every kind in between.
Back to friends and enemies
and in some ways they are all alike.
Back to gossip and crushes and dating,
Back to desks and sitting for hours on end.
Back to white washed walls,
Back to homework and backpacks,
Back to pronouns and formulas,
Back to reading and back to lockers and classes,
Back to dictionaries and journals and essays.
Back to learning,
Back to school.

Hannah Gregor, Grade 8
Little Miami Jr High School, OH

Cancer

Cancer is a terrible disease
If you get it, it can kill you with ease
It kills lots of skin cells
One thing you want to hear is church bells
Chemotherapy makes you lose your hair
But locks of love makes wigs to wear
If someone you know has cancer a good thing is prayer
That's an awesome way to show that you care

Jesse R. Werker, Grade 8
Carlisle Elementary/Jr High School, IN

Darkness Surrounds

Darkness befalls upon the world in hate.
The flame of our belief soon turns to dust.
Suffocating all light that is our fate.
Prying upon our fear and on our lust.

Some welcome death over this horrid beast.
There is no hope there only is our fear.
With horrid stench the beast prepares to feast.
And if one flees the beast is always near.

Then the embers of hope are lit once more.
People band together to fight the dark.
Young and old people good to the core.
The light will sear the beast and leave a mark.

With great faith the light prevails to save the race.
Then darkness must once again hide its face.

Noal Ruddy, Grade 9
Archbishop Carney Secondary School, BC

Softball

Softball is fun.
What a blast.
Big yellow balls,
hitting long, skinny bats.
The pitching so fierce,
the running, what fun,
and hitting home runs,
while you're under the sun.
Getting your bunts down,
and then you run, run, run.
Swinging your bat,
and running so swiftly,
like a cheetah on skates,
who moves so quickly.
Your leadoff so fast,
as is your last.
The injuries, they hurt,
but you don't even smirk.
Winning or losing,
that doesn't matter,
as long as it's fun, and there's lots of laughter.

Cortney Moore, Grade 8
South Vienna Middle School, OH

Bullies

Bullies monsters they are
Pulling your hair and calling you names
Wedgies are given
Michael Dominguez, Grade 7
Sudlow Intermediate School, IA

Apology

I was proud of you,
Yet I knew what you were thinking.
I asked you not to do it,
But you went and did it anyway.
I trusted you before,
Now so much now.
It was your entire fault,
I couldn't help but blame you,
And now, almost a year later,
We speak for the first time.
It will never be the same,
Between you and me.
We used to talk every day,
We were so close.
You should feel sorry.
I believe you are because
You didn't do it again.
I am sorry because
It will never be the same.
Rachel Phillips, Grade 9
Leeton Middle and High School, MO

Chores

Chores are very boring
Aren't very fun
They will not stop
Until everything's done

You may get an allowance
Or you may not
But no matter what
You should have to sweep or mop

It is very boring
And not very fun
There's never any break
It has to be done

Dishes are the worst
Clothes are the best
They all have to be done
With very little rest

If you are lucky
You're parents are rich
They can afford a maid
Named Betsy or Rick!
Logan Keyzer, Grade 8
Otsego Middle School, MI

Joy

Joy smells like cookies in the oven.
Joy sounds like waves crashing against the shore.
Joy tastes like lemonade on a hot day.
Joy feels like winning a first place trophy.
Joy looks like playing football in the backyard.

Jordan Quisno, Grade 7
Fairfield Middle School, OH

The Knife of Death

I woke up this morning with the sun shining down,
But something surrounds me like a black cloud.
This camp is a zoo, though orderly arranged,
Really these Nazis must be deranged.
The taste of thin blood is in my mouth,
While the stench of death is in the air.
As we walk the crematoria looms in front of me
With the frozen ground around it like ice on my feet.
As we eat our rations that taste like cardboard,
We hear gunfire in the distance.
Then we hear a thud like a building falling down
While a dusty haze blocks the view of American soldiers.
The tangy scent of blood wafts through the camp
And on our bunks we feel the vibration
Of American tanks; our liberation.
The clean and fresh American uniforms
Rustle in the wind little butterfly's wings.
As the camp is cleaned up the scent of spring flows through the air,
While in the field beside us tasteful herbs grow.
The knife that danced around our necks is gone.
The knife of death has stopped its song.

Charles Estle, Grade 8
Parkway Middle School, OH

Battle

On top of the mountain, above the valley,
Throughout the crowd, they are awaiting for the battle that is soon to come.

Near the river, within the mountain range,
Under the blazing sun, the crowd hears people yelling out in the distance.

Past the horizon, against the pale-blue sky,
Throughout the land, the war-cry is shout out.

Into the valley, amid the trees,
With weapons and shields, the two armies collide.

After the battle, inside the valley,
Underneath the stars, the dead bodies of brave warriors lay there.

In view of the bodies, despite the cold,
Instead of warriors, the weeping families stand near.

Without happiness, with no reason to live,
In the darkness, why is there death?

Brett Durlock, Grade 7
Algonquin Middle School, MI

A Brand New Book

She calls to me
Whispering her sweet words
She draws me in with her brand new smell
Her glossy cover dances in the light
She jumped into my arms
Waiting to be taken home

Morgan Ebbing, Grade 7
New Albany Middle School, OH

I Am...

I am a girl who loves to ride horses
I wonder how the run will be
I hear fans in the stands cheering me on
I see my horse give it all I got
I want to clock at fifteen
I am a girl who loves to ride horses

I pretend someday I will be a professional barrel racer
I feel like I am flying around the barrel
I touch the horn for a little support
I worry I will get thrown off
I cry when I make a good run
I am a girl who loves to ride horses

I understand that I will not always make a good run
I say to myself I can do it
I dream one day I will be pro
I try my very best
I hope my horse will always love me

Kelby Schneider, Grade 8
Wainwright High School, AB

Nervous

Defenseless,
Like a mouse trapped with fear.
Standing there quivering to the bone,
Shaking,
Shivering
And shattering, my legs are stone,
I start...

But my blank mind holds me back
Sweat trickling
Down my burning hot neck,
Panic pricking me like a thousand needles,
Butterflies filling up my wrenched tight stomach
Raging like waves smashing the shore.
I try to find my voice but
Coconuts are clogging the back of my throat
Trying to hold it back.
Timid tense and twitchy
My wicked heart's pounding,
Wishing wildly
To disappear!

Lydian Martin, Grade 7
Linwood Public School, ON

Elizabeth Taylor

She was the actress of the day
Talent incomparable, a face of a goddess
We saw her grow up
And each day the screen loves her no less

From *Lassie* to *Velvet*
Set her status to a child star
Would soon bring great things
And take her so greatly far

She'd appear with the biggest of people
Newman, Hudson, and Dean
Her popularity soared
As one of the greatest actresses ever seen

A life of glamour and fame
And heartbreak too
Throughout her life
She'd say eight times "I do"

She is one of the Seven Wonders of the World
The girl who could swear like a sailor
Her name is the
Miss Elizabeth Taylor

Tristan Thompson, Grade 9
Southwest Jr High School, AR

Basketball: The Prodigy

Walking into the gym
Where hopes and dreams are made
I slide on my shoes
And get ready to play

The adrenaline of what to do next flowing through my mind
The urge to win and the will to thrive
Feelings emotionally and physically flowing to become one
All players fighting to be top gun

Lights,
Bleachers,
Fans
Basketballs pound the ground,
And sneakers screech
Coaches yelling and parents cheering

This is my game
Winning: the dream
Losing: pure shame
And that's why I play this amazing game

Jalen Rhea, Grade 7
New Albany Middle School, OH

Winter

Winter
cold, long
snowboarding, skiing, snowball fighting
In the snow, snow balls, gloves, boots.
throw, duck, aim
white, melty
Winter

Jonathan Byrd, Grade 7
Fairfield Middle School, OH

The Prairies

I am from the wheat fields,
blowing softly in the wind.
I am from the quiet lakes,
ripples going softly by.

I am from the soft skies,
stars dancing gracefully.
I am from the small towns,
sprinkled across the prairies.

I am from the placid streets,
people waving constantly.
I am from the railroads,
trains blowing their horns.

I am from the hot days,
spent by the pool.
I am from the cold grass,
crunching beneath your feet.
I am from the prairies,
…I miss it…

Keenan Lang, Grade 8
Weledeh Catholic School, NT

Hope

When the moon is new
And darkness falls
The stars are few
Your hope has squalls
Scared are you

Suddenly! a glimmer!
The sun is rising!
The night's cinder
Flaring into the day's fire
Hopeful are you

Blaire De Wilde Kohler, Grade 9
Royal Oak High School, MI

Hamlet

Who killed my father
Mother married the killer
Hamlet will kill him.

Randy Scroppo, Grade 7
Hamlin Upper Grade Center, IL

I Cannot Live Without My Sisters

I just can't live without my sisters
Sometimes they bug me, sometimes they hug me
Before we would play, today we have our own ways
I will always have big sisters to always have to LOVE and listen to
Although sometimes I wish I was an only child
I don't know what I would do without my sisters
Having sisters means I will always have a friend
As I look back on memories of my life
I remember my sisters and all the times we had together
As I look up to my older sisters
I wish they were just like me but that won't matter
If they are with me through good times and bad we will always stick together
I love my sisters dearly and I could not see my life without them
I just wish one was with me
But she will always be with me in my heart if I please
Now please let me be alone with my sisters
With the wind blowing through the trees and the nice cold breeze
But I will always know that my sister Jenna and my sister April
Will always love me through the heavens and the Earth
And be near my side forever and ever in my heart
And in the lands and I will always LOVE them

Kendra Nerad, Grade 8
St Ansgar Middle School, IA

Winter Day

Winter is the reason I want to go outside.
It lets me have fun,
While I watch the snowflakes
Run from the sky,
Gently landing in the soft white blankets that cover the ground below.

Others fall frozen on my tongue,
It gives me chills,
Now wanting the sun.
After the chills are gone, the thrills come back again.
To run and play on that winter day!

Michael R. Schmitz, Grade 8
Blanchester Middle School, OH

Where I'm From

I am from the flower garden filled with bees.
I am from the school with friends who make fun of dorky teachers.
I am from the family of sports.
I'm from the hillbilly, don't care what you look like at home.
I'm from the musical notes coming out of the stereo.
I'm from the stayin' up late watching movies on the weekends.
I'm from the barefoot outside country life.
I am from the sunrise, early bird, get my day started routine.
I am from the scary, haunted stuff that most people don't believe in.
I'm from the playing in the sprinkler in the sun,
From the garden where we plant and work.
I'm from the family who laughs, jokes, and just wants to have a good time.
I am from my mom and dad.

Shannon West, Grade 8
Little Miami Jr High School, OH

If

If you can strike out, but forget about it right there,
Then go back and hit the game-winning home run.
If you can give all your money away to charity to show you care,
And go back home and still have fun.
To value others' life as much as yours,
But still love yourself with all your heart.

If when you lose it all,
It means nothing to you,
You have proven to all,
That you can just start new.
If you wake up with a smile,
Life will be more worthwhile.

If you realize,
That we only fall,
To get back up.
You have passed life's greatest test,
And when you finally have to rest,
You realize that life was the best.

Travis Wolf, Grade 7
New Albany Middle School, OH

I too, Sing America*

I too, sing America

As I approach the shoot
Automatically recommended to take off my clothes,
Only under wears and heeled-up boots
No spoken words or special roles
Just do a dance, strike a pose.

I too, sing America

No intelligence to show, no brains to have,
Just strip myself of dignity as soon as I arrive.

I too, sing America

They give me no history, no freedom of speech,
Just degrade me. Frustration.
Not pleasing myself, no inspiration.

I too, sing America

Please give me my rights
I'm just like you
A human who's bright.

Di'Aujonaj Harrell, Grade 9
Gwendolyn Brooks College Preparatory Academy, IL
*Inspired by Langston Hughes

Up North

Birds chirp from the treetops,
And leaves rustle in the breeze,
We hear the humming of boats
And the crackling of campfires.

The sun shines brightly in the big blue sky,
Waves splash to the shore,
Boats pull kids on tubes and water skis,
And jet skis zoom on by.

Fishermen sit hopefully in their boats,
While vacationers swim and splash in the water,
And little kids play in the sand.
Up north is my favorite place to be.

Laura Robertson, Grade 8
Boulan Park Middle School, MI

American Dream

Immigrants try to cross the border
for a better life just around the corner.
While the border patrol is guarding,
immigrants try to look out so nobody is watching.
"Aliens" as they are called,
are the reason why this country doesn't fall.
Working for a family to feed,
money is all they need.
Paid at work the minimum wage,
they feel that their check just won't change.
Darkness you see in a white man's eyes,
hatred he has among these guys.
Hiding from immigration in their houses,
a raid is what this causes.
Police say bad people they seem,
but they are just looking for the American Dream.

Neftali Calderon, Grade 9
Goshen High School, IN

Just Because

Just because I like soccer
    I don't need to be good
    I'm not afraid to kick your soccer ball
    I'm not going to give up just because it hurts

Just because I like soccer
    Don't think I'll quit
    Don't be afraid to play me
    Don't think you can get past me

Just because I like soccer
    I'm not any better or worse
    I sometimes hurt when I fall
    I'm not going to give up

Just because I like soccer — I just try my best!

James Robinson, Grade 8
Wainwright High School, AB

Karate

Beating your opponent
To win a match
Learning the steps
Like a baby's first step
Learning to not fight
But to protect yourself
Getting hit is part of the experience
Falling down is part of life
And you just get right back up again
And block that next punch

Alexandra LaPointe, Grade 8
Wainwright High School, AB

Beat It or Burn It

I hated that dresser
But finally I got a new one
It's cool, come see!
It has a huge mirror,
8 drawers and a cool trim.
Not sure what color,
But still cool.
My other dresser
Was way different.
The mirror wasn't straight
And the drawers were broken
So we might break it down
Or burn it to the ground.
We could use the wood
To light a fire,
I have to watch for splinters
Those things hurt!

Taryn Randles, Grade 8
Covington Middle School, IN

Zuzu: My Wonder Dog

I wake up and get out of bed,
Miserably knowing school's ahead,
But there's always hope waiting for me.
It's Zuzu; My Wonder Dog.

She wags her tail and looks at me,
Looks at me with her big brown eyes,
She's like the silver lining in the sky,
It's Zuzu: My wonder Dog.

After school I then walk back,
Carrying homework in my pack,
As I walk in the door I see
Zuzu: My Wonder Dog.

After homework, after bore,
I play with my dog having fun.
I'm the sky and she's the sun.
It's Zuzu: My Wonder Dog.

Taylor Ortiz, Grade 7
St Matthias/Transfiguration School, IL

Skateboarding at the Park

going up and skateboarding at the park
riding in the air
everybody's watching sitting on a chair
going up and down the hill and flying in the air
you fell you crashed you're laying on the ground

Connor Meyers, Grade 7
Fairfield Middle School, OH

A-Train

I'm done at the park, gotta get to class,
Almost 7 pm, gotta get there fast,
What's the quickest way?
Walking, bus, subway, I'll catch the A train,
God knows that's always the fun way.
There's always that rank smell,
The kids dancing trying to raise money,
The Asian guy selling light up toys, the sights are always funny.
Like the kid whining to go to the bathroom,
The guy preaching about God,
The guy singing to himself, we all pretend to listen and nod.
The people who are sleeping before they hit the seat,
The people making a living doing whatever they can,
The man reading the *Wall Street Journal*, that big business man.
The drunkie walking around aimlessly, the homeless guy living in *his* seat,
Everyone racing to a chair, wanting to relieve their aching feet.
The people rocking out to their iPods,
That person yelling on their phone,
Not that anyone wakes up, so why should he lower his tone?
One more stop to go, not that this wasn't a pleasant ride,
I'll see these characters tomorrow, rush hour will never subside.

Yogita Singh, Grade 9
Maharishi School of the Age of Enlightenment, IA

Just Me…

I am funny and loud most times, but not always
I wonder how different things will be as an adult
I hear the pen that writes the story of my life gliding on the paper
I see the things that could've been
I want to succeed in everything that I love to do
I am funny and loud most times, but not always

I pretend that nothing ever changes
I feel sad because the clock that measures our good times is set too fast
I touch the torch that lets us try again
I worry that high school will change who we are
I cry because no matter what there are some things I could never change
I am funny and loud most times, but not always

I understand that there are some things I will never understand
I say "Don't let fear hold you back"
I dream that life won't get more complicated in the future
I try not to judge people
I hope that we will all have fun in high school
I am funny and loud most times, but not always

Casey Jettinghoff, Grade 8
Otsego Middle School, OH

Stars

Stars, stars
everywhere.
Up in the sky
and in the air.
They come out at night
and that's the only time
they are in sight.
They sparkle and shine
they make me feel divine!

Juliana Lupis, Grade 8
St Clare Catholic Elementary School, ON

Lies

Lies whirl around like a never ending twister.
They make your thoughts blurred and confused.
They make you turn this way and that
As if you were on a one way road
That leads to tears and confusion,
Sadness and hate.
The emotions run around
Tagging everyone in the traffic of lies.
When no one tells the truth,
Madness.
It turns into a mystery that only a witness could solve.
Then…disaster.
The lies double
In sneak attack.
No one knows what's happening
Till someone tells the truth.
Then…it starts all over again.

Renee Nowicki, Grade 7
Warrensburg Middle School, MO

Remember

I walk into his small empty room
Feeling the tears burn my face
Before, he kept monsters away; my safe place
I look down and I can see he is scared
He sees my tears as he squeezes my hand
Telling me everything will be okay

As he falls asleep I stay by his side
My mind is filled with thoughts
I remember loving all those summers
Complete with camping and four-wheeling
I remember loving all those old stories
When he was young and fearless

Remember loving when he was home
Playing in the flowers, eating sweets
Quickly my thoughts fade away
A man in white tells us he is in a better place
Never will I have new times to say
I remember loving

Kelsey Lee, Grade 9
Cannon Falls Sr High School, MN

Love

Love is the most beautiful thing in the world.
Love is always right in front of you.
Love lifts your soul to the sky.
Love is a glimpse of heaven.
It makes life worth living;
makes every day count.
Love is magical.
It's good.
Love
is wonderful.
Love is pure.
It's like a dream
you never want to end.
Love is a way of life.
Love is an unspoken bond between people.
Love comes naturally and from the heart because,
love is the most beautiful thing in the world.

Brooke Vierling, Grade 8
Shakopee Area Catholic School, MN

Thought

If a thought is something that nobody will know,
It is personal to each and every person
You cannot take back what you think
Whether it is good or bad
They are always with you
Haunting your every move
Just like ghosts
Right now
Yes
This second
Just like that
A thought was thunk
By you and me both
Again and again until a new
What will be thought after this one?
We may never know until the time comes
If a thought is something that nobody will know.

Amber Daly, Grade 8
Shakopee Area Catholic School, MN

My Family

My family is like a variety of dogs,
Living together like a pack.
My dad is like a German Shepherd,
Big and strong, a great leader
My mom is like a Golden Retriever,
Gentle and loving, a great mother.
My sister, Emily is like a Chihuahua,
Thin and timid, yet loving.
My other sister, Erin is like a Jack Russell,
Energetic and happy, fun loving.
I am like an Alaskan Malamute,
Energetic and strong, a great friend.

Sarah Kaiser, Grade 7
Queen of Peace School, OH

Perfection

Perfection
Who needs history? It's over now.
Who needs God? He's only as real as you make him — like the monsters under your bed.
Who needs the government? They just give my money to lawyers to further their career.
Who needs friends? When you could have money.
Who needs parents? When they only hurt you with their painful divorces.
Who needs themselves?   When all we dream about is being someone else.
Who wants history? If we have the present.
Who wants God? He just limits you.
Who wants the government?   Its lawyers don't care about us, just themselves.
Who wants friends? They're just another liability.
Who wants parents? "He's the one." No, he's the third "one."
Who wants themselves? When they could just lose themselves to everything.
Who needs history? Everyone, it always repeats.
Who needs God? I do, I can't live without hope.
Who needs the Government? Everyone, do you want the murderers to be free?
Who needs friends? Everyone, how could you live without them?
Who needs parents? Everyone, who else is going to teach you. For better or worse.
Who needs their self? I do, and whether you realize it yourself, so do you
Remember you're all perfectly flawed. Perfectly incomplete. Perfectly doubtful. Perfectly angry.
Perfectly your self. Perfect whether you know it or not so hate, love, cry, scream: but don't give up.

Sam Huntley, Grade 9
West Jr High School, MO

The Holocaust

Heavenly God,

I pray to you God up high, to keep Hana safe as much as you can try.
As the invasion of Hitler has brought so much sadness and despair, Hana is in need of all your care.
She was very athletic don't you see, she had so much life in her so much she could be.
She was sent away from her town Nove Mesto, and sent away to the place of shattered souls The Ghetto.
I felt her pain as they grabbed her trembling hand,
As she heard strikes of screaming and crying she couldn't quite understand.
She was sent on a train, she didn't know where she was going she felt so much pain.
Her beautiful hair was shaved, would she ever be saved?
She smelt the poisonous gas sneak out among her,
They took her belongings including me, what they were doing she couldn't quite see.
I found out later what went on, how Hana left us why she is now gone.
Those stalls they thought were showers, were actually gas chambers.
The Holocaust is now past, but the broken hearts felt in torture will always last.
I pray to you God up high to keep Hana safe as much as you can try,
As the world is filled with sadness and despair, we are all in need of your care.
Amen.

Alana Vandelaar, Grade 7
St Mary Separate School, ON

Grandpa

It's hard to see you go, but we all know that you're in a better place. I'm glad you're in no more pain anymore, and that you ran to Heaven's gate; to be in paradise. I just wish I could see your smile, scooter, cane, hands, slippers on your feet, you reading your book, and playing war with me. Hugging and loving me. I just want to see you again. With love from all who miss you, we love you and miss you.

Claire Lieburn, Grade 9
Hilliard Davidson High School, OH

Nine Eleven

On 9-11 it was a dreadful day
So many problems so much hate
Ohh — how many people lost their way
But all we could do is sit and wait

I still remember when the second plane hit the tower
There was nothing but a gust
It was a teardrop shower
The city was covered in grief and dust

All day the disaster was on the news
As the tower fell down
Everyone was listening to the blues
News spread across even to the smallest town

As most people went on with their lives
Some people no longer had wives.

Patrick Draves, Grade 8
Wainwright High School, AB

The Sixth Connecticut

Untrained soldiers
Going into battle.
Through the woods they hear their command.
They know there's no chance of victory,
But on they go, unto death.
Guns start firing, killing.
In the field
These untrained soldiers
Are taken off guard
And scattered like the prey of a hunter
Over the now bloody field.
They went in facing the barrels of guns.
They welcomed death, as one would welcome a friend.
The untrained soldiers
Knew nothing of war, knew no chance,
Knew they walked to their death, but showed no fear.
These noble warriors of freedom willingly marched to death.
These men were thought to be cowards,
But are called that no more.

Stephen Wilmot, Grade 9
Bishop Dwenger High School, IN

Damian

I walked down the long lonely halls with anticipation,
to see what had come the day before
You were there wrapped up all nice and snug,
As if you were lying on a soft white cloud.
Your eyes were big and bright,
like the stars that shine in the dark night sky.
As small as your gentle hands were,
you held me tight while you slept,
As if you never wanted me to go.
I never knew you yesterday,
But now holding you in my arms,
I feel like I know so much.

Acacia Abraham, Grade 8
Holy Cross Regional High School, BC

We'll Find a Way to Play

We all have played baseball
At one point in time,
Even those less fortunate
Who had not a dime
But that didn't stop them
From playing a good game of ball
Even without umpires
They made their own calls
Whether it was a broomstick
A branch or a pole
They were determined
To play ball was their goal
A chair at first
And at second
A box at third
And then there was home
Whatever they needed to create a strike zone
Though the things that they used
Might not have been the same
But they did whatever needed
To play their favorite game

Josh Reckmann, Grade 8
Highland Middle School, IL

Creative Juices

When I need the creative juices to flow
I know just where to go
I head to the fridge
It is my bridge
To get the juices going
So when I need them flowing
It's hard to choose between orange and apple
But usually I choose Snapple

Eric Dansart, Grade 7
St Gerald Elementary School, IL

Alex*

Alex is different
Alex has Down syndrome
Down syndrome has no cure
But Alex is still my cousin
People may look at him and think he's a scary person
But he's not
He's a nice, funny person
He loves helping me pull a prank on our cousin, Brad
I wish people would see him for who his, not for what he has
I wish we could find a cure for Down syndrome
I wish his wish could come true
His wish is to be normal
Alex is different
Alex has Down syndrome
And I love him all the same

Shannon Westmoreland, Grade 8
St Katharine Drexel School, MO
*Dedicated to Alex Thompson

Freeze

When I'm with you
I can see right through
That nothing else matters
All else shatters

I look deep into your brown eyes
No need for lies
I'm the luckiest person ever
I hope we'll stay together forever

You're not my possession
Just merely an obsession
I look in your eyes and am lured
And all pain is cured

When I'm by your side
There's no need for lies
You are a summer breeze
When I'm with you I want time to freeze

When I'm with you I am free
You mean everything to me
Tyler Hardisty-Levesque, Grade 8
Shevchenko School, MB

She Said He Said

She said hello
He said goodbye
She said clean
He said dirty

He said Chiefs and Indians
She said princes and princesses
He said dark
She said light

He said running
She said skipping
He said snake
She said hamster

She said tea parties
He said video games
She said love
He said eww!

They said KIDS RULE!
Janelle Breeckner, Grade 7
New Albany Middle School, OH

Grass

Grass is very green
Many, many blades of grass
Grass is very dry
Christopher Caldwell, Grade 7
Isaac Newton Christian Academy, IA

Excited

It's like you're about to blast off in a flame, waiting for it to come.
Before you know it, your heart is pounding like an eight cylinder engine.
It's like lightning flashing — it's here,
Your legs are jittery like flustered ribbon.
You want your feet to move but!
It's like they're glued to the ground.
Gigantic grabbing glue!
Finally you begin to impel
Your legs start to jump like a kangaroo,
Then!
YOU'RE GONE
WITH THE RAFT OF EXCITEMENT!
Andrew Moser, Grade 7
Linwood Public School, ON

Cameo Rose Crowe

I am helpful and supportive.
I wonder what it's like in Heaven.
I see the light in the sky.
I hear the songs the angels sing.
I want to feel what it's like in Heaven.
I am helpful and supportive.

I pretend to fly like a bird in the cloudy sky.
I feel the clouds touching my skin.
I touch the rain as it falls.
I worry the world will eventually end.
I cry because I realize there are people in the world that are homeless and ill.
I am helpful and supportive.

I understand life won't be what I want it to be.
I say "Live life to its fullest."
I dream that when I cease, I will go to Heaven.
I try to help others that are more needy than I.
I hope everyone will eventually have a great life.
I am helpful and supportive.
Cameo Rose Crowe, Grade 8
Otsego Middle School, OH

Hockey

Bone crushing, fists whacking, sticks smacking
it's hockey.
You hear the home crowd cheer like a pack of wolves howling.
Slicing, slashing, skates,
it's hockey.
After a bone crushing hit the glass is shaking like a jack hammer,
whacking whistling, wind in your face
it's hockey.
The sound of the puck smashing against the goalie's equipment
is like the sound of a blazing bullet.
big, bullet, shots
it's hockey.
Hockey is the best sport in the world.
Austin Denstedt, Grade 7
Linwood Public School, ON

The Song of America

These colors don't run, these colors don't cower,
These colors stand and fight, they don't hit the shower.
These men flew up, and marched for the miles,
They swam through the waters, though the bodies grew in piles.
No man can say, that this fighting is simple,
Each choice we make, can have a deadly ripple.
We fight for the right, stand up to the wrong,
We defend all the innocent, with our great song.
This song of America, of the colors we fly,
Is a symbol of courage, of all those that die.
It members the brave, the courageous and strong,
It tells of the battles, fought hard and long.
Oh this song we sing, does not wither or fade,
It dwells in the hearts, of all the ones that laid.
This song is not sung, but felt from within,
It is the song of America, the ones who will win.

Nathan Wilkins, Grade 9
BOSS Buckeye On-Line School for Success, OH

Back into the Sea

Oh, please little child help me back into the sea,
I've been lying here all day baking in the sun,
I am nearly spent, only a little life remains,
Please child, just scoop me up and throw me into the sea,
You've probably heard bad things about my many arms,
No, please don't go away, I need you, please come back,
Oh, thank you child, I am very much obliged,
No, wait, stop, don't go away. I didn't mean it, really,
Oh, please stop crying, please o' please don't cry,
Just leave me now, I can't bear to see your tears,
I'll just lie here till dusk when high tide comes in,
And takes my jelly, lifeless body back into the sea.

Olivia Broussard, Grade 8
Haynes Academy for Advanced Studies, LA

Summer

On the ground you see flowers,
The day starts with the sun.
Flowers bloom with power,
The day ends with lots of fun.

When you walk outside you see the trees,
You go outside and walk.
You run across the grass and feel free,
While you walk I talk.

We feel the heat and swim,
Outside there's only heat.
When you swim you feel like you always win,
When you're inside with lemonade it tastes so sweet.

The summer days are done,
Summer is over, but school is yet to come.

Lorena Retana, Grade 7
Bristol Elementary School, WI

To Be in Paris

The city where you speak entirely French
and where you can sit on a comfy bench
watching millions of people walking on by
aside with all the delicate butterflies

The delectable aroma of rich pastries
running down every street's bakeries
there are true artists making paintings
from near and far
it doesn't matter exactly where you are

You wonder if this is all for real
its not just an ordinary deal
you sit on the edge of your dream in the sky
to get to Paris, if you could only just fly

Natalie Maddalena, Grade 8
Mary Ward Catholic School, ON

Night Sky

An immense gray cloud gives way
To other things here to stay
And wink at all benignly
While some people finally
Realize how our world is small
But part of a universe much larger.

Some thought the stars tell of the past
Or perhaps the future, in contrast
A few ponder their existence
While others care not for their subsistence
But merely lie down and feel
Like looking on forever.

The stars have always been
A factor of amazement within
The human mind and perception, which
Cannot help but be bewitched
By whatever is up there;
Fiction, future, or art.

Mihir Pande, Grade 9
Troy High School, MI

Notre Dame

My first visit to Notre Dame Campus I was only three.
Every return trip to ND — I knew it's the place for me.
Touch Down Jesus,
the Grotto, or
The Golden Dome…
There is no other place I want to roam.
Football, basketball, swimming, lacrosse
Activities abound you'll never be at a loss.
Even though there are many places I can go
Notre Dame will surely make me glow!
My college goal — A Notre Dame Degree
To receive an education of extreme quality!

Lauren Markovich, Grade 7
St John the Baptist Elementary School, IN

I Am a Fallen Angel

I am the distraught and confused
I wonder how many people will be saved
I hear death toll
I see people's souls drifting
I want to help them
I am the distraught and confused

I pretend not to hear their screams
I feel a deepening depression
I touch the hearts of many
I worry for the people
I cry tears of sadness
I am the distraught and confused

I understand the looks on their faces
I say life isn't fair, but death is worse
I dream about life after death
I try not to care
I hope the days stay bright
I am the distraught and confused

Kia Kienitz, Grade 9
Marinette High School, WI

The Steps I Take

Such a difficult task…
Truly difficult.
Though it may hurt, and it may be messy,
I take on challenges others cannot.
I go on many adventures, and as a shoe,
I will discover the world.

Julia Truong, Grade 8
Beverley Heights Middle School, ON

Forever Be Mine

From the moment we met,
I just knew.
I could never find another,
I was meant to be with you.
When our eyes first met,
to an inseparable gaze.
I knew at that moment,
I could stare into them for days.
Little did I know,
as the weeks began to pass.
My time with you became frequent,
I had no idea how long this would last.
Now you got me hooked,
My heart burns for you.
I could never lose you,
For I don't know what I'd do.
So I finally state,
one clear last line.
I will love you forever,
will you forever be mine?

Jolene Perron, Grade 9
General Amherst High School, ON

Armchair Traveler

Here I am, I'm in my room as bored as I could be;
So out I go, onto the plane, off to Italy.
After seeing the Coliseum and the Tower of Pisa that leans,
I catch a jet to Alaska to see some mountain scenes.
I take a train down to Canada to watch Niagara Falls;
Then I make a trip to Paris to visit some shopping malls.
I am pleased with the outcome of my shopping spree,
So I visit the Queen in England to have a cup of tea.
I decide I've had enough of Europe so I travel to Ancient China,
To bike along its Great Wall then head over to Carolina.
I lazily soak up the last few rays of the vibrant sun,
Before heading back to my house after my day of fun.

Abby Wright, Grade 7
Kortright Hills Public School, ON

Freedom

The air was brisk on that November day,
I was on the horse and we started to walk but soon picked up the pace,

We both knew that it was time to play,
We thundered around as the wild wind whipped my face,

I knew that it was just the horse and me and as I took a breath, I felt so free,
The seconds wore on, but it felt like a lifetime,

Everything else had just seemed to stop,
I took one last lap around, and finally came back down to the ground,

Everything else came back and was as busy as could be,
But you see, that feeling will always remain inside of me,

Freedom!

Mollie Wang, Grade 7
Bristol Elementary School, WI

An Average Day on the Enterprise

Here on the Enterprise the recruits are always fidgets,
But Cpt. Kirk still gives them the courage.
For at any moment they could attack those fearsome Klingon frigates,
But even they those Klingon foes cannot discourage.

Then they attack, the shields go down,
Gordy then uses the La Forge maneuver.
The Klingon Captain begins to frown,
As the ships reveal and are scooped up like manure.

The Klingons begin to board the ship,
And they went down with their pink alien blood.
Both captains go head to head as Kirk gets hit on the lip,
But the Enterprise prevails as it always should.

The Enterprise continues its journey of exploration,
In case some other alien race claims universal domination.

Ethan Costello, Grade 7
Bristol Elementary School, WI

Summer

Lazy days of sun
Oh what fun
To play and run
Heads will clear
No more fear
Of looming illness
Only joy and happiness
The sun will soothe our soul
And isn't that the ultimate goal

Warm feet and skin
Make me want to swim
School's out no doubt
Children laughing running free
Makes me want to be happy
You see I am not like them
Friends are special
Summer is too

Luke Dias, Grade 8
Individual Home Program (Woodland), IL

Friends

We all have friends that are perfect for us
This is the person we can tell anything
When you feel there is no hope
This friend will always be there
When you feel sad inside
They bring a smile
True friends forever
And ever
Amen
True friends
Changing things everyday
Our faces will age
But forever young we stay
True to each other and ourselves
We will have our problems through life
It would be so hard living without you
We all have friends that are perfect for us

Abby Bohn, Grade 8
Shakopee Area Catholic School, MN

What If

What if one day somebody told you,
That they had cancer,
Would you break down and cry,
Would you think what your life would be without them?
Would you change your life?
Become nicer,
Tell everybody or keep it to yourself,
Or would you help them,
Give them support
Hold their hand when they need it,
And don't let them give up,
What would you do?
What If

Katie Burke, Grade 8
New Glarus Middle/High School, WI

Mother and Daughter

No matter where, you're always there.
Through wear and tear, you'll always care.
I love you for the things that you say and do:
From saying "Sure, I can help you"
To teaching me all about what's true.
I know, from when you look at me,
That all the love you give is free.
It comes with no catch or hidden fee.
It doesn't even come with a guarantee,
That the love will be reciprocated by me.
True love is something hard to find,
Because many who seek it are blind.
They think that you find true love in a fairy tale,
That is why they all will fail,
True love is what you and I have:
Sometimes it may seem to wax and wane,
And sometimes it seems like just a pain,
To put up with each other.
But I know that forever and ever I will love you,
Because that's what a daughter should do,
For a mother as wonderful as you.

Lindsie Green, Grade 9
Francis Libermann Catholic High School, ON

New York Lights

The shimmering glow of the street lights,
The Empire State building was an enormous height,
The smell of the musky car exhaust,
This city is huge and I feel lost!
Overwhelmed by the feeling of it all,
People look dressed to attend a ball,
Business men and women scurry down the street,
I'm surprised they don't trip over each other's feet.
A place I hope to one day visit,
I hear this place is exquisite,
The place of lights I yearn to see,
The one and only New York City!

Alexa Gordon, Grade 8
Mary Ward Catholic School, ON

The Field

P icking fresh smelling daisies from the soft ground
E xamining an enormous cloud rolling on by
A nts crawl by hurrying to their tall dirt mound
C attails stick out in a nearby pond
E very creature is like a graceful swan
F eeling so free is overwhelming to me
U ltraviolet rays shine all around and make my skin warm
L eaves dance in delicate circles
N othing on Earth could be as peaceful as right now
E ven the grass moves like wiggling worms
S omething tells me this moment is fading
S o I will cherish it while it lasts

Samantha Noel, Grade 9
Hazelwood West Jr-Sr High School, MO

Nervous

My legs are shivering like an earthquake,
In front of the school.
My face, red like a beet.
I'm just a statue standing
On the stage
With a dry mouth,
Blank mind
Like an empty sheet of paper.
One…word…at…a…time.
Just waiting for the minute
That it is over.
My face just sweating more and more.
When is this going to be over?
I mumble to myself.

Simeon Martin, Grade 7
Linwood Public School, ON

Tick Tock Goes the Clock

Tick tock goes the clock
My life is ticking away
Ticking and tocking
Feeding on every minute
Of every hour
Of every day
So let that clock keep ticking
And tocking
Until my life passes away.

Megan Esposito, Grade 7
Stanton School, IL

Her

When I see her
She stands out
From the crowd
She is so beautiful,
All smiles,
No frown,
The closest
I have ever known love,
She must have
Come from above
She lights up my day,
She keeps lighting my way,
She has a great soul,
The only one to make my heart whole,
She has a great heart,
I don't ever want us apart,
The more we talk,
The more I know,
Who knows where we will go,
Forever with her I want to be,
It will always be her and me

Jeromy Marsh, Grade 8
Goshen Middle School, IN

dancing

dancing
crazy, fun
expressing, funky, making
feelings, creativity
singing

Leslie Marcum, Grade 7
Fairfield Middle School, OH

The World Is…

The world is scary.
It's cruel and mean when you're a teen.
But when you know God
You feel like you can do anything.
So, don't worry, don't fear,
Because He is near.
The world is full of battle and war
But so are we,
We have to fight Satan.
But God is there to win it all.
So pray and you will not fall.
The world is full of wonders.
Heaven.
The world is a place
Where you have to fit it
Or people will put you in your place.
Act like someone else, not yourself
And it will work out wrong.
Been there, done that and that's a fact.

Jette Carr, Grade 8
St Pauls Lutheran School, IL

Reminiscing

Loud noises, disturbing lights
Fun-filled nights and petty fights!
I miss you my sibling
And all the giggling
The shoving and scuffling
The pinching and punching
I miss the teasing,
And the teaching!
The nights are quiet
The weekends long.
I thought it will feel better
But it just feels wrong.
Your visits are rare
I guess it is the fare.
Life goes on.
And before long
We'll be miles apart
Only meeting on holidays.
So I might as well say
I miss you so much now.

Manesha Sampath, Grade 9
Troy High School, MI

Love

You hug me tender,
Love me splendor.
Too many words to describe,
You make me do the jive!
Hoping to see you again,
I sit to wait for my friend.
Then I give you a shove,
The very kind of Love.

Cami Cashwell, Grade 7
Galesburg-Augusta Middle School, MI

Grandma

A grandma's someone special,
A person very sweet,
Someone always close to you,
Every day of the week.

She'll be your shining star,
In those times of need,
She'll fill your heart with love,
Whenever you please.

But my grandma's different,
She's better then all the rest,
Someone very special to me,
The very very best.

She's always happy,
Never sad,
Never lets the pain show,
But deep inside her big old heart,
I really hope she knows,
That she means way more to me,
Way more it's true,
I love her so very much,
And I know she loves me too.

Natalie Piemonte, Grade 7
Westfield Community School, IL

Cedar Point

For a reward
Because of my chores
to the rollercoasters
My family and I went to Cedar Point.
Over the hills
down we go
from ride to ride
We went on rides all day long.
Near the end of the day
for all the fun times and rides
off we go
My family and I went home.

Aaron Sanders, Grade 7
Algonquin Middle School, MI

The Great Fight

When I'm by your side, nothing can go wrong,
But when I'm not, that feeling is gone.
That feeling just makes me want to run and hide,
At least until I'm back by your side.

You lay there in that bed,
While those people just said,
You're not going to last long,
Your time alive is almost gone.

Your big blue eyes show no fear,
Not even shed a single tear,
When you go to sleep tonight,
You are finally going to give up the fight.

Tomorrow you will have no pain,
All that you will have is all the love that you will gain.
Don't fear tonight,
Because, you are going to see a great sight.

Bryanna Mater, Grade 8
Sandusky Middle School, MI

Ode to a Lobster

I have a favorite food; it is ugly at best
Before I scare you off; you better hear the rest

It is creepy as a monster; it is red as a beet
If you go near it in the ocean; you better watch your feet

They crawl around the ocean, but catching them is a chore
You trap them in a crate and bring them to the kitchen door

"Screech!" says the lobster, as it's dropped into the pot
I like eating these tasty creatures, when they're nice and hot.

From head to toe, the lobster is really very sweet
When you eat a lobster tail, it is a tasty treat!

Its crusty, crunchy claws, are best when dipped in butter
Once I've finished one, I've got to have another!

John Taylor, Grade 7
St Philip the Apostle School, IL

Sunflower

Life is a sunflower,
It starts out small then it grows
It starts out low
From the roots down below
It gives people joy when they see a small sunflower
Striving to live
Winter comes and that's the day
The sunflower won't come up
To show the world how to smile again

Meghan Moore, Grade 8
Olentangy Liberty Middle School, OH

Califrizoo

Califrizoo is fun to say
Especially when you say it in a bouncy sort of way

With a Califrizoo, I could be a star
Jamming on stage with a bright pink guitar

I could be a psychologist, waitress or moose
With a Califrizoo, you get what you choose

I could weight lift or taste test, go golfing or sing
You can go anywhere and do anything

Wanna sell lemonade? Wanna burn trash?
With a Califrizoo, you get what you ask!

There's no late fees, no weekly funds!
You just get free, nonstop fun!

Get yourself a Califrizoo!
Do all the things that you want to do!

Rachel Slevin, Grade 9
Shenandoah High School, OH

Love Comes Around

L ove comes around
O ver and over again
V ery soon you'll understand
E veryone takes a chance

C hances are worth it
O r sometimes they are not
M oon, sun and stars are compared a lot
E very star represents the chances
S un and moon represents you and the person

A lot of times you have a smile on your face
R eally happy meeting different people different race
O h most of the times we realize our love is going to die
U nderstand, it could come back alive
N ow you know that loves comes around
D eep down inside you have found

Ivelisse M. Cosme, Grade 8
Lakeside Jr High School, OH

When You're Gone

When you're gone I can't stop crying, my heart's in two
I need you here with me,
I can't stop thinking of you.
I need you here when I cry, but you're not here.
I miss you, I miss you so much,
you're not here, you've moved on.
Every night I cry myself to sleep knowing you're not here.
I never got to know you well or really say goodbye.
And now I wish I did for I've heard so much about you.
No way to bring you back.
Now that you're gone!

Kassie Menzies, Grade 7
Weledeh Catholic School, NT

Daddy

Dear Daddy, I am 1 year old today; yeah, I've been around one whole year; I had a big party today; all my family was around; well almost, you weren't here.

Dear Daddy, I just turned 5; I can ride a bicycle now; I started school today; everyone got to bring their mommy and daddy to school but not me; you weren't here.

Dear Daddy, I am now a 10 years old; yep, I reached double digits today; I am a big girl now; Mommy is proud; you would be too, but you're not here.

Dear Daddy, I am a teenager now; a proud 13 year old; I had my first kiss today; I am thrilled; I doubt you would be, but it doesn't matter; you're not here.

Dear Daddy, I just turned 16; I can drive now; a real, big girl; I remember you talking about being a big girl; I remember your promises to help me drive; to be with me when I got my license; empty promises but still promises.

Dear Daddy, I graduated last week; I looked for you; I waited to hear you make fun of me in my gorgeous green robe, but I couldn't find you; you weren't there.

Dear Daddy, I'm out of college already; I have a boyfriend; I think I love him; I wish you could meet him; of course you would have a shot gun in hand, but you're not here.

Dear Daddy, I walked down the aisle today; yep, your daughter got married; I hoped you'd show up; to give me away to my husband, but I walked alone; you weren't here.

Dear Daddy, I got my first job; I am 26 now; I am an English teacher; you would be proud, but you're not here.

Dear Daddy, Mom died today; I cried, I cried hard; I looked to you for comfort; I still could not find you, because you weren't here.

Dear Daddy, I am dying now; I have lived a long life; I could always live longer; I would continue looking for you, I never gave up, I never would, my faith barely wavered, but you still are not here. You were never here; I sometimes wonder if you ever were.

Dear Daddy, I love you, even though you were never here.

Cara Tompot, Grade 9
Westlake High School, OH

Where I'm From

I am from the MIT graduating class of 1999, from the wrong apartment and a forgotten laundry room.

I am from rugby games, full of mud and excitement.

I am from the festivals and museums that taught me that "T" doesn't come in cups and it's possible to ride a dinosaur.

I'm from a place of spaghetti and mushrooms with a cardboard fireplace just to keep the magic alive.

I'm from Guinness ice cream, green pancakes and Vets with no animals.

I'm from the scars on my back and arms, memories of a bent needle and a broken bike.

I'm the whisper of the water in Lake Michigan, the tallest sand dune, standing like a challenge waiting to be defeated.

I'm from Way Out West, Nottinghamshire, the Wild and even the 50's.

I've chased a gang of bandits, defeated a sheriff hungry for the crown, alien plants, and even Elvis.

I know now that No One Mourns the Wicked, No Good Deed goes Unpunished, I can Dance through Life and Defy Gravity.

Brigid Ogden, Grade 8
Karrer Middle School, OH

When Love Doesn't Count

When love doesn't count, how are you left to give? Your all — when your all — is gone? When love doesn't count — why do we scream? We try to hide the pain — so we fight — and become mean…

When Love doesn't matter — it's then when we all hate — We show no respect — for each other's feelings. When we push, and pull, and break one's heart — when we fight to let go — we ignore the hold — it is tearing us apart —

When love doesn't count — I've got nothing left to give — my words go unsaid — my mind cannot dream — I've been blocked by defeat, sadness, and low self esteem…

I've been blocked by my hate — my hate for myself — I've been blocked by others who want to knock me down — it's sad when you let others take your crown…When love doesn't count — it does not make you a winner — it makes you look sorry — just like a ruined beginner — you're a hopeful in the clouds — lusting for the rain — lusting for the feelings of joy — and passion — all the same.

I'm wishing I were you — and you're wishing you were me — looking on the other side, for what you want — is not how you become fulfilled. I'm learning, as I grow up — to not let another take my place. I am here — and I'm not going anywhere. I'm becoming a new person, I'm leaving the old me behind — I need to grow from my mistakes — In order to grow — I need to be…So with that being said — many thoughts can cross my mind — and as I've thought of this many times…When love doesn't count — then nothing should count at all — because without it — well…We all seem to fall.

Ranequa Kelley-Boyd, Grade 9
John Glenn High School, MI

Stage Bright

Entering a stage with a full house,
Loaded on with makeup,
Dressed up all beautiful,
The audience is staring back at me eagerly waiting.

Looking at my cast smiling with pride,
Reciting the lines over in my head one last time,
I feel very confident and so do the people around me,
This is the day…where all the hard practice pays off.

The stage is bright with the light shining down on me,
The sweet smell of hairspray fills my nose,
The unpleasant smell of dirty dust fills my nose as well,
I feel ready to begin.

I feel a little nervous…
Until I say my very first word with volume, clarity, and poise,
I hear the sound of babies crying and applauding,
Bravo!

Rachael Sparks, Grade 7
New Albany Middle School, OH

I Am From

I am from soccer
Games, from dusk to dawn

I am from
The wide-open ocean at Myrtle Beach
With the sand under my feet,
The sun above me
And the cool breeze that sways next to me

I am from
Saying "What the fish"
From me to my friends

I am from
Mid-Ohio
And so many races
With the smell,
The noise,
And the very hot temperature

Trey Hicks, Grade 7
New Albany Middle School, OH

Friends

A friend is someone who is always there,
Right by your side,
To comfort you with pride,
You share laughs and nights,
You show affection and fights,
Trust them with everything you have,
The good ones and the bad,
One day your friend will be no longer here,
Just know that they shared something so dear,
A friend is always there.

Gabby Aucoin, Grade 8
Mount Carmel Academy, LA

I Am…

I am a teenage girl who's fallen in love
I wonder if I even know what love is
I hear your voice soft, and gentle
I see your eyes staring back at mine
I want you to know everything about me
I am a teenage girl who's fallen in love

I pretend I don't like it when you tease me
I feel your arm slip around my shoulder
I touch your hand just to feel close
I worry sometimes this feeling will end
I cry at night after a disagreement
I am a teenage girl who's fallen in love

I understand you would do anything for me
I say I don't care what others think of us
I dream about you night and day
I try not to let my jealousy get to me
I hope someday you'll be mine forever
I am a teenage girl who's fallen in love

Chloe Nelson, Grade 8
Wainwright High School, AB

Red

Red is a red apple and red socks.
Red feels warm.
Red tastes like bright red strawberries.
Roses and cinnamon smell red.
Red is the sound of embarrassment and cherries falling.
Red is red markers, cardinals and red carpets.
Falling is red.
Running is also red.
Red is a red apple.

Maureen A. Charbeneau, Grade 7
Algonquin Middle School, MI

Pure

Chaotic thoughts spawn complete harmony
Toil giving way to symphonic pleasure through
Ink, trembling fingers guiding a
Broken hand across the paper that
Makes me whole.
Penned syllables expressing what cannot be
Spoken, typed vocals producing some kind of
Solace in troubled times.
My savior, my sanctuary, this
Hideaway, refuge, my only heaven,
Losing consciousness to just
Write, letting it all fade away in
Place of something so much more
Pure, more whole, more completely
Put together, without which
I would be lost.

Colleen McBride, Grade 9
Northville High School, MI

Starting Something

Maybe we should sneak away
You and me up in the hay
We'll sneak away just you and me
Our hearts are stolen, but souls still free.

I'm in love, so are you
Put together, that makes two
That's all we need to start something
We'll show them all it's not a fling.

Let's start something, something new
Something crazy, something true
We can take a risk and dive on in
I just can't wait to begin.

Katie Hill, Grade 9
Shenandoah High School, OH

Climbing the Invisible Stair

Moon luminescent in the night
lighting the path to
the mountain in the sky.
Steeply climbing to the clouds,
invisible stairs.
The mountain in the sky,
shifting in the moonlight.
Vertical slopes covering the moon,
hiding the glow,
blocking the path,
climbing on the invisible stair
in the sky.
Walking on the mountain,
walking through time.
On the path winding upward,
shifting,
changing,
On the mountain in the sky.

Christina Wutzke, Grade 9
St Dominic Catholic High School, AB

Soaring

If you can handle losing,
But still hold your head high.
If you are proud of accomplishments,
And are still humble around others.

If you pursue your goals,
And live life to the fullest,
If you help others around you,
And truly respect them.

If you do unto others
What you want them to do unto you.
You will fly with the eagles,
Both respected and free.

Coby Burckard, Grade 7
New Albany Middle School, OH

War

War is like a cavity that keeps coming back,
those soldiers take bullets in their backpack.
They use those bullets to kill other men,
they march in line, ten by ten.

Troops would play songs to let people know,
to reload their guns and get ready to blow.

A soldier's gun can shoot very far,
it can kill those enemies who look from afar.
The guns looked like it had a mind,
because they would hit people in the eye.

Bombs sounded like firecrackers exploding in the sky,
when they hit the troops it was like saying goodbye.
Those evil tanks would come right at you,
when they would shoot they would blow your brains right out of you.

Children and their mothers would be crying on their bed,
because their father is lying on the ground dead.
Their tears would drip, drop, drip, drop on the ground,
just because their loved ones would never come back to town.

Kevin Pereira, Grade 8
Beverley Heights Middle School, ON

My Calm Place

Soft whistles of wind floats weightlessly through my canopy of trees,
The rustle from the wind upon bark lined branches allow the leaves to quaver.
A multitude of color swirls about me,
Trees splatter the ground as if an artist would with a paint brush and a canvas.
Some leaves land on the timeless bridge that is forever cast into an infinite twilight,
Others land in the babbling brook that opens his mouth to speak with his sister lake.
Wafting smells of forest pine and oak fill my nose,
Clears my mind and relaxes every muscles in my body.
I lay upon my twilight bridge,
Creaking boards as I walk like music in my ears.
Rough as the wood may be it has absorbed much of the morning's light.
Lady warmth wraps her arms about me and I am forevermore content,
But woe it was not to last the piercing shrill of my cell phone startles me,
I must leave now, however this is not in vain,
For, if one was never to leave, oh how would they ever return?

Victoria Hetchler, Grade 9
Clintonville High School, WI

Blue

Blue is icy and cold and joyful.
Blue is the taste of blueberries.
Smoothies and the ocean smell blue.
Blue is the sound of blue jays and the running water in rivers and streams.
Blue is heaven, the sky, and the great lakes.
Hoodies are blue.
Winter days are also blue.
Blue is my birthday.

Mario LaFata, Grade 7
Algonquin Middle School, MI

When He's Gone

She sits on the porch, twisting her hair
Wishing he was with her, wishing he was there.

She knows he had to go, that they had to part
But it feels like she's missing a piece of her heart.

Fighting was something he wanted to do,
He wanted to show them, he wanted to prove.

To prove that he's strong, to prove that he's brave
He promised her that he'd be back someday.

But now she's not sure, it's been a while
She gets through every day with barely a smile.

But she knows he's coming back, it's not too late,
He'll be here soon; she'll just have to wait.

Elaina Jones, Grade 8
Sandusky Middle School, MI

Life

Like the sun you have your time to shine;
To show your radiance.
You are seen and loved.
Full of life and vibrant as ever.

Like the sun you have your time of darkness.
Eclipsing your brightness.
Going unnoticed.
In a blanket of darkness.

Sarah Borgen, Grade 8
Prairie View Middle School, IL

What I Figured Out

What I figured out today
Was not the same as yesterday.
Every tear that falls from my
Face.
Is a piece of me breaking apart,
Becoming weak,
Not being able to speak.
It's all too hard and too confusing most times
I feel woozy.
To me no one understands, if
Someone was just there,
Then life would be fair.
I wonder if people even think about
Kids who are like me, who don't live
With their parents and wonder why,
But don't understand when I cry.
A lot of people try, but don't succeed,
But is it that they didn't try enough,
Or is it because we act like we are too tough?

Anyssa Rodriguez, Grade 9
Royal Oak High School, MI

Black

Black is death and destruction
A funeral
Fear, anger, hate, and rage

A bullet leaving a gun
A wall holding names of soldiers lost at war
A single teardrop falling to the ground

Like planes crashing,
And towers falling
Like oxygen-less air you breathe in and choke on

Like poison
A lump in your throat
The pain of loss and sorrow

Black erases a smile; a life

Mary Strickler, Grade 7
Virgil I Grissom Middle School, IL

I Am…

I am the one who changed everything
I wonder if I'll come back
I hear your voice in my head
I see your tears stream down your face
I want our friendship to never end
I am the one who changed everything

I pretend I'm there with you
I feel your pain as we move through life apart
I touch your hand as we walk together
I worry how much I impacted your life
I cry when I think about the day I left
I am the one who changed everything

I understand this is what it had to be
I say that I'll move back someday
I wish that day would be tomorrow
I try to imagine what it would be like if I was there
I hope you can forgive me
for leaving when you needed me most
I am the one who changed everything

Tessa Burzuk, Grade 8
Wainwright High School, AB

Beauty Everywhere

A golden glow filled the room
The colourful colours bounced off the walls
Looking out of the window
The waves crashing
Into rough rocks below
The aureate orb, half sunk into the distance
Throwing an array of colours
Into the sparkling water
Two dolphins splashing merrily near the horizon
Just in front of the glowing ball of flames.

Raghavi Ravi, Grade 9
Troy High School, MI

No!

I wish I could
I wish I would
Find a backbone
And put it in
Just so that
The ones I know
Would not walk
All over me

They make me do
Things that I wouldn't
If they hadn't asked
I always cave
No matter what

Until one day
I was asked
To do a drug
And on that day
I found my spine
And I said no

Kelly Hill, Grade 7
Fairfield Middle School, OH

Mexican Beach

Crashing waves and a salty taste
Colorful fish and cool, smooth sand
I can't be late, so I must haste
To go to the spot where I love to stand

A golden bird with blue tipped feathers
Screaming out his native call
Swing on a rope that tethers
Standing there, proud and tall

Cool, fresh, oceanic air
Red ball of light falling now
All the salt dried to my hair
Looping birds, I wonder how?

Nothing farther out of my reach
Then the great and wondrous beach

Marnus de Vos, Grade 8
Wainwright High School, AB

A Family at Home

A family at home
A dog on the floor
A mom and a dad
A kid equals more
A mess in the kitchen
A dog looking sad
A dad looking mad
A family at home

Megan Poirier, Grade 7
Algonquin Middle School, MI

Cool Breeze

Chilly as we walk through the windy park
On top of roofs there were forming icicles freezing.
On a crazy night that was as black as the Grinch's heart.
Lively we had to move faster as our hearts were beating.

But on cold nights such like this
Running seems to make a lot of sense.
Ending up safe in the warm and toasty house
Exclusively hoping the temperature will go north and not south.
We were zooming to see the fires smolder
Brrr we said enraged if it were any colder.

Sidney Webster, Grade 9
Hazelwood West Jr-Sr High School, MO

I Am

I am
Loving, dreaming, joy
I love my friends and their personalities
Joyfulness is important to me
Sensitivity is important to me
Thoughtfulness is important to me
The ability to show mercy is a good thing
Hurtfulness is bad but can be good because when you are hurt,
you know how bad it feels and will be more kind
The world is becoming more hateful
Happy days come less often
People don't enjoy life enough
Now you know who I am

Angela Bumstead, Grade 7
St John Lutheran School, MI

Never Ending War

As the days go by, the lives start to dwindle
I can't begin imagining what citizens see when they look out their window.
The soldiers' families being torn apart
Pain and fear is growing in the children's hearts.
They say help will come from the United States
How can this be true when all the people feel hate?
Infants and teens losing their moms and dads
Some are losing everything they ever had.
Our president just wants to send over more women and men
How long until he realizes that it's time for the war to come to an end?
The fighting has gone on now for seven years
All of this time has drawn a few too many tears.

Weapons of mass destruction is what brought us to war
But the belief of that is no more.
It seems as if this war is now religious
To most, that is quite ridiculous.
Our troops should no longer be over there
The men and women fighting should be home if anywhere.

Kelly Rud, Grade 9
Boyceville High School, WI

High School

You walk around
Every move
Every breath you breathe is watched
People pick on you
Make fun of you
Show you you're no good
A battlefield

Hollowed hallways
Filled with endless souls
Some with hearts
Some with minds
Most enjoy pain

Endless opportunities
Choices of being on the right side or the wrong
Your future depends on this
High school

Chelsea Forster, Grade 9
Gleneagle Secondary School, BC

In a Land...

In a land with plants and trees
In a land where one can never displease
In a land where there is no wrong
In a land where birds sing their song
In a land where there is no death
In a land with no last breath
In a land with no weapons, no knives, no dirks
In a land where captains do not smirk
In a land with no social class
In a land where men and women do not clash
In a land with no rules to ensure
In a land with no need to be mature
Where there is breeze all day, and stars all night
With the mates, there is no fright
In a land with friendship, long last
In this land, it has a mast
The highest peak, the highest tower
Where there is no higher power
In this land, as it plummets to sea
This is the land in which I want to be.

Yumna Zaidi, Grade 7
Hubert H Humphrey Middle School, IL

Vacation

One winter morning I woke up on a ship
And my sister told me we were gone on a trip.
We had left all that infuriating snow behind!
I couldn't get the thought out of my mind
I looked up ahead and spotted our destination
This was going to be a great vacation
I was thrilled to spot sandy beaches and palm trees,
As I sat on the ship, enjoying the breeze
My mother came by and gave me ice cream.
And I woke up with a start, it was all a dream.

Zahra Talat, Grade 8
Villa Maria High School, QC

American Soldier

The horror
The horror
Nazis think they have the right
to kill the Jews who will not fight.
Nazis think their plan will succeed
but really the Americans will make them plead.
The war goes on day to night
to give the Jews their light.
The closer they get the harder to bear
the nasty smell that's in the air.
As they free the Jews from their prison
I see them cry
and wonder why
and ask is this just a big lie?
As we feed potato peels and moldy bread,
they would never stop to thank us, but just eat
that is when I knew the Nazis were beat!
I was so happy for those who had survived
but cried for those who died.

Bryce Bedwell, Grade 8
Parkway Middle School, OH

Am I, Forgotten?

Am I as transparent as the glass window?
Am I a little stone at the bottom of a vast sea?
The piece of old gum flicked off your fingertip?
Maybe, I am.
I feel rolled over, left in the hard snowy ground
Waiting...
For the frost of death.
My heart drops like a rock, in an unforgiving sea.
I do something amazing, only to have it punched out of me,
Like I'm fighting with a world class boxer...
And I'm losing.
My grumbling and complaining fade away, like the stars,
Washed out by darkness.
BANG, CRASH, CRUNCH!
I stomp my feet, trying for some attention, it doesn't work.
My hopes shatter like a pop fly through a window.
Suddenly I stop caring.
Sitting lifelessly, like a light bulb with no shine.
Am I a patch of dead grass in a field of flowers?
Am I the shadow in the corner?
Maybe, I am.

Darci Jones, Grade 7
Linwood Public School, ON

Sports

running
shooting, skating
sweating, kicking, deking
hitting, catching, throwing, diving
sports are so fun and have lots of things to do.

Adrian Mammoliti, Grade 8
St Clare Catholic Elementary School, ON

Page 279

Chains

Chains could mean different things to different people.
To some when they first hear chains, the first thing they think of
is the type of chains that G's wear with all the diamonds,
but that shows that their minds are limited,
there are family chains better known as family trees, you know parents.
There are also chains of slavery, yes, you've seen them in movies and shows,
slaves with chains around their wrists and ankles, two by two or just one whole line
but there are good chains, friend chains that can't be seen but are there.
Friend chains can also be thought of as a bond.
They take a long time to make and when you work hard
on trying to keep them they can never be broken even if the person is gone.

Michael Bennett, Grade 8
St Peter Catholic High School, ON

Last Day of School

I walk into the school
Knowing this is the last time I will be here as a student
I am happy summer will begin
At the same time, I am sad this is the end of these great three years of middle school
I think about how next year will be so much different
I say goodbye to teachers and friends
I write "Have a good summer, good luck in high school" in yearbooks
Teachers' rooms are packed up
I see trash cans filled with binders and papers
On the bus ride home kids are yelling and screaming
School papers are flying out the windows
I realize middle school went by so fast
I just can't wait for summer to begin

Lindsay Jones, Grade 8
North Rockford Middle School, MI

I Am

I am thoughtful and dark.
I wonder if I'll make it through.
I hear a guiding voice, but I can't understand its language yet.
I see a golden light, but it is blocked out with problems and tasks.
I want to see where I'm going clearly.
I am thoughtful and dark.

I pretend to know what I want.
I feel frustrated when I can't solve my own puzzle.
I believe one's future is determined by their willpower.
I worry that I will lose hope and allow distractions.
I cry when I seem to have lost sight of my unknown goal, and my beliefs turn out to be lies.
I am thoughtful and dark.

I understand I need to work hard.
I say I will start, but I don't.
I dream that everything will be clear for me again,
Or that at least I will lose the knowledge that I never wanted.
I hope this fog will disperse from my mind.
I won't let the little faith I had slip.
I am thoughtful and dark.

Anchshana Haridas, Grade 7
New Albany Middle School, OH

Infinity Pool

Your breath swells inside trying to flee
Scramble to escape
Keep swimming up
It seems endless
Forever going
Never stopping
You see a smile
It glimmers
Like a diamond on display
Aqua, blue, indigo
Suddenly you forget
All the pain gone only beauty
Things can only get better
You were there and you were stuck
I got you out
The deep depression gone
Happiness took its place
Out with the old in with the new
Cheerfulness colors your room
You made the right choice
Because I am Infinity Pool
Kennedy Johannsen, Grade 8
South Middle School, WI

I Am From…

I am from the river,
where we fish in the spring.

I am from the bush,
where we hunt.

I am from the Skidoo races,
where we bet on the races.

I am from the cold winters,
where we stay inside.

I am from Fort Providence.
Jamie Norwegian, Grade 8
Weledeh Catholic School, NT

Crying Angel

There she lies on the heaven floor
With her hair scattered all over her face,
And she cries the sweet sorrow
Pearls rolling down her rose red cheeks.
Her eyes cry the mysterious misery,
Her face has no graceful glory.
Sadness has drowned her,
And grief is all she knows.
She lies on the heaven floor,
She is a crying angel.
Prachi Regmi, Grade 8
The Valleys Senior Public School, ON

The Smoke of a Million Corpses*

"Death and despair!"
Cries the smoke in the air
The smoke of a million corpses

Pushing that vile cart
Like a cart at the mart
A man and a wife and their child
No grave, no remembrance
No notice to be filed
The smoke of few more corpses

The Sonder revolt
The SS locked up
Behind deadlock and bolt
The furnace goes boom!
No more to let go
The smoke of a million corpses
Josh Millikan, Grade 8
Covington Middle School, IN
*Written from the perspective of
Joseph Gani

He's Gone

He's not here anymore
He flew on wings like eagles
To somewhere better
We all miss him, love him
Wish he was here
He was great
Fun loving
Always could make you smile
Helped us through
He could dance
Was a super hero to us
This is something to help me remember
Remember him
I just have one thing to say
As a tribute to him
"I respect you"
Kellen Schneider, Grade 7
Stilwell Jr High School, IA

Softball, a Lovable Sport

S tealing bases
O ut of the park
F oul balls
T ournaments
    every weekend
B ase running
A ction filled
L oud cheering
L ovable sport
Lindsay Haven, Grade 7
Fairfield Middle School, OH

Unkept Promises

Being there
keeping secrets and
holding hands.
You promised you would do these things
but you broke your promise.
Crying myself to sleep
and shedding tears
is all I do.
I promised I wouldn't cry
I guess I broke *my* promise.
When I look in the mirror all I see
is your selfish expression.
What happened?
You let go but
I didn't
it's your fault
I was there the whole time
you lied
you cheated
I just wanted to let you know
I'm still not over you!
Jessica Sanders, Grade 7
Weledeh Catholic School, NT

Extraordinary

There are so many things
That are ordinary
We take them for granted
That's the thing that's scary
A simple rainbow cheers you up
As does a smile for good luck
A hug, a kiss, handshake hello
A simple time to be mellow
They happen so often
We hardly notice them
But if we look closer
They'll stand out like a gem
A water fight out on the lawn
A simple sunrise out at dawn
A day to spend with your best friend
When you're crying, a hand to lend
Occurring every day
To them we aren't wary
What they really are is
Extraordinary
Erica Huhta, Grade 7
Sebeka Secondary School, MN

Tears of Joy

There are tears of joy
They are magically made
Happy as can be
Jesse S. Trupiano, Grade 7
Algonquin Middle School, MI

To Mom on Mother's Day

Mom,
How would I get along without you?
You wash my clothes,
Take care of me when I'm sick,
And buy me things that are new.
You do that plus more,
Put up with three kids in the store,
And I wonder, how?
How do you do it?
Since I was a baby to now,
And beyond,
You've been there to support me,
To care for me,
And the dogs!
We've got three!
Not to mention the other siblings, too!
I look up a lot to you!
So Mom,
On your day,
Feel free to relax!
Today, I'm working for you!

Kaitlyn Richards, Grade 7
Minooka Jr High School, IL

Wolves

Wolves; fierce predators
Run wild in the forests
Stalking their doomed prey

Cassie Brossard, Grade 9
LeRoy-Ostrander High School, MN

Bully

I sit here in the silence;
No one here to comfort me.
The storm has come,
The storm has gone.
The world to me is now dead;
    It is dead.

It appeared out of nowhere,
Like a hungry cheetah;
Bringing fear to everyone in its path,
Until there was no one left to destroy.

It had no compassion, it did not care,
All it wanted to do was bring fear
And despair into our lives, once again.

I sit here in the silence;
No one here to comfort me.
The storm has come,
The storm has gone.
The world to me is now dead;
    It is dead.

Charlotte Julian, Grade 9
Mulgrave School, BC

I Am...

I am a sensitive girl who wants to the change the world.
I wonder if our world will suffer from global warming.
I hear the people of the future screaming for help.
I see the smoke coming from factories go into the air and then disappear.
I want to think that it's all a dream.
I am a sensitive girl who wants to change the world.

I pretend that global warming is just my imagination.
I feel the need to help the world.
I touch the soil of the earth.
I worry that in the future it won't be like that.
I cry when I watch *An Inconvenient Truth* and see the polar bears suffer.
I am a sensitive girl who wants to change the world.

I understand that we are all trying to change.
I say that what we are doing now is not enough.
I dream that the world is a clean and happy place.
I try to help as much as I can.
I hope that global warming will stop.
I am a sensitive girl who wants to change the world.

Brittany Pileggi, Grade 7
St Clare Catholic Elementary School, ON

I Am Emily Gorder

I am Emily Gorder daughter of Howard and Lynda Gorder.
I am a sister to Jessie Gorder.
I am an owner to Slim my dog.
I am a best friend to many people.

I see my family all around me telling me that they love me.
I see my favorite color (lime green) everywhere,
on my walls, on my clothes, and outside.
I see my best friends, all the little boys in my neighborhood,
playing and inviting me to come out with them.

I hear my dog barking for me to come play with him.
I hear squeals of joy when I join my little neighborhood friends.
I hear my friends and all of the gossip about the "hot guys."
I hear my phone ringing off the hook with everyone I love on the other side.

I feel very loved and welcomed by my friends and family.

Emily Gorder, Grade 8
Stewartville Middle School, MN

Inside My Pocket

There are many things inside my pocket…
There are bottle caps, shoe strings that came off my shoes
There is a little toy mirror I got in a happy McDonald's meal
There is lip gloss and a stick of gum
There is my cell phone and the babysitting money I got that day
There is a piece of paper with a boy's phone number
But no matter how old I get I know one thing that always stays in my pocket.
It is a little wooden cross to remind me that I am being watched and protected.

Caitlin Moore, Grade 9
Mater Dei High School, IN

The Stain Glass Moon

Moon shimmering,
It peaks from the shadows,
The moon reveals itself,
Showing off radiant light,
Shining through open doors,
Spread across the universe in seconds,
Glistening spotted by different eyes,
Everyone's eyes,
Mirrored from place to place,
Covered with a coat of glass,
Sponged with the hand of stars,
Painted with God's texture,
The wolves rejoice,
The clouds burrow,
The spotlight set,
Hourglass ready to stop,
The tool of survival,
The reflection of hope,
The signal of faith,
An indication of *Life*,
As we knew it.

Elizabeth Backus, Grade 8
South Middle School, WI

Sorrow

I have to fake a smile
It's cold, coarse, crusted into my face.
There are too many hands all here to say good-bye.
My soul feels weak, hanging down like a kite without wind
The music starts to play, sad, dreary but it keeps on coming.
People come up in ones and twos
All trying to make light of it,
My laugh is cold, broken, reused
Like a CD you've heard a million times
The preacher comes up and starts the homily
As she speaks my eyes well up with tears
It feels like Niagara Falls is gushing down my face
The casket closes
I'll never get to see his face, hear him laugh
Gone!
NO! Not now, never, why did you die?
My mind and body shiver as I try to adapt to death.
My heart is heavy like a weight weighing me down.
My world is empty
A little piece is missing.
You have left our Earth forever!

Kara Lumgair, Grade 7
Linwood Public School, ON

God

G ood for God is never a choice, it's what God does.
O f all things to believe in, God is the number one.
D eath occurs, you then meet God in eternal life in Heaven.

Jane Keohen, Grade 8
Shakopee Area Catholic School, MN

Summer Storm

In the lush, humid rainforest
Is where the fierce summer downpours
Can come in like an airplane
And disappear like a magic trick.
The infinite bright, blue sky
Seems to be swallowed whole
When the growing, gray rain clouds
Roll in like a storming sea
With the terrible tyrannous sound
Of the roaring thunder it contains.
The exotic, dark green trees and plants
Do not seem to understand why the animals hide
From such a replenishing downpour.
The ultimate amount of rain water
Fills the rivers and streams
And seeps through the fertile, rich soil.
And after all of this, the bright, blue sky comes out
Now as a calm sea.
In the teeming, humid rainforest.

Jesse Allen, Grade 7
New Castle Middle School, IN

My Big Brother

I will always love you don't ever let me lie.
You are my big brother you always help me shine.
Even when I'm sad you always make me smile.
Your hugs last forever when the pain is just a little while.
You always know just what to say, even on a cloudy day.
You give me words of encouragement,
You help me out and tell me it will be ok.
You are always fighting and most of the time you win.

You are my big brother Jesse I know I'm going to win,
I'm going to be a wrestler I owe some of it to you.
You told me I can make it, now I know I can too.
The obstacle will become harder will you hold my hand?
So now that I've shared this with you, please just let me say.
I love you Jesse with every passing day.

Nina Fields, Grade 7
Fairfield Middle School, OH

I Believe

I believe in love.
I believe in your love.
I believe that our hearts are one.
and we can fly.

We can fly to the moon and sun.
We can fly to the stars and above.
We can ride our love anywhere in the universe.
As long as we believe in it.

So come with me my love.
Together we will go beyond infinity.
We will fly above the clouds.
Together forever.

Hailey Van Mullem, Grade 8
Templeton Middle School, WI

Who Am I

Am I just a puddle of water
Or am I just a leaf on a tree
Am I an eye that's trying to see

Am I sitting on the doorstep
Waiting for feet
To put mud all over me

Nothing but wind expressing toward my body
Trying to find a comfort zone
To fill my lonely home

It's right there I just can't touch it
I am somebody, I can feel it
I'm just out of reach
It's like my legs won't use its feet

Leaning, leaping and trying to jump
To land a powerful punch
Toward the box of bad luck
That was stopping me from speaking up

Elyssa Ely, Grade 7
Young Elementary School, IL

Not Knowing

You saw me when I was born.
Then you left me the next morn.
You tried to talk to me very often.
But back then you were in Boston.

I grew up and you grew older.
Seven years later you came back, and it was colder...

You didn't know me all that well.
Then we began and apart we fell.
You were happy and curious,
I was mad and furious...

You walked in like nothing was wrong.
We hadn't talked in so long!
Well no more do you know me,
For sooner or later you'll see...

That I have grown up proud and tall,
And soon you'll be nothing
But bones...and a skull.

Emily Wintermote, Grade 8
Washington Middle School, WI

Jesus My Friend

A cross and a man
A hill and a crowd
The sky grew dark,
and the weeping grew loud
"Forgive them Father"
They heard Him say
Some taunted louder
Some turned away
A mother, her love
so pure, so true
She gave Him to me
She gave Him to you
For the weight of my sins
His life had to end
Jesus my Savior,
Jesus my friend.

Kiley Magee, Grade 9
Southwest Jr High School, AR

Index

Author Autograph Page

Author Autograph Page

Author Autograph Page

Author Autograph Page

Author Autograph Page

Author Autograph Page

Author Autograph Page

Author Autograph Page